VIKING FUND PUBLICATIONS IN ANTHROPOLOGY
edited by SOL TAX

Number Forty-One

CERAMICS AND MAN

CERAMICS AND MAN

EDITED BY FREDERICK R. MATSON

ALDINE PUBLISHING COMPANY / *Chicago*

This volume comprises one of a series of publications on research in general anthropology published by the Wenner-Gren Foundation for Anthropological Research, Incorporated, a foundation created and endowed at the instance of Axel L. Wenner-Gren for scientific, educational, and charitable purposes. The reports, numbered consecutively as independent contributions, appear at irregular intervals.

First published 1965 by

ALDINE PUBLISHING COMPANY

320 West Adams Street

Chicago, Illinois 60606

Printed in the United States of America

To the memory of

PAUL FEJOS

A man of vision and great accomplishment

PREFACE

THE PLANS for the symposium "Ceramics and Man" developed in conversations with Dr. Paul Fejos in the months following the stimulating 1959 conference on "The Application of Quantitative Methods in Archaeology" which was organized by Drs. R. F. Heizer and S. F. Cook. The purpose of the proposed meetings, as formulated by March, 1960, was "To evaluate the contribution of ceramic studies to archaeological and ethnological research." This was to be accomplished by:

1. Bringing together, with ceramics as the focal point of discussion, archeologists and ethnologists with special skills and detailed regional knowledge.

2. Trying to achieve through them some interpretative cross-fertilization. Often scholars obtain useful perspectives that enhance their own work by learning in detail and discussing some of the processes and social factors involved in ceramic work, ancient and contemporary, in geographic areas unfamiliar to them.

3. Attempting a critical stocktaking of ceramic contributions to archeological and ethnological research.

A list of suggestive topics was prepared to indicate the nature of the problems that might be considered in the preparation of papers for the conference. It was recognized that in the ultimate publication—this book—the original plans would be significantly altered because of the specific contributions made by the participants in the symposium and the nature of the discussions at Burg Wartenstein.

It was found best to limit the discussion of ceramics in this symposium to unglazed pottery, which constitutes the most abundant and useful portion of the ceramic spectrum in anthropological studies. Glazes, glasses, enamels, brick, faience, fritted pigments, cements, and plasters were regretfully excluded.

A preliminary Planning Conference was held at the New York headquarters of the Wenner-Gren Foundation for Anthropological Research on the afternoon of March 3, 1961. Twenty-five people attended this meeting at the invitation of Dr. Fejos. The date was selected to coincide with that of the Foundation's banquet at which the Viking Fund medals were awarded, so as to take advantage of the presence in New York of scholars who might not otherwise have been able to participate in the discussions. The list of participants in the Planning Conference, together with Dr. Rouse's summary comments presented at Burg Wartenstein, are included in the next to last chapter of this volume. A transcription of the Planning Conference discussions was sent to all members of the symposium at the time that their preprinted papers were distributed early in the summer.

Seventeen archeologists and ethnologists representing ceramic interests and experience in several parts of the world were invited to participate in the symposium on "Ceramics and Man" at Burg Wartenstein. At the last moment Dr. Zaky Iskander was unfortunately unable to attend because of archeological problems arising in connection with the construction of the Aswan Dam, but his paper was discussed and is published in this volume. Dr. Vanden Berghe was called home suddenly, but in his regretted absence his extensive series of slides was shown and his paper discussed. Dr. Heine Geldern and Drs. Ralph and Rose Lilien Solecki attended some sessions of the symposium as participants while they were guests at the castle.

The symposium on "Ceramics and Man" was held at Burg Wartenstein in sunny early fall weather from September 2 to 12, 1961. Sessions to discuss the preprinted papers of the participants who encircled the large green baize-covered round table were held morning, afternoon and at times in the evening, each member of the conference serving as chairman and initial discussant at one of the sessions. All participants brought with them slide collections to illustrate not only their papers but also their current field work, so additional meetings were arranged at which they could be viewed. The discussions were recorded on tape thanks to the skillful arrangements and monitoring cared for by Mrs. Lita Fejos, Miss Patricia Curran, and Mr. and Mrs. Steve Montanye. Dr. Margaret B. Matson acted as secretary and supplied notes which were invaluable when transcripts were later prepared from the tapes for use in the revision of the papers.

Dr. and Mrs. Fejos with their thoughtful hospitality gave us a wonderful day of touring and dining in Vienna at the mid-point of the conference. Another time we had a late afternoon tea at the top of the Sonnwendstein ski lift above the Semmering Pass, and several of us enjoyed climbing down the mountain after sunset. The evening spent in the ruins of one of Burg Wartenstein's towers listening to a recording of "Tosca" was memorable. Our three *heuriger* evenings with the *Teufelsgeige* and accordion, and the lovely Viennese songs so charmingly sung by Mrs. Ilse Schlag, also remain as happy recollections of the informal aspects of our symposium.

The arrangement of the papers as they appear in this volume is regional. Following Dr. Ehrich's paper, which provides an anthropological framework of reference for the others, the archeological, ethnological, and technological ceramic studies begin with those from the Americas, in recognition of the major pioneer work published by Dr. Linné in 1925, *The Technique of South American Ceramics*. Then follow those from Europe, North Africa, the Near East, and one from southeast Asia. In most cases the authors made use of their detailed ceramic knowledge of a region as a base from which to suggest or demonstrate some of the broader applications of ceramic data. For the purposes of the symposium and these reports we have intentionally isolated or emphasized the ceramic aspect of anthropological studies, well aware of the limitations of such a procedure. The materials presented in the papers and the topics indicated in the summary of the discussions are not encyclopedic; they represent only some phases of the almost world-wide use of ceramics. It is hoped that these reports may suggest productive approaches and some precautions in the uses of ceramics in the study of man.

Following the symposium, several members incorporated materials from the transcribed discussions when revising their chapters for publication. Other pertinent data from the transcriptions have been brought together in the last chapter in a topical manner without reference to a particular chapter. All participants had the opportunity to make final minor revisions on their papers and additions to their bibliographies in March, 1964, if they chose to do so. The papers by Mlle. Balfet and Dr. Vanden Berghe, originally presented in French, have been translated into English to conform with the policy of the Viking Fund Publications in Anthropology, and the translations have been edited and approved by the two authors. Dr. Trachsler selected two ceramic problems to discuss at the symposium, so these are here presented separately.

Mrs. Paul D. Holtzman, Mrs. Marjorie Shaffer Rubash, Miss Kathy Rusnak, and Miss Deborah Schubert were of great help in the preparation of the materials for publication.

We as a group wish to dedicate this volume to the memory of Dr. Paul Fejos, who was so keenly interested in the more effective use of ceramic data in anthropological research.

FREDERICK R. MATSON

CONTENTS

CONTENTS

CERAMICS AND MAN

CERAMICS AND MAN: A CULTURAL PERSPECTIVE

ROBERT W. EHRICH

THE CONTEXT OF DISCIPLINES

THE TOPICS of the various papers listed for this symposium, together with others suggested at the preliminary session held at The Wenner-Gren Foundation on March 3, 1961, cover an extremely wide range and, at first glance, seem to present the unco-ordinated contents of a ragbag of individual interests. It may be possible, however, to see them as facets of a broad and coherent pattern if we view the general theme of these studies from the perspective of cultural context. Since culture, as we here use the term, is primarily an anthropological concept, we must first restate the general nature of anthropology and its subdivisions, and we must consider its relationship to pertinent allied fields before we can bring the subject of ceramics and man into focus against a general background.

In the American and English sense, we can define anthropology as the comparative study of man and his works. This statement of course refers to man as a biological animal on the one hand, implying the field of physical anthropology, and to man as a cultural being on the other, and thus the field of cultural anthropology.

For the general purposes of this paper we will disregard the whole field of physical anthropology. It is true that effigy pots, vase paintings, figurines, clay statuary, and the like do give indications of racial difference, anomalies, disease symptoms, etc., but these are cultural reflections of what people saw and incorporated in their customs, rituals, records, and aesthetic traditions. Although physical anthropologists may make use of some of this material, it seems unlikely that ceramics, any more than any other cultural item, had a specific effect, either accelerative or decelerative, upon human evolution—upon human physique, population increase, disease, or the like—over and beyond the general effects of culture as a whole.

In viewing the field of cultural anthropology for this symposium, we must bear in mind that we approach the subject from two orientations: (1) What do ceramics mean to the investigators as tools of analysis? (2) What do they mean as cultural items to their makers and users?

When we use the term "culture" in a general sense, we refer to the learned patterns and mechanisms by which mankind has attempted to adjust itself to the natural world and to the problems of group living, and when we use it in its particularistic sense of *a* culture, we connote the total way of life of a given people (Taylor, 1948, pp. 98–99).

1

Because of this dual orientation of analysis and meaning, it seems justifiable in this context to divide the field of cultural anthropology into *ethnography*, the detailed study of the cultures of distinct groups; *ethnology*, the comparative study of culture; and *archeology*, the study of past cultures and civilizations based upon their actual remains. Within this framework ethnography supplies most of the data from which comparative ethnologists work and, in this sense at least, is a subdivision of ethnology. The actual significance of the ceramic industry to its makers and users is essentially an ethnographic problem involving the values and outlook of one particular society at one particular time.

The discipline of ethnology shows two broad faces to the world: one of historical orientation—whether evolutionist, diffusionist, or historical particularist—and one non-historically oriented, which starts from the foundation of functionalism and then adds superstructures of institutional patterns, economic patterns, values, interaction patterns, culture change, culture and personality relationships, and the like. Although also concerned with general principles, the non-historically oriented schools are more ethnographic in their approach, for they are primarily concerned with how cultures work as functioning wholes in relation to the social group; and although ethnographers do generalize, ethnologic studies tend to be more comparative in outlook.

As the third subdivision of cultural anthropology, archeology has three broad methodological categories of research emphasis which frequently overlap. We can typify these as *historical research*, in that archeology is also concerned with sequence and chronology; *paleoethnography*, in that it seeks to describe, insofar as possible, the culture of a particular society at a particular time; and *paleoethnology*, in that, by painstaking comparison of synchronous data, geographic distributions, and sequential changes, the archeologist attempts by inference to reconstruct the still more remote past as well as the origins of the culture under study, in exactly the same manner that the comparative ethnologist works with data from the ethnographic present.

If we extend our field of cultural inquiry beyond the conventional limits of cultural anthropology with a view to analyzing a body of data such as that afforded by ceramics, we must first clarify the differences in outlook between the conventional historian and the historically oriented ethnologist and archeologist. Here the main cleavage lies between the historian's major historiographical emphasis on people and events in sequence, as against the anthropologist's major concern with cultural history in both its written and unwritten phases in which people or events serve chiefly to mark divisions in culture sequences or rearrangements in external contacts that lead to new directions of culture change.

As this symposium will certainly demonstrate, the study of any facet of culture, such as the ceramic industry which we now consider, will extend beyond the elastic limits of anthropology into other academic disciplines. We can thus view ceramics from the standpoint of sociology and of folk and peasant economics as Foster treats them in his paper, as a creative art as well as an industrial one, or as an element in art history. In the same manner some other disciplines, such as the study of folklore, that bridge the gap between anthropology and other fields may also have relevance.

CONCERNING ARCHEOLOGICAL AND
ETHNOLOGICAL INFERENCE

Although the above formulation presents a series of rather clearly distinguishable facets, we must remember that these are conceptual and that any body of data or any particular problem may well cross the barriers of several or all of them. The purpose of this paper, then, is to take the general category of ceramics and view it as a part of human culture in an attempt to see the wider implications of what we actually do when we pursue some particular question in this field.

Granting that a completely rigid schematic approach may be possible but is largely inadvisable because of the multiple aspects of any given body of ceramic data, let us attempt to proceed in a reasonably orderly manner and begin with the orientation that treats ceramics from the point of view of the investigator.

First, if we accept Webster's definition of ceramics as (1) "the art of making objects of baked clay . . ." and (2) "articles formed of clay in whole or in part and baked," we are obviously dealing with an area of what British anthropologists call "Technology" and American anthropologists call "Material Culture."

American anthropologists use the term *culture trait* to indicate a culture item comparable to others on the same level, even though it may be somewhat complex. A suggested analog is that of a cultural molecule. *Culture complex*, on the other hand, refers to a group of more or less closely related traits that form an operational pattern. Whether we consider a body of ceramics as a trait or trait complex depends to some extent on the level of abstraction from which we may be making our comparisons or analyses. Thus, although we may recognize the inherent complexity of the ceramic industry as a trait complex in any society or group of societies, if we compare the Paleolithic and Neolithic periods with regard to the inventory of their industries, then the presence or absence of a ceramic industry, which is our chief concern, relegates it to the status of a culture trait on this level of inquiry. As soon as we move to a more explicit level in order to compare techniques of pottery-making and types of pots produced in pottery-using cultures, we are *ipso facto* working with ceramics as trait complexes (Ehrich, 1950, pp. 471–72). Since the field of archeology shares most of its methodological assumptions with ethnology, the following discussion applies to both fields and should obviate the necessity of excessive repetition.

A basic consideration in the comparison of culture traits with regard to tracing cultural contact by trade or diffusion, the recognition of historical derivation, or the persistence of tradition, rests upon the doctrine that the more complex the similarities, the less the probability of independent development and the greater the likelihood of either direct or indirect connection and/or continuity. Furthermore, as in any good classification, the greater the number of resemblances and the greater the intensity of those resemblances, the greater is the degree of presumed relationship. Also involved here are the "criteria of quality and quantity" of the Kulturkreislehre (W. Schmidt, 1939) and, within the field of ceramics proper, the "adhesions" of relatively irrelevant ceramic elements that contribute to the building up of significant and distinctive patterns. It is from such combinations of characteristics or the presence or absence of highly specialized or unusual individual traits that we draw inferences relating to the types of culture contact and continuity such as stimulus diffusion, direct migration diffusion, trade, acculturation, and the like. Our progression, however elliptical, must inherently begin with a detailed descriptive classification permitting relatively simple and direct inferences (Thompson, 1958), and advance through more complex associations and multiple possibilities of interpretation on a continually ascending scale of abstraction.

We must remember, however, that the pattern of resemblances will vary with differences of emphasis in different cultures. Generally, for example, simple geometric patterns such as hatched or cross-hatched triangles on painted pots may recur in different areas and at different times, thus suggesting that they may not be related; but when they occur in contiguous territories at approximately the same date, they may well become a diagnostic characteristic for the assessment of diffusion, contact, common tradition, culture area limits, and the like. It is difficult, for example, not to see some relationship between the sharply profiled, stemmed bowls of Middle Bronze Age Tarsus, where the pattern decoration occurs above the shoulder (Goldman, 1956, pl. 287, pp. 168, 169), with those of like date from Phylakopi (Phylakopi, 1904). When we add the presence of the "butterfly" or "double axe" pattern, the complex of resemblance increases. Likewise, in Cilicia and North Syria the appearance of similar designs on spouted pitcher forms characteristic of the Anatolian Highlands demonstrates linkage rather than happenstance. In similar vein, the combination of the technical production of wheel-made grey ware, the characteristic form of pedestaled bowls, the doughnut-like rings on the stems, and the copying in clay of metallic rivets and the like, all in association, builds up to the inescapable conclusion of some kind of relationship between the Minyan Grey Wares (Mellaart, 1958, pp. 15–21; Childe, 1947, p. 73; Childe, 1950, p. 149; Ehrich, 1954, p. ix; Goldman, 1954, p. 75; Ward, 1954, p. 137) and those of Tepe Hissar (E. F. Schmidt, 1937). In this second instance the emphasis is on technology and form rather than on decoration. The mere addition of a "teapot" shape adds to the complexity of resemblances between Tepe Hissar and the Aegean, and strengthens the inference of some type of contact or continuity.

On the other hand, although the simple Neolithic bowls of the Middle Danube are practically indistinguishable from some made by the Indians along the Mississippi River, the rest of their ceramic complexes are sufficiently different to obviate any close generic relationship. Here are chance similarities due to the operation of the principle of limited possibilities in the simplest form of pottery—handmade, smoothed, open-fired bowls.

For the most part, however, we can regard ceramic objects as being inherently so complex that by analyzing visible technical characteristics such as form, style, technique and patterns of decoration, we can make reasonably accurate attributions of the culture complex to which they belong or belonged, and we can do so because each of the categories we observe is capable of so many possibilities of variation. To translate this into numerical terms, let us take a very modest number of categories (such as: type of manufacture; degree of firing; tempering material; surface treatment; location, type, and number of handles or lugs; total shape; body profile; types of base, neck, and rim; technique, field, and pattern of decoration) and allow twelve basic features with five possible variants in each. The number of possible combinations of these features, provided that there is a positive observation in each of the twelve categories, is 5^{12}. The actual number of such potential variations is, of course, infinitely greater (Ehrich, 1950, p. 476).

At the same time, the transfer or extension of certain cultural emphases may provide clear-cut recognition symbols of relationship and make more detailed analysis relatively unnecessary. No one, for example, who has seen the angular tracery patterns appearing on cloth or painted on bodies or wood by the Indians of the South American Montaña could fail to recognize them when they appear painted on their pottery as well (Steward and Métraux, 1948, Figs. 82–86 on pp. 588–89). The Tiahuanaco Horizon style in Peru gives us an archeological case in point. Textile patterns also appear on pottery from several other Peruvian periods.

It is the combination of technological and stylistic factors occurring in shifting patterns of association and resemblance that lays the groundwork for ethnologic and paleoethnologic inference.

If we take the deliberately scored and roughened jars with burnished rim band that we find in the Late Neolithic Řivnač complex of Bohemia and compare them with those from the later Early Bronze Age Unětice jars, we can see close enough resemblances to permit inferences of historical connection, and differences enough to separate them without question. Analogous modifications of other types also seem recognizable.

At Homolka, a fortified site of the Řivnač period, occasional identifiable Early Bronze Age (Unětice) sherds appeared in assemblages from closed units consisting of pits and huts that contained an overwhelming predominance of Eneolithic material of the terminal phase of the Řivnač occupation. At the time of the symposium, this situation permitted certain tentative ethnographic interpretations, particularly since very early Unětice pottery shows traces of Řivnač styles and techniques. It seemed that these associations probably demonstrated contemporaneity, and we therefore concluded that Homolka must have survived as a functioning Eneolithic village which coexisted for a while with Early Bronze Age settlements.[1]

---

1. As this article goes to press, the case for establishing the contemporaneity of Řivnač and early Unětice settlements appears to be increasingly improbable. The validity or lack of validity of this particular association at Homolka is really of no importance in this context, for true or false, the principle remains the same, and this type of interpretation seems well substantiated by the instances described in the ensuing discussion.

If this had proved to be the case, a further question would have remained. How could we explain the actual processes of diffusion by which these essentially derived styles appeared in the corpus of a conservative pottery tradition? The wares themselves were locally produced and showed no very great technical innovations. Among the identifiable jar fragments with deliberately roughened surfaces were some with characteristic Unĕtice finger-streaking. There was no reason to suppose that these vessels were imported or copied locally because of any real or fancied superiority in aesthetic quality or utility.

If it should have been established beyond question that at least some of these typologically Bronze Age vessels were actually contemporaneous with the late Eneolithic occupation of the site, the most logical explanation would then have been that since Late Řivnač and Early Unĕtice settlements existed cheek by jowl in this area, some degree of intermarriage had almost certainly taken place. We need only have postulated that either the potters were women living in a patrilocal society, or men living in a matrilocal one, to have a situation in which diffusion took place through the spread of the pottery-makers rather than of the pots. Furthermore, such individuals living in a new milieu would, for a period of time at least, have retained some, if not all, elements of the aesthetic and technical tradition to which they had become accustomed and, in the long run, might well have had some impact upon the pottery styles of the community as a whole.

The fact that the people of Homolka protected their strongly situated village with a fortification wall, apparently against contemporary groups with other cultures (probably Saxo-Thuringian Corded Ware people, Bell Beaker people, and perhaps even Early Unĕtice people), presented no basic contradiction. In a lecture referring to the disappearance of Neanderthal Man, the late Professor Hooton once said, "When different peoples come into contact, they may fight, but they will always breed," and he has paraphrased this in writing (Hooton, 1946, pp. 338–39). In the Kirkuk Liwa of North Iraq, for example, where Arabs, Turks, and Kurds coexist in neighboring but ethnically distinct villages, a fair amount of intermarriage continually takes place.

If we extend this inference about the traceable effects of intermarriage from the limits of a single village to larger areas, we can expect to find zones of admixture between neighboring areas of distinct pottery traditions. Dr. Evžen Plesl of the Archaeological Institute of the Czechoslovakian Academy of Sciences has called my attention to such an area of admixture between the Late Bronze and Early Iron Age territories of Urnfield and Tumulus Burial tradition. This area lies along the Elbe Valley north of its confluence with the Vltava or Moldau (Böhm, 1925; Plesl, 1960, 1961).

During the course of the symposium discussion, Rouse reported finding such a zone of overlap lying across the middle of Puerto Rico with distinctive and separate ceramic traditions found at each end of the island (Rouse, 1951, p. 260 and Fig. 3). Van der Waals called attention to a similar compact stretch in the Rhine Valley where a mixed pottery tradition resulted from the meeting of Corded Ware–Battle Axe people on the one hand and Bell Beaker people on the other. Mellaart said that a diagonal line could be drawn separating western and central Anatolian pottery in sites occupied at the end of the 3rd millennium, but that an admixture of traits occurs southeast of Tuz Golu. Here the large spouts and wheel-made wares of West Anatolia and the smaller spouts and handmade pottery of the central region both occur. Furthermore, the names of the traders and the place names given in the Kultepe texts definitely establish that West Anatolian Luvians and Central Anatolian Hatti inhabited the area at the same time.

In more broadly theoretical terms, such situations may help to establish the boundaries between archeologically defined culture areas of the past. In a schematic sense, as described in the older ethnological literature, they should fall where the admixture of traits between two culture areas is approximately even, but in general we must consider them as zones rather than as lines on a map. (Dixon, 1928, pp. 24–25; Kroeber, 1939, pp. 4–7; Wissler, 1938.)

In commenting on the suggestion that intermarriage may be recognizable in the pottery of a single site, Solheim described a possible case in a burial site in the Sarawak delta of Borneo, in date approximately A.D. 600–1100. Here for a brief period, pottery forms, especially the handles, were copies of Chinese types but were made locally. The handles did not adhere well to the vessel walls, and their production soon ceased. In the local historic situation, women have traditionally made the pottery and Chinese men have often come into the area and married local women. Solheim suggested that perhaps the local wives struggled to imitate Chinese styles in a technique unfamiliar to them and that subsequently local born offspring had no interest in the Chinese styles, which soon died out.

The symposiasts also discussed inferences that could be drawn from the presence of Roman pottery in several parts of Europe, especially in border areas,[2] and also the impact of the Crusades in the Mediterranean and the Near East together with ceramic traits brought back into Europe by the Crusaders.

Another type of inference on a broader scale comes into play when ceramic similarities merely represent one element in a much wider nexus of resemblances. It has long been recognized that there are many culture traits that are shared by the Indians of northern North America and the people of the northern tier of the Eurasiatic continent. If we take into account such traits and trait complexes as forms of shamanism, bear ceremonialism, the flat drum, etc., it is hardly surprising to find pottery that is strongly reminiscent of the Eurasiatic Pit Comb—and other wares. Although definitive interpretation of this so-called circumpolar complex has not yet been established, the ceramic resemblances would seem to reinforce its inherent validity. This is still a matter of debate and the question remains open,[3]

2. Recently, in his review of D. M. Wilson's *The Anglo-Saxons* (1960), H. J. Fleure (1962) wrote, "Early arrivals (perhaps Roman mercenaries and migrants escaping Slav pressure) were sometimes young men who took to wife native women, so that one gets Roman features on Saxon pots . . ." This is apparently Fleure's construct, for I have been unable to find any clear-cut expression of this in the volume itself.

3. For an hypothesis suggesting diffusion from Europe westward, particularly with regard to possible Ertebølle–Boreal Archaic and Late Neolithic–Early Woodland relationships, see Kehoe (1962).

yet the ceramic complexes of the southeastern United States and of the Hopewell, Ohio, tradition show many traits in common with Southeast Asia and Japan. For the most part there are very marked discrepancies in their dates, with the American series falling one to two thousand years later than those of the Far East. Thus we are again faced with the alternatives of convergence through the mechanism of limited possibilities, or diffusion plus conservatism in the maintenance of ceramic tradition. As our archeological evidence accumulates, we should be able to arrive at a definite conclusion. A recent paper by Estrada, Meggers, and Evans (1962) calls attention to the multiple ceramic resemblances of the Valdivia culture on the coast of Ecuador to that of the contemporary Middle Jomon period of Japan and to continental eastern Asia of that time. There seems to be no question but that this culture must be a transplant that occurred between 3000 and 2000 B.C. Here we seem to have one definite link in our evidence, but many more are still missing. For ceramic data bearing on the question of later Transpacific contacts see Estrada and Meggers (1961). Using exclusively ceramic data, Coe (1960) has not only convincingly pinned down diffusion between Middle and South America during the Formative stages of the Nuclear civilizations of the New World, but he has also suggested the possibility of their derivation from a southward extension of a Woodland base.

Up to this point we have been regarding ceramics, and specifically pottery, as a basis for making paleoethnological inferences. It now seems advisable to mention briefly those qualities of ceramics which make them such a valuable tool for the archeologist. In addition to the possibilities of innumerable variations, the life of a pot in a given culture can usually be considered to be short and, once broken, it becomes almost indestructible as a piece of evidence. Because archeologists do work so much with material culture, they have a tendency to forget that they are working with the tangible cultural remains of what once were groups of living people. Although some ethnologists do conceive of culture as subject to its own laws regardless of people, an archeologist must bear in mind that his primary concern is with the inferences he can draw concerning the groups of people represented by the cultural remains with which he is working.

We draw closer to the meaning of ceramics to the maker when we remember that when we find relatively identical ceramic complexes on the domestic handicrafts level over a wide area, we are dealing with groups of people who share a common aesthetic tradition. We must also remember that, aside from such simple and broad considerations as that a flat plate is a poor receptacle for soup, the actual shape of a pot has rather little relationship to its purpose. True, a pinched spout makes for ease of pouring, a narrow mouth for covering and sealing, and the like, but in a general sense there are many potential ways of meeting a particular need —such as steadiness. A pot may stand on any of a hundred bases, and certainly numerous bases have appeared. What we have, then, is a conservative and probably largely unconscious allegiance to a culture pattern or style that seems "right," rather than a similarity enforced by a functional necessity.

In the attempt to define culture groups or to delimit areas in which traits may be shared, specialized types of ceramics may offer good diagnostic traits for the recognition of culture areas or cotraditions, either for a single period or through time (Bennett, 1948; Ehrich, 1956; Rouse, 1951, 1954). The clay wall nails and glazed bricks of Mesopotamia are a regional example, while the glazed wall tiles used from Turkestan across North Africa to Spain indicate the diffusion of a diagnostic element across the major area of the Islamic World.

Another type of diffusion indicative of contact and culture borrowing, but not necessarily indicative of close cultural relationship, is evidenced by the spread of the potter's wheel, and inferences drawn from wheel-made pottery are often on an expanding level of ethnological inference. The presence of such pottery suggests strongly that the society using it has made the shift from home manufacture for immediate domestic use to a reasonably distinct pattern of economic and somewhat industrialized specialization, at least to meet the demands of peasant markets as Foster suggests. It is no accident that with the appearance of the wheel the areas of pottery stylization expand and the pottery becomes more uniform, but that changes of style, when they occur, are apt to be more sudden and drastic, with less conservative persistence of tradition. The changeover from Hallstatt to La Tène ceramics, though slow in Central Europe (Filip, 1956), became almost complete and, although some La Téne characteristics persisted in modified form during the Roman-Barbaric period, the pottery changed completely with the influx of the Slavs and the establishment of the Slavic wares. Analogs to such changes in style are, of course, numerous in our own highly industrialized culture which tends to foster "planned obsolescence."

On a somewhat different level, we must also move from dealing directly with relatively simple, specific, ethnographic data to very much wider considerations. The presence of baked clay weights and whorls, for example, is normally taken to be prima facie evidence of weaving. In given areas, the date of their appearance suggests the borrowing of this craft or the influx of a people who were already conversant with it. We know, however, that weaving of various degrees of complexity was practiced in pre-Columbian times, and that types of spinning varied from the simple thigh rolling of thread for the hanging warps of the northwest coast of Canada to a spindle product for the looms of Peru. Since the textile industry of Peru has long been cited as one of the bodies of data suggestive of pre-Columbian contact across the Pacific, the appearance of clay spindle whorls has definite relevance as a trait in a trait complex that is found in both the Old World and the New. A recent diffusion of the spindle whorl over Bering Strait seems out of the question, so we are left with a piece of ceramic evidence that is caught up, not only in the specific question of Transpacific contact, but in the wider philosophical question of the nature of man—which formerly took the labels of his psychic unity versus his relative uninventiveness—as translated back into interpretations of independent invention versus diffusion. The whole problem of Transpacific contact in pre-Columbian times is still far from settled. My only purpose in adding this note on spindle whorls is to add a ceramic trait to an already established trait complex that has figured as an important element in the wider discussion of cultural resemblances between the Old World and the New, and the cultural processes which brought them about.

It seems significant that, at the preliminary New York meeting, the question was voiced by Griffin as to whether New World pottery as a whole might not have been derived from the Old World, at least via stimulus diffusion, over and beyond the problems of the circumpolar complex mentioned above (Edmonson *et al.*, 1961, and comments). If this suggestion proves to be the case, the nexus of ceramic data widens and poses still further questions concerning clay figurines.

With regard to the functional aspects of such objects in their immediate ethnographic context, whether ethnologically or archeologically approached, we can legitimately draw inferences from their patterns of occurrence. In the Middle East and in the Aegean, figurines of marble and of baked clay are of very considerable antiquity in the settled villages and towns. There, because of their numbers and the circumstances of their appearance, it seems perfectly legitimate to attribute to them some degree of magico-religious significance. This, of course, is reinforced by the continuing use of such figurines from Mycenaean through Greek Geometric times, down to their known ritual use in Greece and Rome, when their character is less generalized and the definite recognition of particular deities becomes possible. Carrying this inquiry further, we find large numbers of figurines in use in the Danube basins during the Neolithic period, at a time when there is a presumption of strong influx from and contact with Asia Minor. In the complex are also found the so-called "Ishtar beds" considered to be of Anatolian origin. Whether some of the schematic-type Vinča figurines can be tied to the Cycladic idols on the basis of style, or whether we have here a parallelism of conventionalization, poses a specific problem in a wider field.

But how shall we interpret the sporadic appearance of figurines in the area north of the Danube where we face a different cultural tradition? At the site of Homolka, Bohemia Řivnač culture, early 2nd millennium B.C.), for example, we have two small, human, clay figurines found on a shale slab in one pit, and fragments of three or four tiny, crude, animal figurines from other hut units. These may well have been children's toys, although we cannot rule out the possibility of magico-religious significance. This type of archeological inference has been posed by Bullen (1947) in her treatment of both ethnological uses and archeological occurrences of figurines and miniature pottery in the North American Southwest. There miniature pots are made for the children but are also included to insure good luck in the firing process and, among the Hopi at least, are used as an offering to the dead if the potter meets a funeral. The association of occasional crude figurines with miniature pottery in the Řivnač culture obviously has no direct connection with the Southwestern Pueblo and Navaho peoples, and here we are dealing with the principles of limited possibilities and chance resemblance. By extending the inquiry to include the reopened discussion of possible Transpacific contacts (bearing in mind the possibility of Old World derivations for all New World ceramics) we come to the extended and demonstrable ritual use of figurines in Central America. Can such figurines be brought into such a discussion along with the other traits and complexes so frequently cited?' (Ekholm, 1953; Estrada and Meggers, 1961; etc.)

HISTORICAL DOCUMENT AND HISTORICAL ANALOGY

Up to this point we have been directing our attention primarily to some aspects of ceramics with reference to the ethnographic, ethnologic and paleoethnographic and paleoethnologic data. Most of our examples have come from prehistoric and protohistoric archeology with some transgression into historic and current data as analogies in order to demonstrate certain methodological and conceptual usages as they are applied to the inferential reconstruction of cultural history. In this sense, then, we have been largely confining ourselves to the field of cultural anthropology.

Our next step is to reverse our current procedures and, starting with the clear application of ceramic analyses to historical problems, to work backward from known contexts to the interpretation of undocumented ones. In this sense, ceramics, as well as other forms of material culture, become historical documents which supplement the written sources and, provided that some information is available as to place, maker, or cultural context, they are of value—whether accumulated by antiquarians, by ethnologic or artistic collection, or by archeological excavation.

We can use this material to fill in gaps in the record of reasonably well documented periods. Trade patterns in the Mediterranean during Classical times are traceable through the distribution of stamped handles on amphorae indicative of the wine trade. (Eftimie, 1959; numerous articles by Virginia Grace; etc.) The widely distributed red wares of the Roman period, particularly those that bear maker's stamps, also reflect the degree of intensity of trade contact.

In earlier less documented and undocumented periods we can still pick up some historical clues. In the eastern Mediterranean, for example, recognizable Minoan objects, including pottery, are found on the Greek mainland, mainland objects in Egypt (viz. the Tell-el-Amarna Mycenaean pots), and Egyptian objects in Crete. A reasonable inference drawn from this set of circumstances is one of circular or point-to-point trade. Current and historical analogies are numerous. Arab dhows start with a load of Basra dates and spend the better part of a year trading in the Indian Ocean, some going as far as Indonesia. And there is the continuing pattern of exchanges in the eastern Mediterranean today. As one who has shared deck passage on a Khedivial freighter with 2000 sheep and 1500 goats from Turkey en route to Syria, to what was then Palestine, and to Egypt, and watched other commodities being loaded at the ports of those countries, I can attest that this tradition is alive. Shiploads of grapes moving from Crete to Athens may well continue a much older and established pattern.

It seems almost certain that the Bronze Age pots that suggest such a trade were containers rather than trade objects in themselves. Large jars may have held wine, oil, condiments, or some other commodity, and the smaller decorated vessels may well have been forerunners of the Madison Avenue packaging for perfumes and unguents today.[4] (In the symposium discussion Weinberg cited the archeological evidence from Rhodes which shows that during the Late Bronze Age some Mycenaean settlers from the Greek mainland clearly took over the sea trade from Crete.)

A further historical parallel with obvious cultural implications for more dimly recorded periods is the well-documented 19th-century China tea trade. One standard run was to start from New England with manufactured goods and to trade en route for rum at Barbados, for furs on the northwest coast of Canada, and for tea, silks, china and other luxuries in China before starting on the long journey home. Not only were family fortunes made and social stratification accentuated but, in terms of material culture, the influx of Chinese wares into New England provides concrete documentation. To what extent the popularity of the willow pattern and its subsequent debasement through cheap local copies or inferior wares made in Japan and England stemmed from this trade and reflected changes in class structure and culture outlook is primarily a question for art historians and sociologists. The so-called Chinoiserie in England and America at that time represents a definite merchant class subculture which is documented by the Chinese trade wares and their English imitations. With the rapid disappearance of the wooden ships, the silks, the tea itself, and the other perishable organic substances, these Chinese wares, imported grave figures, and the like, are rapidly becoming our only surviving tangible evidence apart from the written records. Conversely, in China we have the effect on ceramic designs of wares expressly made to meet the demands of European and American markets (Beurdeley, 1963). However, the broad distribution of copies, local and other, is a phenomenon that is frequently observable in much simpler archeological contexts, such as the local copies of Bell Beaker and Corded Ware Beakers in Central Europe, or the obviously local styles and wares derived from Minoan and mainland sources found in the Middle and Late Cycladic levels of Phylakopi.

Ceramic materials can be used to document known historical events either in specific situations or in general ones. Pottery dating to roughly 700 B.C. found at Tarsus in association with a level of destruction thus correlates nicely with the historical information that Sennacherib destroyed Tarsus in 697 B.C. and provides supplementary evidence (Goldman, 1937, p. 276). On a broader level, the appearance in the Near East of Iron Age clay figurines of horses and saber-carrying riders wearing pointed caps lends credence to reports that Scythian horsemen were mercenaries, particularly since triangular-sectioned bronze arrowheads with basal barbs and socketed two-edged types also appear at approximately the same time in the same area (Sulimirski, 1954, pp. 296–97, 305, etc; Goldman, 1937, pp. 276 ff., Figs. 33, 36; 1938, p. 51).

Luxury trade articles such as the glazed tiles found throughout the Islamic world from Central Asia to the Mediterranean have already been mentioned. Glazed ware from identifiable centers like Samarra cover much of the same terri-

---

4. For a particularly intriguing demonstration of this, see Merrillees' paper (1962) "The Opium Trade in the Bronze Age Levant."

tory. Glazed tile in Mexico mark the spread of this trait beyond the limits of the Islamic world. Its path originally led westward across North Africa and then northward into Spain where it was introduced by the Moors. Christian Spain then served as a secondary center of diffusion, and it is thus not at all surprising to find these tiles in what was formerly a part of the Spanish Empire. The correspondence of Mexican Primavera ware with Spanish Majolica represents much the same process. In like manner, the wide distribution of Hellenistic wares in the towns of that period documents the spread of the Greek tradition under Alexander and its continuance as a dominant force in the more civilized centers under his successors. Roman wares, too, indicate the extent of Roman trade and power.

The analysis of a ceramic corpus may eloquently show the actual cultural impact of a conquering or dominant political power on the way of life of a submerged population, and the extent of effective domination may to some degree be measured by it. In the southwestern United States, for example, the conscious attempt at "Americanization" or acculturation of the Pueblos is reflected in their pottery by such items as English style teapots, European floral patterns, and the like. The recrudescence of native style ceramics, although artificially stimulated and enforced by trade demands, still has a very real social and cultural significance in reinforcing the ethnic "self-identification" of individuals and the solidarity of the group.

A conservative tendency in ceramics made on the household handicraft level and the fact that stylistic change can become more rapid and complete with industrialization have already been mentioned. We made this point particularly with reference to the potter's wheel, but politically organized craft training can produce the same effect. Such ceramic similarity was produced by the trained potters of the Inca Empire, and their output has an almost mechanical stereotypic regularity although they were unfamiliar with the wheel. The ceramic record by itself bears witness to the thoroughness of deliberate culture leveling by the Incas (Mason, 1957, pp. 104–5; Rowe, 1946, pp. 287, 329). The situation in Cilicia was quite different, for here we apparently have a culturally unstable crossroads area where industrialized crafts spread through the countryside quite rapidly (Ehrich, 1956, p. 8). Tarsus, which was obviously a key town, is distinctly Hellenistic in the Hellenistic period, Roman during Roman times, and Islamic and Turkish once the Turks came into the area. There is very little local distinctiveness or carryover in the ceramics of these periods. Under the Hittite Empire the ceramic corpus is markedly Anatolian in character. All of these changes coincide with known historical shifts in the power structure. On the basis of such historical correlations it seems reasonable to suggest that the sudden influx of Cypriote Iron Age wares—definitely made in the kilns of Tarsus and found on the surface of practically every habitation mound in Cilicia (Gjerstad, 1934; Goldman, 1937, pp. 271–2; 1938, pp. 40–41)— may well indicate a strong but temporary domination of the whole area by Cyprus. Wheeler's study of *Rome Beyond the Imperial Frontiers* concentrates on trade, but it also brings into focus the rapid attenuation of influence on local ceramic styles once the potters were beyond the limits of political control with diminishing cultural contact (Wheeler, 1955, pp. 211–12). The distribution of Tiahuanacan elements in pottery from Bolivia and the Argentine suggests a parallel situation.

ETHNOGRAPHIC ASPECTS IN CONTEMPORARY CIVILIZATION

As we shift our focus again, this time with emphasis on the orientation toward the meaning of ceramics to the maker and user, we still must remain on an analytical level. Elements of technology persist as vital criteria, and various aspects of social structure and outlook are of prime importance. Thus, in our historical and contemporary contexts we can make some broad and obvious divisions within the field of ceramics in terms of function in the society. Among these are ceramics for industrial purposes, ordinary household use, and special occasions in household use, as well as wares which may have some incidental use but which are primarily aesthetic objects from the point of view of both the maker and the purchaser. To these we must add the amorphous class of ceramic objects, once functional but now in general disuse, that are collected for aesthetic or status satisfactions.

Ceramics for industrial purposes may be designed to meet specific engineering needs such as insulation, construction, packaging, and for specialized uses such as flowerpots, sewer pipes, and the like. Functional domestic ceramics may range from roof tiles, used since antiquity, and baked bricks for both industrial and domestic construction, through cooking wares to table china in routine use, whether public or private, lamps, flower containers, and toilet bowls. These are ceramics which are geared to the daily round. There is no prohibition against such articles having aesthetic value, and certain artists and potteries have established reputations for turning out well-designed products. On the other hand, we have much that is of low quality both technically and/or artistically, intended for the uncritical mass market. To tableware we can add the gimcrack ashtrays of the "Gifte Shoppes" and the various horrors of the souvenir trade.

In addition to the everyday ware, however, we must consider good china, often kept in reserve and used only on special occasions. Such sets are usually from potteries with a well-earned reputation for high quality products—Sèvres, Lowestoft, Wedgwood, Lenox, and the like. The reputation, limited production, and high price of these wares render them a status symbol both in respect to the ability to have them, and the implied sophistication necessary to appreciate them properly. The inclusion of antique china through antiquarian proclivities often assigns some coarser wares of an earlier day to an equivalent category, but the aesthetic tastes of the buyer and user may be the dominant factor. Many American women who moved westward to more primitive living conditions carefully preserved their good china as symbolic of a more gracious and sophisticated past and as a contact with the more urbane East. Once this tradition had become established, good china was included among the heirlooms, and precious china became a mark of family continuity. As a documented example of the diffusion of a special class of ceramics we may here have another lead for interpreting historically undocumented distribution.

Another special class with a variable range is that of personalized ceramics. Some pieces of this nature are easily recognizable while with others it must remain a matter of conjecture and definition. It is not unusual to present a distinguished foreign visitor or local celebrity with some specially made piece of porcelain as a commemorative gift (*viz.* the plate designed for Sir Leonard Woolley), and in many historically oriented museum collections we find ceramic objects that were associated with known people or past events. Commissioned pieces belong in this category as do those with personal names, such as the friendly gifts of Mexican potters or the Classical Greek vases bearing love names. The commissioned types range from monogrammed china services through vessels and plaques with individual or family coats of arms, possible portraits such as the Bellarmine jugs of sixteenth-century Germany, joke pieces, and the like. From these, of course, it is but a step to ordering run-of-the-mill pieces with perhaps a request for a particular color or some other less clearly identifiable aspect. The Bellarmine jugs find a closer analogy in the modern Toby-type jugs which delineate a particular figure, such as General MacArthur, but are mass produced for wide and general sales. In this sense they would hardly belong to the personalized class, for the portrait becomes merely a highly popular design.

In the general category of ceramics as a medium of aesthetic expression, the emphasis is on the object itself rather than on its use. We can start with such obviously decorative items as the Dresden figurines and run through a whole gamut of continuing tradition where an earlier significance may have been lost. Although the values attached to the Dresden figures or the modern ones from Copenhagen are only social and aesthetic without religious or magical overtones, the question arises whether the same can be said as unequivocally for the genre figures of Tanagra, Myrina, and other Classical sites. In all of these instances, the figurines were factory produced.

The individual and independent craftsman is essentially in conflict with the machine-like production of a large pottery, and today's artist-potter expresses himself through creating new forms with varied techniques, new associations, special glaze combinations, and unusual painted, incised, and plastic decoration. Far from adhering to accepted cultural prescriptions, the advanced ceramist struggles to break with his immediate cultural limits by incorporating style elements from other cultures or by expressing his own creative urge. Much of this kind of individuality still stays within the bounds of recognizable craft canons, but some products tend to be much more extreme in type. There is always the question of how far the imagination of the present-day craftsman is inhibited by unconscious adherence to ingrained, culturally defined, aesthetic standards and how far his product is conditioned by his estimate of what he can sell. A further ramification stems from the interchangeability of materials which releases him from the limitations of clay. In our present civilization we have better technical control and a wider range of substitutes than our predecessors, but this merely increases the number of choices. While we solemnly note the class significance of the use of materials in the Inca Empire and elsewhere, we often forget the status we attach to some of those that we ourselves use, as well as to the possession of objects created from them by craftsmen of "name."

We must remember that our current cultural stress on individuality results, at least in part, from the concern in the West and particularly in America with the psychology of the individual and his need for self-expression. In this sense, certain ceramic craftsmen properly belong in the current art world for they are applying themselves to the field of creative art. It is, however, somewhat paradoxical and more than a little ironic that a first class ceramist who achieves a distinctive style and technique soon finds that he is not only repeating himself but that he is attracting followers or copyists. In other words, while an artist struggles to project himself through unique creations, his inventiveness is not inexhaustible, and he is likely to become the fountainhead of an industrialized or commercialized style of the same nature as the one against which he is rebelling. He may himself transfer his ceramic creativity to other media, or furnish designs to be executed by others. We are then confronted with what approximates a horizon style that cuts across several specialized crafts and industries in our own society. Among them the field of ceramics plays a major role.

SUMMARY

It has been my purpose in this paper to present a coherent pattern in which specific studies relating to ceramics and man might find a place. My thesis is that, since the whole field of ceramics is a trait complex in the material culture sense of the ethnologist, the culture concept of the cultural anthropologist should provide the most comprehensive means of approaching the subject. We may thus view ceramics from the comparative standpoint of ethnology, from the more particular one of ethnography, from the sequential and documented associational one of history, from elements of all three as reflected in archeological evidence of the past, from contemporary institutionalized forms and values of aesthetic production and appreciation in the artistic sense, and from varying types of social significance.

Seen in this light, the topics dealt with in this paper and in those that follow all find a place in this broader unified pattern.

BIBLIOGRAPHY

BENNETT, W. C.
1948. "The Peruvian Co-Tradition." In *A Reappraisal of Peruvian Archaeology*, assembled by W. C. Bennett. Memoirs of the Society for American Archaeology, No. 4: 1–7. (Supplement to *American Antiquity*, Vol. 13, No. 4, Pt. 2.)

BEURDELEY, M.
1963. *Chinese Trade Porcelain*. Rutland, Vt.: Tuttle. (Published in 1962 as *Porcelain de la Compagnie des Indes*. Fribourg: Office du Livre S. A.)

BÖHM, J.
1925. "Bylanský hrob ve Střešovichích." *Obzor Praehistorický* IV (Niederlův sbornik): 11–23.

BULLEN, A. K.
1947. "Archaeological Theory and Anthropological Fact." *American Antiquity*, 13:128–34.

CHILDE, V. G.
1957. *The Dawn of European Civilization*. London: Kegan Paul.

COE, M. D.
1960. "Archaeological Linkages with North and South America at La Victoria, Guatemala." *American Anthropologist*, 62:363–93.

DIXON, R. B.
1928. *The Building of Cultures*. New York: Charles Scribner's Sons.

EDMONSON, M. S., *et al.*
1961. "Neolithic Diffusion Rates." (with critical comments) *Current Anthropology*, 2:71–102.

EFTIMIE, V.
1959. "Imports of Stamped Amphorae in the Lower Danube Regions and a Draft Rumanian Corpus of Amphora Stamps." *Dacia* (n.s.), III: 195–215.

EHRICH, R. W.
1950. "Some Reflections on Archaeological Interpretation." *American Anthropologist*, 52:468–82.

1954. (ed.) *Relative Chronologies in Old World Archeology*, pp. i–x. Chicago: University of Chicago Press.

1956. "Culture Area and Culture History in the Mediterranean and the Middle East." In *The Aegean and the Near East, Essays Presented to Hetty Goldman*, Saul S. Weinberg (ed.), pp. 1–21. Locust Valley, N.Y.: J. J. Augustin.

1963. "Further Reflections on Archaeological Interpretation." *American Anthropologist*, 65:16–31.

EKHOLM, G. F.
1953. "A Possible Focus of Asiatic Influence in the Late Classic Cultures of Meso-america." In *Asia and North America: Transpacific Contacts*, assembled by M. W. Smith. Memoirs of the Society for American Archaeology, No. 9:72–89. (*American Antiquity*, Vol. 18, No. 3, Pt. 2.)

ESTRADA, E. and B. J. MEGGERS
1961. "A Complex of Traits of Probable Transpacific Origin on the Coast of Ecuador." *American Anthropologist*, 63:913–39.

ESTRADA, E., B. J. MEGGERS, and C. EVANS
1962. "Possible Transpacific Contact on the Coast of Ecuador." *Science*, 135:371–72.

FILIP, J.
1956. "Keltové ve Střední Évrope (Die Kelten in Mitteleuropa)." In *Monumenta Archaeologica* V. Prague: Czechoslovak Academy of Sciences.

FLEURE, H. J.
1962. Review of "The Anglo-Saxons" by D. M. Wilson. *Man*, LXII: p. 95, Item 166.

GJERSTAD, E.
1934. "Cilician Studies." *Revue Archéologique* (ser. 3), 6:155–203.

GOLDMAN, H.
1937. "Excavations at Gözlü Kule, Tarsus, 1936." *American Journal of Archaeology*, 41:262–86.
1938. "Excavations at Gözlü Kule, Tarsus, 1937." *Ibid.*, 42:30–54.
1940. "Excavations at Gözlü Kule, Tarsus, 1938." *Ibid.*, 44:60–86.
1954. "The Relative Chronology of Southeastern Anatolia." In *Relative Chronologies in Old World Archaeology*, R. W. Ehrich (ed.), pp. 69–85. Chicago: University of Chicago Press.
1956. *Excavations at Gözlü Kule, Tarsus.* Vol. II. *From the Neolithic Through the Bronze Age.* Princeton: Princeton University Press.

HOOTON, E. A.
1946. *Up From the Ape* (rev. ed.). New York: Macmillan.

KEHOE, A. B.
1962. "A Hypothesis on the Origin of Northeastern American Pottery." *Southwestern Journal of Anthropology*, 18:20–29.

KROEBER, A. L.
1939. *Cultural and Natural Areas of Native North America.* University of California Publications in American Archaeology and Ethnology, XXXVIII (reprinted 1947). Berkeley: University of California Press.

MASON, J. A.
1957. *The Ancient Civilization of Peru.* Harmondsworth: Penguin Books (Pelican Book A395).

MELLAART, J.
1958. "The End of the Early Bronze Age in Anatolia and the Aegean." *American Journal of Archaeology*, 62:9–34.

MERRILLEES, R. S.
1962. "Opium Trade in the Bronze Age Levant." *Antiquity*, XXXVI: 287–92.

PHYLAKOPI
1904. *Excavations at Phylakopi in Melos Conducted by the British School at Athens.* Society for the Promotion of Hellenic Studies, Supplementary Papers, No. 4. London: Macmillan.

PLESL, E.
1960. "Vztahy Severočeská sídelní Oblasti k Sasku v Mladší Době Halštatské (Die Beziehungen des Nordböhmischen Siedlungsgebiete zu Sachsen in der Jüngeren Hallstattzeit)." *Památky Archeologické* 51:539–60.
1961. "Přeživání Lužického Základu do Mladohalštatského Obdobi na Pohřebišti v Libochovanech, Okr. Litoměřice (Das Weiterleben der Lausitzer Grundlage auf dem Gräberfeld in Libochovany, bez. Litomerice in der Junghallstattzeitlichen Periode)." *Ibid.*, 52:219–28.

ROUSE, I.
1951. "Areas and Periods of Culture in the Greater Antilles." *Southwestern Journal of Anthropology*, 7:248–65.
1954. "On the Use of the Concept of Area Co-Tradition." *American Antiquity*, 19:221–25.

ROWE, J. H.
1946. "Inca Culture." *Handbook of South American Indians*, 2:183–330, Bulletin 143. Washington, D.C.: Smithsonian Institution, Bureau of American Ethnology.

SCHMIDT, E. F.
  1937. *Excavations at Tepe Hissar, Damghan.* Philadelphia: University of Pennsylvania Press.

SCHMIDT, W.
  1939. *The Culture Historical Method of Ethnology.* New York: Fortuny.

STEWARD, J. and A. MÉTRAUX
  1948. "Tribes of the Peruvian and Ecuadorian Montaña." *Handbook of South American Indians*, 3:535–656, Bulletin 143. Washington, D.C.: Smithsonian Institution, Bureau of American Ethnology.

SULIMIRSKI, T.
  1954. "Scythian Antiquities in Western Asia." *Artibus Asiae*, 17:282–318.

TAYLOR, W. W.
  1948. *A Study of Archaeology.* Memoirs of the American Anthropological Association, No. 69. (*American Anthropologist*, Vol. 50, No. 3, Pt. 2.)

THOMPSON, R. H.
  1958. *Modern Yucatecan Maya Pottery Making.* Memoirs of the Society for American Archaeology, No. 15. (*American Antiquity*, Vol. XXIII, No. 4, Pt. 2.)

WARD, L.
  1954. "The Relative Chronology of China through the Han Period." In *Relative Chronologies in Old World Archaeology*, R. W. Ehrich (ed.), pp. 130–44. Chicago: University of Chicago Press.

WHEELER, SIR M.
  1955. *Rome Beyond the Imperial Frontiers.* Harmondsworth: Penguin Books (Pelican Book A335).

WILSON, D. M.
  1960. *The Anglo Saxons.* Ancient Peoples and Places, No. 16. New York: Praeger.

WISSLER, C.
  1938. *The American Indian.* New York: Peter Smith. (Rev. ed., 1950)

THE ETHNOLOGIST AND
THE AMERICAN INDIAN POTTER[1]

S. LINNÉ

IN 1908 Erland Nordenskiöld, while at Rio Pilcomayo on the Bolivia-Argentina border, once heard the Mataco Indian storyteller Na-Yás recount how Creation was divided between the Christians and the Mataco (Nordenskiöld, 1910, p. 104). Their ancestors had dwelt together in a big house where everything was to be had that a Mataco could dream of. But the Christians went away, taking with them all the good and useful things. They left behind only a few mean trifles such as earthen pots and the like—and that is why the Mataco are so poor. This tale is modern—Indians who never beheld the splendors of the whites entertain quite different views and estimates of their pottery. A brief stroll in the strange world of myths shows that benevolent culture heroes taught the Indians how to manufacture the earthen pots so vital to their existence. Thus both the Toba and the Mataco tribes, all on Rio Pilcomayo, were actually indebted to mythical teachers for their knowledge of pottery-making (Métraux, 1946, p. 86). The Paressí and the Yagua in Brazil as well as the Jívaro of Ecuador had supernatural powers to thank for the fact that they knew how to make earthenware (Métraux, 1948, p. 359; Steward and Métraux, 1948, p. 627). The Cuna on Panama's Atlantic coast boast of a multiheaded collection of culture heroes who specialize in different fields. One of them, of course, is the inventor of pottery-making (Nordenskiöld, 1930, p. 673).

POTTERY-MAKING, A FEMALE OCCUPATION

Despite the fact that the representatives of the powers of the unknown who taught the Indians to make pottery were of both sexes, the women excelled at it.

1. The title is vague. As an Americanist I have in this little sketch stuck to the American Indians. Even with this restriction, my contribution of limited size would be comparable to a bunch of flowers picked in a hurry by a wanderer through a meadow in bloom.

I have refrained from making use of all those extraordinary publications written by George M. Foster, the foremost specialist on technical questions of Mexican ceramics. Since Foster was one of the symposium lecturers, I naturally did not want to pick flowers from his garden. Neither time nor place would suffice, as from various points of view Foster's studies of modern Mexican pottery are exhaustive and bear out one of the old sayings: "What he doesn't know about pottery it isn't worth knowing." And not to completely alter the planning of my modest contribution to the conference, I wish to limit myself by listing those works of Foster of which I ought to have availed myself: (Foster, 1948a, 1948b, 1955, 1959a, 1959b).

The fact is that among all Indians a strict division of labor occurs between the sexes, and pottery-making is a virtually exclusive female occupation in tribes outside the high cultures. Thus every woman should have been able to make ordinary utility ware for the kitchen, but both experts and dabblers were found in every community. There are data from South American Indians attesting to the achievements of specially gifted women who were master craftsmen of repute and expert producers of coveted pottery.

Whether or not the women were the potters on the Peruvian coast in pre-Columbian times has long been a matter of speculation. The ceramic craftsmen here were artists by the grace of God in the vanguard of the world elite. As reasons militating against the probability that they were women, some very farfetched and implausible explanations have been advanced. Those ancient Peruvians certainly sported no Victorian views as to human behavior in general. The inferences of their "pornographic" pottery are unknown to us. Arthur Posnansky, who cannot be accused of lacking imagination, attributed the morally offensive features to the debasement of the mind caused by the Peruvians' practice of cranial deformation; and, in turn, attributed the tribe's extinction to this immorality. Posnansky's theory is shared by no one (Posnansky, 1925, pp. 67–74, pls. 8–16).

In 1889, according to Hans H. Brüning (1898, pp. 259–60), itinerant potters appeared in the northernmost Peruvian coastal strip. They hailed from a region where pottery was one of the chief sources of income. In order to escape expensive, troublesome, and risky transportation, the potters themselves peregrinated and settled down in places having usable clay and markets for their products. Junius B. Bird states that "most of the coastal valleys and the highland basins of Peru contain deposits of exceptionally good clay for making pottery. These clays are of fine quality, easily worked . . . without further modification . . ." (Bennett and Bird, 1949, pp. 245–46). Only simple utility wares were produced, and working methods were not very involved. The raw material consisted of a semi-spherical lump of clay with a concave underside. It was put on a rounded stone and beaten out by means of a wooden paddle which had a rectangular surface. During the beating the paddle was regularly dipped in water. After the pot was shaped, its rim was strengthened by the addition of a coil of clay. Then the pot was smoothed and polished, and after drying was fired in a hole in the ground. The fuel consisted of dried goat and cattle dung. The pots were packed in the dung which, when lit, developed an intense heat.

In the Ethnographical Museum of Sweden at Stockholm we have some simple, sooty cooking pots from tombs at Ancón excavated in 1883 by Hjalmar Stolpe, first regular head of the Museum (Fig. 1). Their shape resembles the utility ware produced by Brüning's potters, and their modeling probably was accomplished in a similar fashion. The mummies in these tombs were wrapped in attractive cloths of types typical of this section of the coast during Late Ancón, Middle or Late period of the Central Coast.

FIGURE 1
Clay pots—cooking pots—from tombs at Ancon, Peru
(Ethnographical Museum of Sweden, Stockholm).

THE POTTERS OF THE HIGH CULTURES

The question of whether the potters within the high cultures were male or female can be answered to some extent by examining their descendants, the pottery-makers among the Quechua and Aymara of our own time. Among the Quechua, pottery production is concentrated in certain areas. Both males and females are potters but the majority are males (Mishkin, 1946, p. 433). Among the Aymara, pottery-making is a male occupation although women assist chiefly by modeling certain kinds of simpler vessels, usually bowls (Tschopik, 1946, p. 536).

The division of labor between modeling and firing the ware on the one hand and decorating it, on the other, is not mentioned. Yet it is not unreasonable to assume that the pottery of the Peruvian coast is the result of the joint efforts of at least a couple of ceramic craftsmen. To model a stirrup-spout jar calls for exceptional craftsmanship plus "tradition." The exquisite decoration of the pots—graceful animals and bucolic scenery and races, mythological representations, and naturalistic battle scenes—must have been done by an initiate in the tradition and the cult who was at the same time a great artist—that is, if we give "artist" its old-fashioned meaning: an individual capable of and willing to represent something comprehensible to the common man or something which will deepen the insight of those already versed in iconography.

The same may be said of those technically quite simple Maya vessels which, however, are real masterpieces considering their painted decorations. It is just as unlikely that a potter should understand the complicated iconography and the hieroglyphs as it would be for a man trained in the religious systems to deal with the simple technique of pottery. From the craftsman or woman to the art-creating priest there must have been a long social step. The same could very likely be said about the ceramics of Teotihuacán: A technically simple pot which I found during an archeological excavation in the region of Calpulalpan in the state of Tlaxcala has a decoration in relief produced by a learned artist. He must have been very familiar with the calendar and the religious conceptions (Fig. 2). It is not easy to determine how the decoration was done. Most likely the pot was made in a mold which must have been built up around the original figure, probably a solid piece of clay.

Stuccoed and painted tripods are found at Teotihuacán and also at Kaminaljuyú in Guatemala (Kidder, 1946, Figs. 204–7). This pottery must be considered as a collaboration between extraordinarily skillful potters and intellectuals also prominent in art. The resemblance between the tripods from Teotihuacán and those from Kaminaljuyú is very great in form, technique, and decoration. This cannot be explained by trade, as transportation would damage the decoration on the loose, thin stucco. It might be an example of the traveling potters mentioned in the introduction to this paper. The differences may be an adaptation to the personal taste of the buyers. The painting of the decoration was not the job of the potters.

FIGURE 2
Clay bowl found at Las Colinas, State of Tlaxcala, Mexico.

On the other hand the Thin Orange Ware and the Plumbate Ware must both have been brought by trade from some still unknown distant centers. The clay used in both is unique. For many years I have tried to find the center where the Thin Orange Ware was manufactured. According to Mrs. Carmen Cook de Leonard it can be found somewhere in Tehuacán in the state of Puebla, but she has not been specific as to place. It is indeed strange that the solution to this most fascinating problem is postponed year after year. If, for instance, Dr. Shepard and Mrs. Cook de Leonard could be encouraged to work on this problem, together with some archeologist specially trained in ceramics and supplied with a portable laboratory, then perhaps this puzzling problem would soon be solved.

During the discussion of this paper Miss Shepard gave a splendid summary statement concerning "Plumbate Ware." She has edited it for inclusion here.

Plumbate is another ware that affords an excellent opportunity for the study of trade, imitation, and diffusion because of its technical specialization and stylistic elaboration. The extremely hard, semivitreous slip of Plumbate is perhaps the most interesting technical development of New World pottery. It is a reminder of the technique of Classic Greek Black-on-red and Terra Sigillata pottery. But the Indians lacked Old World potters' control of firing, consequently there are many poorly fired pieces that show the characteristics of the clay slip clearly. The incised geometric design is highly stylized and the effigy representations can be identified as Mexican in origin. The ware is widely distributed, extending from Tepic, Nayarit, Mexico, in the northwest through the Valley of Mexico, Guatemala, and Salvador to Nicaragua. A large proportion of it has been found in El Salvador and Guatemala, and for many years there was a debate as to which of these areas was its center of distribution. The answer has been indicated by the discovery of an early form that is restricted in distribution. This is from the west central highlands of Guatemala. I have argued that all Plumbate pottery had a single center of distribution because of the uniformity of paste, which is distinctive, being tempered with a finely ground vitrophyre. When examined in thin sections the pastes of pottery from Central Mexico, Yucatan, Guatemala, and Salvador cannot be distinguished; pastes of the typical local wares are quite different, and vitrophyre does not occur in some of the areas.

There has been some confusion on the matter of source of production in recent years because of the beautiful imitations of Plumbate made by Robert Sonin. Since he used clays from different sources for slip, the argument was advanced that the pottery could have been made in different places. This fact that fine-textured clays that will vitrify in the Indians' firing range are widely distributed was well recognized in 1948 when the Plumbate report was written, but the argument of unity of origin does not rest on similarity of surface appearance but on identity of paste. Only archeologists unfamiliar with the evidence were misled by the hypothesis of multiple sources.

In the course of study of some four hundred vessels in museums and private collections, seven non-Plumbate vessels that in earlier years had been illustrated in publications as Plumbate were found. They were unmistakable and poor imitations. The potters attempted to copy style but adhered to their own techniques; for example, they incised before, instead of after, slipping. I found no specimen in which there was clear evidence of an attempt to imitate the semivitreous appearance of the slip. The lustrous surfaces of imitations were obtained by polishing, a common technique far removed from the Plumbate technique of dipping in a slip that dried with a natural luster. Occasionally semivitrified vessels in styles unrelated to that of Plumbate have been found; these are in all probability the results of accidents of firing, rather than attempts to imitate

Plumbate by non-Plumbate potters. From present evidence, therefore, it appears that Plumbate Ware was seldom imitated despite its wide distribution in trade. Certain similarities in form and design between Plumbate and Fine Orange Ware[2] raise the question of diffusion. Brainerd referred to these similarities as indicating relationship, but the primary sources of attributes and the interaction between the styles is yet to be studied. Consequently Plumbate pottery still offers excellent opportunity for research.

Characteristic of the pre-Columbian high cultures is an astonishing consistency regarding ceramic modeling and decoration. A mere sherd from Chimú, Nazca, Teotihuacán, the Maya, Aztecs, or Inca, at once betrays its origin. Each by itself also fills exacting aesthetic demands from our viewpoint. The modeling of each one by some gifted artist is unquestionable, yet the fact that they were accepted without "modernizations" to speak of through generations is most remarkable. Pottery was brought to Teotihuacán from many export centers. Strangers—for instance, Thin Orange Pottery—appear in the same burials with Teotihuacán ware of the purest kind (Fig. 3). They never influenced each other.

The Aztecs, herrenvolk of Mexico at the time of the Conquest, dwelt in a well-organized world. They dominated a large portion of Central Mexico from the Atlantic to the Pacific. The subdued peoples regularly paid minutely stipulated tribute of various kinds to the capital, Tenochtitlan, on whose ruins the central part of the Mexico City of our day is built.

In the huge, well-organized marketplace at Tlatelolco in the northwestern part of the city, close by the mightiest of the many temple pyramids, merchandise of many kinds was put on sale. Here surely you could have acquired Cholula pottery, a luxury for the well-to-do. That the price was high is obvious. Bernal Díaz del Castillo, one of Hernando Cortés' comrades-in-arms, relates that Moctezuma's table was decked with Cholula earthenware either red or black (Díaz del Castillo, 1904, Vol. I, p. 280) and that there was pottery of all imaginable kinds in the marketplace. What is preserved in museums transcends all praise. This is everyday or fiesta pottery (for there is no indication whatever of any connotation of a cult function)—utility ware sublime in shape, beautifully decorated, and functional in practice. These potters had tackled in earnest one of the worst stumbling-blocks of utility ware—the dripless spout—and succeeded in producing it. How well? At any rate, to no lesser degree than our potters of today (Fig. 4). Once more the ethnologist has to record the fact that America's potters within the high cultures held their place in the van of the contemporary world's elite. We do not know, however, if these very fine wares were imported. They have nothing in common with Aztec pottery either in style or in decoration. It is out of the question that they should have been made by the same Aztec masters who together with the Mixtecs occupy an outstanding position in the history of handicraft. It has been taken for granted that this is a case where pottery was imported from the Mixtecs, but as yet we have no real proof for such an import. Petrographic investigations of

2. "Thin Orange Ware" is the term preferred by Dr. Linné. Dr. Shepard, however, uses the more general term, "Fine Orange Ware."—F.R.M.

potsherds from the Valley of Mexico with reliable information as to their find-spots could undoubtedly solve the problem. Either the clay would tell us that the pots in question were imported or that they had been made by clever craftsmen brought to the valley where they used the local clay.

The European invasion meant disaster to the aesthetically accented pottery, for Indian art cannot stand Europeanization—it succumbs helplessly. Tourists are offered sorry travesties of popular art, whose sole merit is that they are technically inferior, hence short-lived.

Antonio de Mendoza, first Viceroy of Mexico (1535–50), had copies made of pre-Hispanic pictograms which in part may have belonged to the Aztec state archives or central fiscal authority. They show the kind and quantities of tribute collectively due from groups of villages and deliverable at Tenochtitlan—grain,

FIGURE 3
Tripods from Teotihuacán and strangers appear in the same burials
(Ethnographical Museum of Sweden, Stockholm).

FIGURE 4
A Mixtec pitcher from Tenochtitlan,
the Aztec capital.

honey, incense, blankets, uniforms, feathers, gold, etc. These pictograms are obviously far from complete, yet only one of them comprises vessels which may be of clay: four hundred pieces of a certain kind suitable for chocolate-drinking, four hundred without specified use (Kingsborough, 1831–48, Vol. I, Pl. 49; Vol. VI, p. 38). Legitimate purchase of the imported ware cannot be ruled out. The national capital scarcely could have lived exclusively on fiscal tribute and domestic production—supplies were also brought home by trading expeditions.

One section of Codex Mendoza shows, by means of the expressive pictographs, how boys and girls were educated. The boys were taught no household chores while the girls learned spinning, weaving, cooking, etc. In vain we look for pottery-making. This essential ware and consumer article certainly had been produced in the Valley of Mexico, where excellent clay is to be had in many spots, or was imported to the capital. Out in Lake Texcoco, where the Venice of America had been developed, an occasional potter or two must have found the going hard. The heavy hand of the State rested also on taste. Judging from certain pottery types and painted decorative patterns, a modest evolution occurred during the two hundred-year history of the Aztecs. By the time of the Conquest, at least some of the Aztec potters—or those supplying the Aztec market—had progressed from linear decoration to certain naturalism, using birds, fish, and flowers as decorative elements.

In the Inca Empire the herrenvolk at Cuzco, Peru lorded it as supreme arbiters of taste, style, and everything else. The same ceramic types occurred from Ecuador down to Chile. That the heterogeneous population of the realm should entirely conform to the taste of the rulers is not to be expected. But state-employed potters, or suppliers to official establishments and authorities, or the representatives of the Cuzco rulers around the country, had to produce certain stipulated types. The pottery types of the official style were few yet functional and noble in their stringently compact form. Standardization had been aimed at and achieved.

If the potters of the Inca realm toiled according to the decrees of the temporal powers, their earlier counterparts in the Teotihuacán culture heeded the bidding of their own theocratic rulers. In this metropolis in the Valley of Mexico, the biggest city in the America of those days, charged with cult atmosphere, there had evolved a remarkable pottery type which, like that of the Aztecs or the Inca a millennium later, is wholly unique. The cylindrical tripod with a flat base, conical lid, and decoration incised after firing and filled with cinnabar, is the hallmark of the culture. It must have been an abomination to a potter, though ideal to an artist laboring with metal, but in Teotihuacán there were no metals. At about this time the paradise of Tlaloc, the God of Rain, was represented in a mural. Here is life and movement—people dancing, singing, and bathing in the land of the happy dead. But the decoration on the pottery consists of rigid symbols. The ceramic craftsman had to incise and scrape out the hard shiny surface, figures, concepts, and ideas which are forever lost to us. Every detail had to cover about one-third of the cylinder surface—all that could be seen at one time. Only the most skilled ceramic craftsmen could manage such a delicate problem. Here was a case not of art for art's sake but of art for utility. The decorations were standing supplications to the life-giving divine powers of Rain and Water. The potter scarcely could have found an intellectual source of joy in his products. Behind the cult concepts reflected in the skeleton-texted representations of divinities, there lay invocations of the mythical powers for protection against crop failure and misery. The cosmic powers, the deities dwelling in the Unknown or sweeping over the earth carried by rain clouds, must have been a harmonious and docile tribe. At least this impression is gained by a detailed analysis of the potter's representations—quiescent apparitions, yet regrettably correct in functionary fashion, stiff and rather boring. The craftsmen of Teotihuacán never dramatized their deities, for just as display of one's own emotions was taboo, such display was inconceivable in the case of the gods.

Names of rulers are in abundance in pre-Columbian America. They are, however, only names—in a few cases legendary apparitions. Those wonderful portrait urns created by great ceramic craftsmen during the Mochica epoch in the northern coastal valleys of Peru represent people about whom we know nothing— who will eternally remain anonymous.

THE SILICEOUS TEMPERING OF POTTER'S CLAY

In order to prepare potter's clay, various tempering materials may at times be added. By experience, potters know what should be mixed into it. Sand is most common, but fine-crushed potsherds are a frequently occurring substitute. On the Amazon, its tributaries and their tributaries, as well as in Guiana, the clay is mixed with highly siliceous burnt bark to prevent undue shrinkage and cracking of the ware. There is no sand available and to crush sherds in wooden pestles—rock does not exist—is difficult. The burned bark resembles sand, and unburned it is hard and resistant as a prime clay vessel should be—the matter is settled. Practical experience and magical concepts co-operated. The quantity of the admixture varied, but one part bark silica and three parts clay seems to have been the proportion most common. The admixture was less when the bark was deemed extra fine by the potter. With a pocket lens it is sometimes possible to see the silica crystals in such bark (Linné, 1925; 1932).

Siliceous plants are common in tropical America, especially in the Amazon Basin. Highly siliceous are the genera *Chrysobalanus, Moquilea, Grangeria, Hirtella, Lecostemon, Licania* and *Turiuva*. They all belong to the family *Rosacea* (Lovering, 1959, p. 784). Pottery made of clay tempered with such biological silica (SiO_2) is of good quality and this can in fact be felt: it is dry, granulated, hard and firm. In thin sections of such pottery, icelike siliceous fragments are visible at a moderate magnification (75 times). Returning from a study trip in 1913–14, Erland Nordenskiöld brought home some samples of the bark used as tempering material to produce strong pottery by the Chacobo and the Cavina, two Indian tribes in the Bolivian lowland. When part of the dry bark sample was burnt the very scanty ash from the organic substances could be blown away. The bark used by the Cavina contained 48.63 per cent silica (SiO_2) which amounted to 95.97 per cent of the weight of the ash. But the Chacobo would not give away the secret to the suspect white man. They gave him bark which after burning yielded only 3.48 per cent of ash very deficient in silica. But thin sections showed that there was something wrong here: the Chacobo pottery was just as silica-tempered as that of the Cavina. In Göteborg ten years later (1923) I disclosed the trick. Nordenskiöld, Indian among Indians, had noticed the knavery and taken a sample of the ash that was to be mixed into the potter's clay. It proved to contain 98.5 per cent silica. To give the stranger a sample of the bark would have been to surrender the patent. With the aid of the ash alone he could not possibly have located the tree. Most likely it was bark from a tree of the species *Licania*, perhaps one of the premier silica accumulators of the plant kingdom (Lovering, 1959, p. 785).

The Carajá on the Rio Araguaya in Brazil, according to Fritz Krause (1911, p. 282), mixed burned and crushed sponges into the potter's clay. Curt Nimuendajú, renowned expert on Amazon ethnography and archeology, in a detailed letter to me (March 17, 1926), supplied numerous intriguing data pertaining to the freshwater sponge, or, more correctly, sponges *Parmula batesii* Carter and *Tubella reticulata* Carter, so essential to potters. At least the first-mentioned occurs profusely in the many affluents of the Amazon, its size approximately that of a man's head. In the dry season the number desired is easily obtained. Women potters close to Santarém on the lower course of the Amazon used dried and crushed sponges. At Obidos, farther up the river, the women potters knew that these sponges formerly had been used, but the method was now discarded because the hands were injured when the clay was kneaded. Here it seems a transition to silica from burned bark had occurred.

Nordenskiöld brought home a sponge from the Canichana on the Rio Mamoré in the northeastern Bolivian lowland. Even though these Indians were so deculturized by 1908–9 that they had virtually only their language left, they mixed crushed sponge into the clay in the old fashion when making pottery (Nordenskiöld, 1911, p. 83).

All freshwater sponges have a skeleton of needle or sausage-shaped siliceous spicules that consist almost exclusively of silica when dried. The needles of *Parmula batesii* are 0.3 to 0.4 cm. in length. If a sponge is heated, the cohesive organic substance disappears and the sponge disintegrates into a mass of spicules. Yet neither burning nor crushing, as mentioned by Krause, is likely to have occurred when the clay was prepared from which the archeological vessels were formed. Exposed to sudden strong heating, the siliceous needles shattered. When they were embedded in the ware it was a different matter since the pottery was relatively slowly heated. The majority of the sponge needles in the archeological pottery are intact. Possibly the sponges had been allowed to rot in a vessel filled with water, and the spicules had settled on the bottom in the form of fine sand. When the sponge needles were intact they constituted a reinforcement in microsize, and a potter's clay thus prepared was splendid material not only for those who shaped utility ware but also for artists with bold and uninhibited ideas. Nimuendajú's collections of ancient pottery from the lower course of the Amazon, notably at Santarém, are assignable to the latter category and are counted among the rarities in the South American archeological collections in Göteborg's museum.

With the aid of a thin section of archeological pottery from, say, Santarém, the ethnographer can obtain a message, as it were, from the potter deceased centuries ago. The thin section of the master's work which he has before him tells of its creation. We know how the clay was treated to become of first quality. A thin section taken from an appropriate spot, for instance at the profiled opening of a vessel, may show that the sponge needles have arranged themselves in two main directions. Control tests on other parts of the vessel show that this is no mere coincidence. The needles within a portion of the tested piece cut the section surface at right angle; within the other portion they stand parallel to the surface. The thin section shows that the silica needles in the clay near the exterior surface have aligned themselves horizontally, and this has occurred because the implement shaping the rim has exerted pressure on the clay: the needles have assumed a position according to least resistance. The needles belonging to the inner side of the vessel stand at an angle of 90° to the others. The profiled rim was formed with the aid of some implement, probably a piece of calabash rind in the edge of which a pattern was cut to fashion the vessel's rim. From British Guiana, Im Thurn (1883, p. 276) describes the operation:

To smooth the edge or lip of the vessel, a piece of the shell of a calabash is used. A piece is carefully cut out from one side of the shell, so that the space left exactly corresponds with the intended lip of the vessel. By means of this nick, the shell is then fitted on to the edge of the vessel, and is passed round its circumference. This of course smooths away any inequalities in the clay, and leaves a perfectly smooth edge. In

the same way, either a projecting ledge or a groove is sometimes made in the soft clay
by way of ornament, entirely round the body of the growing vessel. In such cases, according as a ledge or groove is to be made, a groove of the required shape and size is
made in the edge of the calabash-shell, or a projection is left on its edge.

Tests have shown that the needle-shaped siliceous spicules released from the
aforementioned sponge completely tally with those in archeological pottery. If
the needles are exposed to relatively high heat, for instance, by being heated over
a hot spirit flame, they blacken. Whether the time of heating is of consequence has
not been established. Should the answer prove negative it is easy to choose between the two modes of firing the pots which would apply here: an open fire or
some form of primitive kiln. In the latter case the pot is placed on some sherds and
surrounded by firewood placed so that it forms a cone which is then covered by
large pieces of heavy bark. The fire is lit in the innermost layer. A number of
fieldworkers have observed the firing in this manner. The able Indian researcher,
Theodor Koch-Grünberg, writes that the fire gets "nach innen konzentriert und
entwickelt eine enorme Hitze" Koch-Grünberg, 1909–10, Vol. 2, pp. 226 ff). Yet
there are other technicians who think that the open fire momentarily creates
greater heat. This matter once established, we shall be able to follow with a rather
high degree of probability an Amazon archeological pot from clay to finished
product.

In the Rio Uruguay there is a closely related sponge, *Uruguaya corallioides*,
which, according to Antonio Serrano (1950, p. 39), once was used in the production of potter's clay. Unfortunately he is overly laconic, inasmuch as this is a most
interesting observation. Within the Amazon River system, a discovery or invention is likely to spread quite easily. However, in this case the degree of communications between the Rio Araguaya and the Rio Uruguay is an intriguing problem.
In the case of pottery the regrettable fact is that mere superficialities have been
noted while authentic data thus far is scarce; hence many potters may have used a
sponge admixture but there is no record of it.

If the ethnographer collaborates with the archeologist, the latter's research will
show that biological silica is a later improvement of an older ceramic technique.
There are reports of Indians in Brazil who themselves are using bark in their
pottery-making, while this new method of producing pottery was unknown to
earlier generations. Artifacts from two archeological culture strata found by
Nordenskiöld in Mound Velarde in Mojos, North Bolivia, showed that a biological
silica admixture was not known in that region and time. There was no trace of
either a bark or a sponge admixture.

SHAPE AND DECORATION

The student of the pottery of Peruvian coastal cultures—be it from an artistic,
technical or religio-scientific viewpoint—is bound to feel relieved when he becomes acquainted with the potters among the Chané and the Chiriguano in eastern Bolivia on the border of El Gran Chaco. In every respect the potters of the

coastal cultures lead the way among all the world's craftsmen in this field. In certain cases the construction of the masterpieces is still a mystery, nor has the purpose which the vessels served been established—still one is fascinated by the terrifying pictures of demons and fabulous animals involved in dramatic battles.

During his explorations in 1908–9, Nordenskiöld found that while the Chacobo to the north on the Brazilian border knew of only three kinds of earthen pots (Fig. 5), the Chané and the Chiriguano had several hundred different pottery types (Nordenskiöld, 1911, p. 110). The fact that the pottery of one tribe showed a high aesthetic and technical level while it was little developed in another tribe does not necessarily mean that the former possessed a standard higher in every respect. But it is only natural that erroneous conclusions of this kind would be drawn from archeological remains. It is noteworthy that the pottery of Mojos, the lowland part of Northeast Bolivia, modern as well as archeological, lacks ears. This practical detail exists to the south among the Chané and the Chiriguano. This and other elements indicate influence from the high cultures to the west. Pottery-making devolved upon the women, who vied with one another at the feasts to deck their tables with attractive pottery. According to Nordenskiöld, the State Ethnographical Museum of Sweden (Stockholm) has the finest collection in the world. Each and every woman could make a pot but some of them were obviously more adept than others. In their craftsmanship all were conservative. They varied the traditionally inherited ornamentation, refusing to strike out in new directions. By means of simple outline sketches Nordenskiöld classified 146 different types of pottery from the Chané and the Chiriguano as well as 54 with independently de-

FIGURE 5
The Chacobo Indians in Bolivia, 1909, knew only three kinds of earthen pots
(Ethnographical Museum of Sweden, Stockholm).

veloped decoration painted before firing (Fig. 6), (Nordenskiöld, 1920, pp. 148–62).

If the admirable female craftsmen of the Chané and the Chiriguano were reluctant to tamper with grandmother's modeling and decorative elements, a contrary attitude was demonstrated by the Hopi woman, Nampeyo, wife of one of the workers who in 1895 helped Jesse Walter Fewkes excavate Sikyatki, a large prehistoric city or pueblo, in Arizona. The date of the destruction of this once grandiose habitation has not been established but the regrettable disaster is likely to have occurred some time in the fourteenth century. Nampeyo was a potter as skilled as she was spirited. She studied the earthenware recovered, and examined all sherds in detail. Technically and aesthetically, it is one of the best examples of the potter's art in the Southwest. She began to make pottery of the same shape and decoration as those of the prehistoric specimens. The rest of the potters in her pueblo joined her and the new ware completely displaced the types of earthenware that had formerly been produced. She became founder of the Sikyatki school of pottery.

When I interrogated Alfred Vincent Kidder, eminent archeologist and specialist in this field, concerning Nampeyo, he said that she had approached far too near to the originals. To distinguish Nampeyo's products from the archeological specimens proved impossible. Fewkes (1919, p. 218) feared that these imitations could easily pass as genuine when produced on a large scale and offered for sale in the antique shops of New Mexico and California. According to him, it might in time prove difficult to distinguish between the work of Nampeyo and her colleagues and the genuine findings from the Hopi prehistoric period.

Nampeyo, however, was no mere imitator, and she developed new elements while her imagination closely recreated the Sikyatki sense of form and decoration. She was not just a technician but a theorist as well, and she developed into a creative artist. In her excellent study of pueblo pottery, Ruth L. Bunzel writes (1929, pp. 41, 56):

To quote Nampeyo, the founder and leading spirit of the Hopi school of decoration: "The best arrangement for the water jar is four designs around the top,—two and two, like this (indicating on the floor the arrangement). The designs opposite each other should be alike." Her own work clearly showed her preference for this type of arrangement. . . . "When I first began to paint, I used to go to the ancient village and pick up pieces of pottery and copy the designs. That is how I learned to paint. But now I just close my eyes and see designs and I paint them."

It was quite a coincidence that Nampeyo happened to refashion both the form and decoration of the pottery she produced. Her female colleagues followed her. The clock was turned back, the pottery of the dead city was resurrected. This may have been a unique phenomenon, yet if something similar has ever occurred in other areas in prehistory, then any resurrectionist would be likely to make archeologists tear their hair.

According to Anita Brenner (1931, p. 93): "The domestic pottery of Culhuacan is a locally differentiated development of Aztec domestic pottery." The painted

FIGURE 6
Vessels of different shapes from the Chané
and Chiriguano Indians in Bolivia.

decoration here differs from typical Aztec decoration by being quickly and often carelessly and slovenly applied, contrary to the rigid and exact delineation characterizing typical Aztec design. The dissimilarity is probably due to the fact that Culhuacan, an ancient village site in the Valley of Mexico, was a pottery center producing for exportation. It was here chiefly a case of hurriedly producing earthenware in quantity, especially bowls with or without legs. That decoration was not entirely dispensed with was no doubt due to the fact that a vessel without decoration seemed unfinished. Hence a technique was developed which satisfied both producer and consumer. "This technique shifted the control of the design from the eye, or mind, to the hand, and the operation of automatic motor habits affected profoundly design-content and composition, and developed new designs and compositions by transforming previous forms and arrangements calligraphically."

Under more primitive conditions, haste does not affect the decoration because it does not exist. New decoration may be the result of the production method—but unintentionally so. Bowls with flat bases are often modeled on a support leaving neat imprints of plaited mats, cloth, or banana leaf, while rounded vessels, if modeled in a basket, show basket imprints. In the case of archeological pottery, the producer unwittingly supplies data concerning mats, textile products, and baskets. A banana leaf imprint attests to the fact that the bowl, perhaps an archeological specimen, is post-Columbian—the banana being a recent arrival in the New World, introduced by the Spanish. From San Miguel on the Rio Guaporé, Nordenskiöld in 1909 acquired a large earthenware plate with a flat bottom. It was reportedly recovered from land just brought under cultivation. The bottom carried a very clear imprint of a banana leaf (Nordenskiöld, 1924, p. 130, Fig. 31). The vessel must be post-Columbian.

Finger-impression ornamentation is another mode of decoration directly connected with a production method common in America. Spherical vessels, jars, or urns were built up with coils of clay laid successively one on top of the other. One roll was pressed tightly on the preceding with the thumb and index finger, and in this fashion regular rows of little dents were formed. They were smoothed out on the interior but retained on the exterior. When this mode of decoration became popular—on a cooking pot it might prove practical for a variety of reasons—the finger-impression technique was frequently developed to astonishing perfection. This was the case in the southwestern United States and in South America. Utility vessels finished in this way are less apt to slip when handled, and when used as cooking pots they absorb heat more quickly than smooth-surfaced vessels since the surface area is so much much larger.

Long ago Erland Nordenskiöld pointed out that finger-impression ornamentation in South America occurs in the distribution area of the Tupi-Guarani tribes (1919, pp. 215–18). He said that this method of decoration came from the Guarani Indians and through them was subsequently disseminated, spreading westward on the slopes of the Andes. Instrumental in this connection were the Chiriguano when, in the early part of the sixteenth century, they migrated from Paraguay and subdued the tribes settled on the slopes. These were strongly affected by Andean influence, for they acquired decorative elements typical of the Inca pottery as well as other elements found on wares from pre-Columbian cultures in Argentina, northern Chile and southern Peru. For centuries these elements were copied, but finger-impression elements also survived.

FORMING AND SHAPING VESSELS

It would take us much too far to account, even in summary, for the building-up processes. Brought together, the observations by ethnologists and archeologists in addition to the studies of ceramic specialists scientifically or technically trained would run to a tome of respectable size. From terse reports by men in the field or from Franchet's "Céramique primitive"—now a classic—the observations have evolved during the past fifty years to such heights as Shepard's *Ceramics for the Archeologist* (1956), the most important studies by Frederick R. Matson on Ceramic Technology, Marriott's *María: The Potter of San Ildsfonso* (1948), Thompson's *Modern Yucatecan Maya Pottery Making* (1958) or Fontana's *Papago Indian Pottery* (1963).

Where, when, why, did the first potter start his trade? These are questions on which plenty of time and thought was wasted in the infancy of ethnographic science. Then the foundations were laid for the refined research methods of our day, and most·of it has been transferred to the fascinating and sometimes amusing curio cabinet of unrealistic theories.

Karl von den Steinen, eminently successful explorer, ethnographer and museologist, advanced a notable theory concerning the origin of pottery-making (Steinen, p. 216). Clever yet incredible, it never lacked adherents. The Indians kept clay for body painting in baskets, the clay hardened in the sun—a prototype for pottery was a fact. When the clay vessel was put in the fire it became a pot.

That pottery actually was molded in baskets is shown by bowls recovered in the course of archeological work, particularly in northwestern Argentina (Boman, 1908, pl. 2; Bruch, 1911, Fig. 71). These bowls are the best reproduced of a number by no means small. The list I published in 1925 can be extended with new arrivals from different parts of America, all testifying to the fact that they were modeled in baskets (Linné, 1925, p. 97).

An easier way of achieving an earthen vessel than by hollowing out a lump of clay and gradually raising the sides, finally getting a simple pot out of the lump, is scarcely conceivable. This very simple method of pottery-making was observed in relatively recent times by Tessmann (1930, p. 765) among some tribes between the Rio Yapurá and Rio Putumayo. Many additional instances can be adduced. The potters on the Peruvian coast, referred to by Brüning as earlier mentioned, made use of a development of this method.

In 1927, at Puturgandi, or Ustúpu, capital of the independent Cuna Indian Republic in Tule, Panama, I had occasion to watch a woman making an incense burner, *sianála*. But a finished specimen never appeared because at every stage in the manufacturing process she craved more cash. When my purse in due course was empty, she simply knocked the prospective burner back into the same lump of clay it originally had been. Otherwise her method was to model the main portion from a larger lump and then add suitable bits of clay for foot and upper part. These she baked together with the main portion, shaping her product with dexterous fingers.

That the coiled technique represents the climax of a lengthy evolution is most probable. The method has been described by innumerable travelers, yet I believe that Walter E. Roth's narrative (1924, pp. 131–32) takes the prize. It is a brief, pregnant account. Every stage can be followed as though by captions to a nonexistent film which in simple pictures plus the author's reactions becomes a reality to us. From a circular level foundation of clay the edges were raised. On a board a dozen coils of clay had been made ready. One coil is now taken and placed around and inside of the everted edge of the preceding. They are pressed together. The next coil is put on and pressed together, and so forth.

Julio Tello, eminent Peruvian archeologist, has paid much attention to the technical problems connected with the production of the peerless pottery of the coastal cultures (Tello, 1938, pp. 12–37). As far as I can see, his studies—including solutions of theoretical problems—can be considered successful. Only he who has access to pottery of intricate construction, smashed by *huaqueros*, or professional native grave-plunderers, has a chance to study the marvelously adept building-up technique. Tello had data to go by, and his interpretations and suggestions serve as a good start for a professional ceramic specialist who has to solve all problems.

Two defects in the technical know-how of Indian potters have always been pointed to: they could not glaze, and they did not use a potter's wheel. But objections have been raised to the contention that they lacked the potter's wheel and the claim has been advanced that Yucatan's potters had a prototype of the potter's wheel. Independent of each other, the potters of the New and the Old World should have been on their way to respectively reaching the same goal: a time and labor-saving implement by the aid of which an unlimited number of products exactly alike could be achieved.

The Indian "potter's wheel" has a turnable foundation. The authentic type is a fast-rotating disc in the center of which a pressed-on lump of clay is drawn up to the shape desired. The vessel is given exact contour by means of a mold held against its surface during the turning. For rim profiles, such implements were once used, as earlier mentioned, on the lower Amazon. Indian pottery is built on a foundation which can turn as the vessel is rising. This foundation may have been a basket, a small board, a mat, a piece of cloth or, simplest of all, a banana leaf. It provided a level base. A rounded vessel could have been modeled on the preserved bottom remaining from some disaster met by an erstwhile pot and then built up further with coils or strips. These two methods are seemingly related but have actually nothing in common. The turner turns, the Indian builds—even if the foundation can be turned rapidly. In Indian America the potter's wheel is not the end of an evolution but something novel—a revolution and the No. 1 enemy of creative art.

SENSE OF HUMOR

The ability to laugh is a characteristic of man, declared François Rabelais four centuries ago. This privilege reserved for man was very sparingly taken advantage of by the Indian potter. He could not at first reproduce sense impressions and when he got that far he was not allowed to. The fact is that Cult and State held the potters of the high cultures of ancient America in an iron grip, and giving vent to some little sense of humor would be laughing in the wrong place. During the Mochica and Chimú epochs the superb ceramic craftsmen in the coastal valleys of northern Peru created, as mentioned, portraits of rulers and warriors; they reproduced everyday people fishing, weaving, battling, as well as fruit and animals—fabulous animals and frightful demons—a culture-historical textbook of a unique kind. But rarely a tacit joke or stealthy smile is hinted at. The burial urns of the Zapotecs in Oaxaca are to be seen by the thousands or tens of thousands in Mexican museums and private collections or in the ethnographical museums of all the world. Technically often masterpieces, they usually represent a human figure more or less ornately decorated. Yet even if some of them represent deities, they should be able occasionally to betray some human emotion. One figure in the Ethnographical Museum at Stockholm, wearing the image of Ueueteotl, old God of Fire, as a pectoral, seems to smile at the resemblance between himself and the godly image (Linné, 1938, pl. 4).

In western and northwestern Mexico, masterful ceramic craftsmen have shaped a variety of figures—men and animals—with singular freedom, vivacity, and inventive ability. These artists were unfettered by cult or state decrees or inhibiting tradition. With joy and humor they created expressive snapshots without parallel in the history of the world's art.

It is almost touching when, among a lot of earthenware rigidly and doctrinally built up, one suddenly comes upon a specimen showing a genuine sense of humor. In the large Costa Rican archeological collections at the Stockholm museum there is a sizable vessel having on one side a rounded hollow outcrop. Out of a hole a curious animal is peering. The lengthy neck ends in a face larger than the opening (Fig. 7). Never risking the loss of its head, the animal is able to survey his environment undisturbed. A jest, pure and simple—and a rarity.

SUMMARY

In conclusion I shall adduce one more example. An archeologist finds a sherd with several holes. Magic? Scarcely, for one hole had sufficed to make it suitable to accompany the owner to the world of the dead. Whether the interpretation is correct or not, instances of this sort abound. When the holes have been drilled after firing it is a case of a cracked pot having been mended by holes drilled on each side of the crack and tied together by means of a ligament in the way one would tie his shoes. Today this practice is confined chiefly to cracked decorated calabashes. A sherd recovered from the Chané, the Mataco-Vejos, or the Chiri-

FIGURE 7
Clay vessel from Costa Rica.

guano, came from a steam-cooking contrivance: a bowl with holes in the bottom placed atop a cooking pot (Nordenskiöld, 1920, Figs. 16a, 16b). But had this sherd been recovered in Mexico—for instance, in the mountain villages of Guerrero —it would have been a piece of a smashed sieve or colander for washing the maize boiled in lime water. I saw such sherds used when on a trip from Chilapa to Oaxaca in 1948. On the other hand, a sherd of this sort recovered in the Mexico Valley is likely to have been part of a *tlemaitl* or "fire arm"—Aztec incense burners in the form of large ladles with a pierced blade. In Yucatan, too, incense burners—rounded vessels on high conical feet—were and still are produced.

Here and there in the foregoing I have attempted to show that the ethnographer is likely to be of some use not only to ethnography but to archeology as well. Some archeological pottery problems can be solved by study of methods still practiced. Forty years ago when I began to study the technique of South American pottery, little or nothing had been done systematically in this field. Since that time, highly skilled specialists at work in laboratories with superb equipment have achieved results then never dreamed of. Numerous problems have been solved, yet a great deal remains to be done.

Anyone devoting himself to the revelation of technical tricks and the recognition of technical practices now forgotten, or about to be so, is frequently apt to be regarded by theorists and desk savants as a mere tradesman. Yet these tradesmen furnish theoretical master builders solid and verified material for their constructions, which otherwise could easily prove to be castles in the air. Willard Libby, 1960 Nobel laureate in physical chemistry, might appear as an "honorary tradesman" to the theorists. As a rule, the life expectancy of theories is brief. On the other hand the secrets wrested by the ethnographer from ancient craftsmen and inventors via their latter-day descendants constitute firm and enduring stuff.

BIBLIOGRAPHY

BENNETT, W. C., and J. B. BIRD
1949. *Andean Culture History*. New York: American Museum of Natural History, Handbook Series, No. 15.

BOMAN, E.
1908. *Antiquités de la Région Andine de la République Argentine et du Désert d'Atacama*. 2 vols. Paris: Librairie H. Le Soudier.

BRENNER, A.
1931. *The Influence of Technique on the Decorative Style in the Domestic Pottery of Culhuacan*. Columbia University Contributions to Anthropology, Vol. 13. New York: Columbia University Press.

BRUCH, C.
1911. *Exploraciones Arqueológicas en las Provincias de Tucumán y Catamarca*. Buenos Aires: Revista del Museo de La Plata, Vol. 19.

BRÜNING, H. H.
1898. "Moderne Töpferei der Indianer Perus." *Globus* (Braunschweig), 74:259–60.

BUNZEL, R. L.
1929. *The Pueblo Potter*. New York: Columbia University Press.

DÍAZ DEL CASTILLO, B.
1904. *Historia Verdadera de la Conquista de la Nueva España*. 2 vols. Mexico. Oficina Tipográfica de la Secretaría de Fomento.

FEWKES, J. W.
1919. "Designs on Prehistoric Hopi Pottery." *33d Annual Report of the Bureau of American Ethnology*, pp. 207–84. Washington, D.C.: Smithsonian Institution.

FONTANA, B. L., et al.
1963. *Papago Indian Pottery*. Seattle: University of Washington Press.

FOSTER, G. M.
1948a. *Empire's Children. The People of Tzintzuntzan*. Washington, D.C.: Smithsonian Institution, Institute of Social Anthropology, Publication No. 6 (Printed in Mexico).

1948b. "Some Implications of Modern Mexican Mold-Made Pottery." *Southwestern Journal of Anthropology*, 4:356–70.

1955. *Contemporary Pottery Techniques in Southern and Central Mexico*. Middle American Research Institute, Publication No. 22:1–48. New Orleans: Tulane University.

1959a. "The Copotepec *Molde* and Some Associated Problems of the Potter's Wheel." *Southwestern Journal of Anthropology*, 15:53–63.

1959b. "The Potter's Wheel: an Analysis of Idea and Artifact in Invention." *Ibid.*, pp. 99–119.

FRANCHET, L.
1911. *Céramique Primitive*. Paris: Librairie Paul Geuthner.

IM THURN, E. F.

1883. *Among the Indians of Guiana*. London: Kegan Paul, Trench and Co.

KIDDER, A. V., J. D. JENNINGS, and E. M. SHOOK

1946. *Excavations at Kaminaljuyú in Guatemala*. Washington, D.C., Carnegie Institution of Washington, Publication 561.

KINGSBOROUGH, LORD

1831–48. *Antiquities of Mexico: Comprising Facsimiles of Ancient Mexican Paintings and Hieroglyphics*. 9 vols. London: Robert Havell.

KOCH-GRÜNBERG, T.

1909–10. *Zwei Jahre unter den Indianern*. 2 vols. Berlin: Ernst Wasmuth A.–G.

KRAUSE, F.

1911. *In den Wildnissen Brasiliens*. Leipzig: R. Voigtländers Verlag.

LINNÉ, S.

1925. *The Technique of South American Ceramics*. Göteborgs: Kungl. Vetenskaps–Och Vitterhets–Samhälles, Handlingar, Fjärde Följden, Band 29, No. 5.

1932. *Contribution à l'Etude de la Céramique Sudaméricaine*. Tucamán: Revista del Instituto de Ethnología, II:199–232.

1938. *Zapotecan Antiquities*. Stockholm: The Ethnographical Museum of Sweden (n.s.), Publication No. 4.

1942. *Mexican Highland Cultures*. Stockholm: The Ethnographical Museum of Sweden (n.s.), Publication No. 7.

LOVERING, T. S.

1959. "Significance of Accumulator Plants in Rock Weathering." *Bulletin of the Geological Society of America*, 70:781–800.

MARRIOTT, A.

1948. *María: The Potter of San Ildefonso*. Norman, Okla.: University of Oklahoma Press.

MÉTRAUX, A.

1946. *Myths of the Toba and Pilagá Indians of the Gran Chaco*. Philadelphia: Memoirs of the American Folklore Society, Vol. 40.

1948. "The Tribes of Mato Grosso and Eastern Bolivia." *Handbook of South American Indians*, 3:349–60, Bulletin 143. Washington, D.C.: Smithsonian Institution, Bureau of American Ethnology.

MISHKIN, B.

1946. "The Contemporary Quechua." *Handbook of South American Indians*, 2:411–70, Bulletin 143. Washington, D.C.: Smithsonian Institution, Bureau of American Ethnology.

NORDENSKIÖLD, E.

1910. *Indianlif i El Gran Chaco*. Stockholm: Albert Bonniers Förlag.

1911. *Indianer och hvita i Nordöstra Bolivia*. Stockholm: Albert Bonniers Förlag.

1919. *An Ethno-Geographical Analysis of the Material Culture of Two Indian Tribes in the Gran Chaco*. Comparative Ethnographical Studies, 1. Göteborg.

1920. *The Changes in the Material Culture of Two Indian Tribes under the Influence of New Surroundings*. Comparative Ethnographical Studies, 2. Göteborg.

1924. *The Ethnography of South America seen from Mojas in Bolivia*. Comparative Ethnographical Studies, 3. Göteborg.

1930. "Cuna Indian Religion." *Proceedings of the 23d International Congress of Americanists*, pp. 668–77.

POSNANSKY, A.
1925. *Die erothischen Keramiken der Mochicas und deren Beziehungen zu occipetal deformierten Schädeln*, 2:67–74, pls. IX–XVI. Frankfurt am Main: Abhandlungen der Frankfurter Gesellschaft für Anthropologie, Ethnologie and Urgeschichte.

ROTH, W.
1924. "An Introductory Study of the Arts, Crafts, and Customs of the Guiana Indians." *38th Annual Report of the Bureau of American Ethnology, Smithsonian Institution.* Washington, D.C.: Smithsonian Institution.

SERRANO, A.
1950. *Los primitivos Habitantes de Entre Rios.* Paraná: Ministerio de Educación.

SHEPARD, A. O.
1956. *Ceramics for the Archaeologist.* Washington, D.C.: Carnegie Institution of Washington, Publication 609.

STEINEN, K. VON DEN
1897. *Unter den Naturvölkern Zentral-Brasiliens.* Berlin: Dietrich Reimer.

STEWARD, J., and A. MÉTRAUX
1948. "Tribes of the Peruvian and Ecuadorian Montaña." *Handbook of South American Indians,* 3:535–656, Bulletin 143. Washington, D.C., Smithsonian Institution, Bureau of American Ethnology.

TELLO, J. C.
1938. *Arte antiguo Peruano, Inca,* Vol. 2. Lima: Museo de Arqueología de la Universidad Mayor de San Marcos de Lima.

TESSMANN, G.
1930. *Die Indianer Nordost-Perus.* Hamburg: Memoirs of the Society for American Archaeology, No. 15. Friederichsen, DeGruyter & Co.

THOMPSON, R. H.
1958. *Modern Yucatecan Maya Pottery Making.* Memoirs of the Society for American Archaeology, No. 15. (*American Antiquity,* Vol. XXXIII, No. 4, Pt. 2.)

TSCHOPIK, H., JR.
1946. "The Aymara." *Handbook of South American Indians,* Vol. 2:501–73, Bulletin 143. Washington, D.C.: Smithsonian Institution, Bureau of American Ethnology.

THE SOCIOLOGY OF POTTERY:
QUESTIONS AND HYPOTHESES
ARISING FROM CONTEMPORARY MEXICAN WORK

GEORGE M. FOSTER

IN examining the voluminous ethnographical literature describing the manufacture of pottery, one notes with surprise how little attention has been paid to the social, cultural, and economic settings in which the work is done. Most descriptions deal with techniques and processes of manufacture, and with design elements. But beyond telling which sex makes pots, most accounts reveal little about such things as the status of the potter in his or her society (except, of course, in Indian caste studies), how potters look upon their work artistically and economically, standards of workmanship and the range of variation within a community, and, above all, about the processes that contribute to stability in a tradition, which make for change, and which may be involved in the dying-out of a style. Yet, from the standpoint of archeological interpretation, these and other "sociological" points are just as important as are styles and construction methods.

In this paper I deal comparatively with a variety of phenomena of this type, which fall logically into two principal categories. The first has to do with the potter's position in his or her society. Here I am interested particularly in two questions: What status is assigned to potters by their society, and how do they themselves look upon their position and work with respect to non-potters? And, are there personality characteristics of potters that differentiate them from the other members of their social groups? The second category of phenomena comprehends the dynamics of pottery-making. Here I look for answers to the questions of what makes for stability or promotes changes in style, and what factors are involved in the dying-out of a technique or form. The data and hypotheses are offered in the hope that they will be helpful to archeologists by suggesting the probable validity of various inferential conclusions. For example, Anna Shepard speculates whether the makers of Plumbate Ware found in Mexico and Central America recognized the demands of special markets (1948, pp. 113, 114). The fact that contemporary Mexican village potters (and potters in many other lands) produce different wares for different markets substantially increases the probability that this inference, to explain a differential distribution of styles, is correct. On the other hand, her speculation that the industry may have ceased because of exhaustion of clay supplies (1948, p. 144) seems unlikely in view of the lack of evidence of any such contemporary event. But when we know that specialized wares sometimes are made by secret processes known only to a few potters, and that informal "patents" or "copyrights" are often respected, then her alternate suggestion (1948, p. 144) that the work of these specialists was disrupted beyond repair, possibly by their being driven from the clay sites, seems entirely reasonable.

To cut the descriptive and comparative task to manageable size, I limit myself largely to pottery-making in peasant societies. This means that potters are part or full-time specialists, that they form recognized groups (as in craft villages) or classes or castes (as in India), that they produce primarily for a market rather than for home consumption, and that productive techniques are significantly more advanced than the simple coiling or hand-modeling methods, and the open-firing, that characterize most primitive peoples. For inferential archeological value, therefore, the descriptions and hypotheses apply primarily to areas where similar conditions presumably prevailed—the centers of high cultures—rather than to regions inhabited by simpler tribal peoples. The point of departure is Mexico, and especially the village of Tzintzuntzan, on the shores of Lake Pátzcuaro in Michoacán, 250 miles west of Mexico City, where I have studied pottery-making more intensively than elsewhere.

I think it likely that in Mexico more pottery per capita is produced and that more forms, designs, and colors are found, than in any other part of the world of comparable size. Methods of production are equally varied, and range from the simplest coiling and hand-modeling techniques to the use of the wheel to make fine Majolica (Foster, 1955; Thompson, 1958). Although Spanish acculturation has in greater or lesser degree influenced contemporary techniques, except in marginal areas, it is clear that the pottery tradition itself long antedates the Conquest. As today, there must have been villages then largely devoted to the single industry, which traded their wares commercially over wide areas.

Most Mexican pottery is made for utilitarian purposes: for kitchen uses such as storing water and cooking food, for eating, to hold chicken and animal food, and to grow flowers and herbs. But significant amounts are artistic: made to be given as gifts, to be sold in religious fiestas for religious and secular purposes, as toys for children, and for other more specialized purposes. Increasingly, of course, the tourist demand is taking wares. The most common productive unit is the nuclear family in which husband, wife, and children co-operate in the entire process, from mining the earths to selling the finished product. The small-scale workshop with entrepreneur and a few hired hands is far less important, and real factories are limited to a few towns such as Puebla. In short, in Mexico today we find a vigorous, dynamic, varied pottery tradition which plays a major social and economic role in the lives of the people, and which consequently provides an ideal vehicle to explore general problems in pottery sociology.

Tzintzuntzan falls into this general pattern. When I first studied the community in 1945 there were 1200 inhabitants. Of the 251 households with a male head-of-family, pottery-making was the only economic occupation in 94; it was a part-time occupation in 53 more. Of the 22 households with a working female head-of-family, pottery-making provided the livelihood in 16. In other words, 60 per cent of the people depended entirely or in part on pottery-making. In 1960 the total population had grown to 1800, but the distribution of occupations was about the same, and pottery continued to be equally important.

Vessels are formed either in concave pottery molds in two halves divided vertically, or over convex "mushroom" pottery molds (Foster, 1948a, pp. 79–100). They are fired in the primitive circular Mediterranean kiln with open-topped pot chamber separated from the firebox by a grate. Men alone gather clays and firewood. Women alone grind the glaze, presumably because this is *metate* work, and only they use this grinding stone. Both sexes prepare paste, mold pots, decorate them, participate in firing, and help with selling. Most production is utilitarian, and consists of glazed casseroles, tortilla griddles, and cooking pots. A red-slipped *tinaja* ware, burnished and painted, is the traditional water-storage jar, and beginning about 1940 an ancient, although post-Conquest, white glaze ware began to be elaborated in form and design. Pottery is made in all parts of town, but most of the griddles come from one barrio which is inhabited almost completely by potters. Non-potters live in the other sections of town, intermingled with potters.

When I first knew Tzintzuntzan in 1945, all potters were familiar with the basic techniques, regardless of the particular objects they customarily made. All produced ware destined for the market, ware done according to a good, substantial, honest standard. With a half dozen or fewer exceptions, all potters were artisans rather than artists, and few made any effort to surpass commonly accepted standards of good work. No individual marks of manufacture were used, but every potter recognized his or her work, and that of many other villagers as well, by variations so minor that they usually escaped the eye of the ethnologist. Potters, when asked who the best potters were, usually agreed on half a dozen people, both men and women. But these people were not particularly envied or emulated; it was just that they did things a bit better than most.

Tzintzuntzan pottery competed for the local Pátzcuaro market, 10 miles away, with that from the village of Santa Fe, five miles farther from the market. Lesser competition was offered by wares from more distant Michoacán towns, and even from as far as Guanajuato. Men and women drove pack mules and burros to the big Friday market, although it was beginning to be realized that trucks and buses offered cheaper transportation. Eighteen potters also were muleteers who carried their products and additional purchased ware to more distant places. Eleven more men were full-time muleteers, and seven more split this occupation with other forms of work, a total of 36 men so engaged, or, on a proportional basis, about one muleteer for every five pottery-making families. Most muleteers made trips of not more than a week on regular schedules, usually to market towns in the tierra caliente where either clays are not good for pottery or where people prefer to work at other things. The longest trips were to Petatlán, Guerrero, 150 airline miles away on the Pacific coast. Journeys to that point required about a month for the round trip. On these long trips muleteers worked more or less like tramp steamers, picking up and selling local cargo as they worked along their trade routes. Obviously, a bulky, heavy relatively inexpensive product like pottery could not be taken by muleback to such a distance and sold at a price sufficiently high to compensate the muleteer for his original cost and time.

Pottery-making is a hereditary craft, passed down in family lines through either the father's or the mother's side, or both. But since there are no secrets in traditional wares, anyone can learn to be a potter. Non-potter wives taken both from Tzintzuntzan and other towns often take up the craft to help their husbands and some, like Doña Andrea Medina, become outstanding. Non-potter husbands from Tzintzuntzan and other villages also often become potters if they have no other means of support.

Most of the social characteristics of Tzintzuntzan potters are duplicated in scores of other Mexican pottery villages, which in turn seem to have much in common with pottery-making communities in other parts of the world. What does the evidence tell us about the position of potters in Mexico, and in societies in other places? Tzintzuntzan is essentially a classless town. Potters participate fully in civic and religious activities, they intermarry freely into non-potter families, and they appear to be in no way distinguished from other people. Most Mexican peasant villages are classless like Tzintzuntzan or, if they are larger, they are semi-classless. Yet, wherever pottery is made, potters appear to deprecate themselves, and they are looked down upon by non-potters. Time after time Tzintzuntzan potters have remarked to me, half by way of apology and half by way of stating an obvious fact, "Here you find us in all this dirt." "*Es nuestro destino*" ("it's our destiny") is the way they refer to their work. Opportunities for giving up pottery are slim, because of an absolute limit to agricultural lands, and the lack of other types of occupations. Men who can leave pottery-making by renting or purchasing agricultural lands do so, and almost everyone agrees that farming or store-keeping is preferable to the traditional craft.

In Acatlán, Puebla (Foster, 1960), Herón Martínez, one of the two most progressive potters, commented to me that potters were the lowest people in the social structure of this town of 14,000 people. "If it weren't for foreigners like you who appreciate art," he said, "the work wouldn't be worth doing. Here at home nobody appreciates the beautiful things we make." Potters in other Mexican towns have spoken to me in the same vein. They feel they are low class, that their work is dirty, and that they are looked down upon by other people, and that their artistry (real or imagined) goes unrecognized by their fellows. Other anthropologists have noted the same situation. In the famous pottery town of Tonalá, near Guadalajara, Mrs. May Díaz has found a picture comparable to Tzintzuntzan: potters are near the bottom of the social scale, except for a few entrepreneurs who do not themselves work at pot-making. Silva Rendón has noted that in Riotenco San Lorenzo, Cuauhtitlán, pottery-making is dying out because most of the men have become farmers, and "only the most destitute continue to be potters" (1950, p. 225). In Santa Maria Atzompa, Oaxaca, another classless town, the potters, who as full or part-time specialists comprise over half the families, are economically less secure than non-potters (Hendry, 1957, p. 129), and potters feel their work is dirty and "piglike" (Hendry, 1957, p. 227).

How do potters rank in other countries? The data, not surprisingly, show much variation. In the famous Guatemala pottery town of Chinautla, on the outskirts of Guatemala City, Ruben Reina finds that potters—all women—enjoy high status, and their water jars are much appreciated over a wide area. The work is quite profitable, and this perhaps explains their good status (communicated). Tangkhul Naga pottery-makers are prosperous, and wear clothing beyond the means of most villagers, of a type worn almost exclusively by headmen and other well-to-do people (Betts, 1950). In western Tibet potters are reported as being high caste and enjoying better living standards than many other groups (Asboe, 1946, p. 10).

Yet a cursory survey of the literature suggests the Mexican picture is more often true. In direct contradiction to Asboe, the Millers say the Tibetan potters are one of the few outcaste groups (1955, p. 3). In Assam they are described as ranking below the castes that have always been purely agricultural (Gait, 1897, p. 5). Within the Indian caste system the position of potters varies from relatively high (for artisans) to quite low. In Central India, pottery-making is described as one of a group of occupations that is messy or ridiculous rather than polluting, below agriculture but above work having to do with dead things or bodily emissions such as tanning or sweeping (Mayer, 1960, p. 75). In Tunis, where the small workshop system is utilized, the entrepreneurs enjoy a status corresponding to their financial success, but the potters themselves are recruited from among the poor classes (Lisse and Louis, 1956, p. 173). Potters in the Spanish province of Salamanca are described as very poor and of the most humble condition (Cortés y Vásquez, 1953, p. 57). In contrast to Chinautla in Guatemala, the aged female potters of San José, Peten, rate low in the local stratification scale. Dr. Reina writes me that "these old ladies are very happy this year because I have paid them much attention."

I believe that more intensive fieldwork will indicate that the position of potters in peasant society generally is not high, and that given reasonable alternatives, a majority of potters will try to abandon the profession. The explanation for low status probably is found in the combination of average low income and the feeling that the work is "dirty."

As a corollary to this hypothesis I suggest that as a group, potters are more conservative in basic personality structure than are their non-potter fellow villagers. By this I mean not only that most potters are reluctant to try new pottery methods, but that as a class, potters are more resistant to innovation of all kinds than are non-potters. The most striking evidence supporting this hypothesis is from Tzintzuntzan. In 1959–60 I set up a file of innovators, putting on cards the names of all people who were first or among the first to adopt new practices. These practices, unimportant in themselves, included such things as the ownership of a bicycle, a garden hose, kerosene stove, phonograph, radio, or steel plow; the practice of improved agricultural methods such as composting; the use of new pottery techniques and the production of new styles; and many other material and non-material items. As the list took shape I realized that, except for pottery innovations themselves, almost no potters appeared as innovators, even though they constituted 60 per cent of the population. But this was an impression-istic hunch. Was there any way, quantitatively, to see whether there was substance to this lead?

Data from my 1945–46 fieldwork offered the necessary information. At that time a complete village census had been taken, which included much information on house characteristics. Utilizing such criteria as the presence of a latrine, a raised plank bed, the type of lighting, and the source of water, I had plotted all houses on a scale running from 0 to 10 points, the highest number being assigned to the most comfortable and hygienic houses. When, in 1960, I checked the names of the owners of the 22 houses in category 10, I found not one belonged to a potter. The same was true of owners of houses in categories 9 (7 cases) and 8 (also 7 cases). Only when category 7 was reached did potters appear as house-owners. Thus, the top 36, or 15 per cent of the total of 248 recorded houses, all belonged to non-potters, although in proportion to occupational distributions, 10 per cent, or about 24, should have been potter homes. Economic limitations have something to do with this picture, but this in itself is not a sufficient explanation. The use of a latrine and a plank bed, both of which require little or no money, would give the poorest family a rating of 6. Yet, although many potters had both electricity and running water, none had the combination of criteria to place them among the owners of the most comfortable and healthful homes. By contrast, farmers, fisher-men (almost all Tarascan Indians), shopkeepers, and day laborers were all listed in the top categories. Only potters did not rise above category 7.

Since 1945 a few potters have begun to innovate, but most of their innovations are in pottery techniques and designs. A dozen potters have established roadside stands to sell to Mexican and American tourists, and the most successful of these have abandoned pottery-making for full-time commerce. Their homes have been improved, and they begin to take their place among the town's leaders. But they are no longer potters. This suggests the possibility that when a generalized innova-tion-bug bites a potter there is a good chance he will cease to be a potter. Many of the potters who have been successful in developing new styles and forms for the market have made few changes in their personal lives: they continue to sleep on reed mats on drafty, dirty floors, meet bodily needs in patios, and otherwise show little evidence of a basic change in outlook. This is not invariably so. A few who have hit upon salable designs use their profits to send their children to school, to improve their homes, and to take a more active part in village life. But they are the exception.

The Tzintzuntzan data raise two questions: (1) are potters in other communities also more than ordinarily conservative, and (2) if so, why? The evidence seems to me strongly to suggest conservatism of potters as a class.[1] Tonalá, Jalisco (Mexico), on the outskirts of Guadalajara is a larger edition of Tzintzuntzan; the

---

1. It should be noted that conservatism manifests itself on two related but distinct levels: conservatism with respect to innovation in pottery, and the more general conservatism char-acterizing basic personality structure. Here I am interested in the latter type of conservatism, although from the literature, the two cannot always be distinguished.

same basic productive techniques are used, but the level of artistry is appreciably higher. Much of the best ware popularly believed to come from Tlaquepaque is, in fact, made in Tonalá, largely in family workshops. Of the 859 households for which Mrs. May Díaz has data, in 31 per cent pottery-making is the sole occupation of all adults, and in an additional 22 per cent one or more family members make pottery, so that 53 per cent of the families derive all or part of their income from this industry. Tonaltecan potters, like their Tzintzuntzan fellows, appear to be notably conservative in basic personality. For example, of the 15 original subscribers to electric power service, only one was a potter, and he a part-time worker at that. Of the 25 families that paid for water when the first public system was installed, only three were potters, two of whom were part-time workers. Of the eight men who subscribe to Guadalajara newspapers, only one part-time potter is included. In tracing the names of the first people to have such innovations as radios, bicycles, television, a washing machine, gas stove, or bathroom, potter families appear in the same reduced proportion. As in Tzintzuntzan, the innovations that occur among potters are almost entirely in pottery-making itself. These are adaptations in shape, and in design, but always within the limits of known pigments. Pottery innovations tend not to occur in shaping techniques, glazing, and firing (communicated by Mrs. Díaz).

In Guatemala, Ruben Reina describes the Chinautlecos as conservative, in spite of their commercial success, and the same is even more true in San José where the potters are the poorest people and have made the least progress noted in the community (communicated). Lisse and Louis (1956, p. 173) describe Tunisian potters as enemies of innovation who like to work alone, with their families, without outside influences. The master potter is said to be a traditionalist in his techniques, reluctant to modernize his installation, fearing machines and modern apparatus which he does not know (Lisse and Louis, 1956, p. 176). Here conservatism appears to refer specifically to attitudes toward pottery techniques rather than to basic personality.

Assuming, for the sake of argument, that potters in peasant societies are conservative as a class not only in their work, but, as in Tzintzuntzan, in basic personality structure as well, can we adduce a possible reason? I believe so. This reason lies in the nature of the productive process itself, which places a premium on strict adherence to tried and proven ways as a means of avoiding economic catastrophe. Pottery-making is a tricky business at best, and there are literally hundreds of points at which a slight variation in materials or process will adversely affect the result. A slight difference in raw materials, in glazes, in paints, in firing temperatures—any of these may mean that a week or a month's labor is in vain. Hence, economic security lies in duplicating to the best of the potter's ability the materials and processes he knows from experience are least likely to lead to failure. A premium is placed on hewing to a straight and narrow productive path. Straying very far from one side to the other is apt to mean economic tragedy. *If* the potter is skilled, and *if* he uses only tried and true methods, he has a relatively good chance of predicting the outcome. He knows about what his production of salable ware will be each period and since, in Tzintzuntzan at least, pottery is sold almost immediately, he knows how much he will realize from his work. I suggest that the productive process and the economic situation place a premium on not trying new things, and that this breeds a basic conservatism, a caution about all new things that carries over into the potter's outlook on life itself.

Contrast the potter's situation in Tzintzuntzan with the farmer and the fisherman. To succeed in these fields technical skill obviously is important. But, however competent the farmer or fisherman, he lacks the control over the outcome that characterizes the potter; there is an element of uncertainty with which he cannot cope. Too much or not enough rain or plagues of insects may ruin the crops of the most careful farmer. Lake levels rise and fall and the fish come and go in mysterious ways over which the fisherman has no control. Luck, in addition to skill, is more important to the farmer or fisherman than to the potter. Perhaps this leads both groups to a greater willingness to gamble on other things as well. Their conservatism, while marked in all peasant communities, is perhaps not quite so built-in as is true (I believe) of peasant potters.

Supporting evidence for this hypothesis comes from several sources. Speaking of Tonalá, Mrs. Díaz says the potter cannot afford to experiment with different clays and glazes because the danger of losing a whole kilnful of ware is too great an economic hazard (communicated). Lisse and Louis (1956, p. 176) describe the fear of the potter each time he fires his kiln; here up to two months of work go into a single firing, and the product, if successfully completed, may be worth as much as 200,000 francs. This is not a setting that encourages radical experiments. That the potter's personality may be reflected outside the field of pottery is also suggested by Reina's data on Chinautla. Here the few families who have tried pottery innovations have also innovated in other areas: they have become Protestants, or have joined the Third Order of San Francisco, and by so doing have rejected the traditional *cofradía* religious fiesta pattern (communicated).

I now turn to the problem of pottery dynamics. If peasant potters are basically conservative people, as suggested, it is logical to expect that, in the absence of strong motivation, pottery styles and production techniques will change but slowly. This is frequently true, and the potter's resistance to change has been recorded in many places. Tschopik, for example, speaks of a "remarkable ceramic continuity" in the northwest Titicaca Basin, which demonstrates the persistence of an Aymara tradition over a span of five centuries (1950, p. 196). In nearby Bolivia, Goins speculates about the lack of an urge to experiment he noted among the potters of Huayculi in the Cochabamba Valley. Here men make pots on the Spanish wheel, while the women grind glazes, aid in painting, and are the principal sellers in town markets.

It strikes me as a very curious thing that there should be in Huayculi no invention of new designs whatsoever, and no urge to experiment, except on the part of the village drunk, and even his creative talent is lost when he is sober. The men, who have worked out the designs, are clearly craftsmen rather than creative artists; and the women, who for the most part apply the designs, are just as clearly wives and daughters interested in getting the job in hand finished and out of the way. But why is there no one to disrupt the total uniformity, out of impatience if nothing more? The answer does not lie in the realm of art or craft or design, nor in any generality like "the weight of culture" or "habit." Is it easier, or better, or inevitable for a Quičhua to conform? (Goins, 1954, p. 218).

Resistance to new techniques appears to be as common as resistance to new designs—perhaps even more so. The resistance to the use of the wheel, even with good opportunities to learn, is particularly noteworthy, and it leads one to wonder how the worldwide distribution of the wheel has come to be as extensive as it is. In Tzintzuntzan, for example, the Mexican government operated a trade school in the 1930's, and for a year a master potter from Jalisco taught the use of the wheel. Not one potter changed from the traditional mold techniques. Rendón relates a similar example in Ticul, Yucatan, where a Oaxaca potter who taught the wheel made no inroads on the kabal technique, which has sometimes, erroneously, been described as a protowheel. Other things taught by this potter also were rejected (Rendón, 1947, p. 110). In the 1860's a well-intentioned Britisher tried to introduce the Indian wheel to Tibet,

but so little interest did the Booteans feel in an instrument which they were told would greatly expedite their business and diminish their labor, that not one individual ever took the trouble to come and look at it after it had been made. . . . (Olson, 1954, p. 15, quoting Capt. R. B. Pemberton, "Report on Bootan," *Political Missions to Bootan*, Calcutta, 1865, p. 74).

Elsewhere I have speculated about the factors that encourage or discourage the introduction of the wheel. In Tzintzuntzan, I think the relative rapidity with which pots can be made with molds, and the lack of congruence of motor patterns between those of this system and the wheel, is a major factor (Foster, 1948b, pp. 368–69). To abandon traditional methods, and to take the trouble (and interim economic loss) to master the wheel represents a major break. I suspect that when non-wheel using potters have adopted the wheel it is because the traditional methods have fallen far short of meeting market demand, and drastic steps have had to be taken to save a livelihood (Foster, 1959b, p. 113).

But much of the current distribution of the wheel may be due to quite a different process. Tschopik (1950, p. 201) points out that in such Peruvian centers as Arequipa and the Iça Valley, Spaniards set up pottery workshops and hired Indian potters who were taught the use of the wheel to make wine jars. The same history accounts for the wheel-made Talavera of Pueblo, Mexico; and in many other parts of the country, such as Oaxaca City, where the wheel is used, the workshop organization leads me to believe the origin was the same. Perhaps some of the spread of the wheel in the Old World is due to small-scale entrepreneurs who knew the wheel, and who, in setting up workshops, taught their employees to use the wheel. If one's livelihood is dependent upon learning a new technique, a greater effort will be made than if it is a matter of personal choice. Again, there is good evidence to suggest that it is often easier to teach a person an entirely new craft than to persuade a competent craftsman to make major changes in his traditional methods. The novice has no preconceptions to set up resistances to new ideas.

With respect to changes in pottery styles, most studies treat the subject as an artistic problem: the role of the unusual person who experiments with her media, searching for new designs and new combinations, which in turn attract the attention of less inventive artisans who follow this lead. In other words, change comes because the potter is trying to please herself. This may very well be true of tribal potters, where production is for home consumption, or trade or barter on a small scale within a limited area. It is also true, to some extent, among peasant potters. In the few instances of comprehensive accounts of peasant potter villages there is always mention of one or several people who are true artists, who derive an aesthetic satisfaction out of superior work, and who like to try new things for the pleasure of doing so. Natividad Peña in Tzintzuntzan is one such person (Foster, 1948a, pp. 95–99), and Hendry names two potters in Atzompa who appear to be true artists (1957, pp. 233, 242).

But in spite of the presence of an occasional potter-artist in peasant societies, the evidence suggests that market demand rather than artistic urge is the primary cause of change. Peasant potters look upon themselves as artisans, and upon their work as simply an occupation whereby one earns a living. In Atzompa, Hendry (1957, pp. 225, 230) finds that, for the vast majority of people,

pottery is simply a task to be performed, a part of the daily routine along with cooking, cleaning, and other domestic chores, and carried out with about the same degree of enjoyment. . . . Disinterested enjoyment does not figure prominently among the Atzompeños' reasons for taking up and practicing the craft. By their own admission, the potters derive little pleasure from their work and few find it intrinsically interesting. If the aesthetic emotion is lacking, so too are its consequences since for the vast majority pottery making is reproduction rather than creation.

These words are equally applicable to Tzintzuntzan, and doubtless to all other peasant pottery-making towns. Clearly, this is not an environment in which an aesthetic urge flourishes. Artisans are not artistic innovators, almost by definition.

The stimulus of the market, on the other hand, can easily be seen, and it is fairly well documented. In most parts of the peasant world, pottery is sufficiently plentiful so that the buyer has great choice. In the Pátzcuaro market, for example, the ware of two or three hundred potters, at the very least, is available for selection, and purchases are made only after the most minute examination of a variety of pieces. Obviously, the successful potter is the one who satisfies the customer, regardless of what he or she may think of the artistic merits of the product. Again, when a man or group of men set out on a trading trip of 150 or more miles, it is clear that they must carry merchandise with market appeal.

The precise role of the market as a change stimulus is difficult to appraise, because the tourist demand, which is producing great changes, is in most places a recent phenomenon. In contemporary Mexico, the tourist trade beyond question is the active force that is producing a florescence in pottery forms and designs—

some good, much bad—that is scrambling the traditional village styles to the point where recognition and classification will become almost impossible. The first specific change of which I have record occurred in Tzintzuntzan in about 1940 when Natividad Peña, at the suggestion of a tourist guide, developed a white-glazed painted ware called *loza blanca* from an earlier and simpler white-glazed style. In recent years the best Tzintzuntzan potters have developed new products which have little or nothing in common with the ware I knew in 1945. Sometimes in desperation, new paints and glazes are tried, in the hope that a lucky combination will give the potter a market winner; and when good luck occurs, every effort is made to conceal the method. One young potter returned from Mexico City with the secret of oxygen-reduced black ware; for six months his sister importuned him to reveal the method, but only after she spied over the wall separating their houses, and saw him at work late one night, was she able to duplicate the product.

Changes in a pottery-making town in Guerrero stem from the requests of curio dealers in Taxco, Acapulco, and Mexico City. Potter merchants return with new designs requested by shop owners, and quickly these designs become standardized (communicated by Peggy Golde). In Acatlán, Puebla, Herón Martínez made major changes in his production in response to the demands of dealers in Oaxaca and Puebla. His now-famous black ware resulted from the desire of a Puebla dealer to have a source closer at hand than Coyotepec, near Oaxaca.

In Atzompa, Hendry writes (1957, p. 253) that economic factors in large part determine the types of pottery made, and that the desire to exploit the tourist market is one of the few incentives for innovation. She gives the example of several women who have changed the kinds of ware they make because they felt something other than their traditional styles would sell better. One woman gave up casseroles and took up pots because her husband felt they were more in demand, and another, who failed to follow her mother's custom in making the big *apaxtles* (very large casseroles) because they were too hard to make, subsequently changed her mind because she found they sold so well (Hendry, 1957, p. 195). In another home an American tourist asked to have a special order made up of a number of identical square casseroles, in contrast to the traditional round ones. To be sure of achieving the same size and shape for all pieces, plaster molds were made, so that a change (for this family) in technique as well as style resulted. Subsequently, as an experiment, the family offered a few square casseroles for sale in the Oaxaca market, found they went well, and so have continued to make this type (Hendry, 1957, p. 235).

In other parts of the world the demands of outsiders have wrought significant changes in styles. The Europeans in Port Moresby, New Guinea—hardly tourists—provide a sufficient market so that women in nearby pottery towns "now make pottery to entirely novel designs" (Groves, 1960, p. 5). Lisse and Louis (1956, p. 224) describe the Tunis potters who try to attract visitors by the creation of original objects. Reina (communicated) describes the attempt of a few Chinautleca women to introduce new figures for tourist sale, and the statues produced at the suggestion of an archeologist! But the most skillful of the young women to do this ultimately reverted to traditional ware because of the force of public opinion. She was branded as an unreliable potter who played with toys. At a different cultural level, the demands of white purchasers as early as 1890 caused new pottery forms to be made by Yuman potters, and indigenous forms to be discontinued (Rogers, 1936, p. 1).

Without doubt, a vigorous tourist market speeds up the processes of change beyond what they would otherwise be. At the same time, I feel certain that the same motivation—the desire for good sales—has worked to produce change since the time when pottery-making first became a commercial process. The best evidence for this seems to me to lie in the common practice whereby potters make different products for different markets. In 1949 in a big pottery-making town in Spain, La Rambla in Córdoba province, I was shown pieces labeled "sevillanas," "cordobeses," and others with town names. Each represented, I was told, the product that was in demand in these towns. In the same country, in Salamanca province, specialization for recognized markets is so developed that complete lines for local home consumption are not made, and potters must buy wares from other towns for domestic use. In Ciudad Rodrigo, the *cazuela portugués* is produced to sell in towns in the neighboring country (Cortés y Vásquez, 1953, p. 15). Pottery is hawked over the surrounding countryside from burro-back, up to a range of about 150 miles. In Tzintzuntzan, until recent years, several families produced specialized wares called *pinípites* and *porcelanas* used for serving the festive *pozole*, a hominy-and-pork dish mandatory at fiestas in most of Michoacán. Several conservative villages on the south shore of Lake Pátzcuaro were willing to pay premium prices for these dishes, so production was oriented toward this limited market.

Traditional commercial producers also recognize other kinds of market differences, and special forms are made for special occupational functions, or for religious purposes. Hallifax long ago pointed out how Punjab potters make *mats* for dyers, huge vessels four feet high and three feet broad, designed to hold indigo. Other containers are made to meet the needs of sugar manufacturers and tanners (Hallifax, 1894, p. 40). In forested areas of Mexico, small pottery cups are made to sell to tappers who draw off sap to be made into turpentine, and in mining areas small crucibles are made for silver casting. Annual fiestas also offer special market opportunities toward which major production may be directed. Pottery biblical and other figures for use in Christmas *nacimientos* or *belenes* (nativity scenes) are made in Latin America and Mediterranean countries. In Juchitán, Mexico, colorful and bizarre painted human figures are made to be sold as New Year's toys (*e.g.*, Covarrubias, 1946, facing p. 294). Surprisingly similar figures, which are whistles, called *Siurells* are made by one family in Sa Cabaneta, on Mallorca, to be sold at religious fairs (*verbenas*), and particularly on the day of San Marcial, when they are named *pitos de San Marsal* (author's field notes). There are, unfortunately, relatively few recorded instances of these kinds of differential production for different markets. I suspect the rarity is due to failure to ask questions rather than to a real absence of the phenomenon.

The stimulus of the market can explain much of the process of innovation in pottery styles, and perhaps also in productive techniques. The market may also operate to stabilize traditional designs, in both a positive and a negative fashion. The positive influence I have in mind is illustrated by the very widespread belief that food cooked in pottery, or even in special kinds of pottery, tastes better than food cooked in metal vessels. In Mexico, for example, it is generally felt that the most savory dishes are those cooked in earthenware pots, and even in big cities a great deal of everyday cooking is done in this fashion rather than in aluminum pans, which are relatively cheap and easy to acquire. In Spain, Cortés (1954, p. 147) tells how, in Salamanca province, certain foods are believed to reach their peak of perfection only if cooked in casseroles made in Perezuela, a fact which presumably will maintain the industry there long after the economic need might otherwise disappear. Apparently similar opinions are held in India: Aiyappan reports that in Wynad (Malabar), the hand-modeled pots of the tribal Urali are thought to be better for cooking than the wheel-made pots used for other purposes (1947, p. 59). It seems likely that, to the extent this preference remains, the Urali will continue to meet market demands with traditional products.

The negative fashion in which the market may act to maintain traditional forms is through the absence of a competitive situation. That is, where a market is essentially non-competitive, there is no particular stimulus pushing potters to come up with a new or better product. Goins' (1954) speculation about why no Huayculi potter breaks out of the bonds of tradition appears to substantiate this point. In this Bolivian town, it will be remembered, in spite of a vigorous pottery tradition, the artistic spirit seems lacking, and the nearby city market seems to have no influence. There is another pottery-making town five miles from Huayculi, but here only *ollas* are made, which are not made in Huayculi, so that in fact there is no competition between the two pottery-producing centers. Presumably the market for Huayculi products remains strong, and there is simply no need to push beyond the limits of a satisfactory economic system. The potters are craftsmen with a good sale and no significant competition, and they see no need to change their methods or designs.

In my experience it is a rare potter who, without unusual stimulus, is much interested in how other potters work or what they make. In the famous Oaxaca pottery town of San Bartolo Coyotepec, Maximino Mateo is one of the most competent of all workers (Foster, 1959a, pl. 2). But when I recorded my notes after spending a day with him in 1958, I remarked that he was a careful artisan, but not an artist. He did the most careful burnishing of anyone whose work I saw, but always within a narrow style range. He attempted new designs only when they were requested by buyers, and after meeting this demand he reverted to his traditional designs for which there was a good sale. He had never been to nearby Santa María Atzompa, and he had no curiosity to see how potters work there (techniques are significantly different). He had seen the wheel in use in Oaxaca City, thought it was faster than his spinning *molde* method, but it didn't occur to him to try it.

The next question I wish to raise is how far wares may be traded in a traditional pottery economy. For archeologists interestd in the distribution of styles, this is a point of particular importance. Obviously, there can be no general rule. Where safe water transportation is available, considerable distances may be easy. With burros or mules, it may be that greater distances can be achieved than when ware is carried on the human back. Yet the long trips made by Mexican *huacaleros*, carrying pottery and other merchandise in crates on their backs, show that long distances on foot are quite possible, given the demand. I have found few reports about actual distances to which pottery is carried by the primary seller. Dorman says that among the Wagoni and Wandendehule of southern Tanganyika, where most pottery is made for local use, the one exception are big beer-drinking vessels known to be especially well made in one village; these are traded up to a distance of 30 miles (Dorman, 1938, p. 98). The Salamanca burro-back range of 150 miles is, rather surprisingly, identical to the maximum range of muleteers in Tzintzuntzan before the truck replaced burros. Motu pottery, carried by boat from towns in the Port Moresby region, is traded to a distance which, on the map, measures about 150 miles. The people who buy this ware in enormous quantities in turn distribute it farther inland and along the Gulf of Papua (Groves, 1960, p. 8). Although these three instances hardly constitute a sample, they suggest that, given a market, animals or boats, and reasonably peaceful conditions, pottery of recognized quality can easily be traded up to 150 miles by the makers or original sellers before lesser distribution may carry it to more remote places.

The final point in this paper deals with reasons why pottery styles may decline or disappear. The reasons, presumably, are not peculiar to pottery, but apply to other arts and crafts as well. Here it is interesting to turn to the speculations about the loss of useful arts in Oceania, in the studies of Rivers and Thurnwald. Rivers points out that many of the objects used in everyday life in Oceania are made by specialists, whose skills and practice come down in hereditary lines. "It is only necessary for such a limited body of men to disappear either as the result of disease or war or through some natural catastrophe, to account for the disappearance of an art" (Rivers, 1926, p. 200). He points out that in the Papuan Gulf, in Massim, and in New Caledonia, pottery is made in only a few places, and that extermination by warfare or natural catastrophe of people who make it could eliminate the supply over a large area. He goes so far as to suggest that a volcanic catastrophe may have led to the loss of pottery in northern New Hebrides, where sherds are found beneath volcanic scoriae (Rivers, 1926, p. 201). Certainly, a specialized ware made in Pompeii would have disappeared. This admittedly would be exceptional, but Rivers (1926, p. 203) asks the question: if useful arts can be completely lost, is it not much more likely that, for the same reasons, deterioration or change reflected in archeological sequences might not occur? Solheim (1952, p. 2) also suggests catastrophe as the cause of disappearance of pottery-making in parts of Melanesia.

Thurnwald (1932, pp. 121, 127), in discussing handicrafts in general, points out that special skills are limited to certain families, and that not all specialists share in the culture to the same extent. Arguing from the famous case of the disappearance of canoes in Torres Strait, where the only family of skilled builders died out in 1896, he suggests that a sudden fall in standard dexterity can be explained in similar fashion. Pottery-making in Santo is cited as a specific example.

There is evidence to support this hypothesis as one among various explanations. González Marti (1933, p. 164), for example, describes the 1609 expulsion of the Moors from Spain as " the death sentence" for the Majolica of Valencia. Ceramic decorations became poorer and poorer for lack of direction, and finally almost disappeared. Subias Galter (1948, p. 67) explains some of the deterioration: the eagle becomes a simplified bird, various flowers all become simple carnations, and what had been sophisticated art descends to the level of folk art.

The previously-mentioned Siurell figures of Mallorca are made by the members of a single family who have done this work for generations. Most figures are modeled by an old woman who took up the craft when she married. Her four sons gather the raw materials and prepare the paste, paint the figures, fire them, and sell them. The wives of the four sons have tried to make the figures but have done badly and are not continuing. When I visited the workshop in 1950 I speculated in my notes that the Siurells might die out since there were no likely candidates to carry on.

Sometimes secrecy limits a skill to a single or a few families, and sometimes other potters respect what amounts to primitive patents. In several Costa Rican villages, daughters learn pottery-making from their mothers and in turn pass the craft to their daughters. Special emphasis is placed upon the individual household style. A woman or a household which has developed a certain distinct type of vessel decoration or which produces, for example, clay figures instead of pots, tries to retain such a trait within the family. Strangely, Hendry reports the same phenomenon in Atzompa where it is felt that what is invented by a particular family belongs to that family and its descendants. The feeling of "ownership" of new forms is so marked that there have been instances in which people have married or proposed marriage in order to obtain the right to make certain kinds of wares (Hendry, 1957, pp. 237–38). In these kinds of situations the dying-out of a line or the abandonment of the craft would not mean loss of a useful art, but cumulatively, the process could go far to explain changes in archeological pottery sequences. This precise thing has taken place in Atzompa where, formerly, the members of a single family made *barrilitos*, barrel-shaped vessels as high as a person. When the family died out this particular style died with them (Hendry, 1957, p. 126).

In 1945 in Tzintzuntzan, as pointed out, there were no true pottery secrets. If certain people had given up the occupation, what might the results have been for a hypothetical archeological sequence? Natividad Peña was the artist in white-glazed painted ware; she had learned it from her mother, Doña Andrea Medina, much surpassing in skill her teacher. In turn, she had taught a younger brother, whose wife was just taking up the work. If these people, for any reason, had found they could not sell *loza blanca*, or if they had moved away or given up the work for other reasons (*e.g.*, Natividad today makes very little, because she and her husband have prospered to the point where he could buy land to farm, which is a higher prestige occupation), it is unlikely that anyone else in Tzintzuntzan would have continued this tradition. For several years Natividad was, for all practical purposes, the key person upon whose work the continuation of the tradition depended.

If the two or three men who made the most artistic red-slipped burnished ware had given up the work, a significant deterioration in style would have been noted, but the basic technique would have remained; and with sufficient market demand, other skillful drawers might very well have restored the art. On the other hand, this ware today is far inferior to what it was fifteen years ago. The reason seems to be lack of discrimination among buyers, who are satisfied with inferior pieces.

The expansion of the tourist market in Tzintzuntzan has produced a flowering of styles. A potter who hits upon a new technique in coloring or glazing jealously guards his secret, so that pottery-making knowledge is no longer universally shared. For several years only one, and then three or four people, knew the oxygen-reduced process that makes a superb black finish. If, during this period, these people had given up pottery, had died, or had moved away, the style would have disappeared and, in a hypothetical archeological sequence it would appear as the briefest intrusion. Knowledge of several other new glazes and colors is limited to one or several families, so that if the few people who know such secrets give up the work, the style will disappear.

These Tzintzuntzan data suggest a hypothesis of possible inferential value in archeological reconstructions: in a period of pottery style and production technique stability, all knowledge will tend to become universal, and there will be no trade secrets. Under these conditions, pottery styles are not likely to die out as the consequence of what happens to only a few people. Conversely, in a period of active experimentation to develop new styles and improved techniques, pottery secrets will appear which will increase the probability of loss of techniques and styles after very short periods of production, as a consequence of something happening to the person or people who alone control the secret.

SUMMARY

In societies characterized by markets, potters are full or part-time specialists whose major production is for sale rather than home use. Their social position varies, but it tends toward the lower rather than the upper end of the ladder. With respect to the pottery process, potters appear to be more conservative than members of other occupational groups. This may be due to the fact that the pottery process itself demands a "conventional wisdom" in which economic security lies in duplicating tried and true methods. In Mexico, at least, the potter's conservatism is reflected in a strong reluctance to innovate in many other areas of culture; an essentially conservative basic personality structure seems the rule.

Stability and change in pottery styles can be examined within artistic and economic frames of reference. In peasant societies here considered it is suggested that the vast majority of potters are artisans, not artists, and that market conditions are more important than artistic motivations in maintaining stability and producing change in styles. The tourist market is a particularly important factor in contemporary pottery-style changes; but long-standing specialized production for known markets, both specific towns and areas, and for specialized purposes, indicates the traditional importance of economic forces. Markets explain the diffusion of the same pottery over wide areas; and a range of at least 150 miles from the source, carried by the producer or original middleman, is recorded in widely separated parts of the world.

Pottery forms and production techniques change as a result of market demands. Under conditions of little technological and stylistic change, pottery-making techniques are available to all members of a village who wish to know them; hence, losses are not apt to occur as a consequence of something happening to specific people. Under conditions of rapid change, pottery-making secrets appear, known to only a few people. At such times disappearance of a particular style or technique can more easily occur than during periods of little change.

BIBLIOGRAPHY

AIYAPPAN, A.
1947. "Handmade Pottery of the Urali Kurumbars of Wynad, S. India." *Man*, 47:57–59.

ASBOE, W.
1946. "Pottery in Ladakh, Western Tibet." *Man*, 46:9–10.

BETTS, F. N.
1950. "Tangkhul Naga Pottery Making." *Man*, 50:117.

CORTÉS Y VÁSQUEZ, L. L.
1953. *La alfarería popular salmantina*. Salamanca.
1954. "La alfarería en Pereruela (Zamora)." *Zephyrus*, 5:141–63. Salamanca: Centro de Estudios Salmantinos, Universidad de Salamanca.

COVARRUBIAS, M.
1946. *Mexico south: the Isthmus of Tehuantepec*. New York: Alfred A. Knopf.

DÍAZ, M.
1960. Unpublished field notes on Tonalá, Jalisco, Mexico.

DORMAN, M. H.
1938. "Pottery Among the Wangoni and Wandendehule, Southern Tanganyika." *Man*, 38:97–102.

FOSTER, G. M.

1948a. *Empire's Children: the People of Tzintzuntzan.* Washington, D.C.: Smithsonian Institution, Institute of Social Anthropology, Publication No. 6 (Printed in Mexico).

1948b. "Some Implications of Modern Mexican Mold-Made Pottery." *Southwestern Journal of Anthropology,* 4:356–70.

1955. *Contemporary Pottery Techniques in Southern and Central Mexico.* Middle American Research Institute, Publication No. 22:1–48. New Orleans: Tulane University.

1959a. "The Coyotepec *Molde* and Some Associated Problems of the Potter's Wheel." *Southwestern Journal of Anthropology,* 15:53–63.

1959b. "The Potter's Wheel: an Analysis of Idea and Artifact in Invention." *Ibid.,* pp. 99–119.

1960. "Archaeological Implications of the Modern Pottery of Acatlán, Puebla, Mexico." *American Antiquity,* 26:205–14.

GAIT, E. A.

1897. "The Manufacture of Pottery in Assam." *Journal of Indian Art,* 7:5–8.

GOINS, J. F.

1954. "Huayculi: the Quichua of Cochabamba Valley, Bolivia." Unpublished Ph.D. dissertation, University of California, Berkeley.

GOLDE, P.

1961. Personal communication on pottery manufacture in Guerrero, Mexico.

GONZÁLEZ MARTI, M.

1933. *Cerámica española.* Barcelona and Buenos Aires: Editorial Labor, S. A. Colección Labor No. 338.

GROVES, M.

1960. "Motu Pottery." *The Journal of the Polynesian Society,* 69:3–22.

HALLIFAX, C. J.

1894. "The Pottery and Glass Industries of the Punjab." *Journal of Indian Art,* 5:35–42.

HENDRY, J. C.

1957. *Atzompa: a Pottery Producing Village of Southern Mexico.* Ph.D dissertation, Cornell University. Ann Arbor, Michigan: University Microfilms, Publ. No. 22, 199.

LISSE, P. and A. LOUIS

1956. *Les potiers de Nabeul: Étude de sociologie tunisienne.* Tunis: Publications de l'Institut des Belles Lettres Arabes, 23.

MAYER, A. C.

1960. *Caste and Kinship in Central India: a Village and Its Region.* Berkeley and Los Angeles: University of California Press.

MILLER, R. and B. MILLER

1955. "Further Notes on Tibetan Ceramics: a Preliminary Field Report." *Far Eastern Ceramic Bulletin.* 7:1–5.

OLSON, E.

1954. "More about Tibetan Ceramics." *Far Eastern Ceramic Bulletin* 6:14–17.

REINA, R.

1961. Personal communication on Chinautla and San José, Guatemala.

RENDÓN, S.

1947. "Notas sobre la alfarería indígena de la península de Yucatán." Mexico, D.F.: *Revista Mexicana de Estudios Antropológicos* 9:107–23.

1950. "Modern Pottery of Riotenco San Lorenzo, Cuauhtitlán." Middle American Research Institute, Publication 15:251–67. New Orleans: Tulane University.

RIVERS, W. H. R.

1926. *Psychology and Ethnology.* London: K. Paul, Trench, Trubner.

ROGERS, M. J.

1936. *Yuman Pottery Making.* San Diego: San Diego Museum Papers, No. 2.

SHEPARD, A. O.

1948. *Plumbate—a Mesoamerican Trade Ware.* Washington, D.C.: Carnegie Institution of Washington, Publication 573.

SOLHEIM, W. G., II

1952. "Oceanian Pottery Manufacture." *Journal of East Asiatic Studies* (The University of Manila), 1:1–39.

SUBIAS GALTER, J.

1948. *El arte popular en España.* Barcelona: Editorial Seix Barral, S.A.

THOMPSON, R. H.

1958. *Modern Yucatecan Maya Pottery Making.* Memoirs of the Society for American Archaeology, No. 15. (*American Antiquity*, Vol. XXIII, No. 4, Pt. 2.)

THURNWALD, R.

1932. *Economics in Primitive Communities.* Oxford: Oxford University Press.

TSCHOPIK, H., JR.

1950. "An Andean Ceramic Tradition in Historical Perspective." *American Antiquity*, 15:196–218.

RIO GRANDE GLAZE-PAINT POTTERY:
A TEST OF PETROGRAPHIC ANALYSIS

ANNA O. SHEPARD

INTRODUCTION

ABOUT thirty years ago Pecos pottery was chosen to test the archeological significance of ceramic technological analysis. To review that study now
seems like rattling the skeleton in one's closet: reminders of things neglected and things that should have been done differently are not pleasant. But an
occasional reassessment of methods is necessary and it is especially desirable at this
time when so many new analytical procedures are being introduced. It is worthwhile to consider how our methods and results would compare with those of the
thirties if we were analyzing Pecos pottery today.

Methods are of secondary interest, however, compared with the interpretations
of culture history that can be based on technological analysis. During the planning
conference on "Ceramics and Man" held in New York, March 3, 1961, Dr. Fejos
commented that he visualized the symposium "more or less as an appraisal of the
significance of ceramics for man. What ceramics had made possible for man to
do . . ." The query, how has the potter's industry influenced man, might well
serve as a milepost on the trail of ceramic investigation. Description and classification, identification of materials, study of techniques, and analysis of decorative
design are the first steps taken with our eyes on the trail to avoid stumbling. When
we turn to the study of ceramic history and development, their course and causes,
our stride becomes easier, and when we come to think of the effect of clay working on man's development, we have become aware of our surroundings and the
purpose of the journey

The petrographic analysis of Pecos pottery and of Rio Grande Glaze-Paint
Ware to which it led was an early step in a discipline that calls for close co-operation between archeologist and analyst. The footing of those steps was tested with
great caution, and it was only gradually and with grave doubts that the direction
in which they seemed to be leading was accepted. Today the results seem less
startling. This change in attitude is a reminder of the fact that change is a normal,
continuing process. In the course of this process it is important to know what to
preserve from the past and what to discard.

Several distinct circumstances favored the technological study of Pecos pottery.
First, was the relation of archeologist and analyst. The archeological background,

62

as well as the stylistic features and relative dating of the types, was known to me from the start, and throughout the study there were frequent opportunities for exchange of information and discussion with Dr. Kidder. This was an inestimable advantage. Second, the history of the ware was exceptional because its unique decorative technique required a lead ore that was restricted in occurrence. Third, the geological diversity of the region from which the potters obtained clays, non-plastics, and pigments greatly facilitated the location of sources or source areas of these ceramic materials. Consequently, this investigation was a specific, not a general, test. This fact will be borne in mind when deductions are drawn.

THE GEOLOGICAL SETTING

The Upper Rio Grande Valley of New Mexico is the locale of a well-defined Pueblo subculture. The physiographic and geologic features of the region afford strong contrasts. The principal formations and localities that enter this account of Glaze-Paint Ware are illustrated in Figure 1. To the east, the valley is bounded by the Sangre de Cristo Range. Peaks in this range rise over 13,000 feet, and pre-historic settlements stopped where the valley floor meets the mountain flank. To the west are the Jemez Mountains, a huge caldera or crater. Thick deposits of ash on the Rio Grande side of this crater form the Pajarito Plateau, which is deeply dissected by a series of canyons. In prehistoric times, Indians took advantage of the ease of excavating artificial caves in the soft ash of the canyon walls in order to establish dwellings, and they farmed in the narrow canyon floors. There are lenses of air-borne ash from the Jemez eruptions in the sedimentary beds of the Rio Grande Valley north of Santa Fe. These deposits have afforded both pre-historic and present-day potters a source of tempering material.

Along the course of the Rio Grande itself are a series of basalt flows that have issued from a number of vents. This rock also supplies a tempering material, and its use has continued down to the present. Southwest of Santa Fe and east of the Rio Grande is still another geologic province that played a role in prehistoric culture. Its northern edge is marked by the Cerrillos Hills from which the Indians mined turquoise, and its southern end by the ore-bearing Ortiz Mountains. These are igneous formations, and the rocks are intermediate in composition between the rhyolitic ashes of the Jemez eruption and the basalt flows of the river valley. Moreover, they are crystalline rocks that cooled at depth. In the diagrams of this paper the term "andesite," used in the original Rio Grande Glaze-Paint report (Shepard, 1942), has been retained to avoid confusion, but it should be understood that the rocks include a wider textural range than is implied by this term; more coarsely crystalline rocks and porphyries are common. Dikes of these rocks, which extend into the Galisteo Basin to the east of the Ortiz Mountains, were an important source of a tempering material that has afforded an important link in the reconstruction of the ceramic history of the Upper Rio Grande Valley.

There are distinctive classes of clay in each of these provinces. Montmorillonitic

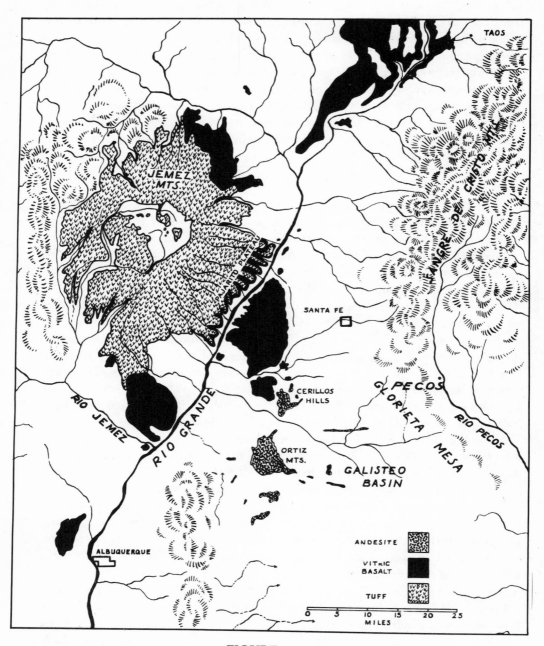

FIGURE 1

Section of the Upper Rio Grande Valley; physiographic features and geologic
formations pertinent to the development of Glaze-Paint Ware.

clays, which form from the alteration of volcanic glass, are found on the Pajarito Plateau. Sedimentary clays along the river are red-firing, whereas the clays of the Cretaceous deposits in the Galisteo Basin are buff-firing.

Geographically, Pecos is just outside this area, on the upper waters of the Pecos River which drains the lower central part of the Sangre de Cristo Mountains. It is northeast of the Galisteo Basin and separated from it by Glorieta Mesa, which forms a high precipitous wall on the Pecos side. Although, as the crow flies, it was only twenty-five miles from Pecos to the nearest settlement in the Galisteo Basin, the steep trail up the mesa made it an arduous trip.

When the study of Pecos pottery was commenced, we were unaware of the significance of these various geological features. Pecos was a large and important settlement. It had been occupied from about 1300 to 1838, and as far as we knew pueblo communities were economically, as well as politically, independent. At the inception of the technological analysis, we assumed that we were studying the history of pottery-making at Pecos during the long course of its history and that, after the introduction of the technique of producing a glaze paint, this was a self-contained history.

THE ARCHEOLOGICAL BACKGROUND

The excavation of the ruins of Pecos by A. V. Kidder holds a unique place in Southwestern archeological history. It established a new era in archeological method because it was the first extensive test in this area of the principles of stratigraphy. Nelson (1914) had introduced stratigraphic methods in his Galisteo Basin explorations a few years before work at Pecos was commenced. He had given a splendid demonstration of its value (Woodbury, 1960), but the scale of his operations was limited and the conditions were much less favorable than those at Pecos. In fact, Kidder chose Pecos as the site for the long-term exploration (sponsored by the Phillips Academy, Andover) because it had been lived in continuously longer than any known ruin in the Southwest. In Kidder's words, Pecos ". . . gave rise to the hope that remains would there be found so stratified as to make clear the development of the various Pueblo arts, and thus enable us to place in their proper chronological order many other Southwestern ruins whose culture had long been known, but whose time-relations one to another were still problematical" (Kidder, 1924, p. 1). Physical conditions were also favorable. Pecos occupies a small mesa, and the population was concentrated within a limited area. Refuse was dumped over the edge of the mesa and the heaps were confined, rather than broadly scattered. Another important consideration was Pecos' geographical location on the edge of the buffalo plains, which gave it a strategic position for trade between the peoples of two cultures.

Excavations, commenced at Pecos in 1915, were interrupted from 1917 to 1919 by World War I but were resumed in 1920 and continued through 1925. During the first season, efforts were concentrated on a main rubbish heap which proved to be twice as extensive as anticipated and much more complex. But the work was also extremely rewarding, and before explorations were interrupted by the War, the sequence of pottery types had been worked out and published (Kidder and Kidder, 1917). We will be concerned here only with that part of the sequence during which Glaze-Paint Ware was the dominant painted pottery.

Rio Grande Glaze Paint is one of the few true glazes produced by the American Indian, but its use was limited to decorative design, hence the term. It was not originally discovered by Rio Grande potters. The Kidders established stratigraphic evidence that Rio Grande people had obtained Glaze-Paint Ware in trade with Little Colorado people before they learned to produce it.

During the Rio Grande Glaze-Paint period—roughly three hundred and fifty years—potters modified their style in simple, easily recognized ways; in particular, they toyed with the rims of bowls, their standard painted-ware vessel form. Changes in slip color and design pattern accompanied the rim modifications. The earliest type bore a red slip, but even before the rim was modified, a yellowish or buff slip appeared. At first the glaze was heavily pigmented and often only semi-glossy; it held the line of application like a matte paint. On later types it was lighter colored and more vitreous, and eventually the design was often obscured because the glaze had become fluid enough to run during firing. Beginning extensively in Glaze III, decoration was elaborated by the use of matte red paint for bold motifs that were outlined in glaze paint.

These various stylistic changes, although unmistakable, were less useful than rim form as classificational criteria. The six sequent types which the Kidders defined and numbered in chronological order were therefore based primarily on rim shape (Kidder and Kidder, 1917) (Fig. 2). Since these types occur in ruins throughout the Glaze-Paint area, they have afforded an extremely useful relative dating scale. In later years they were renamed in accordance with the current taxonomic system (Mera, 1933), but in this discussion I will adhere to the Kidders' nomenclature because it is more easily born in mind.

Kidder's detailed, systematic, and logical description of design elements and structures (Kidder and Shepard, 1936) stands today as a model of design analysis and also as an excellent example of the possibilities of deciphering design from remnants on sherds when the patterns of entire or restorable vessels are used as a key. Kidder's comprehensive and meticulous study of style gave a clear picture of developmental sequence, but it cast no doubt on the supposition that the first five glaze types were Pecos products.

Kidder's manuscript on Glaze-Paint Pottery was nearing completion in the early thirties when I was casting about for a means of testing the archeological significance of petrographic analysis of pottery. The suggestion that this geological technique would afford a satisfactory means of defining the composition of pottery had been made in the late twenties by Dr. Arthur Coe Spenser of the U.S. Geological Survey and was elicited through the keen interest and searching, scientific spirit of Wesley Bradfield. It was not until after Mr. Bradfield's death that I was prepared to test the method in archeology. I did not then know of Linné's study of South American ceramics, published in 1925, and could only claim that optical

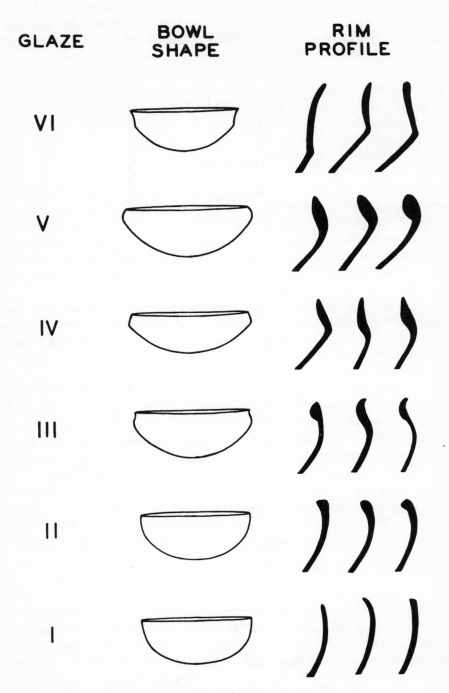

FIGURE 2
Shape and rim profile of Glaze-Paint types
from Pecos (Kidder classification).

petrology offered an accurate method of identifying the mineral inclusions in pottery. As far as anyone knew at that time, the Pueblo Indians added sand when they needed to reduce the shrinkage of clay. It could be a tedious chore to distinguish sands from different drainages. Despite the uncertainty of results, Dr. Kidder offered Pecos pottery for the test. Throughout the study he contributed to its success by his enthusiastic interest, his ready co-operation when background archeological information was required, and his keen and good-natured jibes when unorthodox hypotheses were advanced.

THE TEST

At the outset Dr. Kidder submitted representative sherds of each type for thin sectioning and analysis. The results were unanticipated and I was cautious; consequently, I had over 500 thin sections when the study was completed. The project was undertaken during the Depression when funds for equipment were short, and it was well advanced before we acquired a binocular microscope, which enabled me to distinguish major temper classes and recognize anomalous pastes, thus greatly reducing the number of thin sections required.

The principal constituents of paints and glazes were determined by microchemical methods, and one quantitative analysis of the glaze was secured. In addition, the refractive index of a large number of glazes was measured in order to estimate percentage of lead and learn if there had been a significant increase of flux in the later glazes.

Tests of physical properties were made in order to compare pastes, to distinguish clays by their firing properties, and to ascertain if there were any significant changes in the quality of pottery during the course of Pecos history.

A survey of the ceramic resources of the area constituted an important part of the study. An extensive collection of clays was tested, and the distribution of the various tempering materials was traced with the aid of geological maps.

Finally, many experiments were made using local materials and non-kiln firing to ascertain the conditions under which the properties of the pottery could be duplicated. In this connection, firing methods of contemporary Pueblo potters of the Rio Grande Valley were observed and their firing temperatures measured.

RESULTS

Petrographic analysis showed considerable variety in paste composition. Moreover, the tempering material in a significant proportion of the pottery could not have been obtained locally. Nearly all Glaze I, a type in vogue for at least fifty years, was tempered with igneous rock, chiefly andesites and diorites that occur in the Galisteo Basin, but basalts were also well represented in Glaze I Red, although not in Glaze I Yellow. Potsherd temper was rare and limited to Glaze I Red. The absence of sand- or sandstone-tempered pottery was especially noteworthy because pottery that preceded Glaze-Paint Ware was tempered with this common, local material.

The later Glaze-Paint types, II through IV, were tempered principally with sand or sandstone, but a small amount of rock-tempered pottery persisted. Even this minor representation of rock was absent from Glaze V, the very abundant type, which is stylistically distinctive of Pecos. Finally, the last type, Glaze VI, which was so poorly represented that Dr. Kidder had considered it a possible intrusive, was entirely rock-tempered.

The quantitative chemical analysis showed that the glaze is essentially a lead glass colored with a variable amount of iron and manganese, Glaze I Red being the most strongly pigmented. The range of indices of the later glazes is distinctly and consistently higher than that of the early ones. The high proportion of flux indicated, explains their greater fluidity. From the experiments in reproduction, it was found that galena, which has silver-colored cubic crystals that would attract the Indian, required stronger oxidation than is usually attained with prekiln wood firing. A vitreous paint could be produced much more easily with cerrusite, the carbonate of lead. This mineral is reported from veins in the Ortiz Mountains.

The physical tests gave no indication of either improvement or deterioration in the serviceability of Glaze-Paint Pottery during the period of its manfacture; there were no significant trends in hardness, strength, or porosity. The most interesting result of these tests was the correlation of buff-firing clay with andesite and diorite temper.

INTERPRETATIONS

The difficulty of explaining the large percentage of igneous rock in Glaze I pottery is best expressed in Dr. Kidder's words (Kidder and Shepard, 1936, p. xxiii):

Two years ago I had written for inclusion in the present volume, a discussion of the development of the local decorative art based on the supposition that all the pottery found at Pecos, with the exception of a few patently imported pieces, had been made there. I realized, of course, that certain artistic stimuli had come from exterior sources; but I believed that in general the ceramic history of the pueblo could be worked out, so to speak, on the ground. But Miss Shepard has now demonstrated that several very important types of pottery contain ingredients which could not possibly have been procured in the valley. It is her opinion that the thousands of vessels concerned were brought to the pueblo in manufactured form.

If this was actually the case, we are faced by the necessity for a drastic rearrangement of ideas regarding the status of the ceramic industry, not only at Pecos, but throughout the Southwest. It has always been assumed that potting was one of the regular household tasks of every Pueblo woman; that each town was in this regard self-sufficient. But if whole classes of pottery, such as Glaze I and Biscuit, were imported, we must postulate an extraordinary volume of trade and allow for a compensating outward flow of other commodities. Furthermore, we must believe that the production of vessels at the source of supply was much greater than was needed for home consumption, in other words, that rudimentary commercial manufacturing was practiced.

Petrographic analysis had revealed a condition of which stylistic analysis had given no hint. The satisfaction that I took in this result was somewhat offset by the fact that the evidence was only circumstantial. Although trade offered the simplest explanation of the findings, there seemed to be no way of proving that the foreign material found its way into Pecos in finished vessels and not as raw material. It was not enough to argue that there was too much of this rock-tempered pottery to have been made by women from Galisteo and Rio Grande pueblos who had married into Pecos, or that Pecos potters would not continue to adhere so strictly to the practices of the people from whom they learned to make glaze ware that they would import the temper. We tread on dangerous ground when we decide what was reasonable or logical for prehistoric potters to do.

Circumstantial evidence continued to accumulate, however, as the study progressed. After the chief pottery types had been analyzed and we were arguing the question of trade in pottery versus import of raw material, Dr. Kidder submitted for analysis a handful of sherds that he called Glaze I Red Degenerate Phase. This variety appeared toward the end of the Glaze I Red period and was rare; a less thorough archeologist might have overlooked or ignored these sherds, considering them accidental failures, because the slip was dull in color and soft, and the glaze was imperfectly vitrified. But Dr. Kidder wondered why potters, who had been making good quality Glaze I Red for generations, should lose their skill and produce this poor pottery.

Paste identification indicated a different interpretation. This was the first Glaze-Paint pottery from Pecos tempered with the local sand and sandstone; it was immediately followed by the light slip types which were made mainly from local material. The inference was clear: Glaze I Red Degenerate Phase represented Pecos potters' first attempts to use glaze paint. Characteristics of slip and glaze marked these sherds as the failures of beginners, who did not have good red slip clay, were unskilled in firing methods that would produce complete oxidation, and had not learned to obtain a sufficiently high temperature to produce a fully vitrified glaze. The type was renamed Glaze I Red, Late Phase. It is a rare experience to find the first steps in the production of a new kind of pottery; only an archeologist with rare acumen finds it.

The theory of trade also found support in other types of pottery that contained material foreign to Pecos. Thus, a contemporaneous type called Biscuit because of its soft, porous body, was heavily tempered with volcanic ash. It is best represented on the Pajarito Plateau, the locality of volcanic tuffs. Especially interesting was a sherd-tempered type, Galisteo Black-on-White that immediately antedated Glaze-Paint Ware. Pecos potters had plenty of sherds on their refuse heaps; they did not have to walk twenty-five miles for them, but the sherd temper of this particular Black-on-White pottery did not come from Pecos. It was in part from rock-tempered cook pots. Pecos' cook pots were sand-tempered whereas those of the Galisteo Basin were rock-tempered. Galisteo Black-on-White was known to be most abundant in the Galisteo Basin, but not until its composition was revealed by the petrographic microscope was it suspected of being a trade ware in Pecos.

Finally, the correlation of buff-firing clay with andesite temper supported the interpretation of this rock-tempered pottery as trade. If one argued that rock rather than pottery was imported, one would have to assume the importation of clay also and explain why buff clay was always used with the rock imported from the Galisteo Basin and never with the basalt from the Rio Grande Valley, but this argument was not seriously pressed.

The hypothetical outline of Glaze-Paint-Ware history at Pecos rested largely on petrographic data. Rock-tempered Glaze I Red and Yellow suggested that Rio Grande potters had been using glaze paint for some time before Pecos potters learned the secret of its production; it took the span of time during which a style developed and waned. The lag could not be attributed to lack of appreciation of the shiny paint on the part of Pecos people because they secured the pottery in great quantity; it was, in fact, their principal fine ware and together with Biscuit Ware—almost certainly an import also—constituted the only slipped and painted ware of this time, a time when, it would seem, Pecos potters were somnambulant.

But when glaze paint was finally made in Pecos, it was the unskilled Pecos potters themselves who took the step, not experienced potters who had married into Pecos from villages where the technique had long been practiced. Moreover, Pecos potters were quick to learn the technique; by the time a new style became established, their pottery was outwardly indistinguishable from that of villages where the tradition was well established. The small amount of rock-tempered pottery in the two subsequent types at Pecos gives an idea of how much pottery might be brought into a village through friendly exchange. There is no reason to believe that this friendly exchange ceased during the time that Glaze V was made, even though rock temper is absent from this type. Pecos potters had now become originators, but their tastes were somewhat flamboyant, and people in other villages did not care to imitate them. So when Galisteo ladies visited Pecos and tendered a small gift, it was a Glaze IV, not a Glaze V, bowl.

After their Glaze V splurge, Pecos potters lost the art of glaze painting; but they still valued the pottery, and for a short time before its complete disappearance they once more obtained it in trade. It is not surprising that the art of glaze painting was lost because this was a Time of Trouble, the time of Spanish Conquest and settlement. It is more than likely that the Spaniards gained control of the mines from which ore for glaze paint had been secured; not only did the ware cease to be made, but eventually even memory of the secret of its production was lost.

FURTHER TESTS

The petrographic analysis of Pecos Glaze-Paint pottery elucidated the history of the ware at one large and important but marginal site. It also raised many questions regarding the course of ceramic development in the region as a whole. How was the technique of glaze-paint decoration introduced and how rapidly did it spread? What was the extent of the area, where were the chief centers of production, what was the volume of trade in it, and was trade in pottery stimulated by this glossy paint that was so new to the people? It was fun to speculate because we had found a method that promised answers.

Some comparative material was examined during the course of the Pecos studies, in particular Nelson's collections from the Galisteo Basin. A few years later, a site on the western margin of the area, Unshagi, was excavated under the sponsorship of the Museum of New Mexico (Reiter, 1938). Glaze-Paint Ware comprised a small percentage of the pottery at this site. Was it trade ware, a local product, or mixed in origin? Surface features did not give the answer. When Reiter submitted sherds for petrographic analysis, a number of tempering materials were found, but there were only a few sherds made from the paste that characterized the contemporaneous, local Black-on-White Ware, a crystal ash temper not found elsewhere. The answer seemed clear with respect to Unshagi. Glaze-Paint Ware was obtained from a number of sources and only a little was made locally. The variety of pastes in the trade pottery emphasized the need for a more extensive survey of the upper Rio Grande Glaze-Paint area.

In order to pry into the question of centers of production, it was necessary to rely on surface sherds, for not even test trenches had been run in many parts of the Glaze-paint area. Fortunately, the collections of the Laboratory of Anthropology's surface survey of the Rio Grande Valley afforded an opportunity to examine samples from all of the principal sites in the area. Although the survey collections were not made for purposes of statistical study, it seemed worthwhile to analyze them in order to formulate problems more explicitly and to obtain some basis for judging the possibilities of answering them.

A factor in the decision to undertake the paste classification was the ease with which it could now be made. The experience obtained in the analysis of the Pecos material enabled me to rely primarily on the binocular microscope for identification. The paste of the entire laboratory collection of 14,700 sherds from 170 sites was therefore examined. It was possible to identify the tempering material of 90 to 95 per cent of the sherds. The results were summarized by districts in order to estimate frequencies of occurrence. These districts were defined by similarity of paste composition. A further simplification was made by combining related types in groups: Glaze I Red, the introductory type, with its dark slip varieties constituting the Early group; followed by the light-slip types, Glazes I Yellow, II, and III, designated the Intermediate group; and types IV, V, and VI, the Late group. The errors of sampling were minimized because comparisons were made within these groups, rather than between them. Furthermore, with respect to paste composition, the sample was completely random.

The results of the analysis were summarized in a series of maps showing the distribution of the various classes of tempering material in relation to natural resources and the changes in paste composition with time. Three of these diagrams, slightly modified, will indicate the nature of the evidence. I have omitted that part of the area south of Albuquerque because it is less well known archeologically, and I had no opportunity to familiarize myself with the geology.

Three major classes of tempering material were found in Glaze I Red pottery, and there was at least one district where one of these was present in the majority of sherds: sherd in Albuquerque; crystalline basalt in Zia; and andesite, andesite porphyry, and diorite in Galisteo (Fig. 3). In all of the other districts more than one material is prominent. A new material not found in Pecos, vitreous andesite, occurs in small quantity in the Bernalillo district.

To interpret this diagram one must bear in mind that it summarizes ceramic history during the course of several generations while a new technique was being introduced. Undoubtedly, the art of glaze painting was learned earlier in some districts than in others. Both geographic location and amount of Little Colorado trade pottery point to settlements of the Albuquerque district as the cradle of Rio Grande Glaze-Paint pottery. This is the only district with a strong preponderance of sherd temper, although some occurs in all the other districts, being best represented in the nearest ones and weakest on the periphery of the area.

One might expect sherd to be the chief tempering material of Glaze I Red in the Galisteo Basin settlements because it was here used for the antecedent Black-on-White Ware. Instead, this sample shows that, by some quirk, igneous rock had become the accepted temper for glaze ware. It was not a total innovation for these potters, having been used for cook pot paste.

The geographic distribution of andesitic rock points to the Galisteo as the district where pottery tempered with this rock was indigenous. On the other hand, it is unlikely that Galisteo potters would have trekked ten or fifteen miles for basalt when they had rock at their doorstep. The basalt-tempered pottery of the Galisteo district can therefore hypothetically be set down as trade pottery. This leaves 60 per cent of indigenous Glaze I Red pottery.

Turning to Pecos, we seem to have an anomalous situation. It has a higher percentage of andesite-tempered Glaze I Red than Galisteo, from which this pottery presumably came. The answer to this conundrum is that Galisteo obtained basalt-tempered trade pottery before Pecos did and had a larger quantity. But as soon as Glaze-Paint-Ware production went into full swing in the Galisteo, this district became Pecos' main supply source.

There is little doubt that in the Zia district, as in the Galisteo, Glaze-Paint pottery was soon produced locally and the technique became well established. Beyond this, there is little point in speculating about the meaning of basalt temper because the distribution of the varieties of basalt was not traced, and there is insufficient basis for judging the center of production of vitric basalt-tempered pottery.

The paste distribution of the intermediate types (Fig. 4) shows great changes: (1) The Albuquerque district is unrepresented; the sample of these types in the collection was too small for statistical treatment. Moreover sherd temper has disappeared from the region as a whole, and (2) andesite and diorite tempers have notably increased, especially in their home base of the Galisteo Basin, but also in every other district except Pecos.

The sand temper of Pecos is unique, a fact consistent with the postulate of its

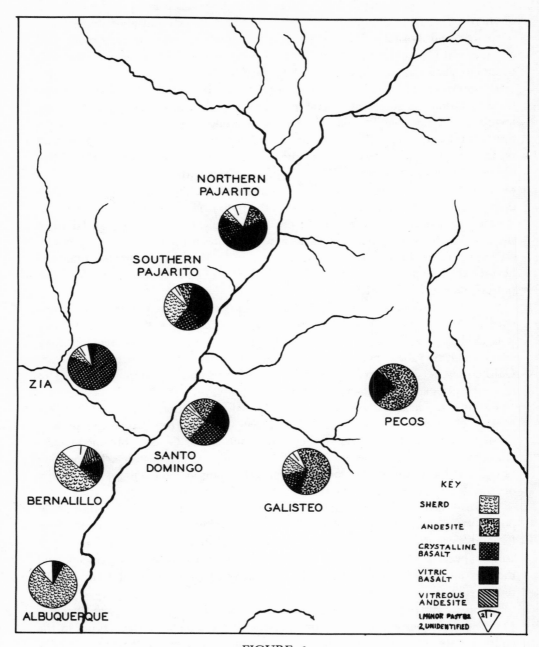

FIGURE 3
Distribution of the chief classes of tempering material in
the Early group of Glaze-Paint types.

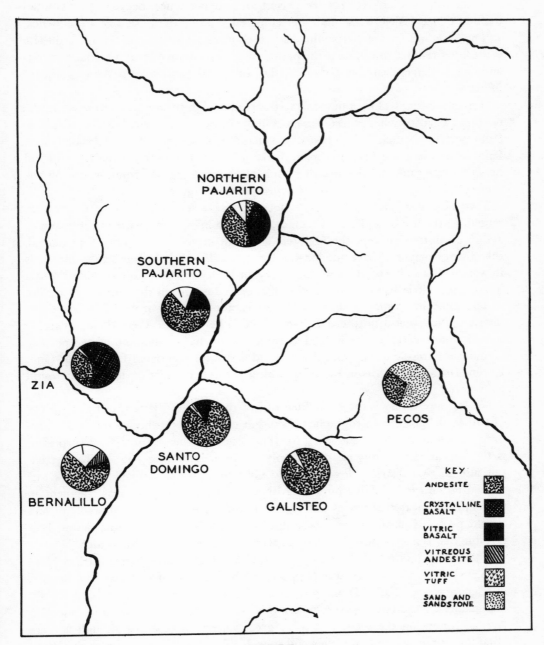

FIGURE 4
Distribution of the chief classes of tempering material in
the Intermediate group of Glaze-Paint types.

independence at this time. The diagram shows more than the 3 or 4 per cent of andesite which characterizes its period of independence because the samples include Glaze I Yellow, an andesite-tempered type of the period of dependence.

The situation in the Bernalillo district contrasts with that in Pecos. Andesite is the chief temper throughout the period, whereas a unique local material, vitreous andesite, which appeared in Glaze I Red of this district, does not show a significant increase.

It is interesting to find a new material introduced in this period, vitric ash in the northern Pajarito where there was an abundance of volcanic ash but not of Glaze-Paint pottery; in fact, Mera (1940) considered these settlements outside the Glaze-Paint area. Vitric ash first appears in the later types of the Intermediate group and heralds the significant changes that took place in temper distribution during the succeeding stage represented diagrammatically in Figure 5.

Two new districts appear in the north, and the southern Pajarito is unrepresented. In the use of andesite as temper, there is a marked decrease in the percentage in all districts except the Galisteo, although in volume of pottery produced, this district may still have headed the list. Crystalline basalt is as strong in Zia as it was in Glaze I Red. But there is very little crystalline basalt outside the Zia district and vitric basalt had virtually disappeared except in the northern Pajarito.

The most interesting change is the appearance of new materials in northern districts, Picuris and northern Pajarito. Picuris has so little Glaze-Paint Ware, it would almost certainly be judged as trade on this basis, yet some of the pottery contains an arcosic sand, quite distinct and easily differentiated from Pecos sand. Except for a few sherds in the neighboring Rio Arriba district, it was not found elsewhere.

No less interesting is the devitrified tuff of the northern Pajarito. It is a variety of tuff to delight the petrographer because it contains a distinctive mineral, tridymite, which serves as a trade mark for the pottery of this district. Most surprising is the appearance of this paste, not only in the neighboring Rio Arriba district, but also in two districts down the Rio Grande. It seems unlikely that this tuff floated down the river like pumice. Although I have seen it only as fragment in pottery, it is clear that it was not vesicular; furthermore, it is an altered tuff and would probably disintegrate too readily to be carried far in sizable lumps. Is it possible that this little marginal district was producing pottery for trade?

The overall picture of the Late styles is clear. In six out of eight districts 75 to 80 per cent of the pottery was tempered with one class of material, and in each district save one (Santo Domingo) that material is known to have been locally obtainable. Of the two districts where this generalization does not hold, one, Rio Arriba, is new on the scene and has a great variety of pastes as though it were obtaining glaze ware from hither and yon. It even has some that bears the Pecos mark of style (Glaze V) as well as that of temper. Pecos had not been an exporter of pottery, but here it was jumping into a new market.

The other district with a variety of pastes, Bernalillo, presented an anomalous situation in the preceding period. The vitric andesite, interpreted as local material,

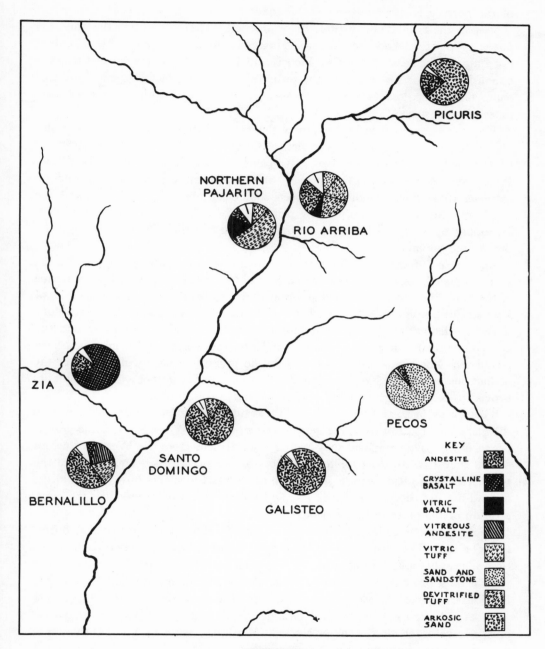

FIGURE 5
Distribution of the chief classes of tempering material in
the Late group of Glaze-Paint types.

is now only slightly stronger than in the Intermediate period, whereas nearly half of the pottery is still tempered with andesite.

Despite the rise of new centers of production, Galisteo was still the chief exporter of pottery. Andesite-tempered pottery is present in appreciable quantities not only in the new districts of Picuris and Rio Arriba, but even in the well-established one of Zia, and it is the principal class in the neighboring district of Santo Domingo. Possibly Santo Domingo had a source of andesite that we have missed in our survey.

The stages summarized in these three diagrams have been named from chronological relations. In terms of hypothetical Glaze-Paint-Ware history, they might be renamed: (1) Introduction of glaze-painting, (2) Central control of Glaze-Paint Ware production, (3) The rise of independent centers. The distinction between these stages would have been somewhat blurred had I followed the usual stylistic classification, which places Glaze I Yellow in the early class. Grouping by paste composition has not slighted the time factor; it only shifts the dividing points.

Some years after the analysis of the Laboratory of Anthropology collection was completed, excavations conducted by the Museum of New Mexico at Kuaua in the Bernalillo district afforded an opportunity to study stratigraphic samples of Late group pottery. Some 2000 sherds examined with the binocular microscope showed a definite trend in paste composition with consistent decrease in andesite and compensating increase in vitreous andesite, for which local origins had been postulated. This was a district where I did no groundwork in geology, hence the deductions were based on distribution. It was significant that vitreous andesite proved to be the principal temper of cook pots in this district.

The survey of paste-type distribution was supplemented by additional work on the glaze directed toward three general questions: (1) When Rio Grande potters began using glaze paint, did they secure raw pigment from the Western Pueblos or did they have to discover local sources of ore before they could imitate the ware? (2) When Rio Grande production came into full swing, how many sources of lead ore did the potters have? (3) Did potters intentionally modify the composition of the glaze in later periods?

These questions called for different attacks. Qualitative or quantitative differences between Western and Rio Grande glazes had to be defined before the question of possible initial importation of raw glaze paint could be answered. Copper was the most promising element; F. G. Hawley had found moderate to high copper in Western glazes (Hawley and Hawley, 1938), whereas our spectrographic analyses indicated that in the Rio Grande glazes, copper was usually present as only a trace or, at most, a minor element. Mr. F. G. Schoffman and I, therefore, made quantitative microchemical determinations of copper in twenty-one samples, separating the copper microelectrolytically and determining it photometrically. Fourteen Western glazes in our sample contained moderate to high copper, but only two of the Rio Grande samples contained moderate copper; we detected none in the others (Shepard, 1942, p. 222). The two samples with moderate copper were from Glaze I Red of the Albuquerque district where we thought the first Rio Grande Glaze-Paint Ware was made. The copper determinations, therefore, lent support to the hypothesis of initial use of bartered paint.

Determining whether ore from one or more sources was used for the Rio Grande paints was difficult. The possibility that ore from different outcrops would differ in trace elements seemed the most promising lead, and spectrographic analysis the most practicable method of investigation. Through the courtesy of Dr. G. R. Harrison and Mr. Rockwell Kent III, of Massachussetts Institute of Technology, 117 glaze-paint samples were analyzed. The results showed no qualitative differences that we could interpret in terms of sources of ores, but even though the analyses only differentiated major, minor, and trace elements, they gave promising indications that percentages of diagnostic minor and trace elements would mark glazes from different sources.

The question of intentional modification of the composition of the glaze in the Late period was given a preliminary test by quantitative microchemical analyses of ten samples, five each of Early and Late types. In these analyses lead was separated microelectrolytically; iron and manganese were determined photometrically; and silica, alumina, calcium, and magnesium were determined by wet microchemical methods. The increase in lead in the Late glaze was clear; percentages in the twenties and thirties characterized the Early type, whereas they jumped to the fifties and sixties in the Late type. There was a decrease in alumina and a slight decrease in silica in the Late glazes. These elements would all affect the fusibility of the glaze. Manganese was lower in the Late than in the Early glazes, but there was no significant change in iron oxide. The change in color of the glaze was caused, therefore, by more complete solution of the pigment as well as by change in composition. The analyses of the alkaline earths suggested a local differentiation in composition, of interest in relation to the question of sources of ore. The change in composition of the Late glazes may have resulted from use of ore from different sources, from selection of ore from a single outcrop, or from refinement and compounding of the pigment. It would be interesting to know if potters had compounded pigment for the Late glazes. The analyses indicated possibilities of answering this question. Tracing the history of the glaze was challenging and the preliminary results were encouraging, but the problems were difficult, the sampling was inadequate, and the methods of analysis employed were time consuming.

A HYPOTHETICAL RECONSTRUCTION

Paste analysis of the Laboratory of Anthropology collection was undertaken primarily to formulate explicit questions. Rather than summarize the work by a series of questions, I shall attempt a brief hypothetical reconstruction of the history of Glaze-Paint-Ware manufacture in the Upper Rio Grande Valley.

About A.D. 1250, Indian traders from the Little Colorado River Valley found that the showy red pottery with glossy black paint from their home towns was popular with Rio Grande people; the paint was unlike anything these people had seen before. The traders bartered principally with the villages they first reached on entering the Rio Grande Valley, but they sometimes went farther, and soon the attractive red bowls could be found in all the larger settlements of the valley. Despite its popularity, however, the ware could not be secured in great quantity; it made a heavy pack for the long trek. Although Rio Grande potters were eager to imitate it, they could not find out how to produce the glossy paint; piñon pitch did not work and they could think of nothing else. Finally, a friendly trader agreed to bring them a little of the mysterious paint. It was just a dark powder, and the first bowls painted with it were disappointing, but the potters persisted in their trials and finally succeeded by using hotter fires and better draft. The next problem was to find paint in their own territory. Hunters had noticed patches of various colored earths in the Ortiz Mountains, which had been used as body paint during ceremonials and for Kiva frescoes. Potters now tried these colored earths, choosing those that most closely resembled the bartered paint. After a number of trials they were again successful. These people of the Albuquerque district now had pottery to trade. They sought trade especially with the people of the Galisteo Basin who controlled the turquoise mines, but their ware also passed into all parts of the valley.

To maintain their trade, the Albuquerque people tried to keep secret the source of the paint, but in time it leaked out and then experimenting began in other settlements. At first the Albuquerque style was imitated and a red slip was used. Galisteo potters, however, soon substituted their own light-firing slips because they lacked large deposits of good red clay. Then they thought of making more showy vessels by using red as a filler, thus utilizing their own resources effectively to set a new style that came to be imitated in other settlements.

Not long after they introduced the light slips, the Galisteo people gained control of Glaze-Paint Ware production because the ore outcrops were in territory they claimed. This gave them considerable advantage in trade, and so proficient were they as potters and so well did they guard the pigment outcrops that they supplied the greater part of the Glaze-Paint Ware of the valley for a considerable time. They did not often offer the paint in trade but they were willing to let Pecos people have it in exchange for buffalo hides from the Plains. Pecos potters were soon able to make their own Glaze-Paint pottery but they did not compete with Galisteo potters. The settlements of the Zia district also had access to ore for glaze paint and, like Pecos, made most of their own pottery; they even traded some. A small amount of glaze paint was also secured by people in other districts, but they remained largely dependent on trade with the Galisteo.

In time a change occurred. People in parts of the valley who had not used glaze paint before commenced making Glaze-Paint Ware and even traded it to a limited extent. Just how this change came about, we are not certain— whether ores outside Galisteo territory were discovered or Galisteo people decided to trade in ore. It is clear, however, that this was not only a time of greater independence in production, but was also a period of greater freedom in style. Pecos developed its own style and there were other local styles. Unfortunately the trend did not run its full course; the history of an unusual technique was cut short by the Spanish conquest.

In this hypothetical reconstruction, postulates that can be tested are readily distinguished from those that cannot. Its principal justification is that it highlights areas where investigation would be most practical. For example, if one were to pursue the question of the number of sources of glaze-paint ore, it would be advisable to start with a systematic comparison of Zia and Galisteo glaze rather than to analyze samples from randomly chosen sites.

The principal question is whether the outline of the course of development— a period of introduction and imitation followed by one of centralized control of production, and finally ending in greater independence and diversification—is sound. This is not simply a question of soundness of the thesis that source of tempering material marks place of production. Accurate dating is also essential. We do not yet know that the various types had the same time span in all parts of the area. Specialization resulting from differences in clay resources may have resulted in greater local differences in stylistic history than has thus far been recognized. For example, in localities where there were good red clays, the production of Glaze I Red may have continued after Galisteo people had established the cream-slip types. Just how much such temporal overlapping of types would affect the picture of Galisteo dominance, I am not prepared to say, but the Rio Grande study demonstrated that this problem of relationships can be unraveled when the evidence of paste composition is correlated with dated styles.

EVALUATION OF METHODS

Many new methods of analysis have been introduced since the Rio Grande glaze-paint study was completed. An idea of these can be gained from the journal *Archaeometry*, and from the researches of E. V. Sayre and his associates (1957, 1958, 1959, 1961), and from Aitken (1961). They are principally instrumental methods of chemical analysis. If the glaze-paint study were repeated today with hindsight, would our procedures be revolutionized and what new information might we reasonably expect to gain?

When Dr. Kidder offered Pecos pottery to test the value of petrographic analyses, he unwittingly presented an exceptionally favorable case. Although we knew that the pottery was tempered and therefore satisfactory for mineralogical identifications with the petrographic microscope, we did not realize that special factors had affected production and trade—*i.e.*, the demand for the ware and the requirement of a pigment of limited occurrence, access to which could be controlled. Moreover, the advantages of geological diversity were far greater than we realized. Under these circumstances the key to the story of diffusion of glaze-painting, as well as trade, centers of production, degree of specialization, and control of the industry, was found in paste composition, specifically in the source of the tempering materials. The petrographic microscope is the classic instrument for identification of minerals and rocks. It has not been superseded by any other method and would be relied on as heavily today as it was thirty years ago. It is clear that the story would never have unfolded had we depended on chemical analysis alone; this could not have shown what kind of materials the potter used, and even though differences in composition would have been reported, they would have been meaningless in terms of sources of material.

Although we would choose the same basic analytical tool for the Pecos study today, our procedure would differ. We would make much more extensive use of the binocular microscope for preliminary classification and, in consequence, would require fewer thin sections. Doubtless the extravagant use of thin sections for the pilot study at Pecos has contributed to the erroneous idea that petrographic analysis is too time-consuming and expensive to be practicable.

These generalizations regarding paste analysis apply to tempered pottery. Obviously analytical requirements for untempered pottery made of levigated clay are entirely different.

The second important method of mineralogical analysis, X-ray diffraction, has been developed much more recently than optical petrography and has been employed extensively in geology. Its great advantage is for identification of minerals too fine-grained for optical methods, and its chief limitation in ceramic studies is that crystalline structure is affected when clay is fired. Although X-ray diffraction has been used in a few archeological studies, it has not yet been tested extensively where its contribution to broader questions could be evaluated. If we were studying Rio Grande Glaze-Paint pottery today, we would certainly employ it. We would define the differences in clay composition of different districts, but we could make only partial comparison between these and the potters' clays because Pueblo firing temperatures were high enough to destroy some of the clay minerals. However much a comparison would show, it is safe to say that X-ray diffraction would be a supplementary rather than a primary method in this particular study.

In contrast to the value of petrography in the study of Pecos pottery, most of the tests of physical properties were unnecessary. It may have been worthwhile to test their significance once, but ordinarily they would be used only for special problems, after quick tests had indicated important changes.

Location of sources of tempering material was a major clue in recovering the history of Glaze-Paint Ware. As a general guide, I relied on Darton's geologic map of New Mexico (Darton, 1928), on special geologic reports, and on field trips. Many geologic reports that would have been helpful have come out in subsequent years. The added detail that is now available is well illustrated by the recent report on the geology and water resources of the Santa Fe area (Spiegel and Baldwin, 1963). These reports have not altered the major conclusions originally reached, but they would have facilitated the study. Although the analyst cannot expect to gain from geologic maps the intimate knowledge of ceramic resources that native people have acquired after living in an area for many generations, he has the guidance of geologic principles and knowledge of the relationship of minerals to the type of formation.

The greatest improvements in method would be made in the analysis of the glaze itself. Here it is essential to determine chemical composition, and the problems formulated call for quantitative analysis and identification of trace elements. There have been tremendous advances in instrumental methods of chemical analysis since the glaze-paint study was made. New techniques allow greater latitude in the range of problems that can be attacked, and increase efficiency of analysis immeasurably as well as the possibilities of making quantitative determinations; some are nondestructive. Nevertheless, for a preliminary survey of glaze-paint composition, we would still use the classic method of emission spectroscopy. For some problems, the choice between emission spectroscopy and vacuum X-ray fluorescence spectroscopy might be debated. However, X-ray fluorescence spectroscopy is not sensitive enough for quantitative determination of trace elements, whereas emission spectroscopy requires dilution of sample for determination of major elements. Consequently, several methods might be combined for the quantitative analyses that are essential for investigation of the source of the earliest glaze paint used in the Rio Grande Valley and of the number of Rio Grande sources of ore during the period of full development of the ware. For comparison of lead content in Early and Late glazes, we would try beta-ray back scatter. This method is nondestructive, as well as being quick and simple (Emeleus, 1960). The developments and improvement in instrumental methods have been so rapid that comparisons of sensitivities, limits of analysis, efficiency, and economy should be made at the time that archeological problems are formulated. Of the many new methods that are just being introduced, the Laser microprobe is one to be watched. Without question, the new possibilities of quantitative determination together with more extensive sampling would bring us much nearer than we were in the thirties to solutions of glaze-paint problems.

In addition to being a test of methods, the glaze-paint study illustrates several general points with regard to the conduct of ceramic laboratory analysis. The importance of problem formulation and adequate sampling need not be labored; it is sufficiently clear. The naïve over-optimism of the archeologist who submits a handful of "representative sherds" for identification was understandable thirty years ago, but is no longer.

The advantages of full and free exchange of information and frequent discussion between archeologist and analyst should be equally clear. But there are still archeologists who argue that information relating to provenance, dating, and stylistic characteristics of pottery should be withheld from the analyst in order to avoid influencing his judgments. There are two curious assumptions implicit in this stand. First, that it is essential to guard against the bias of the analyst who is dealing largely with data secured by instrumental means, but that such precautions are unnecessary for the archeologist who must often rely on personal impressions; and second, that the interpretation of data should be left entirely to the archeologist, that he can recognize all implications of results obtained from methods with which he is unfamiliar, and that the analyst has nothing to contribute other than bare facts.

Had Dr. Kidder acted on this idea, the results of the Pecos study would have been very different. The analytical data would have said nothing more to me than that pottery from Pecos contained a number of kinds of tempering material. Dr. Kidder would have undertaken interpretation with severe handicaps: (1) a strong bias—the perfectly reasonable idea, shared by archeologists of that time—that all pottery-using settlements were self-sufficient pottery producers; and (2) the necessity of spending more time on geology than most archeologists can afford. It would have been essential for him to recognize natural petrographic provinces as well as define ceramic practices in those provinces. Granted that Dr. Kidder would have taken a mental somersault, risked the ridicule of his colleagues, and spent considerable time on geology, he still would have lacked the data necessary for meaningful interpretation because I would have thrown up the analytical job in boredom long before it was completed.

GENERAL INFERENCES

Ceramic history has many facets. Even the technological side of pottery production embraces such diverse activities as: (1) improvement in serviceability accomplished by discovery of better clays, refinement of paste composition, and introduction of more effective firing methods; (2) speeding production by the invention of mechanical devices for vessel shaping and of more efficient methods of firing, which in turn open the way for pottery to become an article of commerce; (3) the adaptation of shape and quality to function; (4) the discovery of pigments and glazes which, together with refinement of form and finish, influence the aesthetic aspect of pottery. It is clear that technique influences the economics of pottery production, the functional specialization of pottery, and the potter's role in the development of decorative art.

In the course of history, the various aspects of ceramics have not maintained an even pace. This situation calls for explicit definitions when the term "levels of ceramic development" is used. In the New World, levels of ceramic development have been defined with respect to the surface finish and decorative elaboration of pottery. These levels have never been evaluated with respect to technological development, specialization and commercialization in pottery production, and degree of refinement of aesthetic standards. Our New World view of ceramic development is decidedly myopic because the American Indian never passed many of the major milestones in ceramic history: levigation of clay, construction of permanent kilns, wheel throwing, production of stoneware and hard porcelain, use of glazes and enamels. Ethnologists have recently raised interesting evidence bearing on incipient wheel throwing (Foster, 1959a, 1959b), and our evidence regarding kilns is negative; it is possible that survey with the magnetometer will locate kilns that have been missed in spotty excavations (Aitken, 1961, pp. 16–24). Nevertheless, the quality of American Indian pottery speaks for itself; it is confined to the earthenware stage of ceramic history, and the developmental levels that have been proposed refer primarily to finish and decoration.

Against this backdrop, Rio Grande Glaze-Paint Ware appears as an unusual phenomenon in American Indian ceramic history, but its production was accidental, premature, and abortive. The accidental nature is clear; it was premature because it antedated the invention of a kiln, which would permit potters to control firing conditions sufficiently to produce an all-over glazed ware without excessive loss. Perhaps it was abortive because it was premature, but its history was ended by outside forces, the Spanish Conquest. Nevertheless, in the course of its 350-year history, the developments that occurred were mainly in the nature of decorative modifications: variations of slip color, use of supplementary paints, and minor modifications of shape. The one technical advance that may have been made was in compounding a glaze, but additional chemical work is needed to determine if this was actually done. The important step of using the glaze paint as a slip was never taken. It may have been tried on small pieces and proved unsatisfactory because bits of ash from fuel stuck to it or uneven firing left it only partly vitrified. Whether the cause was technical problems, or short supply of glaze paint, or lack of interest or imagination, Pueblo glazing remained a technique of patterned decoration.

Granted that Glaze-Paint Ware is exceptional and that it was made in an area where ceramic resources favored petrographic analysis, the technological data nevertheless have direct bearing on such questions as the nature and rate of ceramic change, and factors governing diffusion, specialization, and trade. In fact, the evidence is probably clearer because of these exceptional circumstances.

The archeologist's ideas of the nature of ceramic change have varied according to his experience. His "sherd view," or "early period view," pictures ceramic development as a very slow and gradual process. This is the impression gained when one studies pottery made during periods when there were no significant changes. The archeologist is also handicapped when his study is based entirely on sherds because the record of shape and decoration is incomplete. Furthermore, the very methods of classifying sherds—by reference to norms (pottery types)—obscures the record of change. Finally, the student has an incomplete and unbalanced picture if he lacks the facilities and the materials necessary to define the role of natural resources. These limitations should be recognized before broad generalizations regarding the rate and course of ceramic change are made.

The glaze-paint study illustrates the ways in which change in composition of slips and paints with their attendant effects on style are dependent on natural resources. In this area of ceramic development, change comes suddenly with the discovery of a new material and is followed by a more or less gradual process of learning and assimilation. The study also demonstrates that a new technique may be learned so rapidly that its introduction can pass unnoticed in the sherd record of a stratigraphic test.

Laboratory analysis demonstrates the role of natural resources in diffusion. For example, the idea of using a glossy paint would never have borne fruit in the Rio Grande Valley had lead ores been absent. As the idea spread, slip and decoration were modified in adaptation to the materials available in the various districts. This process is most conspicuous in the Galisteo Basin with its introduction of a cream slip.

One of the most interesting questions raised by the Rio Grande Glaze-Paint study is that of the possibility of recognizing the beginnings of commercialization in pottery production. Can we identify the times and conditions under which pottery-making was transformed from a craft practiced for home consumption to an industry producing for the market? This is a difficult matter. The fact that wide trade in Rio Grande Glaze-Paint Ware was not suspected prior to the petrographic study bears witness to the obscurity of evidence of intraregional trade. The petrographic data suggested the hypothesis that control of an essential material led to specialization and the development of an extensive market even at the handcraft level. Glaze-Paint Ware represents a rare kind of specialization in the field of American Indian ceramics. Although it is more easily recognized than others, it is by no means the only kind. Discovery of a clay that has superior properties may be the key to production of a ware that is more serviceable, that meets the requirement of a particular function, or that has the attraction of a rare slip. Exceptional skills, no less than valuable materials, may lead to special-ization. I have postulated an example of this in the distribution of corrugated ware in northwestern New Mexico (Judd, 1954, pp. 236–38).

The difficulty of recognizing this exceptionally interesting transition in ceramic history lies in the fact that extensive intraregional trade results in such an inter-mingling of types in different districts that outward appearances of the pottery give the archeologist no clue to actual centers of production. In some instances, relative frequency of occurrence of wares may actually create an erroneous im-pression, as was so plainly demonstrated in the case of production in the northern districts of the Glaze-Paint area. Under favorable circumstances, sources of material may afford the necessary clues, but the opportunity for petrographic analysis to make a useful contribution depends in no small measure on the thorough integration and cross checking of archeological and laboratory data. This is simply to state, in effect, that ceramics is a complex industry and in order to understand its history correctly we need all possible lines of evidence and the closest possible co-operation between those engaged in its study.

BIBLIOGRAPHY

AITKEN, M. J.
1961. *Physics and Archaeology.* New York and London: Interscience.
DARTON, N. H.
1928. *Geologic Map of New Mexico.* Washington, D.C.: U.S. Geological Survey.
EMELEUS, V. M.
1960. "Beta Ray Backscattering: A Simple Method for the Quantitative Determination of Lead Oxide in Glass, Glaze and Pottery." *Archaeometry,* 3:5–9.
FOSTER, G. M.
1959a. "The Coyotepec *Molde* and Some Associated Problems of the Potter's Wheel." *Southwestern Journal of Anthropology,* 15:53–63.
1959b. "The Potter's Wheel: An Analysis of Idea and Artifact in Invention." *Ibid.,* pp. 99–119.
HAWLEY, F. M., and F. G. HAWLEY
1938. *Classifications of Black Pottery Pigments and Paint Areas,* and *The Chemical*

Analysis of Southwestern Glazed Paint. Albuquerque: University of New Mexico Bulletin, Anthropological Series, Vol. II, No. 4.

JUDD, N. M.

1954. *The Material Culture of Pueblo Bonito.* Smithsonian Miscellaneous Collections, Vol. 124. Washington, D.C.: Smithsonian Institution, Publication 4172.

KIDDER, A. V.

1924. *An Introduction to the Study of Southwestern Archaeology with a Preliminary Account of the Excavations at Pecos.* Papers of Phillips Academy, Southwestern Expedition, No. 1. New Haven.

KIDDER, A. V., and A. O. SHEPARD

1936. *The Pottery of Pecos,* Vol. 2. Papers of Phillips Academy, No. 7.

KIDDER, M. A., and A. V. KIDDER

1917. "Notes on the Pottery of Pecos." *American Anthropologist* (n.s.), 19:325–60.

LINNÉ, S.

1925. *The Techniques of South American Ceramics.* Göteborgs Kungl. Vetenskaps-och Vitterhets-Samhälles, Handlingar, Fjärde Följden, Band 29, No. 5.

MERA, H. P.

1933. *A Proposed Revision of the Rio Grande Glaze Paint Sequence.* Laboratory of Anthropology, Archaeological Survey, Technical Series, Bulletin No. 5.

1940. *Population Changes in the Rio Grande Glaze Paint Area.* Laboratory of Anthropology, Archaeological Survey, Technical Series, Bulletin No. 9.

NELSON, N. C.

1914. *Pueblo Ruins of the Galisteo Basin, New Mexico.* New York: Anthropological Papers, American Museum of Natural History, Vol. 15, pt. 1.

REITER, P.

1938. *The Jemez Pueblo of Unshagi, New Mexico.* Albuquerque: University of New Mexico Bulletin, Vol. 1, No. 5, pt. 2.

SAYRE, E. V.

1959. "Studies of Ancient Ceramic Objects by Means of Neutron Bombardment and Emission Spectroscopy." In *Application of Science in the Examination of Works of Art,* pp. 153–75. Proceedings of the Seminar conducted by the Research Laboratory. Boston: Museum of Fine Arts.

SAYRE, E. V., and R. W. DODSON

1957. "Neutron Activation Study of Mediterranean Potsherds." *American Journal of Archaeology,* 61:35–41.

SAYRE, E. V., A. MURRENHOFF, and C. F. WEICK

1958. *The Nondestructive Analysis of Ancient Potsherds Through Neutron Activation.* Long Island: Brookhaven National Laboratory, Report BNL 508(T-122).

SAYRE, E. V., and R. W. SMITH

1961. "Compositional Categories of Ancient Glass." *Science,* 133:1824–26.

SHEPARD, A. O.

1942. *Rio Grande Glaze Paint Ware, A Study Illustrating the Place of Ceramic Technological Analysis in Archaeological Research.* Washington, D.C., Carnegie Institution of Washington, Publication 528, Contribution No. 39.

SPIEGEL, Z., and B. BALDWIN

1963. *Geology and Water Resources of the Santa Fe Area, New Mexico.* Washington, D.C.: U.S. Geological Survey, Water-Supply Paper 1525.

WOODBURY, R. B.

1960. "Nels C. Nelson and Chronological Archaeology." *American Antiquity,* 25:400–2.

CARIBBEAN CERAMICS:
A STUDY IN METHOD AND IN THEORY

IRVING ROUSE

THE West Indies and the adjacent mainland of South America, including eastern and central Venezuela and the northern part of the Guianas, constitute a single Caribbean culture area. A rather peculiar approach to the study of pottery has developed there, which it is the purpose of this paper to discuss.

Archeologists working in the Caribbean area have found it necessary to concentrate on pottery because they find little else. As in other parts of tropical south America, chipped stone artifacts are virtually non-existent, and ground stone artifacts occur so rarely and vary so little that they provide a relatively poor basis for archeological interpretation. The same is true of bone and shell artifacts, while objects of other materials are rarely preserved in the tropical climate. Pottery, on the other hand, is frequent. It is not uncommon to find as many as 1000 potsherds in a single excavation block that measures two meters square and twenty-five centimeters deep (e.g., Cruxent and Rouse, 1958–59, vol. 1, Tables 9–12).

There are, of course, exceptions to this situation, especially in the Taino culture of the Greater Antilles. But even here, the stone, bone, wood, and shell artifacts offer only sculptured and engraved designs similar to those modeled and incised on the pottery vessels (Rouse, 1948, pp. 535–38). These designs are so much more common on the vessels that, even in Taino culture, pottery provides the key to Caribbean prehistory.

CLASSIFICATION OF THE POTTERY

The Caribbean archeologist is faced with several difficulties in classifying pottery. One is the restricted usage which the aborigines made of the art. With very few exceptions, the sites have yielded only two kinds of clay artifacts: vessels and the thick, flat griddles that were used for baking cassava bread. The latter vary so little from site to site and from period to period that the archeologist must focus his attention on the pottery vessels.

But the vessels are almost all fragmentary. The Indians of the Caribbean area rarely deposited their pottery in graves and they had no permanent buildings in which the vessels might have been preserved. Almost all the pottery is found scattered through the refuse in the form of sherds; and these must have been badly trampled, for there are rarely enough sherds from a single vessel to reconstruct it.

As a result, it is impossible to use vessel shapes as a criterion for classifying the pottery. Elements of shape can be used—for example, Caribbean archeologists have come to pay great attention to rim profiles (e.g., Cruxent and Rouse, 1958–59)—but these will suffice to classify only a portion of the sherds. We need a criterion which will serve as the basis for an overall classification.

In some areas, for example Peru, the nature of the potsherds themselves provides such a criterion (Ford, 1949, pp. 41–43). Unfortunately, the Caribbean potters do not seem to have paid much attention to this. In the West Indies, for example, they did not even add tempering material; they simply used clay which already had a certain amount of grit in it (Horton and Berman, 1941). The sherds vary so greatly in thickness, fineness, color, etc., that it has not proved practicable to classify them into types on the basis of any of these criteria. Again, there are exceptions; e.g., one group of Indians in the Middle and Upper Orinoco Valley mixed sponge spicules with their clay (e.g., Cruxent and Rouse, 1958–59, Vol. 1, pp. 252–53), but such exceptions are rare.

One might have hoped to use painting as the basic criterion of classification, since this has proved to be successful in the southwestern United States (e.g., Colton, 1953, pp. 53–55). Unfortunately, the Indians of the Caribbean area rarely painted the entire surfaces of their vessels, as was done in the southwestern United States; instead, they limited the paint to certain areas of the vessel surface, such as the base, shoulder, rim, or any combination thereof. Hence this criterion cannot be used either, for it would result in assigning too many parts of the same vessel to different types.

Surface finish is another criterion which has been used for overall classification, as in the northeastern United States (Smith, 1950, p. 188). However, the Caribbean potters were also accustomed to vary this from one part of the vessel surface to another; for instance, polishing is frequently limited to the rim, or fabric impression to the bottom of the vessel (Rouse, 1952, pp. 338–39).

The same is true of other elements of decoration. The standard procedure in the Caribbean area was for the potter to divide the vessel into zones and to decorate the zones in different manners (Rouse, 1941, Fig. 6). Thus, modeled lugs might be attached to the shoulder at opposite ends of a vessel; they might be flanked on either side by appliqué figures; the rest of the shoulder might be decorated with incised designs; and the rim itself might be punctated. If one classified unrelated fragments of a single vessel like this according to their decoration, one might have to assign them to four different types, characterized respectively by modeled, appliqué, incised, and punctated decoration.

To be sure, several different types of decoration are frequently found on the same sherds. Would it not be possible, by a study of these concurrences, or of the concurrences of various elements of material, shape, and decoration on individual sherds, to arrive at combinations of material, shape, and/or decoration which might serve as the basis for an overall classification? This has been attempted, but it, too, has been a failure. A few such combinations do occur; a distinctive kind of fine tan ware incised with zoned crosshatching has become a time marker for the first half of the first millennium A.D. on the eastern coast of Venezuela and in the Lesser Antilles (Cruxent and Rouse, 1958–59, Vol. 1, p. 37). But this combination comprises only a small part of the pottery of the time, and we need a method of classifying all of it.

Apparently, the Caribbean potters preferred to vary their vessels as much as possible by employing a large number of alternative kinds of materials, techniques of manufacture, elements of shape, techniques of decoration, and decorative designs, and by making a different choice from among these alternatives each time they produced a pot. In addition, they had a number of options—for instance, they might or might not add a handle to the vessel, or they might not decorate it—and they seem to have exercised a free choice among these options. As a result, the pottery presents an almost endless combination of elements of material, shape, and decoration. The writer has estimated that the Meillac pottery of Haiti contains 192 different combinations of elements of shape alone (Rouse, 1941, p. 85).

In order to encompass such a large number of combinations within a reasonable number of types, it is necessary to make the latter so broad as to be almost meaningless. For example, in classifying the pottery of La Cabrera Site in the Valencia Basin, Venezuela, Kidder (1944) was able to distinguish only three types: La Cabrera Plain, La Cabrera Red, and Valencia Red. Such a classification does not begin to do justice to the rich variety of attributes of material, shape, and decoration which are present in the pottery.

In an attempt to take this variety into consideration, Bennett (1937) used a different approach to the classification of Valencia pottery. He divided the pottery into three categories, bowls (i.e., vessels), bowl handles, and bowl adornos, and made a separate classification for each of these categories. He set up seven different types of bowls, four types of handles, and seven types of adornos. Osgood (1943) adopted the same approach and carried it further (Osgood and Howard, 1943) by establishing different types of rim profile and different "styles" of design.

The writer brought this approach to its logical conclusion by setting up separate classifications for each aspect of the material, shape, and decoration of Caribbean pottery. In dealing with the Valencia pottery, he made nine successive classifications for material, three for techniques of decoration, eleven for shape, and eleven for decoration. Many of these classifications consisted of only a single type, but others contained two or more types, as in the previous classifications of Bennett and Osgood (Cruxent and Rouse, 1958–59, Vol. 1, pp. 175–79). For example, coiling was the only technique of building up the vessel wall, but on the vessel walls there were three types of appliqué work: human faces, vertical ridges, and horizontal ridges.

The usual procedure of classification is to lay a collection out on the table and to separate it into a series of groups on the basis of one or more of the criteria discussed above (Rouse, 1960, Fig. 3). Each group is considered to represent a single type and is given the name of the type, which usually combines the name of a typical site with that of one of the main criteria used in the classification, e.g., the Chaco Black-on-White type. All the specimens fall into one group or another.

In effect, the procedure used by the writer assumes that it is impracticable to discriminate more than a single type of pottery. Therefore, when a collection is laid out on the table, it is not separated into piles according to types of pottery; instead, it is successively classified in a number of different ways: first according to types of material, then according to techniques of manufacture, then according to types of bases, of bodies, of rim profiles, etc. (Rouse, 1960, Fig. 2). Only a portion of the sherds will be utilized in each of these classifications, of course, since not all sherds will be classified, for example, for both bases and rims.

If the Caribbean pottery had included more complete vessels, or if the potters had had less freedom in choosing types of material, shape, and decoration, then we could have utilized both kinds of classification; i.e., we could have classified the collection first according to types of pottery and then have successively regrouped the artifacts according to types of material, shape, and decoration. This is not an uncommon practice; Ford (1952) did both kinds of classification in preparation for his study of prehistoric design developments in the southeastern United States. Unfortunately, this does not seem to be practicable in the Caribbean area.

TYPES VERSUS MODES

Since the procedure of classifying the pottery into types of material, shape, and decoration has been carried to its logical conclusion in the Caribbean area, the research in that area offers a good opportunity to test the value of the method. Is it really worth doing as a complement to the method of classifying pottery according to types, or as a substitute for this method in dealing with broken and extremely variable pottery like that in the Caribbean area?

First, it will be well to define some terms. We have so far been using the term *type* rather loosely, and should tighten the usage for the sake of clarity in the following discussion. Hereafter, the word *type* will be used only to refer to the overall classification of the pottery; i.e., as a shorthand method of saying "type of pottery vessel" or "type of potsherd," depending upon the nature of the material being classified. (The difference need not concern us here.)

Having imposed this limitation, we shall be unable also to use the word *type* in such phrases as "type of material," "type of base," and "type of incised design," and shall need a substitute. The writer has adopted the term *mode* for this purpose (Rouse, 1939, pp. 11–12). Just as the term *type* refers to a kind of pottery, so the term *mode* refers to a kind of material, of technique, of shape, or of design which occurs in the pottery. It is a less clumsy way of referring collectively to these units.

For the purpose of this discussion, it will also be necessary to distinguish classes of artifacts from the types and modes. The classes are the piles of artifacts produced when one sorts a collection on the table. They consist of the artifacts themselves; one can handle them, describe them, and add to them by collecting more artifacts of the same kind. Types and modes, on the other hand, are abstractions from the classes. They consist of the criteria which have been used, consciously or unconsciously, to group the artifacts into the classes. A type or mode, therefore, can be defined by listing its diagnostic attributes but it cannot be described, nor can it be added to, as can be done to a class.

Once a series of types has been established, one can use them to classify a new collection without going to the trouble of actually sorting the pottery into classes. One need only determine which type a given artifact exemplifies by matching the attributes of the artifact with those of the type. One determines the modes represented on a given potsherd in the same way, by comparing the attributes of the potsherd with those of the various modes. The main difference is that a given artifact can exemplify only one type but it will ordinarily exemplify several different modes. For example, a sherd may bear the attributes of a certain mode of rim profile, which might be called the beveled rim, and at the same time, this beveled rim may be incised with a certain mode of design, such as horizontal parallel lines.

Conceptually, then, a type consists of the attributes which distinguish one class of artifacts from another. A mode, on the other hand, consists of the attributes which distinguish one aspect of a class of artifacts, such as rim profiles, from the same aspect in another class of artifacts. Not uncommonly, modes are used in place of attributes to define types. In the northeastern United States, for example, pottery types have been formed by combining modes of rim profile with modes of decorative technique and design (Ritchie and MacNeish, 1949, pp. 100–16). From this point of view, each type may be regarded as a complex of several modes (Rouse, 1960, pp. 317–18).

USAGE OF MODES

Since types and modes are analogous phenomena, they are able to fulfill similar functions in archeological research. The following discussion will illustrate the principal uses to which they have been put.

Identification of artifacts.—The best way to identify an artifact, of course, is to name its type. Lacking types, as in the Caribbean area, one may use modes in their place. We catalog our Caribbean pottery, for example, by naming its modes, as well as its provenance and the culture to which it belongs. This is a more cumbersome procedure than simply naming the type of artifact, but is equally precise.

Description of culture.—It is customary in a report of excavations to present and discuss the types of artifacts that have been found, treating the types found in each component of the site separately if there happen to have been several different occupations. Lacking types in the Caribbean area, we define and discuss only the modes present in each component. This discussion serves as a description of the ceramics of the component, and to it is added, as in other areas, a discussion of the types of non-ceramic artifacts, as well as inferences concerning other aspects of the culture, the whole combining to present as comprehensive a picture as possible of the total culture of the component.

Discussions of types of pottery include a description of the pottery of each type, i.e., of the sherds in each class. In the Caribbean area, this is not needed, since the definitions of the modes constitute an adequate description of the pottery, including, as they do, all aspects of its material, shape, and decoration. Indeed, they have the advantage that they focus attention upon the culturally significant aspects of the pottery, that is, upon the customs of the community, whereas descriptions of pottery classes often fail to discriminate the cultural aspects of the pottery from its less significant details (cf. Shepard, 1956, pp. 97–100).

Classification of culture.—Most archeologists find it advisable to group their components into cultures, known variously as phases, foci, complexes, industries, or styles. This requires a form of classification. The common practice is to compare the components in terms of their "traits" and, as in the classification of artifacts, to group into one class all those components which have similar traits. Ceramic traits, of course, are among the ones used for this purpose. In many parts of the world, they include types of artifacts, but in the Caribbean area, we are only able to use modes. These seem to suffice; we have had no difficulty distinguishing cultures on the basis of modes, especially when supplemented by types of non-ceramic artifacts, by settlement patterns, burial practices, etc.

Since, as was noted in the beginning, we find little else but pottery in the Caribbean sites, we have had to define our cultures primarily in terms of modes, though we have used other criteria whenever possible. This being the case, it has seemed advisable to use the term *style* instead of culture, following a practice of Peruvian archeology (e.g., Strong and Corbett, 1943, p. 49). A style may be defined as the modes which are shared by a group of site components and which distinguish them as a class (Rouse, 1952, p. 327). It is usually given the name of a typical component.

Determination of chronology.—Modes appear to work as well as types in establishing chronologies. For example, we have used them in the Caribbean area to seriate site components in the same way that types are used elsewhere, i.e., by calculating the frequencies of modes from level to level in our excavations and from site to site, and by arranging the excavations in order of the frequencies, on the assumption that all levels which have the same frequencies are approximately contemporaneous (Rouse, 1939, Charts 1–3).

Modes have one advantage over types in this kind of research. The validity of seriation depends upon the degree of consistency among the frequencies of the traits studied; and hence the more traits one is able to use, the more reliable one's seriation should be. Since there are many more modes than types, they provide a better statistical basis for the seriation. On the other hand, modes have the disadvantage that, being elemental units of culture, they are not too distinctive and may easily have been reinvented (Rands, 1961). This is less likely to be true of types, since they are, in effect, combinations of modes, and hence they are a more reliable unit of seriation, when available.

By means of seriation and/or stratigraphy, the archeologist is able to build up a local sequence of components. This, in turn, provides the basis for determining the succession of styles (i.e., cultures) which are represented in the components of the local area. The next problem is to synchronize the local succession of styles with the successions in other areas. Types are not so useful for this purpose because they tend to be limited in distribution. Modes are ordinarily distributed more widely, and hence we have found them particularly useful in synchronizing local chronologies (e.g., Cruxent and Rouse, 1958–59, Vol. 1, pp. 5–6).

Studies of cultural history.—Caribbean archeologists have had no difficulty in tracing the distribution of individual modes from one area to another or from one period to another, and in drawing inferences about diffusion or persistence of modes from the distributions. Linne's (1925) study of the techniques of South American ceramics is a good example; among other things, he was able to conclude that sponge-spicule tempering, to which reference has already been made, was invented on the Lower Amazon and diffused outward from there.

Modes, of course, do not always have independent histories. They may diffuse as complexes, e.g., in the form of types or styles, both of which, as we have seen, are in effect complexes of modes. By studying the history of complexes like these, one is often able to draw inferences concerning movements of people. Examples will be given later in the paper.

Cultural processes.—The research done in the Caribbean area has yielded considerable information concerning certain cultural processes, notably concerning the manner in which ceramics change and acculturation takes place. The remainder of the paper will be devoted to a discussion of these subjects.

THEORY OF CERAMIC CHANGE

During the earlier decades of archeological research in the United States, there was a tendency to handle pottery in the same way as organic remains, i.e., to assume that one type of pottery gives rise to another type in the same way that one species of animal evolves into another (Brew, 1946). This was not illogical, since most archeologists of the period had a background of natural history. It has had some harmful effects upon the development of archeological method and theory, however, for artifacts do not change in the same manner as organic objects. One task of anthropology in general and of archeology in particular is to formulate a theory of ceramic change that will express the differences between variation in ceramic artifacts and the evolution of plants and animals.

Such a theory must start with the concept of culture, since artifacts are cultural objects. One must go beyond the appearance of the pottery to examine the standards, customs, and beliefs to which the artisans conformed in making it. It is these standards, customs, and beliefs which constitute the culture of the community, and only by knowing them will one be able to determine whether a given potsherd belongs to the local culture, is a personal aberration, or has been brought in from another culture as the result of trade.

This is not to deny that the sherds themselves are culturally significant. Whether of local or foreign origin, they were originally parts of vessels used by the inhabitants of the site in their daily life, and description of them is therefore essential to any reconstruction of the local culture. But we are here concerned with change rather than with description, and for this purpose must deal not with the artifacts themselves but with the standards, customs, and beliefs which influenced the potters and, by changing, caused one form of pottery to become another.

An analogy may be drawn to biology. A demonstration that two plants or animals are taxonomically related does not reveal how one changed into the other. To do this, it is necessary to study the genes which governed the change. And just as genes determine the final form of a plant or animal, so the standards, customs, and beliefs to which the potter conforms determine the nature of his vessels.

How does one determine these standards, customs, and beliefs? They may be determined by analyzing the pottery into its constituent parts and establishing the norms for each of those parts, i.e., by the process of forming modes which has been discussed above. From this point of view, a mode may be defined as "any standard, concept, or custom which governs the behavior of the artisans of a community, which they hand down from generation to generation, and which may spread from community to community over considerable distances" (Rouse, 1960, p. 313).

Reverting to the biological analogy, we may note that modes differ from genes in their capacity to diffuse from one culture to another. Genes form self-contained systems that ensure that plants and animals develop in a linear fashion. Modes, on the other hand, are parts of less rigid complexes, capable of fusing together in a manner not possible in the case of plants and animals which do not interbreed.

Types and styles are the units within which modes are integrated. As we have seen, a type may be regarded as a complex of modes, leading to the manufacture of a distinct kind of artifact, for which the potter presumably had a name. In theory, therefore, each type comprises a distinct procedure of manufacture, which the potter probably recognized by applying to it the name of the type of artifact which it produced. At various stages in the procedure, the potter was faced with a choice between several alternative or optional modes, such as design motifs, and these permitted considerable variation within a single type (Rouse, 1960, Fig. 1).

Unlike types, styles do not represent single procedures of manufacture but instead encompass all the procedures of manufacture within their respective communities. If the members of a community had left us a record concerning their style, they would presumably have referred to it as their own local form of pottery, as compared to that of other, foreign communities. But they would also have recognized that certain related communities possessed the same style of pottery as themselves. A style, therefore, may be said to consist of the modes shared by a group of related communities and distinguishing them from all other pottery-making communities.

Types, of course, are analogous to genera and species in biology, whereas styles correspond to animal and plant communities. Within the human realm, styles are also comparable to languages. Each style includes all the community's activities in making pottery in the same way that a language includes all the community's activities of speech. Moreover, both styles and languages form the basis for grouping communities together, in one case because they made the same types of pottery and in the other because they spoke the same language.

The analogy between style and language can be carried one step further. As one moves from the centers of two languages toward their common boundary, the two become more and more alike (unless, of course, their normal distributions have been biased by factors such as migration or a strong political barrier). Styles show similar transitions, either through space or time, and as a result it is often difficult to draw a sharp line between the peripheral forms of two styles, although they may easily be distinguished in their pure states.

CERAMIC CHANGE IN THE CARIBBEAN AREA

At the beginning of this paper, it was noted that Caribbean pottery tends to be so highly variable that it is practically impossible to distinguish the fixed combinations of modes which are subsumed under the name of types. We have attributed this variability to the pottery's complexity in shape and decoration and to the number of alternative and optional modes open to the potter in each of these categories. By contrast, the pottery of other areas is much more integrated, and combinations of modes in the form of types are more easily distinguished. This is particularly apt to be true when the vessels are simple in shape and have overall painted or impressed decoration, so that shape and decoration are relatively unified.

In commenting on this paper at Burg Wartenstein, W. G. Solheim gave an example of the difference from Southeast Asia. Sa Huynh-Kulanay pottery of that region is complex and variable, like Caribbean ceramics. Bau pottery, on the other hand, is simpler and better integrated. It tends to have an overall pattern of decoration rather than a series of discrete decorative units.

One would expect nonintegrated pottery, like that of the Caribbean area and of Sa Huynh-Kulanay, to change primarily in terms of individual modes, whereas changes in integrated pottery such as that of Bau would be more likely to take place in terms of combinations of modes in the form of types. In the Caribbean area, it has been possible to show that modes tend to vary independently both in frequency and in kind (Rouse, 1939, Chart 6).

The Meillac style of Haiti will serve to illustrate this kind of ceramic change. It will be convenient to discuss it in terms of the steps in the potter's procedure, since that is the context in which he himself made the changes.

First, despite the great latitude which the Meillac potter enjoyed, there were some parts of his procedure that permitted no choice of modes; he had only a single way in which to accomplish that particular step. For example, as we have seen, technological analysis of Meillac pottery has revealed that grit was the only tempering material used, and that it did not vary significantly in either quantity or quality (Horton and Berman, 1941). It is the writer's impression that change took place relatively slowly under this circumstance, presumably because it was difficult to replace or add to a single mode.

More commonly, a series of alternative modes were available. The Meillac style contained a series of alternative modes for decorating each part of the vessel surface (Rouse, 1941, pp. 61–81). Change could take place either by replacement of one of the modes in the series, by addition of a new mode to the series, or simply by abandonment of one of the old modes. Change seems to have been easier and faster when there were so many possibilities as this.

Third, some parts of the artisan's procedure were optional. In making a particular vessel, he could either select from among the modes available for that part of the procedure, or he could decide to omit it entirely. For example, the Meillac potter sometimes added a ridge to the inner surface of his vessel just beneath the rim and sometimes left it off. In the former case (but not the latter), he had the further option of leaving the ridge plain or of decorating it with a row of punctations (Rouse, 1941, p. 72). Under such circumstances, change could take place either by addition to or deletion from a series of alternative, optional modes, or by replacement of one optional mode with another.

Finally, there are changes which may best be regarded as deviations from the established modes. For example, the writer was able to distinguish five kinds of incised designs on Meillac pottery. There were, in addition, eight sherds with designs which did not fit into any of the five categories (Rouse, 1941, p. 90). These deviations appear to be derived from the contemporaneous Boca Chica style in the Dominican Republic; it may be speculated that, as time went by, they were accepted by more and more of the Haitian potters and eventually became regular modes in the new Carrier style, which succeeded Meillac in Haiti.

The causes of changes in modes are difficult to determine. Some must be due to diffusion of new modes from foreign styles, as in the example just cited. Others were probably innovations of the local potters, which likewise began as deviations and were subsequently accepted more or less gradually by the rest of the potters (Rouse, 1939, Chart 6). Many modes conversely declined in popularity, as new alternatives and options came to be favored by the potters (Rouse, 1939, Chart 6).

A certain number of the innovations have been caused by modifications in the artisan's procedure. It would have been relatively easy, as already noted, for the potter to abandon an optional part of the procedure or to add a new option without materially affecting the rest of the procedure. Such a change would result in his either dropping all the modes exclusive to that part of the procedure, or adding modes to fulfill the new option. In the latter part of the period of existence of the Cuevas style in Puerto Rico, for example, the potters ceased to decorate the outer surfaces of their vessels with painted designs, and this in turn led to their abandoning a series of techniques and motives which had been exclusively applied to that area, such as white-painted designs (Rouse, 1952, p. 339). A change in one mode sometimes led to changes in another elsewhere in the artisan's procedure. For example, rims beveled inwards and painted red on top were originally characteristic of the Ostiones style in Puerto Rico. Later, the red paint began to be replaced by incision and, in order to accommodate the designs, the potters found it necessary to broaden the bevels by moving them down beneath the rim on the inside of the vessel (cr. Rouse, 1952, Pl. 3, F and N). The new incised designs were derived from a foreign style, presumably Boca Chica in the Dominican Republic, where they occurred on an even broader area, the outer surface of a shoulder (Rouse, 1952, Pl. 5, A–G). In order to compress these designs onto bevels inside vessels, the Ostiones potters had to simplify them (cf. Rouse, 1952, Pls. 5, A and 3, N).

On the other hand, our studies in the Caribbean area do not indicate that a mode occurring early in the potter's procedure determined *ipso facto* the nature of subsequent modes. Clifford Evans (personal communication) has argued that material is the best criterion to use in classifying pottery because the potter selected it before he did anything else and therefore valued its modes over those for all subsequent parts of his procedure. Material does seem to have been important to the potters of the Orinoco Basin in Venezuela, as we have seen, but there is no evidence, for example, that the introduction of sponge-spicule tempering in itself caused the other modes to change. The potters of the Guarguapo style on the Lower Orinoco, for example, continued to decorate their sponge-tempered vessels with the same elaborately modeled and incised designs which the potters of the previous Los Barrancos style had applied to grit-tempered pottery, and they retained many of the same modes of shape (Cruxent and Rouse, 1958–59, Vol. 1, pp. 230–33).

Changes in the uses to which the pottery is put are, of course, also likely to lead to changes in the pottery itself. For example, there is a trend during Period III in Puerto Rico from open bowls with sides flaring outwards, to constricted-mouth bowls with the sides turned inward. This may well have coincided with an increase in the popularity of the "pepper pot," in which cassava juice, meat, fish, and other ingredients were boiled (Rouse, 1952, p. 360).

Certain changes of modes seem to have had their origin in other aspects of the local culture, beyond the ceramics. For example, the marked increase in popularity and complexity of modeled head lugs in the Ostiones and Capá styles of Puerto Rico is evidently due to the rise of the cult of *zemis*, for these lugs resemble the carvings of *zemis* in stone, bone, and shell, and the early sources tell us that the Indians were accustomed to portray their *zemis* on household utensils (Rouse, 1948, p. 535). Other decorative motives, such as reptilian heads, are likewise common to ceramics and to other media (Hostos, 1941, pp. 147–51), but it is not clear whether they originated in ceramics or in one of the other media.

Some factors, of course, limited ceramic change instead of causing it. Many of these were inherent in the potter's procedure itself. The nature of one step in the procedure sometimes imposed limits on the possibilities open to the potter during other parts of the procedure. For example, as has already been noted, Antillean potters were accustomed to divide the surfaces of vessels into a series of areas, usually corresponding to such features of shape as shoulders and bevels, and to decorate the vessels by placing different designs in different areas. This custom would obviously preclude the adoption of overall painted designs, such as occur in other parts of the world.

More often, the nature of one stage in the procedure probably influenced the potter's acceptance or rejection of new modes for another stage, without imposing strict limits on the possibilities. For example, if the artisan was accustomed to dry the vessel thoroughly before painting it, so that the clay became quite hard, he would not be so likely to adopt incision, which can best be done when the clay is wet. Neither would he be so eager to adopt modeling in the round unless he already had a tradition of adding lugs to his vessels.

Certain values associated with each style also seem to have served as limiting factors. For example, throughout its period of existence the Cuevas style of pottery in Puerto Rico had gracefully curved shapes with relatively unobtrusive designs, whereas Ostiones-style pottery had only angular, poorly proportioned shapes with designs which stood out abruptly (Rouse, 1952, pp. 336–44). It is to be presumed that foreign modes or other innovations which did not fit these values were either rejected outright by the local potters or were modified to conform to the local values. Similarly, the potters of the Los Barrancos style in the Lower Orinoco Valley could hardly have accepted the techniques for roughening vessel surfaces which were available on the adjacent Llanos, for they valued smooth, polished surfaces (Cruxent and Rouse, 1958–59, Vol. 1, pp. 198–200, 227–30).

Without such limiting factors, a given style would soon disappear. With them, the Caribbean styles seem to have been able to maintain their identities over considerable periods of time. Unfortunately, our methods of dating are not precise enough to determine the exact duration of different styles, but the evidence suggests that some may have lasted as long as 1,000 years (Rouse and Cruxent, 1963, Figs. 9, 28).

MIGRATION AND ACCULTURATION AS FACTORS IN CERAMIC CHANGE

Since styles include all aspects of the pottery of a community and since they are as distinctive of the community as its language, we have been able to use them in the Caribbean area to reconstruct migrations and to determine the amount of acculturation that has taken place among the peoples studied. Plotting the distribution of our styles in time and space, we found that they occur in series corresponding to the "horizon" and "traditions" of Peruvian archeology (Kroeber, 1944, pp. 108–11; Willey, 1945). A series may be defined (Cruxent and Rouse, 1958–59, Vol. 1, p. 22) as:

a set of similar and contiguous styles. In order to constitute a series, these styles must share many, though not all, of their traits. They must also form a continuous [sequence], extending through either time, space, or both, so that we can be reasonably certain that their shared traits have spread or persisted from one style to another and have not been independently invented in some areas and periods.

Series are more widespread in the Caribbean area than we had anticipated. We have been able to identify twelve of them in Venezuela alone, and they crisscross the country, several of them extending for more than a thousand miles and persisting for more than three thousand years (Rouse and Cruxent, 1963, Fig. 9). Some appear to be the result of migration. Others, on the contrary, probably came into being through trade, intermarriage, or other contact between local groups of people, leading to interchange of modes among the groups and to subsequent resemblances in their styles.

Two examples will serve to illustrate these processes. The first is provided by the archeology of the middle and lower parts of the Orinoco Valley (Rouse and Cruxent, 1963, pp. 112–25). At the beginning of Period II in the local chronology (*ca.* 1000 B.C.), this area was inhabited by Indians of the Saladoid series. Early in Period II another group of Indians, characterized by the Barrancoid series, seized the lower valley, leaving a part of the Saladoid Indians in the middle valley and pushing the rest of them out to the adjacent parts of the Caribbean coast. During the rest of Period II and all of Period III (until *ca.* 1000 A.D.), the two groups of Saladoid Indians who had thus been isolated continued to develop very similar styles of pottery, partially, it would seem, because they had a common ceramic background and partially because they were subject to the same influences from the intervening Barrancoid people. But their pottery became more and more divergent, owing to the geographical separation between them. The Saladoid group in the Middle Orinoco Valley died out at the close of Period III; but during Period IV the group on the coast developed a new series, the Guayabitoid, partially, it would seem, by a process of simplification and partially through diffusion of new ceramic modes from series farther west along the coast.

The second example comes from the island of Puerto Rico in the West Indies (Rouse, 1952, pp. 513–45). Saladoid Indians, splitting off from the group on the Venezuelan coast, colonized this island during the latter part of Period II (*ca.* A.D. 100–300). During Period III, they developed two local styles, Santa Elena in the eastern part of the island and Ostiones in the west. During Period IV (*ca.* A.D. 1000–1500) a new style, Boca Chica, made its appearance in a village site in the central part of the coast, on the boundary between the areas of distribution of the two previous styles. This new style was presumably the result of a migration from Hispaniola, the next island to the west, for its sherds are like the pottery which had developed there during the previous period, and differ sharply from all the local Puerto Rican pottery (Rainey, 1940, p. 113). That it influenced the two local styles, Santa Elena and Ostiones, is indicated by the occurrence of a few of its sherds as trade objects in sites of both of the latter styles. Ultimately, it seems to have caused each of them to develop into a new style, called Esperanza and Capá, respectively. The latter may best be described as blends of modes present in their ancestral styles with modes adopted from the Boca Chica style. This is a good example of the process of acculturation or fusion of styles which, as stated above, differentiates ceramic change from organic change. In the present instance, it contributed to the formation of a new series, called the Chicoid, which ultimately spread through most of the Greater Antilles and into the Bahamas (Cruxent and Rouse, 1958–59, Vol. 2, Fig. 4).

Many styles, of course, cannot be fitted into series. For example, Period III in the Greater Antilles can best be described as a time of local variation in pottery, with fewer of the styles linked together into series than they were during Periods II and IV (Rouse, 1951, pp. 259–70).

It is interesting to note that the Period III styles were not limited to individual islands, as are the modern cultures of the West Indies. Instead, each style spans a passage between islands, reflecting the fact that the Indians traveled by sea, whereas the modern inhabitants communicate more easily overland. Here, we have an example of the way in which cultural ecology may influence the relationships among styles.

EVOLUTION OF CERAMICS

A final comment has to do with general, evolutionary trends. To the writer, it seems that the earliest pottery throughout the Caribbean area was the best. The sherds are finer, harder, and more durable, and are frequently more complex in shape and design. From this point of view, Caribbean ceramics has degenerated instead of evolving through time, contrary to Caribbean social organization and religion, which show marked advances during Periods III and IV in many parts of the area (e.g., Rouse, 1951, p. 259). To explain the decline in ceramics, we may speculate that pottery-making diffused into the Caribbean area from regions to the west where it was more highly developed, and that for some reason the local potters were unable to maintain it at its previous high level of development. Alternatively, the local people may simply have lost interest in pottery-making as they became more concerned with other aspects of culture, i.e., with social organization and religion. Something like this seems to have happened in Peru (Bennett and Bird, 1961, p. 181).

In such degenerative trends we may see another difference between ceramic change and organic evolution. Organic changes are progressive rather than degenerative, until they are cut off by natural selection. In the case of ceramics, however, the human community provides a sanctuary within which change can proceed in either direction.

BIBLIOGRAPHY

BENNETT, W. C.
1937. *Excavations at La Mata, Maracay, Venezuela.* New York: Anthropological Papers of the American Museum of Natural History, Vol. 36, pt. 2:69–137.

BENNETT, W. C., and J. BIRD
1961. *Andean Culture History.* New York: American Museum of Natural History, Handbook Series, No. 15 (first published, 1949).

BREW, J. O.
1946. "The Use and Abuse of Taxonomy." *Archaeology of Alkali Ridge, Southeastern Utah.* Papers of the Peabody Museum of Archaeology and Ethnology, 21:44–66. Cambridge: Harvard University.

COLTON, H. S.
1953. *Potsherds: an Introduction to the Study of Prehistoric Southwestern Ceramics and their Use in Historic Reconstruction.* Flagstaff: Museum of Northern Arizona, Bulletin No. 25.

CRUXENT, J. M., and I. ROUSE
1958–59. *An Archaeological Chronology of Venezuela.* Social Science Monographs, No. 6. 2 vols. Washington, D.C.: Pan American Union.

FORD, J. A.
1949. "Cultural Dating of Prehistoric Sites in Virú Valley, Peru." *Surface Survey of the Virú Valley, Peru.* New York: Anthropological Papers of the American Museum of Natural History, Vol. 43, pt. 1:29–89.
1952. *Measurements of Some Prehistoric Design Developments in the Southeastern United States. Ibid.,* Vol. 44, pt. 3.

HORTON, D., and J. BERMAN
1941. "Preliminary Report of the Technical Analysis of Meillac and Carrier Sherds." Appendix to I. Rouse, *Culture of Ft. Liberté Region, Haiti.* New Haven: Yale University Publications in Anthropology, No. 24:169–73.

HOSTOS, ADOLFO DE
1941. "Reptilian Art Forms and Sympathetic Magic in the Precolumbian Antilles." *Anthropological Papers, based principally on Studies of the Prehistoric Archeology and Ethnology of the Greater Antilles,* pp. 146–73. San Juan, P.R.

KIDDER, A. II
1944. *Archeology of Northwest Venezuela.* Papers of the Peabody Museum of Archeology and Ethnology, Vol. 26, No. 1. Cambridge: Harvard University.

KROEBER, A. L.
1944. *Peruvian Archeology in 1942.* New York: Viking Fund Publications in Anthropology, No. 4.

LINNÉ, S.
1925. *The Technique of South American Ceramics.* Göteborgs Kungl. Vetenskaps- och Vitterhets-Samhälles Handlingar, Fjärde Följden, Band 29, No. 5.

OSGOOD, C.
1943. *Excavations at Tocorón, Venezuela.* New Haven: Yale University Publications in Anthropology, No. 29.

OSGOOD, C., and G. D. HOWARD
1943. *An Archeological Survey of Venezuela.* New Haven: Yale University Publications in Anthropology, No. 27.

RAINEY, F. G.

1940. "Porto Rican Archeology." *Scientific Survey of Porto Rico and the Virgin Islands*, Vol. 18, pt. 1:1–208. New York: New York Academy of Sciences.

RANDS, R. L.

1961. "Elaboration and Invention in Ceramic Traditions." *American Antiquity*, 26: 331–40.

RITCHIE, W. A., and R. S. MACNEISH

1949. "The Pre-Iroquoian Pottery of New York State." *American Antiquity*, 15: 97–124.

ROUSE, I.

1939. *Prehistory in Haiti, A Study in Method.* New Haven: Yale University Publications in Anthropology, No. 21.

1941. *Culture of the Ft. Liberté Region, Haiti.* New Haven: Yale University Publications in Anthropology, No. 24.

1948. "The Arawak." *Handbook of South American Indians*, J. H. Steward (ed.), 4:507–39. Washington, D.C.: Smithsonian Institution, Bureau of American Ethnology, Bulletin 143.

1951. "Areas and Periods of Culture in the Greater Antilles." *Southwestern Journal of Anthropology*, 7:248–65.

1952. "Porto Rican Prehistory," *Scientific Survey of Porto Rico and the Virgin Islands.* Vol. 18, pts. 3–4: 307–578. New York: New York Academy of Sciences.

1960. "The Classification of Artifacts in Archeology." *American Antiquity*, 25: 313–23.

ROUSE, I., and J. M. CRUXENT

1963. *Venezuelan Archaeology.* New Haven: Yale University Press, Caribbean Series, No. 6.

SHEPARD, A. O.

1956. *Ceramics for the Archaeologist.* Washington, D.C.: Carnegie Institution of Washington, Publication 609.

SMITH, C.

1950. *The Archeology of Coastal New York.* New York: Anthropological Papers of the American Museum of Natural History, Vol. 43, pt. 2.

STRONG, W. D., and J. M. CORBETT

1943. *A Ceramic Sequence at Pachacamac.* Columbia Studies in Archeology and Ethnology, Vol. 1, No. 2. New York: Columbia University.

WILLEY, G. R.

1945. Horizon Styles and Pottery Traditions in Peruvian Archeology." *American Antiquity*, 11:49–56.

CERAMIC COMPLEXITY AND CULTURAL DEVELOPMENT: THE EASTERN UNITED STATES AS A CASE STUDY

JAMES B. GRIFFIN

MANY prehistorians and students of ceramics have suggested that there is a general correlation between the quality and complexity of the potters' art and the general cultural level of the society in which the pottery has been produced. This correlation is best seen in certain large areas during the initial development or spread of food-producing societies, before the development of metal containers or before pottery becomes mass produced. There are other judgments which have been made regarding the presence or absence of pottery and the general level of cultural development of the society. For many years the presence of pottery on a site in Europe was one of the identifying markers for whether that site had reached at least the Neolithic level and, in North America, whether the people who produced the pottery also had agriculture. When a Greek black-figured or red-figured vase is seen in a museum the conclusion is obvious that this product has come from a society where the potters' craft has reached a high level of technical and artistic competence, and further, that the society as a whole is advanced, with specialization of labor and many other advanced societal features. If, on one side of this Greek vase there is a Hohokam Red-on-Buff painted jar from the southwestern United States of about A.D. 900, and on the other side a Gerzean Red-on-Buff jar from Egypt of about 3500 B.C., it may be surmised that the potters' craft and the societal level which produced them are more similar to each other than either is to the Greek potter and society.

In the eastern United States we know that pottery appears for the first time about 2000 B.C. and that apparently all of the tribal groups were using pottery by A.D. 1600. Some of the tribes along the eastern and northern margins of the pottery users at the historic period were still producing pottery vessels which had changed relatively little from those of the earliest pottery of the Great Lakes and northeastern area. In the Mississippi Valley, however, there was a striking ceramic development which was in existence at the time of the Spanish and French explorers of the southeast.

THE PALEO-INDIAN PERIOD

In addition to a summary of the pottery development in the eastern United States, I will give a brief characterization of the several levels of cultural development. The first occupants of the area will be referred to here as Paleo-Indians or Early American Hunters. Their remains are found over the entire area at a time period believed to be before 8000 B.C. They were primarily hunters who used fluted projectile points similar to the Clovis and Folsom types of the western Plains. There is, so far, no evidence of structures for shelter, and the sites were apparently temporary camps. Their community pattern has been called "Free Wandering" (Wauchope, 1955). They were organized as single family groups or small bands of related families. Their artifact inventory is rather simple in nature and limited in variety. Their general culture pattern is quite clearly derived from northeastern Siberia, with some modification as the result of the passage of time and the "opportunity of living in the United States."

THE EASTERN ARCHAIC PERIOD

Next is a period of time from 8000 to 1500 B.C. during which there develops what may be called the Archaic stage. There is a gradual change from a primarily hunting economy to a more varied subsistence pattern. Because of the variety of forest, prairie, coastal, riverine, and lacustrine environments, and because of climatic differences in this large area, there are regional cultural traditions, with a higher degree of cultural uniformity through time than are found in the area as a whole. In the early phases of the Archaic there are still only temporary camp sites, but by the middle of the period there is an increase in the number of localities to which the people would return seasonally to obtain certain foods. Toward the close of the Archaic, this cultural practice produces sites with deep midden deposits, some of them up to thirty feet deep. The community structure of this stage has been called "Restricted Wandering" and "Central Based Wandering" (Wauchope, 1955). The society is organized into small bands of multifamily groups. The camp size is normally less than an acre to one or two acres. There is some evidence of circular pole-framed structures, perhaps covered by bark or woven mats, and some evidence of storage pits toward the close of the Archaic. By about 4000 B.C. there is a gradual development of ground stone tools and ornaments. Burials are normally in the village area or may be in an adjacent cemetery. The animal refuse indicates that a wide variety of mammals, birds, and fish were caught, and it is probable that nets, traps and other hunting devices were known.

In the southeastern United States between 2000 and 500 B.C., there are three major areas in which fiber-tempered pottery was made. This is the earliest pottery in the United States and is one of the earliest wares in the New World. There is no known source from which this pottery can be derived. It precedes in time by at least 1000 years the first pottery in western Alaska or in the Great Lakes area. In Nuclear America (southern Mexico to Peru) pottery is known by 2000 B.C., but a connection between these two earliest ceramic areas cannot be proven.

The simplicity of the bowl forms of the fiber-tempered pottery is derived from the stone and probable wooden prototypes. Stone bowls of steatite precede pottery from southern New England to the southern Appalachians, but they tend to disappear as pottery manufacture becomes more common. In northern Florida steatite vessels make their first appearance after pottery had been introduced into the culture.

The fiber-tempered shapes vary somewhat from flat bases and vertical side walls in Florida to hemispherical bowls in Georgia and Alabama (Fig. 1). The ware is low-fired and is often thick-walled. The surfaces of the earliest fiber-tempered pottery are plain or roughly smoothed, but by 1500 B.C. there are three decorative style areas—one in northern Florida, one in coastal Georgia, and one in northern Alabama. The decoration in Florida is by incising in simple linear patterns on the exterior wall of the bowl on a flat lip surface, with some of the designs analogous to those on engraved bone artifacts. In northern Georgia the decoration is by gouging or punching the surface in simple linear patterns. In northern Alabama there are a number of techniques by which the surface is altered such as cutting, brushing, punching, and dentate or comb stamping. This latter technique results in an appearance that is similar to some of the comb ceramic or cardial pottery of Europe. As a ceramic complex this earliest pottery changes very little in forms, decorative techniques, designs, or in manufacturing and firing processes over some 1500 years. There is relatively little pottery in use in the society. It is never placed as burial furniture with the dead.

THE EARLY WOODLAND PERIOD

The Early Woodland cultures of the eastern United States are associated with the appearance of grit-tempered pottery, burial mounds, and an emphasis on burial ceremonialism. Each of these has a different history and is blended with a variety of local Archaic concepts. The time period is from 1500 B.C. to about 400 B.C. The economic base is still hunting, fishing, and gathering but with some slight indications of agriculture based on Middle American plants. There are small scattered villages but some sites are as large as two acres. The few known house structures are circular with pole frames 12 to 15 feet in diameter, but larger structures, perhaps ceremonial, are 45 feet or so in diameter. An increase in population density in some areas is suggested both at individual village sites and from the number of sites of this complex in a given area. There is a marked increase of

FIGURE 1
Common forms of Archaic fiber-tempered pottery.

burial ceremonialism represented by the burial mounds, some of which have multiple log tombs and a height of 70 feet. There are suggestions of status differentiation in the quality and quantity of grave goods and in the burial practices used for the individuals placed in the mounds. Cremated burials are found in the village sites. Significant changes in social and political organization are reflected in the labor direction and control necessary for the mound structures and the circular earthworks that accompany them. While there are some indications of interregional trade during the Late Archaic, there is a noticeable increase of such practices in Early Woodland. The community pattern for most of the Early Woodland complexes is Central Based Wandering, but the Late Adena culture may be called Semi-Permanent Sedentary.

The pottery of the Early Woodland cultures is also a low-fired rather thickwalled product. It has grit temper from crushed rock (including flint) or sand particles added to the clay. It was built up by the coil method and has a simple jar form with either a conoidal or flat base (Fig. 2). The exterior surfaces are either plain, patted with a paddle wrapped with cord, or marked with a woven fabric or textile that has been pressed against the surface. None of the vessels were ever made in a basket. There is little or no evidence that the pottery was ever used as a trade ware and it is almost never associated with burials. It functioned almost entirely as a utilitarian product, was boringly similar in appearance, and was used to boil food in an open fire. This pottery tradition, apparently, was introduced into North America from Siberia some time after 1500 B.C., although adequate documentation of this is still lacking. Pottery of specifically Asiatic origin is known in western Alaska and northwestern Canada by about 500 B.C. The Early Woodland pottery of the Great Lakes and northeastern United States can be dated about 1000 B.C. for its beginning. It is quite distinct in many details from the Early Arctic pottery.

THE MIDDLE WOODLAND PERIOD

During the Middle Woodland period (from about 400 B.C. to A.D. 400) there is a marked cultural florescence which reaches its culmination in the Hopewellian

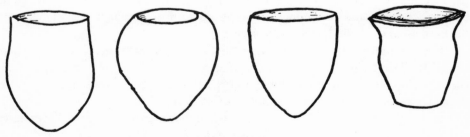

FIGURE 2
Common forms of Early Woodland pottery.

culture of the Ohio and Upper Mississippi valleys. The normal village size is from one to three acres, but the larger Hopewellian sites may cover five acres. The Hopewell earthwork patterns in southern Ohio enclose areas of up to 100 or more acres, and some of the walled "fortified" hilltop enclosures are from one to four miles in total length. There is, then, a marked population expansion as indicated by both the increase in village size and the increased number of contemporary sites. The size and complexity of these geometric earthworks and their accompanying burial mounds compare favorably in size with those of northwestern Europe during the Bronze and Early Iron Ages.

A part of the population expansion is the result of agricultural productivity, but there is relatively little evidence of crop plants preserved to prove it. There is some evidence that the growth and climax of the Hopewell culture occurs in a relatively warm period in the north central United States, and that the Hopewell expansion to the north coincides with a somewhat milder climate favorable to agricultural pursuits on a simple technological level.

Relatively few house sites have been excavated. They are 20 to 30 feet wide and 30 to 60 feet long, and have been preserved under burial mounds. It is not known whether these are ceremonial structures or habitations for multifamily groups. There is an important development of burial ceremonialism with status differentiation apparent. The larger burial mounds are usually elliptical in floor plan and are up to 250 feet long, 150 feet wide, and 30 feet high. They covered groups of primary mounds, some of which are built over circular pole-walled structures, 40 to 100 feet in diameter, that are suggestive of charnel houses. Within them are found log tombs, cremation concentrations in prepared clay basins, and extended and flexed burials. The interred or cremated individuals who enjoyed high status were accompanied by grave goods, some of which were intentionally mutilated. These include clothing, ornaments, and luxury or ceremonial items without practical utility.

There is an impressive increase in the trade and exchange of raw materials and manufactured goods from the Gulf of Mexico to Lake Superior and from the Atlantic Coast to the Rocky Mountains. Many of the foreign raw materials were made into artifacts that are associated with burials. There are clear indications of specialized craft production although this tendency does not reach the level of full specialization of labor. A significant level of artistic ability was reached in sculpture, carving and engraving, in the production of ornamental copper forms, and in a number of widespread art styles.

The community pattern varies from Semi-Permanent Sedentary to perhaps Simple Nuclear Centered. It is possible that some of the major burial and earthwork developments in southern Ohio and the Illinois Valley were erected by the labor of a primary village and a number of subsidiary villages.

From about A.D. 200 to 700 there is a gradual deterioration of cultural intensity in the north central part of the eastern United States, and this is reflected in all facets of cultural behavior. The cause or causes are difficult to understand, but a minor climatic deterioration affecting the reliability of agricultural production may have been important.

Middle Woodland ceramics spread over much of the area east of the Rocky Mountains and a number of regional techniques for altering the exterior surface of the vessel are developed. These are primarily local innovations and do not seem to have been stimulated either from northeast Asia via the American Arctic or from Middle America. In the north, the cord-wrapped paddle is the most common tool used to finish the vessel, but in the southeast, a variety of carved paddles produce the distinctive stamped surface finishes. The same techniques for preparing the clay and firing the vessels, as well as their use chiefly as utilitarian cooking forms, continue on from the preceding period. Most of the vessels are, however, thinner and have finer tempering particles. The lines of juncture between coils are normally difficult to find, and both the exterior and interior surfaces are more carefully treated. Much of the pottery in the Lower Mississippi Valley is tempered with clay particles, some of which are broken potsherds, and the surfaces of vessels in this area and along the Gulf Coast and in Florida are plain.

In the Hopewell culture a number of techniques are employed in decorating the upper fourth to upper half of the outer walls of jars (Fig. 3). Before the incised or stamped design is applied, the surface of the vessel is smoothed where the design is to appear. Both decorated and undecorated jars are used for cooking, storage, and as burial furniture. Some few vessels, made specifically for burial purposes, have none of the indications of domestic use and abuse and are very low-fired. These vessels are small jars or bowls and are decorated over most of the exterior by a graceful curvilinear zoned decoration. The majority of the ornamented Hopewellian vessels are, however, well fired.

The decorative style is also found in bone engraving and on embossed copper plates, and probably was also placed on wood and bark. The symbolic design style of Hopewell pottery spread widely in the eastern United States. Some part of this was accomplished by trade, the actual transport of vessels over considerable distances, or by journeys of potters from one area to another. It does not seem to have been due to population movements.

During Middle Woodland times there is a great deal more pottery produced at each site, and more time and skill are devoted to its manufacture and decoration. There is a marked increase in the importance of pottery for utilitarian purposes and for ceremonial use, and the number of decorative techniques increases, including painting and negative painting. Specialized decorative styles are developed, and there is a clear separation between ordinary domestic vessels and those which received a considerable amount of care and attention to produce an aesthetically pleasing and ceremonially satisfactory product.

The distinctive styles and techniques used by the Hopewell potter to produce her better vessels slowly deteriorated and disappeared by about A.D. 400 to 500 in the northern Mississippi Valley. There gradually comes into being a simplified pottery still in the Woodland tradition which is decorated on the upper body and rim with single cord-impressed designs and with a pseudo-cord decoration. This basic Woodland vessel form, finish, and function continues in the Great Lakes and northeast up to the historic period.

FIGURE 3
Various forms of Hopewellian pottery.

THE MISSISSIPPI PERIOD

The last major prehistoric complex in the eastern United States is the Mississippi culture pattern which was in existence from approximately A.D. 700 to 1700. It was stimulated by the introduction of concepts and religious practices from northern Mexico. There were improvements in agricultural techniques and probably also in agricultural plants, resulting in a sedentary existence with a strong dependence on food production. The community pattern may be regarded as a Simple Nuclear-Centered one with ceremonial structures and deep refuse deposits indicating long and continuous habitation. House and temple structures were of wattle and daub and they were arranged in the village or town according to a regular plan. An outstanding feature of this culture was the earthen temple mound which served as a raised platform on which the major community buildings were placed. The council houses and "temples" were the political and ceremonial centers. The platform mounds were placed on the sides of a central plaza which was the ceremonial center for the tribal community during important recurrent functions or during times of crisis.

This is the period of greatest population density, both in terms of the number of sites and in size of the towns. Some of the larger towns had a population of a few thousand. Many towns had walled fortifications enclosing them which were made of timbers and plastered with earth. Intergroup conflicts were better organized than in preceding periods, and the growing importance of warfare is reflected in the art records of ceremonies and symbolism. A highly stylized religious symbolism spread throughout the Mississippi complex from the Gulf to the Great Lakes and from the Appalachians to the eastern Great Plains.

Elaborate ceremonies and grave goods accompanied the burial of high status individuals in mounds or in cemeteries. The burials were extended, flexed, or bundles of bones. Cremation occurred, but was not common. Trade in raw materials and finished products reached a higher level over the whole area than in the Hopewell or Middle Woodland cultures. There are indications of craft specialists but no true specialization of labor.

In the central Mississippi Valley the pottery associated with the Mississippi cultures reaches a level of variety and quality which has seldom been equaled and hardly surpassed by any group of people on a comparable cultural level. The importance of pottery in the society is clearly reflected in the variety of forms for different functions, in the elaborations of these forms, in the varieties of decorative techniques, in the integration of the vessels into many aspects of the society, and finally, in the striking amount of pottery found in the village sites and as burial goods in the tombs and cemeteries.

A large variety of bowls are used for both utilitarian and ceremonial purposes (Fig. 4). The better vessels are polished, have a red lip or wash on the surface, or are decorated by incising, engraving or painting. Many bowls have appliqué effigy heads placed on the rim with a balancing lip flange opposite the effigy. Some are made into fish effigies or into forms representing other beasts. One of the specialized vessels is known as the salt pan. This is a large shallow basin or shallow pan up to three feet in diameter with straight sides. The salt pans are found in great numbers around the salt springs in the Mississippi Valley, where salt was one of the major trade commodities.

The cooking and storage jars have plain surfaces and globular bodies; many have functional handles. They range in size from small jars about six inches in height to large vessels two to three feet high. This ware is coil-made and is scraped on the interior to produce thin-walled vessels. These latter reflect the need for adequate food storage. Some of the large jars were used as burial urns. When these utilitarian forms are decorated they are usually incised on the outer rim area. They are almost never either slipped or painted. Some of the smaller jars are modeled into effigy forms.

Probably the most striking form in variety and quantity is the bottle, which was

FIGURE 4
Mississippi pottery forms.

given different neck shapes in different regions. It was of considerable importance as a container of liquids and received many modifications in human and animal effigy forms and in incised, engraved, and painted decorations. A number of different styles of tripod supports were attached to them and the best quality of workmanship was displayed in their manufacture. Curiously enough, the Mississippi Valley Indians never learned the comfort of alcoholic beverages. Among the specialized burial vessels are death's-head representations with elaborate painted and incised decorations.

The designs and symbolism placed on the finer vessels has the same import as those which appear engraved on shell and embossed on copper plates. These vessels were prepared for special ceremonial functions and were traded from one area to another. The potters' art in the eastern United States reaches its climax in this period and neatly parallels the cultural climax of the late prehistoric period. With the arrival of the benefits of European civilization, Indian culture enters a period of rapid decline and disintegration.

INTERPRETATION

There has been presented here a perhaps too neat picture of the parallel growth or evolution of prehistoric societies and of ceramic development. It is, however, reasonably close to the truth for the area under consideration. A similar case can be made for the southwestern United States over some 1700 years of cultural and ceramic change following the introduction of pottery from Mexico. In the early simple village societies in three regional areas of the Southwest, a few simple jar and bowl forms occur with relatively little decoration or refinement in the potters art. Over a period of six or seven hundred years, as the societies increase in population and in general cultural level, the potters' art reaches a peak parallel to that of the Mississippi culture but with marked differences in detail. In the North American Arctic, pottery comes in from Asia at its highest level of accomplishment in the Arctic area. From then on it deteriorates, and tends to disappear in areas where it was introduced.

In Middle America the beginnings of pottery are dimly understood, but by and large there is present a significant correlation of ceramic and cultural development. Nowhere in the New World did the development of metal containers supersede and supplant the need for ceramic containers, cooking vessels, or the expression of objects of art. The wheel did not intrude to change a handicraft and an art expression into a manufacturing process and a standardized product.

BIBLIOGRAPHY

WAUCHOPE, R. (ed.)
  1955. "Functional and Evolutionary Implications in Community Patterning." *Seminars in Archaeology: 1955* (Richard K. Beardsley, Chairman). Memoirs of the Society for American Archaeology, No. 11. *American Antiquity*, Vol. 27, 2 (pt. 2):129–57.

ASPECTS OF POTTERY IN TEMPERATE EUROPE
BEFORE THE ROMAN EMPIRE

H. W. M. HODGES

IN THE PAST, European prehistory appears generally to have developed either as an extension of history or of antiquarianism, and European prehistorians have thus tended to follow the methods of art historians when examining ceramics. Morphology and decorative detail are the accepted overriding criteria in establishing the relationship between different ceramic traditions: it would even be fair to say that the actual materials and techniques employed by prehistoric man have only seriously been considered in cases where a particular group of pottery is so outrageously different from others in the same archeological context as to demand some comment. Although the adoption or rejection by prehistoric man of a particular pottery-making technique must have been as much a result of cultural tradition or contact as the adoption or rejection of a particular decorative style, an adequate account of prehistoric ceramic technology in Europe remains to be written, while the technical examination of pottery, far from being the routine matter it should be, is seldom even contemplated. Indeed, when one compares the large number of really excellent monographs dealing with the metallurgy of copper and bronze in prehistoric Europe with the mere handful of technical ceramic studies, one realizes that the basic groundwork yet remains to be done. A measure of this deficiency can be seen in the fact that the late Sir Lindsay Scott, whose chief interests lay in European prehistory, could find only one paper from this field worthy of reference in his contribution on early ceramics in Singer's *History of Technology* (Scott, 1954).

A second contributary factor to this state of affairs is a virtually total lack of any on-the-spot ethnographic material from which to draw. In many other areas, even today, the archeologist is able to study potters at work who are still using basically the same materials and processes as did their ancestors in the remote past; but in Europe, due to the introduction of the crank-driven kick-wheel in the first instance, and later to the general acceptance of industrially produced pottery, this is not possible. The very few cases in which primitive methods of pottery manufacture appear to have survived into this century, as for example in Denmark (Steensberg, 1940) and the Hebrides (Holleyman, 1947), are quite insufficient to allow serious study along these lines.

Wheel-thrown pottery was unknown in temperate Europe until its invasion by Rome or until such time as Rome made itself felt beyond the Imperial frontiers, and thus prehistoric pottery was made by cruder means. Speaking of these earlier methods of manufacture, Sir Lindsay Scott (1954) argues that since clay is by nature amorphous, early pottery simply echoed the shapes of containers made of other materials; at the same time he allows that the methods of manufacture might influence shape, but gives no examples. For the past decade, in an attempt to give students at the Institute of Archaeology a deeper understanding of European prehistoric pottery, they have been instructed to make pottery themselves. The following observations result from watching, in all, about a hundred students at this work. Very few of these had ever handled clay before, and the efforts of those that had have been disregarded.

In the making of pinch-pottery, in which a ball of clay is held in the palm of of one hand and hollowed and squeezed out with the other, the student will initially produce a small hemispheric bowl (Fig. 1:1). As the student becomes more dexterous and more ambitious he will use a progressively larger ball of clay until he arrives at a point where the bowl can no longer be held comfortably in the palm of the supporting hand. At this stage he will more often than not tilt the bowl, supporting it on its side, and continue to thin down the walls of the vessel while rotating it the whole time. As a result of this treatment the base will become conical. This is not a conscious thing—the instructions were to produce a round-based bowl—but is dictated by the shape of the slightly flexed supporting hand (Fig. 1:2).

If he tilts the pot still further and continues to expand the walls, a protuberance may develop (Fig. 1:3), due in this instance to the tips of the fingers of the supporting hand pressing inward on the base. Unintentional variations of form in the upper part of the vessel may also result from the manipulation, most com-

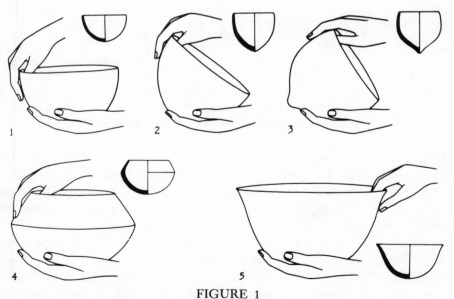

FIGURE 1

Stages in pinch-pottery manufacture that students produced.

monly when the student is concentrating more on producing an even rim than on the precise shape of the vessel. Thus, when the shaping hand is held on the far side of the pot, a sharply defined incurving neck may develop (Fig. 1:4), while, if the hand is on the near side, a flared rim may be made (Fig. 1:5), and this, too, may become defined if the thumb is allowed to press into the body.

These variations recur year after year, and it must be emphasized that they are not consciously produced. Most commonly, in fact, students are only aware that "something seems to have gone wrong." There seems to be no escaping the fact that these features are latent in the method of forming.

One cannot, obviously, make the assumption that because a vessel exhibits one of these features it was, therefore, produced either accidentally or by these means. Equally, it is important to realize that these features can recur as normal variants, and one should be careful not to attach more significance to them than is their due. Thus in Early Neolithic pottery in temperate Europe, at Michelsberg (Childe, 1957, Fig. 133) and Ertebølle (Childe, 1957, Fig. 7), bases that are conical or bear a protuberance may be found; while the same type of base may be seen outside this area, in Spain at El Garcel (Childe, 1957, Fig. 123), and again in predynastic Egypt at Mostagedda (Brunton, 1937, Pl. XXI). Indeed Childe (1957, p. 260), following Schuchhardt's (1909) theory of Skeuomorphism, suggested that these vessels not only copied leather prototypes but actually indicated direct cultural connection. At Michelsberg and at Mostagedda, however, one also finds bowls with incurved necks and round-based beakers with flaring rims, and it would seem on the whole more rational to accept these as common variants of the hemispheric vessel than to insist upon any common cultural ancestry.

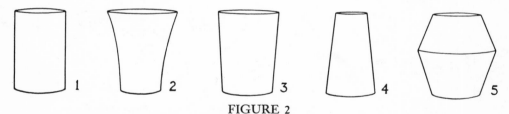

FIGURE 2

Stages in ring-built pottery manufacture that students produced.

When making ring-built pottery there is a very definite tendency to produce a splayed profile (Fig. 2:2), even when every attempt is made by the beginner to produce a pot with perfectly vertical sides (Fig. 2:1). The reason for this seems to be principally that greater care is given to smoothing down the outside than the inside of the vessel, and since the rings are worked downward, an outward warp develops. To overcome this tendency, most students will reduce the diameter of each ring as they add it so that it is slightly less than that of the pot so far built. Even adopting this expediency, a slight splay is general (Fig. 2:3), and some students may attempt to correct this at a late stage, so producing a very characteristic form (Fig. 2:5). Overcorrection throughout, which produces a vessel with a narrower neck than base, does occur—perhaps one student in twenty will produce such a shape (Fig. 2:4).

While it must be admitted that these tendencies are naturally exaggerated among students, at the same time even quite experienced potters admit that it takes considerable concentration to produce a vessel with absolutely vertical sides by this method of forming. Here again there is evidently an inherent tendency in the method of production. A greater splay than was intended may easily result, or, to avoid this, the potter may overcorrect.

Since straight-sided vessels are a rarity in prehistoric Europe, an experiment was recently carried out to see whether this tendency to splay was equally applicable

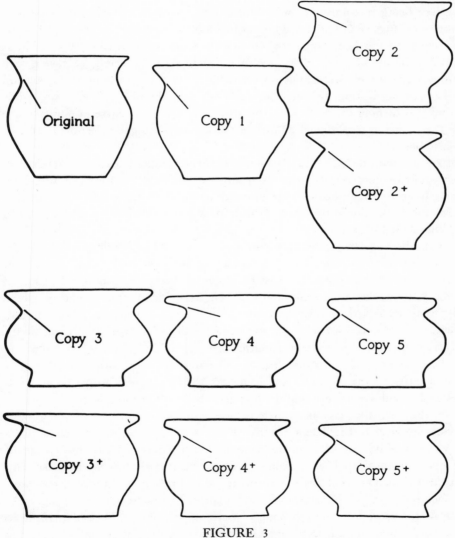

FIGURE 3
Serial copies by students of a simple vessel form.

to rounded shapes. A simple form was taken as a starting point (Fig. 3) and this was copied by one student. The original was then removed, and the copy was reproduced by two other students, independently. The first copy was then removed, and reproductions were made of the second copies, and so on, to provide two sequences. The results illustrate a number of interesting features. Despite a very poor second copy in one sequence, the end-products of each are very similar, and at first viewing, one gains the impression that each copy is just a little shorter and wider than the previous one. In fact, the total width varies little throughout each sequence while the height diminishes with each stage. In other words, due to the greater splay during building the lower part of the vessel, the required girth is achieved in each case that much nearer the base, the sum effect being not only to cause diminution in height, but also to exaggerate the angles of inward and outward curvature—most clearly seen at the angle of the neck, which in the later copies becomes little more than an out-turned rim. It should also be noticed that a distinct foot develops earlier in one sequence than the other. The vessels were built on turntables, and the foot appears to develop as a result of supporting the partly made vessel with the palm of one hand while working and turning the table with the other, the foot thus corresponding to the angle between the hypothenal eminence of the supporting hand and the top of the turntable.

Clearly it would be a drastic oversimplification to suggest that these tendencies alone should be considered when discussing variations in the forms of ring-built pottery. Even so, they must be kept in mind; and one might suggest that initially, for example, variations in the form of neck in Western Neolithic pottery (Childe, 1957, Figs. 133, 147) may not have been quite as deliberate as has sometimes been supposed. The same might be said of beakers as a whole (Childe, 1957, Figs. 83, 107, 108). In fact, the experiment just described is most applicable to what has already been inferred about this class of vessel on purely archeological grounds: repeated copying led to a diminution in height, a widely splaying neck which finally appeared as little more than a rim and, more often than not, a distinct foot.

These observations must lead one to the conclusion that, within obvious limits, comparison of form alone is not a particularly reliable criterion when discussing prehistoric pottery in temperate Europe. Decoration in its various forms is, of course, a different matter, although even here there may well prove to be tendencies in the methods of applying designs that lead to their modification, a field of research that seems to have been little explored to date.

When one turns to the detailed study of ceramics from excavated sites, a number of methods of examination are open to us to determine various aspects of technique: chemical analysis, refiring experiments, and the use of thin sections.

On the whole, chemical analysis seems to be of greater use in answering questions relating to the composition of clays than in throwing light on other technological aspects of ceramics. Although no attempts appear to have been made to use the techniques of chemical analysis on prehistoric pottery in Europe, the method has been shown to be of considerable promise by Miss E. E. Richards (1959) in her examination of Romano-British mortaria.

As a general rule, refiring experiments would seem to be of very little value when dealing with European prehistoric pottery, if only because of the very low temperatures being worked. Nevertheless there may be cases in which this type of examination could profitably be used to determine firing conditions.

The particular advantages of the use of thin sections lie in the fact that one can examine not only composition but also structure. The method has been used sporadically by European prehistorians to study either the inclusions in clay (Thomas, 1952) or structural detail (Stevenson, 1939, 1953), but there has been no long-term policy such as that pioneered by Anna O. Shepard (1956) in the New World. This failure to follow up such a lead is all the more curious since the petrological examination of stone axes, for example, has been one of the major contributions to advances in prehistory in the last decades (Wallis, 1951; Jope, 1952; Giot, 1955).

In the past three years a beginning has been made along these lines at the Institute of Archaeology, London University. The results here can only be summarized, but in general, our method of procedure has been not only to section prehistoric ceramics but also to attempt to reproduce the phenomena we have observed using known clays prepared and fired under controlled conditions (Hodges, 1962).

A. Methods of Forming

If, as suggested above, the method by which pottery is formed can radically affect its shape, it becomes more than a matter of distant academic interest to be able to determine, without reasonable doubt, by what means pottery was indeed formed, and our initial series of experiments was directed partly to this end. Our results suggest the following tentative propositions:

1. A completely homogeneous clay containing little organic matter may leave no visible trace of how it was treated. The join between one ring, or coil, and its neighbor may not be detectable even when one knows precisely where to look for it. In such a clay, too, no visible flow structure may develop, no matter how much the walls of the vessel are drawn up by ribbing or using paddle and anvil. Mercifully, such clays are unknown in European prehistoric ceramics, but in other periods and areas this can be a real stumbling-block.

2. A clay containing much organic matter seems invariably to develop a marked flow pattern when drawn up. This is due partly to small particles of organic substances becoming orientated vertically in the walls of the vessel, and subsequently burning out, and partly to the fact that such clays are seldom homogeneous, in which case small cleavages may develop between different clay entities.

3. The junction between one ring and its neighbor is not invariably visible even when a clay lacks homogeneity. Dirty working conditions, in which the rings may be rolled out on a surface covered with dust, ash, or dry clay, generally results in poor adhesion and a quite distinct join. If the clay is kept clean, however, this junction may be impossible to detect.

Applying these criteria to the limited classes of prehistoric material that we have been able to study we can confirm what R. B. K. Stevenson (1953) has already suggested: our round-based Neolithic vessels were either molded or hand modeled, the necks sometimes being applied; flat-based wares, such as beakers, were built of rings or coils. So far we have no evidence to contradict this statement, but a far bigger sample must be made before we can accept this as a generalization.

B. Surface Treatment

We believe that we can now distinguish in thin section a number of rather different surface treatments, all of which have in the past variously been described as "slips":

1. When a pot has been allowed to dry for a short time it is possible to work over the surface with wet hands and, in so doing, to improve the look of the vessel. The effect is to draw the finer clay particles to the surface, where they are deposited. Sections of such pottery will thus show a highly luminous surface when fired at low temperatures, but if the firing temperature is sufficient to cause a breakdown of the crystalline structure of the clay minerals (say about 850° C), then the surface will appear distinct from the body when seen in section and be isotropic in polarized light (crossed Nicol prisms).

2. Coloring matter—limonite, hematite, or other more or less pure pigments—may be applied at the same time that pottery is given a wet-hand finish.

3. The same types of coloring matter may be applied dry and burnished onto the surface of a vessel.

4. A pot may be slipped either in the finer fraction of the clay of which it is built or a different clay, to which coloring matter may, or may not, be added. Such a coating may be applied by a painting technique as well.

5. Any of these surfaces may be given a final burnish.

Where true slip or painting techniques have been used, not only is the coating invariably thicker than where other methods have been employed, but there results a very marked line of distinction between body and applied or altered surface, save in the case of pots slipped in the same clay as the body, when all signs of demarcation may vanish.

We have examined a large number of vessels that are said to have been slipped, and so far we can find no single prehistoric example in Britain that answers these criteria. Bell beakers, for example, were demonstrably given a wet-hand finish; but the bright red surface that tends to peel from the body, and has so often been called a slip, usually results from the breakdown of the crystalline structure of the clay minerals, the product of a high firing temperature of short duration. Elsewhere on the European continent, bell beakers may well be colored deliberately, using some ferruginous material; but without resort to thin sectioning it might well be impossible to detect those that have from those that have not. From the point of view of origins this information could be critical. Even in the Early Iron Age in Britain, the so-called "hematite slipped wares" are generally only treated with a wet-hand finish and ferruginous coloring matter.

On the whole, polychromy is uncommon in prehistoric wares in temperate Europe, and this is in all probability a reflection of the lack of superficially occurring light-firing clays (Walter Trachsler shows elsewhere in this volume to what lengths prehistoric men were prepared to go to achieve color effects in their pottery). Culturally speaking, renewed attempts in western Europe at different periods to produce multicolored wares should indicate renewed connection with those areas in which painting was more easily achieved because of the variety of available clays.

Body Composition

Most European prehistoric ceramics are of a composite body made of a single secondary clay and a single filler (temper). A study of the filler used may, of course, suggest an origin for the material, and it is to this end that thin sections have most commonly been put. Valuable as this kind of information may be, technologically the choice of a filler is of great importance, too, for this must surely be, to a degree, dictated by tradition.

In most areas there is a wide possible range of available mineral fillers such as flint or quartz sand, as well as organic materials such as shell, which are every bit as effective at the temperatures being worked as grog (pitchers, sherds). Thus, while the occasional use of grog along with some other filler could be accidental or an expediency, the use of grog alone as a filler could point to a tradition developed in some area in which satisfactory mineral fillers were not readily available.

In our experience, while Neolithic wares in Britain do occasionally contain some grog, the vast majority of bodies are formulated with flint, quartz, or naturally occurring sands. By contrast, in our beaker pottery, grog was almost invariably used. Naturally, one would like to know if this generalization holds good elsewhere in Europe, for if it does, might it not suggest that the bell beaker was developed in an area lacking other mineral fillers, such as the loess lands?

This argument would require for its verification the examination of a very wide sample of beaker wares and other Neolithic pottery. So far, we have only been able to study a few sherds of beaker material from Spain.

Firing Conditions

Primitive firing conditions are apt to vary considerably from day to day, depending upon the weather and the condition of the fuel. This is especially true on the Atlantic seaboard of Europe, and is apt to make one a little wary about making generalizations. Apart from soot-soaked wares, one can, however, distinguish between two major types of firing. In the one, the pottery has been submitted to a fairly smoky firing held at a steady but low temperature over a comparatively long period. In such cases there is an evenly graduated burn-out of organic matter throughout the body, while the clay minerals remain completely unaltered. In the other instance, the firing was clearly rapid, achieving a relatively high temperature, while the fire itself was clean-burning. Pottery fired thus has a clear red surface, while the burn-out of organic matter is far from complete and not infrequently shows a marked zoning at varying depths below the surface. In their extreme forms these two types of pottery are quite distinct, although, of course, there exists every manner of gradation between them. Typically the Western Neolithic type of pottery conforms to the first kind of firing, while beaker wares conform to the latter. One might tentatively suggest that while Western Neolithic pottery was fired in a domestic hearth which was fed with fuel during the process, beakers seem to have been fired in a dry brushwood fire that flared up quickly and was soon burnt out.

The differences of firing technique may themselves point to a difference of environment, although not necessarily in Britain, between the Early Neolithic and Beaker periods. A quick-burning fire of the brushwood type might equally imply the use of grass or straw as a fuel, and this in turn might suggest an open environment or at least one not heavily forested as a place of origin for the technique.

Although little work has yet been done along these lines, the results do seem promising. Any conclusions so far arrived at are, of course, tentative. It is hoped that in the future a sufficiently large sample may be made to allow a more positive statement.

BIBLIOGRAPHY

BRUNTON, G.
   1937. *Mostagedda and the Tasian Culture.* London: B. Quaritch, Ltd.
CHILDE, V. G.
   1957. *The Dawn of European Civilization.* London: Kegan Paul.
GIOT, P. R., and J. COGNE
   1955. "Les haches des combat en metahornblendite." *Bulletin de la Société Préhistorique Française,* 52:401–09.
HODGES, H. W. M.
   1962. "Thin Sections of Prehistoric Pottery: An Empirical Study." *Bulletin of the University of London, Institute of Archaeology,* III:58–68.
HOLLEYMAN, G. A.
   1947. "Tiree Cragans." *Antiquity,* 21:205–11.
JOPE, E. M.
   1952. "Porcellanite Axes from Factories in North-East Ireland: Tievebulliagh and Rathlin," Part I, Archaeological Survey. *Ulster Journal of Archaeology,* 15:31–55.
RICHARDS, E. E.
   1959. "Preliminary Spectrographic Investigation of Some Romano-British Mortaria." *Archaeometry,* 2:23–31.
SCHUCHHART, C.
   1909. "Das technische Ornament in den Anfängen der Kunst." *Praehistorische Zeitschrift,* 1:37–54.

SCOTT, SIR L.

1954. "Pottery." In C. Singer, E. J. Holmyard and A. R. Hall (eds.), *A History of Technology*, I:376–412. Oxford: Clarendon Press.

SHEPARD, A. O.

1956. *Ceramics for the Archaeologist.* Washington, D.C.: Carnegie Institution of Washington, Publication 609.

STEENSBERG, A.

1940. "Handmade Pottery in Jutland." *Antiquity*, 14:148–53.

STEVENSON, R. B. K.

1939. "Two Bronze Age Burials." *Proceedings of the Society of Antiquaries of Scotland*, 73:229–40.

1953. "Prehistoric Pot-Building in Europe." *Man*, 53:65–68.

STONE, J. F. S., and F. W. WALLIS

1951. "Third Report of the Sub-Committee of the South-western Group of Museums and Art Galleries on the Petrological Identification of Stone Axes." *Proceedings of the Prehistoric Society*, 17:99–158.

THOMAS, H. H.

1952. (Title not available)

Proceedings of the Devonshire Archaeological Society, 1:175.

EARLY CERAMICS IN THE NETHERLANDS:
TWO PROBLEMS

J. D. VAN DER WAALS[1]

INTRODUCTION

THE SOIL of the Netherlands is poor in natural resources, and Dutch prehistory therefore displays in none of its periods a particular richness in material remains. Yet the variety of soil types in the Netherlands encouraged the coexistence of different cultures within a limited area, and the geographical position of the country on the Scheldt-Meuse-Rhine delta favored connections with cultural centers in central, northern, and western Europe in many periods (Waterbolk, 1962b). Thus, many of the features and problems that confront one when studying prehistoric pottery in the Netherlands pertain to a wider area. Some of these problems touch upon questions concerning pottery and potting in a general sense and appear to have a bearing on the subject matter of the "Ceramics and Man" symposium. Of these, two are presented here to the anthropologist: (1) the post-Neolithic decline in the art of pot-making, and (2) the failure to make use of the potter's wheel until medieval times.

THE POST-NEOLITHIC DECLINE IN
THE ART OF POT-MAKING

Decline in the art of pot-making, evident from the technical or artistic deterioration of pottery, is usually easily accounted for in terms of a general cultural disintegration or as a consequence of interruption of cultural development by calamities such as war. In other cases, possibly more difficult to detect, the changing demands of fashion may be responsible. For the study of pottery as such, internal factors are the more interesting ones since they are indicative of the functions of the pottery in the society—functions that need not be constant. Therefore, whenever a case of conspicuous decline of pottery presents itself to the prehistorian, it is worthwhile to try to detect the factors responsible.

In northwestern Europe a sharp decline in potting occurred in Late Neolithic to Early Bronze Age times. In contrast to the good quality of the Neolithic Wares, the native Early and Middle Bronze Age pottery is so poor that no one

1. The writer wishes to express his gratitude to Dr. J. J. Butler, not only for correcting the English of the text, but also for helpful criticism and valuable suggestions concerning the content.

has ever thought of a better name for it than the German term *Kümmerkeramik*, which, once suggested by Sprockhoff (1942, p. 15), was eagerly seized upon as the only suitable descriptive term. Coinciding with the qualitative decline, the variety of shapes diminished, and at the same time pottery ceased to be an important item found in the graves.

Pottery is one of the most important discriminants of the numerous Neolithic cultures; the degree to which the interpretation of the Bronze Age has been influenced by the eclipse of this discriminant has been recognized by De Laet and Glasbergen (1959, pp. 114–15),[2] but how the decline of pottery-making in the post-Neolithic period is to be explained in itself is by no means clear. Before going into this, we must attempt briefly to characterize this decline. We cannot do this better than by contrasting the *Kümmerkeramik* with the Neolithic Wares, i.e., the pottery of the Funnel Beaker Culture (*Trichterbecherkultur*, abbreviated TRB), the Protruding Foot Beaker Culture (the Northwest European branch of the Battle Axe Cultures, abbreviated PFB) and the Bell Beaker Culture (BB).[3]

A general characteristic of these Neolithic Wares in northwestern Europe is the care with which they are made. This care is notable in the evenness of the tempering; in the comparatively thin walls, evenly coiled throughout and carefully smoothed so that hardly any tempering material is visible on the outer surface; in the regularity of the shape of each pot; in the decoration; and in the firing. There are differences: TRB pottery is tempered with stone grit; PF Beakers sometimes are tempered with a little sand; Bell Beakers have grog tempering. In the fracture, TRB sherds generally show a yellowish outer surface, not strongly contrasting with a light grey core and inner surface. PF beaker sherds may have a dark core and a yellowish-brown inner and outer surface. Bell Beakers invariably have a black core and a yellowish-brown outer and inner surface, which on the outer surface often locally turns to red (due to a "wet-hand" finish and dehydration of iron colloids; cf. the contribution by Hodges in this volume). As to the shapes, the TRB pottery stands significantly apart in being multiform (Knöll, 1959), whereas in the Protruding Foot Beaker and Bell Beaker Cultures the shapes are mainly limited to slender S-profiled Beakers (PFB and BB), more squat "3"-profiled Beakers (BB), and Giant Beakers (PFB and BB; storage pots?; cf. Becker, 1955), to which occasionally are added small "amphorae" (PFB) and polypod bowls and handled mugs (BB). TRB pots may have a ring base, PF Beakers generally have a strongly protruding foot, and Bell

2. If we try to define cultures our attention is directed to other elements such as the form and structure of the graves (Waterbolk, 1961, p. 11), or the bronzes and other grave goods. Thus what we may recognize as a culture in the Bronze Age in our area is not strictly comparable to what we define as cultures in the Neolithic; the material serving as a base for the definition is different. The Neolithic pottery certainly represented traditions within cultures. But the bronzes, for instance, represent metalworking traditions and their sphere of influence, more or less independently of cultural entities.

3. The most complete survey of the TRB pottery concerned is to be found in Knöll (1959); a recent survey of the present state of knowledge concerning the TRB Culture is given by J. A. Bakker (1962). For the PF Beaker Culture and the Bell Beaker Culture and for the mixed PFB and BB groups, cf. Van der Waals and Glasbergen (1955, 1959).

Beakers a flat, often even slightly convex, bottom. Patterns and techniques of decoration also differ. In TRB pottery, there is a dominating verticalism in the patterns, contrasting to the horizontalism that is characteristic of PFB and BB pots. TRB decoration usually is deeply incised or impressed (sometimes with a thread wound core), and incrusted with apatite; PF Beakers are decorated by impressions of cord and/or a plain spatula, and sometimes by grooved lines. Bell Beakers are usually decorated by impressions of a carefully dentated spatula, but grooved lines and cord impressions also occur.

The three Neolithic groups clearly represent three different traditions of potting, even though a certain amount of mutual influence, especially of the PF Beaker and Bell Beaker groups, can be demonstrated. It should be noted that in this case, too, socioeconomic factors may be responsible for the contrast of the multiformity of the TRB pottery with the relative uniformity of the other two groups.

In contrast to these wares, most *Kümmerkeramik* pots are grossly shaped. They are more heavily tempered, often with rather large stone grains that are visible on the surface. The surface is lumpy and may show extremely shallow vertical ribs or striations. The walls are often of uneven thickness even at the same height. The irregularly shaped rims are of uneven height and thickness, for they are just the thinly tapering ends of the walls, even if they are slightly beveled. One gets the impression that the walls are drawn upward rather than built with coils, but it is possible that this drawing-up was done following initial coiling. Bottoms are remarkably flat and often broad, sometimes even forming a splaying foot. There is but little variation in sizes and shapes: all that we have are small to medium-sized pots, usually of simple barrel shape seldom exceeding 20 cm. in height (the height equals or slightly surpasses the diameter of the rim), and deep bowls whose diameters slightly exceed their height. Some of these pots have large vertical lugs, not unlike sausages; a few have a knobbed cord below the rim. They are devoid of decoration, except for a few which show the simplest of fingertip or nail-impressed decoration. In the fracture, a coal-black core between thin yellowish brown surface layers is characteristic.

When trying to estimate the factors responsible for this decline in pot-making, we must first ask whether external causes, such as immigration, or strong internal influences have been at work. To the reader who is not a specialist of European prehistory we must apologize for having to bring in details of northwest European prehistory in order to make our view on this question clear.

Sprockhoff, who was the first (1930, pp. 227–36) to draw attention to the pottery which he later baptized *Kümmerkeramik* (1942, p. 15), originally (1930) thought of it as a continuous development out of the preceding Neolithic Wares, but later (1942, pp. 12–31) changed his mind. Though not positively rejecting the possibility that the *Kümmerkeramik* was made by the descendants of the Neolithic inhabitants of the region, he rejected its derivation from the Neolithic pottery, and pointed instead to strong resemblances with the pottery of the Seine-Oise-Marne (SOM) Culture in northern France. He also cited the stone cists with porthole slabs in Lower Saxony as elements taken over from the SOM Culture. Thus, Sprockhoff visualized an expansion to the northeast of the western European SOM Culture.

It must be admitted that the resemblance of *Kümmerkeramik* to SOM pottery is striking enough. In their classic paper on the SOM Culture, Childe and Sandars (1950, p. 4) specifically mention the thick walls, the poor firing, the rough rock particles of the tempering material, and the thick black core of the pottery. Aside from a general resemblance among the many barrel-shaped pots in both groups, the splaying foot and the slight constriction just below the rim, which are distinctive marks of SOM pots, may also be found with *Kümmerkeramik*.

Nonetheless, Sprockhoff's thesis is difficult to maintain. The SOM Culture is essentially a Neolithic culture. Its closest relative, the Horgen Culture in the west of Switzerland, is stratigraphically imbedded between the (preceding) Michelsberg and the (succeeding) *Schnurkeramik* Cultures. Indirect (trade?) connections in our area with the SOM Culture may be suspected from the dagger-knives of Grand Pressigny flint found with a Late PF Beaker and with beakers of the mixed PFB and BB groups, but such connections fall well before the occurrence of *Kümmerkeramik*, which may begin in Early Bronze Age times, but which is chiefly typical for the Middle Bronze Age.[4] Even if we adopt the theory that the SOM Culture, or at least its pottery, existed into the Late Bronze Age (a possibility left open by Childe and Sandars, 1950, p. 14), strong influences are hardly to be expected. Apart from the resemblance of the pottery already noted, none of the distinctive marks of the SOM Culture enumerated by Childe and Sandars, and hardly anything typical of northern France of the succeeding period, are found in the Bronze Age cultures of northwest Europe. Even the stone cists of Lower Saxony must be rejected: recently Schrickel (1962) showed that these belong to a second horizon of west German stone cists, and thus must be separated from possible SOM influences that are detectable only in the third horizon. Thus, the points of resemblance of *Kümmerkeramik* and SOM pottery are those which might be expected between any groups of coarse and simple pottery made by corresponding techniques. Instead of negative points of resemblance and those apparently conditioned by the techniques of pot-making used, a correlation of specific traits in both groups of pottery should be required to establish the existence of some real connections. Deterioration of pottery indirectly caused by external cultural influences is imaginable; for example, if easier methods of production were adopted, or if the introduction of bronze vessels altered the demand. But direct cultural influence, resulting in the imitation of inferior wares by people who themselves possess fine pottery, is difficult to imagine.

If, then, connections with the SOM Culture must be rejected, can we point to other external influences, or is there reason to claim discontinuity in the development? Some influences from other groups of Early or Middle Bronze Age

4. The writer is much indebted to Mr. O. H. Harsema for valuable indications as to the dating of the *Kümmerkeramik* resulting from a survey of all available data, which is not yet in print.

pottery seem to be present; in this respect we think of the knobbed cords below the rim occasionally occurring on *Kümmerkeramik* pots in the northern parts of the Netherlands, which could represent the influence of Hilversum urns. But this is an isolated trait—the Hilversum Culture, coming from the west and well represented in Belgium and the center and south of the Netherlands, never obtained a firm footing in the northern provinces and adjacent Germany. In the north of the Netherlands, where *Kümmerkeramik* is best known, there is on the whole little reason to think of discontinuity of culture. On the basis of Bronze Age barrow structures, Van Giffen (1930, p. 4; 1956, pp. 115–21) sees continuity in development since Neolithic times. Glasbergen is of the same opinion (De Laet and Glasbergen, 1959, pp. 113, 129).[5]

This then, leads us back to Sprockhoff's initial view (1930), the derivation of *Kümmerkeramik* from Neolithic pottery. If we ask why Sprockhoff's arguments for this derivation are not quite convincing—he himself was, as we have seen, the first to change his opinion—we can give an answer, at least as far as the Netherlands are concerned. By 1930 it was hardly clear that between the periods of the last part of the Neolithic Wares advanced by Sprockhoff (he cited TRB, PFB, BB, and even Rössen) and the period of the *Kümmerkeramik* there is still a gap to be bridged, into which can now be interpolated the "barbed-wire" Beaker pottery (pottery decorated with a thread-wound stamp). This is now recognized to represent a separate group (Modderman, 1955) for which a date in the Early Bronze Age was established both by archeology and carbon-14 measurements (Waterbolk, 1960, pp. 72–74). On the one hand, some of these barbed-wire pots show in their shape and in their simplified decoration several elements characteristic of the Neolithic Wares just mentioned, except Rössen (De Laet, 1958, pp. 103–5). On the other hand, many of the barbed-wire pots are already clearly suggestive of the *Kümmerkeramik* in their general coarseness, thickness of wall, coarse tempering, lumpy character, and texture of surface. Often the shapes with their diluted S-profiles are not far removed from those *Kümmerkeramik* pots that have a narrow base. Moreover, the decoration on this category of barbed-wire pots is minimal, foreshadowing the absence of decoration of the *Kümmerkeramik*. In the center of the Netherlands (where the position and distribution of the *Kümmerkeramik* is not yet well known), very late and debased-looking Bell Beakers of Veluwe type, probably also to be dated close to the Early Bronze Age, herald the *Kümmerkeramik* in their coarse tempering, barrel shape, and thick walls.

A striking decline in the art of pot-making is thus recognized against a background of general cultural continuity, caused by internal or only indirectly by external factors. If we ask what kind of factors these could have been, we have to realize that factual evidence on which to base the answer is extremely scanty, and one can at most give a rough estimate. The demand for pottery for ordinary

5. To these arguments can be added the fact that many cemeteries were continuously in use from Neolithic times throughout the Bronze Age. With respect to the practice of cremation which was believed to make its appearance only on the verge of the Bronze Age, flat graves with cremation burials of the Late TRB Culture and the Late BB Culture have recently been discovered (as yet unpublished).

use must have increased rather than decreased, for according to Waterbolk (1962b, pp. 246–47) a period of more permanent settlement based on more extensive and regular agricultural activities begins with the Bronze Age. This is inferred from the facts that cemeteries remain continuously in use and that, since Early Bronze Age times, plowed soil can be recognized, which means prolonged cultivation in one place. Although there are examples known of wooden vessels used in graves in place of pottery (Schwantes, 1939, Abb. 411–13, 476; Brøndsted, 1958, pp. 57–58), it is unlikely that this occurred on a large scale for domestic purposes. In our area it is certain that pottery was not replaced by bronze vessels. Therefore, we are not inclined to think of decreasing demand as a possible reason for the devaluation of the art of pot-making.

The relative scarcity of material objects of the Bronze Age in our area has been interpreted in terms of general impoverishment. This is inferred from the alleged spread of heather fields at the cost of the mixed forests, from the relative scarcity of bronzes, from the decline of the practice of interring grave goods, and from the impoverishment of the pottery. Our area was certainly relatively poor if compared to Schleswig-Holstein, for example. But was it also poor compared to the conditions in the preceding Neolithic period? The progress made in food production, already referred to, and the character and size of the Bronze Age settlement recently discovered at Elp (Waterbolk, 1961; account of the complete excavation in preparation),[6] are certainly not suggestive of impoverishment. The decline of the grave furniture can as well be accounted for by eschatological changes—the same changes that were responsible for the introduction of several new elements in the burial ritual and for the complexity and richness of structural features of Bronze Age barrows (Glasbergen, 1954). On the whole, the impression one gets is not one of cultural deterioration, and so we should not like to attribute the decline in the art of pot-making to this.[7]

Although most of the *Kümmerkeramik* pots we know come from graves, it is unusual to find a pot in an Early or Middle Bronze Age grave. The preponderance of pottery among the grave goods, which was characteristic of the Neolithic, has come to an end. One could imagine that the decline of this ceremonial function of the pottery was responsible for at least its artistic deterioration. From what is known of Neolithic settlements (chiefly of the TRB Culture) it is clear that the majority of the domestic pottery was void of decoration; such decoration as does occasionally occur is of the same character as the decoration of practically all pots found in the *hunebedden* (the collective megalithic tombs of the TRB Culture). The decoration of this pottery was obviously chiefly required by its ceremonial function. Significantly, the deterioration of the decoration of barbed-wire pots seems to be concurrent with the declining frequency of their inclusion in

6. The settlement of Elp is really of Late Bronze Age date, but there is some reason to believe that it is to be connected with the descendants of the local Middle Bronze Age inhabitants and their traditions rather than with the intrusive Urnfield Culture.

7. Due to the heavy podsol profile, the original floor level of the Bronze Age settlement at Elp (Waterbolk, 1961) had been completely destroyed before excavation, and most of the pottery had perished. The little that is preserved is due to chance finds from deeper holes and pits.

graves (cf., for example, Waterbolk, 1960, p. 74). Even if the declining importance of the ceremonial function of this pottery is responsible for its artistic deterioration, this offers no direct explanation for the qualitative decline. But it is noteworthy that with the reappearance of ritual pottery in the Late Bronze Age, when urns were employed for the burial of cremated bones, a revival took place in the art of pot-making, both artistically and qualitatively. This suggests that the standards of pot-making were more dependent on the importance of the product for ritual uses than for its ordinary domestic role.

THE FAILURE TO MAKE USE OF THE POTTER'S WHEEL UNTIL MEDIEVAL TIMES

The invention of the potter's wheel and its adoption by potters in different parts of the world has long fascinated the anthropologist, and it is difficult to add to the observations that have been made on this point. However, the circumstances leading to the adoption of the wheel could possibly be illuminated by instances where this device conspicuously failed to be adopted, even after its temporary introduction from the outside. A case of this sort occurs in the Netherlands and the adjacent areas, and we propose to examine it. It should be clear from the outset that we use the term *potter's wheel* only in the sense of its being a device for throwing pottery, as defined by Foster (1959) in his fundamental paper on this subject.

The wheel was in use for transport in the Low Countries in Neolithic times (end of the third millennium B.C.; Van der Waals, 1962), but neither imported nor locally produced wheel-made pottery existed before Roman times. In the Roman period it was imported in fair quantity at the legionary fortresses and in a few of the local settlements that were most exposed to Romanizing influences. A few pieces found their way into the countryside. It was then produced in factories in parts of our area that were situated within the boundary of the Roman Empire, as at Nijmegen and Heerlen, shown on the map in Figure 1. In post-Roman times, however, the potter's wheel ceased to be used. Wheel-made pottery continued to be imported in small quantities from the Cologne district of the Rhineland where its production seems to have continued uninterrupted after the collapse of the Roman Empire. In Carolingian and Early Medieval times this import became gradually more important, and was increasingly depended on for wares of better quality. The local potters then contented themselves with making coarser kitchen ware of the *Kugeltopf* (i.e., round bottomed) family, still shaped by hand. It was not until the developed Middle Ages when city life was flourishing, that the potter's wheel was finally adopted—in the extreme south in the 12th century (Bruyn, 1959, 1961),[8] in the north even later.

That the mere presence of the wheel as such does not suffice to induce the local

---

8. The results of the excavations of the wasters' and potters' ovens at Brunssum and Schinveld published by Bruyn are highly interesting since they show the process of the transition from hand-shaping to potting-on-the-wheel within the same workshop.

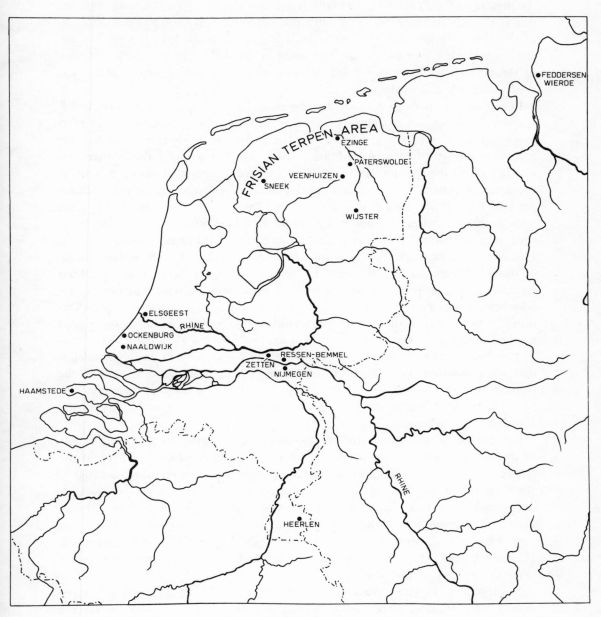

FIGURE 1
Map of the Netherlands showing selected sites from
the Roman to the Medieval periods.

potter to start throwing his wares is exceptionally clear in this case. Since even the presence of the *potter's* wheel fails to produce this effect on the native potters, this is a much stronger hint that only the economic situation and the tradition of the potter are decisive. We can attain a degree of insight into the relative importance of these two factors by examining in detail the history of the adoption of the potter's wheel in two small districts within our area in which somewhat contrasting conditions prevailed.

In our area all pottery continued to be made by hand down to Roman times. From the fifth century B.C. onward, wheel-made pottery was increasingly common in various centers of Celtic civilization, but in the non-Celtic areas potters remained faithful to their own tradition. This is true not only for the Netherlands and the adjacent part of Germany, where we find a culture of rather provincial character in which the events and developments of neighboring cultural centers are but dimly reflected, but it is also true for the areas farther East. Even when some Germanic potters did adopt the use of the wheel under strong Celtic influence, they abandoned it as soon as this influence faded (Otto and Grünert, 1958). Hachmann points to the fact that the distribution of wheel-made pottery north of the Alps coincides broadly with the distribution of La Tène *oppida*, fortified settlements which probably also served as marketing centers. Apparently the wheel-made pottery was dependent on a comparatively high degree of specialization and on a market economy, such as would be expected in the *oppida* but would not be found farther north (Hachmann *et al.*, 1962, pp. 29–42, Karte 2, 4).

The introduction of potting-on-the-wheel in those parts of the Netherlands that were incorporated into the Roman Empire (i.e., the southern part of the country bounded by the Rhine) is quite natural, but it is not fortuitous that the factories for wheel-made pottery have so far been found only at Nijmegen and Heerlen.

Heerlen, the *vicus* Coriovallum of Roman times, is situated in that narrow part of the Netherlands which extends far south into a region which had been in the sphere of Celtic influence, and which in Roman times was much more thoroughly Romanized than the rest of the country farther north. It was also of military importance, since there is evidence of a *castellum* in the latter half of the Roman period. The potter's workshop, of which a part was discovered, was active at least in the second half of the first and in the beginning of the second century A.D. (Goossens, 1909). Its customers presumably lived in the *vicus* itself and in the *villae* in this part of the country.

Nijmegen on the river Waal was the capital of the Bataven, known as Batavodurum, and stood as a somewhat isolated stronghold of Romanization on the frontier in the north. Two potter's workshops have been discovered so far. One is at "De Holdeurn" (Holwerda, 1944; Holwerda and Braat, 1946). It was possibly started as a factory to satisfy the civilian demand, but later it was in all probability in the service of the Tenth Legion, when this had its *castra* at Nijmegen (70–105 A.D.). After the departure of the Tenth Legion it seems to have continued to satisfy civilian demands. The second workshop was discovered inside the town of Nijmegen (Daniëls, 1927, pp. 90–93), and apparently supplied the citizens of Ulpia Noviomagus Batavorum, the successor to Batavodurum after the uprising of the Bataven in 70 A.D. Its pottery was dated by Daniëls toward the end of the first and the beginning of the second century A.D.

The wares manufactured in these workshops belong in part to the family of shapes which became current all over the Roman Empire. Other shapes are in the Celtic tradition. None of the pots in these factories are in the local tradition. From De Holdeurn, three potters' names are known which prove to be Roman in character (Holwerda, 1944, p. 44). Names stamped on lamps from the Ulpia Noviomagus workshop are Celtic. It is certainly questionable whether such names refer to the people who did the actual manual labor, but it is equally questionable whether there were any of the local population among those who turned the wheels in these factories. In the cemeteries of Roman Nijmegen, the old local pottery occurs in the graves in relatively small numbers until the end of the first century A.D. These pots are handmade, conforming to the old tradition; they display but little influence of the new factories and their products (Vermeulen, 1932; Brunsting, 1937; Stuart, 1962). Other than a small number of pots tentatively considered by Vermeulen (1932, pp. 37–39) and Brunsting (1937, pp. 127–29) to represent renderings of the local tradition thrown on the wheel, there is no evidence that serious attempts were made by local potters to throw their wares. In addition, Vermeulen (1932, pp. 121–23) knows of only a few types of handmade ware that clearly show the influence of the wheel-made pottery in their shapes. This picture is confirmed by the Nijmegen settlement finds. Here, too, wheel-made pottery of foreign tradition already predominates in the Augustan period (Holwerda, 1943). The rare handmade pottery is of the same character as that in the graves and hardly occurs after the first century A.D. (Breuer, 1931; Brunsting, 1937, p. 130; Holwerda, 1946).

Much of the same situation is to be found at other settlements in the frontier area that were under strong Romanizing influence, such as Ockenburg near The Hague (Holwerda, 1938) and Haamstede on the island of Schouwen (Braat, 1957). But strongly contrasting with these, other settlements of the same period in the same area and sometimes only short distances away yield but small numbers of sherds of imported wheel-made pottery, whereas quantities of the soft and gritty sherds of local handmade pottery are found. Examples (Fig. 1) are settlements at Naaldwijk (Holwerda, 1936), Zetten (Braat, 1937), Ressen, Bemmel and in the Elsgeest polder (Braat, 1949). They show that the local handmade ware continued to be made throughout the Roman period, and was by no means discontinued in the second century A.D. as one might have thought from the Nijmegen finds.

How can we account for these facts? Life in the countryside in the frontier area was apparently little affected by Romanization. Only a few centers that were of military or economic importance were taken by surprise and rashly acquired the new look of the economic life of a town in the Roman province. In these centers there was a replacement of the old mode of life by the new one rather than a gradual adaptation. Immigrant entrepreneurs set up new workshops in which pots were made by completely different techniques. The pottery-making of old would not even have had a chance to complete or to adapt to the new situation and to satisfy the demand which was rapidly increasing both quantitatively and qualitatively. In the countryside, little changed in the general economic situation and in the standard of living to raise the demand to such an extent that the adoption of the new techniques would have been a necessity; whether, as seen from the economic standpoint, it would have been a *possibility*, available data do not permit us to judge. The situation certainly bears resemblance to that in many a colonial society of our own time. With the collapse of Roman power, the isolated centers of higher economic life disintegrated, and conditions were apparently no longer favorable for the making of pottery on the wheel.

Now let us consider the situation outside the Roman Empire. Few of the trans-Rhenish tribes had as many Romanizing contacts as those living in the northern part of the Netherlands. This is clear from historical sources alone. In the marsh area of the extreme north where the Frisian *Terpen* Culture was flourishing, there was a short intermittent occupation by Roman troops which came to an end after an uprising in 28 A.D. and the withdrawal of all troops beyond the Rhine in 47 A.D. Regular trade contacts with the Roman province began to develop from the later part of the first century onward and lasted into the first half of the third century (Van Es, 1960) as is indicated by numerous finds of all kinds. In the *terpen* (the artificial dwelling mounds in the marsh area that offered protection from high tide until dikes began to be built (*ca.* 1000 A.D.) which were often inhabited continually from pre-Christian times until the present day, a sprinkling is found of sherds from wheel-made pots imported from the Roman province (Boeles, 1951, pp. 490–93, 572–75; Glasbergen, 1948). But from settlements of shorter duration on the peat such as Sneek (Elzinga, 1962) or on the sand such as Wijster,[9] which have been excavated in such a way that all sherds were preserved, we know that in proportion to the local handmade wares, the imported wheel-made pottery was really scarce. Yet, the appreciation for the imported wheel-made pottery is beyond doubt,[10] and even after the breakdown of regular trade contacts, fourth-century wheel-made pots from northeastern France and fifth-century Mediterranean *terra sigillata* bowls occasionally found their way into the *terpen* area (Boeles, 1951, pp. 494–96; 574–75).

Apart from these and other traded wares, and the frequent occurrence of bronze statuettes representing gods of the Roman pantheon, which are more numerous in the marsh area of the northern part of the Netherlands than anywhere else outside the Roman frontiers,[11] Romanizing influences can be seen in

9. We are much indebted to Mr. W. A. van Es for kindly supplying us with information on the results of his large-scale excavations at Wijster.

10. Eggers, (1951), p. 67, Karte 62) brought to light the curious fact that whereas the bulk of the Roman pottery exported to the "free Germanic" tribes is found in a broad zone directly outside the empire's boundary, other exports such as bronze vessels have their main concentration outside this zone, farther north.

11. A corpus of these statuettes is in preparation by A. N. Zadoks-Josephus Jitta, W. J. T. Peters, and W. A. van Es.

the occurrence of great quantities of second or early third century roof tiles of Roman type at two *terpen* sites, and of two *stili,* also in the *terpen* area. At Wijster, on the sand, Roman influences are demonstrable in constructional features of houses and pits. Romanizing influences must also have operated through the Frisians who served in the Roman army (Byvanck, 1935, p. 492). Nevertheless, the Frisian *terpen* culture is on the whole independent in its line of development and has strong indigenous traditions.[12] This is especially evident in the exclusively handmade pottery which imitates the wheel-made products of the Roman province only in a limited number of shapes (Boeles, 1951, pp. 187–88).

It is clear that the economic situation in the northern part of the country did not force potters to start throwing their pots on the wheel any more than it did farther south inside the Empire's border. But here in the north, far better than in the south, we are in a position to formulate our problem differently: Would not the socioeconomic situation in the north have offered a fair chance to a potter who might start a factory for wheel-made pottery? And if so, is it not significant that such factories did not arise, when we know that wheel-made pottery was appreciated and imported, and when we can safely surmise that at least some of the local population must have had a notion of the production methods of potters' factories inside the Roman province?

Already in the first century A.D. the marsh area in which the *terpen* culture of the Frisians flourished was densely populated. Halbertsma (1954, p. 243) gives an estimate for Westergo—a district in the Frisian *Terpen* area of about 800 square kilometers—of a population of about 20,000 people, living in at least 700 settlements.[13] The *terp* of Ezinge, which has been excavated by Van Giffen, must have borne in this period about twenty contemporary farmhouses, some of which offered accommodation for about fifty cows (Van Giffen, 1936). In post-Roman times, according to Halbertsma, a number of the smaller *terpen* were deserted, but the more important ones grew incessantly, so that by about A.D. 700 some of these attained the size of a regular town. At Feddersen Wierde, a *terp* on the coast of northwestern Germany meticulously excavated by Haarnagel (1957), there is proof of workshop specialization already in the second century A.D. Apart from large farmhouses containing stables, a smaller house without a stable was found which proved to have been the home and workshop of a bone carver; in the courtyard of the largest farmhouse, the workshop of a smith was discovered. Feddersen Wierde is in a different culture province, but as far as the economic situation is concerned, it can hardly have differed much from the Frisian *terpen* area.

To put it briefly, we cannot help thinking that the economic situation had sufficiently developed towards shop specialization and marketing to permit establishment of a potter's workshop turning out pottery thrown on the wheel. If the

12. The background and early development of this culture has recently been outlined by Waterbolk (1962).

13. For the distribution and density of the *terpen* in the tidal marsh area, cf. the detailed maps published by Halbertsma (1963).

potters, who by Early Medieval times had established extensive workshops for coarse handmade kitchen ware,[14] nevertheless failed to adopt the wheel, the conclusion seems inevitable that tradition was too strong an opponent. Perhaps one should note at this point the traditional reputation of the Frisians for stubbornness; but one wonders whether a more general principle may not be involved, and whether we have here an instance of the conservatism of the potter so often referred to at the "Ceramics and Man" symposium.

Is it simply conservatism? One should realize that the switch-over almost certainly would have caused a temporary drop in the production of the well-trained hand potter, just as it would take a person who is really skilled in typing with two fingers a long time to attain the same speed when trying to type with all fingers. There is a psychological barrier (how many of the contributors to this volume typed their manuscripts with ten fingers?). One can well imagine that in a situation characterized by a general continuity of cultural development, a shock of some kind in the economic sphere is required to bring about the switch-over to potting on the wheel. In the Frisian *terpen* area, as in general in the northwestern part of Europe, there was continuity of development (cf., for example, Hachmann, Kossack, and Kuhn, 1962), and the required shock evidently failed to come.[15]

14. Several of these workshops have been discovered in the North (near Veenhuizen and at Paterswolde in the province of Drenthe), but none have so far been scientifically excavated. They appear to be situated on the peat, which no doubt served as fuel.

15. The quality of the clay available as a possible factor influencing the potter in his predilection for shaping by hand could not be taken into consideration, since investigations into the ceramic properties of the clays available to the potters in the *terpen* area are lacking so far.

BIBLIOGRAPHY

BAKKER, J. A.
1962. "Relations with the TRB Culture." In J. F. van Regteren Altena *et al.*, "The Vlaardingen Culture," *Helinium*, 2:217–24.

BECKER, C. J.
1955. "Coarse Beakers with 'Short-Wave' Moulding." *Proceedings of the Prehistoric Society* (n.s.), 21:65–71.

BOELES, P. C. J. A.
1951. *Friesland tot de elfde eeuw. Zijn vóór- en vroege geschiedenis.* (2nd ed.). 's Gravenhage: Martinus Nijhoff.

BRAAT, W. C.
1937. "De Hooge Hof. Een Bataafsche nederzetting bij Zetten." *Oudheidkundige Mededeelingen uit het Rijksmuseum van Oudheden te Leiden* (Nieuwe Reeks), 18:22–40.

1949. "Drie inheemse nederzettingen uit de Romeinse tijd." *Ibid.*, 30:23–46.

1957. "Brabers, een inheemse nederzetting uit de Romeinse tijd op Schouwen." *Ibid.*, 38:84–90.

Breuer, J.
1931. "Les objets antiques découverts à Ubbergen près Nimègue." *Oudheidkundige Mededeelingen uit het Rijksmuseum van Oudheden te Leiden* (Nieuwe Reeks), 12: 27–121.

Brøndsted, J.
1958. *Danmarks Oldtid.* (rev. ed). Copenhagen: Gyldendal.

Brunsting, H.
1937. *Het grafveld onder Hees bij Nijmegen.* Amsterdam: N.V. Noord-Hollandsche Uitgeversmaatschappij.

Bruyn, A.
1959. "Die mittelalterliche Töpferindustrie in Brunssum." *Berichten van de Rijksdienst voor het Oudheidkundig Bodemonderzoek*, 9:138–88.

1961. "Die mittelalterliche keramische Industrie in Schinveld." *Ibid.*, 10–11:462–507.

Byvanck, A. W.
1935. *Excerpta Romana. De bronnen der Romeinsche geschiedenis van Nederland,* Vol. II. 's Gravenhage: Martinus Nijhoff, Rijks geschiedkundige publicatiën 81.

Childe, V. G., and N. Sandars
1950. "La Civilisation de Seine-Oise-Marne." *l'Anthropologie*, 54:1–18.

Daniëls, M.
1927. "Romeinsch Nijmegen II. Ulpia Noviomagus." *Oudheidkundige Mededeelingen uit het Rijksmuseum van Oudheden te Leiden* (Nieuwe Reeks), 8:65–111.

Eggers, H. J.
1951. *Die römische Import im freien Germanien.* Atlas der Urgeschichte I. Hamburg: Museum für Völkerkunde und Vorgeschichte.

Elzinga, G.
1962. "Nederzettingssporen van rond het begin onzer jaartelling bij Sneek." *De Vrije Fries*, 45:68–99.

Es, W. A. van
1960. *De Romeinse muntvondsten uit de drie noordelijke provincies. Een periodisering der relaties.* Scripta Academica Groningana. Groningen: J. B. Wolters.

Foster, G. M.
1959. "The Potter's Wheel: an Analysis of Idea and Invention." *Southwestern Journal of Anthropology*, 15:99–119.

Giffen, A. E. van
1930. *Die Bauart der Einzelgräber.* Mannus-Bibliothek 44–45. Leipzig: Verlag Kurt Kabitsch.

1936. "Der Warf in Ezinge, Provinz Groningen, Holland, und seine westgermanischen Häuser." *Germania*, 20:40–47.

1956. "Zur Frage der Einheitlichkeit der Hünenbetten." In *Zur Ur- und Frühgeschichte Nordwestdeutschlands*, P. Zylmann (ed.), pp. 97–122. Hildesheim: August Lax Verlag.

Glasbergen, W.
1948. "Terra sigillata uit de provincie Groningen. Bijdrage tot de geschiedenis van de handel in den Romeinschen tijd." *Jaarverslag van de Vereniging voor Terpenonderzoek*, 25–28 (1940–44):317–68.

1954. "Barrow Excavations in the Eight Beatitudes." *Palaeohistoria*, 2:1–134 (pt. 1); 3:1–204 (pt. 2).

GOOSSENS, W.

1909. "Eene Romeinsche pottenbakkerij te Heerlen (L)." *Oudheidkundige Mededeelingen uit het Rijksmuseum van Oudheden te Leiden*, 3:71–80.

HAARNAGEL, W.

1957. "Vorläufiger Bericht über das Ergebnis der Wurtengrabung auf der Feddersen Wierde bei Bremerhaven im Jahre 1956." *Germania*, 35:275–317.

HACHMANN, R., G. KOSSACK, and H. KUHN

1962. *Völker zwischen Germanen und Kelten.* Neumünster: Karl Wachholtz Verlag.

HALBERTSMA, H.

1954. "Enkele aantekeningen bij een verzameling oudheden, afkomstig uit een terpje bij Deinum." *Jaarverslag van de Vereniging voor Terpenonderzoek*, 33–37 (1948–53): 239–56.

1963. *Terpen tussen Vlie en Eems. Een geografisch-historische benadering.* Groningen: J. B. Wolters.

HOLWERDA, J. H.

1936. "De nederzetting te Naaldwijk." *Oudheidkundige Mededeelingen uit het Rijksmuseum van Oudheden te Leiden* (Nieuwe Reeks), 17:19–37.

1938. "Een Bataafsch dorp bij Ockenburgh bij den Haag." *Ibid.*, 19:11–60.

1943. "Een Bataafsch dorpje bij het Oppidum Batavorum uit de jaren vóór Chr. geb." *Ibid.*, 24:35–58.

1944. *Het in de pottenbakkerij van de Holdeurn gefabriceerde aardewerk uit de Nijmeegsche grafvelden.* Supplement op *Oudheidkundige · Mededeelingen uit het Rijksmuseum van Oudheden te Leiden* (Nieuwe Reeks), 24. Leiden: E. J. Brill.

1946. "Het Bataafsche dorp van het Hunerpark te Nijmegen." *Oudheidkundige Mededeelingen uit het Rijksmuseum van Oudheden te Leiden* (Nieuwe Reeks), 27:5–27.

HOLWERDA, J. H., and W. C. BRAAT

1946. *De Holdeurn bij Berg en Dal. Centrum van pannenbakkerij en aardewerkindustrie in den Romeinschen tijd.* Supplement op *Oudheidkundige Mededeelingen uit het Rijksmuseum van Oudheden te Leiden* (Nieuwe Reeks), 26. Leiden: E. J. Brill.

KNÖLL, H.

1959. *Die nordwestdeutsche Tiefstichkeramik und ihre Stellung im nord- und mitteleuropäischen Neolithikum.* Münster (Westfalen): Aschendorff Verlag.

LAET, S. J. DE

1958. *The Low Countries.* Ancient Peoples and Places, No. 5. London: Thames and Hudson.

LAET, S. J. DE, and W. GLASBERGEN

1959. *De voorgeschiedenis der Lage Landen.* Groningen: J. B. Wolters.

MODDERMAN, P. J. R.

1955. "Laat bekeraardewerk versierd met indrukken van een wikkeldraad stempel." *Berichten van de Rijksdienst voor het Oudheidkundig Bodemonderzoek*, 6:32–43. (English summary, pp. 42–43).

OTTO, K. H., and H. GRÜNERT

1958. "Das Verhalten der Germanen zur Scheibentöpferei in der vorrömischen Eisenzeit." *Jahresheft für Mitteldeutsche Vorgeschichte*, 41–42:389–408.

Schrickel, W.

1962. "Westeuropäische Einflüsse im neolithischen Grabbau Mitteldeutschlands." *Germania*, 40:22–32.

Schwantes, G.

1939. *Die Vorgeschichte Schleswig-Holsteins*. Neumünster: Karl Wachholz Verlag.

Sprockhoff, E.

1930. "Hügelgräber bei Vorwohlde im Kreise Sulingen," *Praehistorische Zeitschrift*, 21:193–236.

1942. "Niedersachsens Bedeutung für die Bronzeizeit Westeuropas," 31. *Bericht der Römisch-Germanische Kommission*, 1941 (II):1–138.

Stuart, P.

1962. *Gewoon aardewerk uit de Romeinse legerplaats en de bijbehorende grafvelden te Nijmegen*. Supplement op *Oudheidkundige Mededeelingen uit het Rijksmuseum van Oudheden te Leiden* (Nieuwe Reeks), 43. Leiden: E. J. Brill.

Vermeulen, W. G. J. R.

1932. *Een Romeinsch grafveld op den Hunnerberg te Nijmegen*. Amsterdam: H. J. Paris.

Waals, J. D. van der, and W. Glasbergen

1955. "Beaker Types and their Distribution in the Netherlands." *Palaeohistoria*, 4:5–46.

1959. "De twee bekerculturen." In *Honderd Eeuwen Nederland*, W. A. Ruysch (ed.), pp. 100–24. 's Gravenhage: Luctor et Emergo.

1962. "Neolithic Disc Wheels in the Netherlands. With a Note on the Early Iron Age Disc Wheels from Ezinge." *Palaeohistoria*, 10:101ff.

Waterbolk, H. T.

1960. "Preliminary Report on the Excavations at Anlo." *Palaeohistoria*, 8:59–90.

1961. "Bronzezeitliche dreischiffige Hallenhäuser von Elp (Dr.)." *Helinium*, 1:126–32.

1962a. "Hauptzüge der eisenzeitlichen Besiedlung der nördlichen Niederlande." *Offa*, 19:9–46.

1962b. "The Lower Rhine Basin." In *Courses toward Urban Life*, R. J. Braidwood and G. R. Willey (eds.), pp. 227–53. Viking Fund Publications in Anthropology No. 32. Chicago: Aldine Publishing Company.

THE INFLUENCE OF METALWORKING
ON PREHISTORIC POTTERY:
SOME OBSERVATIONS ON IRON AGE POTTERY
OF THE ALPINE REGION

WALTER TRACHSLER

THE imitation of an attractive but for some reason unobtainable prototype in more readily available and possibly cheaper material is a phenomenon of considerable anthropological and sociological interest. One aspect of that phenomenon may be taken into consideration here with respect to the general subject of the present publication, pottery—the reaction of the latter to the impact of metal vessels considerably different both in shape and decoration. As has often been pointed out,[1] this aspect is discernible archeologically in many places and at very different periods beginning when metal-casting and the production of metal containers were invented.

Metal vessels made in prehistoric times have survived only under exceptional circumstances. Because of the scarcity of metals (in comparison with potter's clay) and the difficulties of their processing, such vessels were produced in relatively small numbers. Gold, silver, copper, and bronze could be melted down and eventually be given a new shape. If they were lost (or were deposited in graves or sacred places) they risked the danger of disintegration through corrosion—at least those made of non-precious metals.

The more distant from ore-producing centers metal vessels are found, the more their acquisition must have been a privilege of social leaders and the more others must have become desirous of equaling the rich by imitating the outer aspects of their wealth. Imitation may be limited to the taking-over of certain formal elements proper to the prototype (such as specific shape, decorative motifs, surface coating) or may aim at an apparent facsimilation. If the same type of object turns up in different materials, it is not always easy—sometimes even impossible—for the archeologist to determine which of the two represents the prototype. The potter did not necessarily imitate the product of the metalworker, for the opposite could (and did) occur as well. If a ceramic vessel shows formal elements which can be considered neither properly decorative nor functional, but which, on the other hand, would make sense (or must be considered as unquestionably functional) in a metal vessel—such as sutures, rows of rivets, etc.—we may look for

---

1. This point was discussed by Robert H. Dyson, Jr., of the University Museum, Philadelphia, at the planning conference for this symposium.

a metal prototype. Full archeological evidence is, of course, obtained only if the priority of inception can be determined.

A number of archeological examples illustrating paradigmatically the problem of metal imitation in pottery are well known. Among Cretan antiquities there is an Early Minoan earthenware jug with a row of bosses around the body (Evans, 1921, Fig. 47b) which no doubt imitate the rivets of a sheet-metal vessel. There is an earthenware goblet from Knossos (Evans, 1921, Fig. 183b) with the same type of handle as the famous Vaphio gold cup, including a literal imitation of the metal riveting. The queer disk-ornamented handles of Rhodian oenochoë (of the seventh-century orientalizing style) have long been regarded as an invention of a metalworker. In Etruscan pottery there are many examples. The metal proto-types are well known for several kinds of bucchero vessels, earthenware beak-flagons, situlas, cists, and pitchers with tubular-shaped spouts.

For methodological reasons it is necessary to mention also that in many cases where the same formal elements are found in metalworking as well as in pottery, it may be useless to concern oneself with the question of priority. There are, within the complex phenomenon that is called style, creative ideas which find their adequate realizations in different materials and different techniques. Not every hemispherical protuberance on the body of a ceramic vessel is derived from a rivet, nor does every incised decoration presuppose a metal prototype. They may be nothing more than formal elements of decoration, and the more they are assimilated stylistically into the field of creative human activity, the less important the question of their origin becomes. Nevertheless, for transitional eras it can be of considerable developmental interest, reflecting contacts or cross-fertilizations between isolated areas of production, pointing out hidden affinities and revealing energetic promotion.

Iron Age pottery of the Alpine region offers good illustrations of this phe-nomenon. Because of the scarcity of data in the field of prehistory, an analysis cannot be as extensive as one would wish. We regret not having a technologist's collaboration, but teamwork between archeologists, ceramists, and technologists is in many parts of the Old World at its very beginning. Thus the following pages cannot be more than a modest communication of some observations on pottery from a region probably fairly unknown archeologically in the New World.

"METALLIC" SHAPING AND COATING—
AN ASPECT OF URNFIELD POTTERY IN THE ALPINE REGION

In the period between roughly 1200 and 600 B.C., a tremendous boom in metal production and metalworking took place in central Europe. A survey of the archeological material of this period—covering the so-called Urnfields and the later phases of the Hallstatt period—reveals a highly developing specialization in the different branches of metalworking (Kimmig, 1958, p. 55). The availability of metal vessels with their attractive, brilliant surfaces that have punched, em-bossed, incised, engraved, or inlaid decoration apparently influenced contemporary

PLATE 1
Beaker with high cylindrical neck, from
Auvernier (Lake Neuchâtel). Bronze, height
10 cm., max. diam. 10.5 cm. Neuchâtel,
Musée. (Photo taken from the plaster cast
in the Swiss National Museum, Zürich;
Inv. no. 29144, neg. no. 54595.)

PLATE 2
Beaker with high cylindrical neck, from Zürich-
Alpenquai. Earthenware, height 12 cm., max.
diam. 13.2 cm. Graphite coating, band incisions,
flutings. Zürich, Swiss National Museum (Inv.
no. 26783; photo from neg. no. 54596).

PLATE 3
Cup with band-shaped handle, rivets, from
Völs (district of Innsbruck, Austria), tomb
6. Bronze, height 5.7 cm. Innsbruck,
Museum Ferdinandeum (Inv. no. 1991).
(From Wagner, 1943, Pl. 24, no. 1a.)

PLATE 4
Cup with band-shaped handle, from
Wilten, Innsbruck, Austria. Earthen-
ware, height 5.5 cm. Innsbruck, Mu-
seum Ferdinandeum (Inv. no. 9601).
(From Wagner, 1943, Pl. 32, no. 1.)

PLATE 5

Small bowl with repoussé boss ornamentation, from Cortaillod (Lake Neuchâtel). Bronze, hammered, height 5 cm.,
max. diam. 14.7 cm. Zürich, Swiss National Museum
(Inv. no. 6924; photo from neg. no. 54594).

PLATE 6

Fragment of a beaker with repoussé
boss ornamentation, from Völs (district of Innsbruck, Austria). Sheet
bronze (composed of two parts). Bottom and rim missing. Height 7 cm.
Innsbruck, Museum Ferdinandeum
(Inv. no. 1992). (From Wagner,
1943, p. 112 and Pl. 25, no. 3.)

PLATE 7

Plate with imitation bronze studding inside
(cf. Figs. 2 and 3), from Ravelsbach (district of Hollabrun, Austria). Period Hallstatt C-D, earthenware, diam. 25 cm. Horn
(Austria), Hobarth Museum. (From
Pescheck, 1948, Pl. XI, no. 1.)

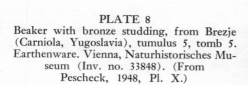

PLATE 8

Beaker with bronze studding, from Brezje
(Carniola, Yugoslavia), tumulus 5, tomb 5.
Earthenware. Vienna, Naturhistorisches Mu-
seum (Inv. no. 33848). (From
Pescheck, 1948, Pl. X.)

pottery production. This is especially true for the era of the so-called Urnfield Culture,[2] which extended from Hungary as far west as eastern France, including Austria, Germany, and Switzerland. V. Gordon Childe (1929, p. 378) characterized the pottery of that period in the Pannonian plain as "definitely metallic both in form and ornament."

The following examples, chosen principally from discoveries in Switzerland, may illustrate the considerable extent to which potters in the Alpine region were also influenced by the achievements of contemporary metalworking, though in the Hallstatt A–B period their region was apparently not influenced in the same direct way as in the Danube Basin and the Balkans, where the new ideas came in with a new invading population.

Without discussing the rather unintelligible ethnic situation in the Alpine region at that time, the fascination of the new production possibilities (and the new way of life and the social regrouping in consequence of it) must have been so imposing that—archeologically recognized in terms of shape and ornamentation —a certain "koine," i.e., a common language in style, was spreading throughout the influenced area, inaugurating direct connections between regions lying as far away from each other as Hungary and Switzerland.

In comparison with the ponderous and often rather clumsy-looking vessels of the preceding period, the Middle Bronze Age (Vogt, 1956, Pl. 7), Urnfield pottery found in Switzerland is more elaborately differentiated both in form and decoration (Fig. 1). The most frequent types are biconical vessels,[3] bowls and dishes, cups (mostly with ring or band-shaped handles), and beakers with wide and high cylindrical or conical necks. The shaping of the vigorously accentuated rim contrasts clearly with the high neck; the preferred decoration is fluting and incision (Pl. 2). Together with the brilliant dark surface, they evoke that "metallic look" which ceramists would hardly term genuine invention in clay, but, far more likely, derivative. (Cf. H. W. M. Hodges' experiments for the building-up of ceramic vessels, in this volume.) It is their general structure which suggests an association with metal, especially with sheet metal. We are tempted to say that Urnfield pottery, to a certain extent, is conceived in terms of metalworkers.

But beyond that, connections can be established by direct parallels. A number of pottery types are represented in identical shapes among the contemporary metal vessels. Bronze cups with band-shaped handles[4] (Pl. 3) have survived in various places; there are copies of them in pottery showing pseudoedges of pseudosheet metals and pseudo-rivets (Pl. 4). The beaker or urn shape which has a hemispherical base, a sharp bend in the lower part of the body, and a high

2. The Urnfield period in Central Europe corresponds to the Hallstatt A–B period (in Paul Reinecke's terms). It is a feature of the Late Bronze Age, covering the time from about 1230 to 800 B.C.

3. Approximate to Villanovan shapes, but also eastern European types, e.g., from the Vattina Culture (end of the Hungarian Bronze Age). (For Tyrolese examples, cf. Wagner, 1943, Pl. 22.)

4. Swiss specimens from Cortaillod (Lake Neuchâtel), Auvernier (Lake Neuchâtel), and Corcelettes (Canton of Vaud) are in the Swiss National Museum in Zürich. (For Tyrolese examples, cf. Wagner, 1943, Pl. 24.)

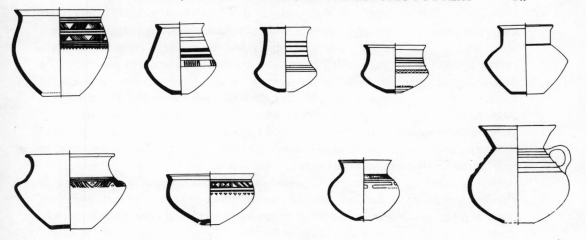

FIGURE 1

Shapes of Urnfield pottery in Switzerland. Incision, fluting,
graphite rubbing (after Speck, 1956, Pl. 11).

and relatively wide cylindrical or conical neck (Fig. 1 and Pl. 2), is also known
in metal vessels in hammered[5] as well as sheet bronze (Pl. 1, 6).

Beside those formal loans, an adaptation of the metalworker's technique can
be recognized in Urnfield pottery. On the basis of observations made on a number
of beakers and urns (of the type shown in Fig. 1 and Pls. 2, 14), I believe that they
were built up in two separate parts—one being the hemispherical base, the other
the cylindrical or conical neck—and that the body was later smoothed by hammering, i.e., by a genuine metal-working technique, but modified for the potter's
use[6] (with a beaker and convex disk or anything corresponding to paddle and
anvil; (Scott, 1956, p. 386, Fig. 228). I suppose that for the shaping of the hemispherical base, molds were used.

A technique never practiced in metalworking in the Alpine region before the
Urnfield period was the inlay of metal wires (gold, silver, copper, even iron)
into incised grooves prepared in the metal surface. (Fine specimens of that technique from the Late Bronze Age are in the Swiss National Museum in Zürich.)[7]
This metalworking technique of wire inlay was adapted to contemporary pottery:
instead of wires, vegetable fibers were used[8] (Pl. 14).

5. E. Vogt describes it as being cast (and not hammered, as was usual for smaller bronze
vessels); we were unable to verify this. (Cf. Vogt, 1930, p. 37, No. 56.)

6. The adaptation of hammering and embossing to pottery is a phenomenon well known also
to ethnologists; thus in Tunisia certain types of large earthenware cauldrons are manufactured
in the same way as metal ones; the potter prepares three different sizes of clay sheets which
then are assembled by hammering. I am much obliged for this communication to Miss Hélène
Balfet (Musée de l'Homme, Paris); she drew my attention to a film by Père O'Reilly, showing
the manufacturing of the vessels mentioned above.

7. E.g., a hilt of a bronze sword from Mörigen (Lake Bienne) with iron wire inlay. Zürich,
Swiss National Museum, Inv. No. 9092.

8. More will be said about this inlay technique in the following paper, "Precursors of Polychrome Painted Pottery."

The most striking aspect of the "metallic look" of the Urnfield pottery is its aim to endow the outside of the vessels with a brilliance equaling that of a polished metal surface. For the first time in the Swiss Alpine region, ceramic vessels received a graphite coating[9] which gave them a surprisingly metallic aspect.[10] The nearly mathematical precision in the shaping of the Urnfield pottery is all the more astonishing because none of its vessels were thrown on the wheel (Bandi, 1956, p. 37).[11] This is clearly shown by an examination of the inside of the pots. Judging from incised decoration produced by a notched tool and running round about the body of the vessel at the same level (Pl. 2), it can be assumed that at least primitive devices for rotating pots were known.

Metal prototypes in the Urnfield period do not provide a universally applicable clue for the understanding of the evolution of contemporary pottery, but they point to metalworking as an important influence in a cultural configuration which, it must be added, on closer consideration turns out to be very complex and which cannot be dealt with here.

BRONZE-STUDDED CERAMIC VESSELS— AN ASPECT OF POTTERY IN HALLSTATT B–C IN THE ALPINE REGION

A hemispherical protuberance on a metal surface may be the visible part of a rivet or stud, or it may be a purely decorative motif, an element of repoussé technique.[12] Both are genuine in metalworking. Rivets and bosses have been imitated in pottery from a very early date, apparently beginning in the eastern Mediterranean (Evans, 1921, Fig. 47a) and developing chiefly in Europe after metallurgy had come to the stage of building up vessels of sheets of metal by means of rivets.

In the second quarter of the first millennium B.C.—or speaking in terms of Central European prehistory, in Hallstatt B–C—rivets as well as boss ornamentation are

9. A graphite coating was not yet known in the region of present-day Switzerland in Hallstatt A; the earliest examples of this technique are from a tomb at Elgg (Canton of Zürich), belonging to the first part of phase Hallstatt B (unpublished materials in the Swiss National Museum in Zürich). The application of graphite to the outside of ceramic vessels goes much further back in time. In Europe it turns up in the Danube region as early as the middle of the third millennium B.C. (Polgar Culture). During the Urnfield period, graphite coating was, of course, not restricted to the region of Switzerland. (For Tyrolese specimens, cf. Wagner, 1943, Pl. 25.)

10. I am very much indebted to Miss A. O. Shepard for having kindly analyzed some sherds of the type in question. Here is the result which she communicated to me in her letter of January 31, 1962: "The sherd marked 'Zürich-Alpenquai' definitely has a graphite treated surface and has been burnished. Graphite plates, which have been spread out with the burnishing tool, can be clearly seen with the microscope. I can not say positively whether the graphite was applied before or after firing because with a low temperature, smudgy fire, graphite would not be oxidized. Since the graphite has only a mechanical binder, some might rub off on the fingers in either case. You may be interested to know that the potters of Coyotepec, Oaxaca, Mexico, rub their black pottery with graphite after firing."

11. Technological studies are entirely lacking so far for Swiss prehistoric pottery.

12. Examples of boss ornamentation from the Early Bronze Age are found in great numbers in the Balkans (e.g., Břesz Kujawskj, Handlova, Nilaveč). (Cf. Childe, 1949, p. 264.)

PLATE 9
Bowl with repoussé boss ornamentation, from Zürich-Altstetten, about 600 B.C. Gold,
height 13.5 cm., max. diam. 24.4 cm. Zürich, Swiss National Museum
(Inv. no. P 17430; photo from neg. no. 5554b).

found in great numbers on band-handled metal cups, on hammered bowls of
bronze or gold,[13] (Pls. 5, 9) on situlas and beak-flagons that are Etruscan imitations.

There are many ceramic vessels of that period with embossing and riveting,
but the astonishing thing is that these decorations are made of metal, of real
bronze rivets and studs. The adaptation of bronze parts to a clay vessel no doubt
raised technical difficulties. Judging from the small number of clay imitations of
riveting and embossing found within the materials of that time,[14] the potters must
not have been content with the steps taken in that direction. Rivet heads and
bosses had to be shaped neatly, contrasting well with their background, otherwise
they would not be recognized as such. So the potters imitated not only formal
elements of metalworking, but even adopted its raw material. They got bronze
studs (or properly speaking, nails) and inserted them into the soft clay to produce
true embossing and riveting on their vessels (Fig. 2 and Pls. 8, 10, 11). The rivets,
of course, were not functional, but decorative. The results are very surprising and
they represent a real enrichment of the potter's decorative resources.

It cannot be determined as yet when and where "nailed" pottery was made
first. Isolated finds from the Urnfield period are known from central and southern

13. Plate 9 shows a most remarkable example of a hammered boss-ornamented Hallstatt gold
bowl found in Zürich-Altstetten. (About 600 B.C.; Zürich, Swiss National Museum.)
14. Literal imitation of repoussé bosses in pottery are found in small number in Moravia
(specimens from Nemčice) and Bohemia (specimens from Trebušice) from the end of the
second millennium. (Cf. Schranil 1928, Pl. IX, No. 12.)

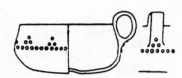

FIGURE 2

Cup with bronze studding from Grafenwörth (district of Tulln, Austria). Graphite coated. The interior has a cross-shaped graphite decoration. Max. diam. 10 cm. (Tulln, Heimatmuseum; illustration from Pescheck, 1948, Fig. 4, no. 1.)

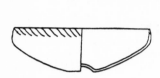
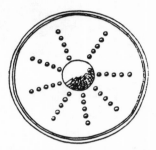

FIGURE 3

Bowl with *imitated* bronze studding from Marz (district of Eisenstadt, Austria). Max. diam. 15 cm. (Eisenstadt Landesmuseum; illustration from Pescheck, 1948, Fig. 4, no. 2.)

Germany[15] and from Switzerland.[16] The results of research by Dehn (1942), Pescheck (1948), and Stjernquist (1958) indicate that studded pottery had an early distribution center in Hallstatt B in Silesia. In Hallstatt C–D this technique was in vogue in the Middle Danube Basin[17] and in the Illyrian and Venetian regions of what today are Yugoslavia and northern Italy.[18] While in the "nailed" pottery from the north Alpine region (Fig. 2) the studs are mostly inserted with their spine into the soft clay surface and arranged there in single rows or simple geometric patterns (Pl. 8), in the Italian examples (Pls. 10, 11) which are more recent, the nails are but hollow hemispherical tops which are pinched

15. Examples from the following regions: Rhenish Palatinate, Rhenish Hesse (cf. Dehn, 1942, p. 123 ff.) and Bavaria (cf. Müller-Karpe, 1957, Pl. 1).

16. The only (and yet unpublished) specimens of bronze-studded pottery in Switzerland found so far are from Cresta near Cazis (Canton of Grisons), a dwelling place which is being systematically excavated by the Swiss National Museum in Zürich.

17. Examples from Grafenwörth (dist. of Tulln), Statzendorf (dist. of St. Pölten), Gemeinlebarn (dist. of St. Pölten), Jois (dist. of Bruck a.d. Leitha). Wildon (Styria), and Maribor on the Drava (Yugoslavia).

18. Examples from Kobarid (formerly Caporetto, Yugoslavia), from the Santa Lucia necropolis near Tolmín (Isonzo valley), from Ljubljana, and Brezje (Krajina).

into the wet clay or stuck to it after firing.[19] They usually make up a more elaborate geometric decoration, sometimes covering the entire body of the vessels,[20] or even form simple figurative friezes.[21] Chronologically they can be placed in the period Este II and in the beginning of Este III, i.e., roughly in the seventh century B.C. (Randall-MacIver, 1927, p. 29).

An outstanding phenomenon within the relationship between metalworking and pottery is the fact that "nailed" pottery was also imitated in pottery; i.e., the bronze studs which first were properly inserted in the clay were reproduced later in the material innate to pottery. Concluding from the preferred decorative motifs of "nailed" pottery, especially in the eastern Alpine region (Pl. 8 and Fig.

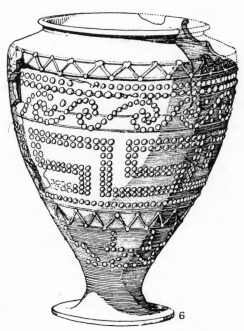

PLATE 10

Vessel with bronze studding, from Este (province of Venice, Italy), period Este II. Earthenware, height 22 cm. Este, Museum (Inv. no. 4962). (From Randall-MacIver, 1927, Pl. 4, no. 3—after a drawing by R. A. Cordingley.)

PLATE 11

Vessel with bronze studding, from Este (province of Venice, Italy), period Este III. Earthenware, height 32 cm. Este, Museum (Inv. no. 2469). (From Randall-MacIver, 1927, Pl. 4, no. 6—after a drawing by R. A. Cordingley.)

19. Stjernquist (1958, p. 149): "Les clous ont parfois été fixé par une pointe centrale, parfois par des griffes au bord du clou . . . . Dans certains cas; les clous ont été collés." Randall-MacIver (1927, p. 16): ". . . little studs of bronze which are set in the clay before burning, and come out of the fire imbedded in the fabric."

20. Este II–III examples mostly from the place of Este itself (province of Venice). Illustrations: Montelius (1895, Pl. 52 [nos. 3, 4, 12], Pl. 53 [nos. 11, 13], Pl. 58 [no. 7], Pl. 59 [no. 17] and Randall-MacIver (1927, Pl. 4 [nos. 3–6]).

21. Examples from Este (e.g., tomb 155).

2), the nail-patterns developed there were taken over *tale quale* in pottery[22] (Pl. 7 and Fig. 3). There is almost no possibility that they were derived from embossed metal vessels since the embossing decorations are very different.

Thus "nailed" pottery of Hallstatt B–C offers an instructive example of cross-fertilization between metalworking and pottery.

BIBLIOGRAPHY

BANDI, H. G.
1956. "Die Kultur der Bronzezeit." In *Die Bronzezeit der Schweiz,* Heft 2 of *Repertorium der Ur-und Frühgeschichte der Schweiz,* pp. 35–41. Zürich: Kurskommission der Schweiz. Gesellschaft für Urgeschichte.

CHILDE, V. G.
1929. *The Danube in Prehistory.* Oxford: Clarendon Press.
1949. "The First Bronze Vases to be Made in Central Europe." *Acta Archaeologica* (København), 20:257–64.

DEHN, W.
1942. "Zwei Gefässe der Urnenfelderkultur mit Bronzezierat vom Rhein." *Altschlesische Blätter,* 4.

EVANS, SIR. A. J.
1921. *The Palace of Minos at Knossos,* Vol. 1. London: Macmillan and Co.

GONZENBACH, V. VON,
1949. "Die Cortaillodkultur in der Schweiz." In *Monographien zur Ur-und Frühgeschichte der Schweiz,* Vol. VII. Basel. Birkhaüser Verlag.

KIMMIG, W.
1958. *Vorzeit an Rhein und Donau. Südwestdeutschland, Nordschweiz, Ostfrankreich.* Lindau und Konstanz: Jan Thorbecke Verlag.

MONTELIUS, O.
1895. *La Civilisation Primitive en Italie depuis l'Introduction des Métaux,* Vol. 1. Stockholm. Imprimerie Royale.

MÜLLER-KARPE, H.
1957. "Münchener Urnenfelder." *Praehistorische Staatssammlung München.* München: Michael Lassleben, Kallmünz Opf.

PESCHECK, C.
1948. "Späthallstättische Kulturströmungen im Ostalpenraum." In *Strena Praehistorica, Festgabe zum 60. Geburtstage von Martin Jahn,* pp. 160–82. Halle a. Saale: Max Niemeyer.

RANDALL-MACIVER, D.
1927. *The Iron Age in Italy.* Oxford: Clarendon Press.

22. Hallstatt B examples from Karmine (dist. of Milice), Comöse (dist. of Neumarkt), Schlause (dist. of Münsterberg). Hallstatt C–D examples from Jois (dist. of Bruck a.d. Leitha), Fischau am Steinfelde (dist. of Wiener Neustadt), Gross-Weikersdorf (dist. of Tulln), Krensdorf (dist. of Eisenstadt), Sopron (Hungary), Ravelsbach (dist. of Hollabrunn). Cf. Pescheck, 1948, p. 164 (map showing localities).

SCHRÁNIL, J.
1928. *Die Vorgeschichte Böhmens und Mährens.* Berlin: Walter de Gruyter & Co.

SCOTT, SIR. L.
1954. "Pottery." In *A History of Technology*, C. Singer, E. J. Holmyard, A. R. Hall (eds.), I:376–412. Oxford: Clarendon Press.

SPECK, J.
1956. "Die späte Bronzezeit." In *Die Bronzezeit der Schweiz*, Vol. 2 of *Repertorium des Ur-und Frühgeschichte der Schweiz.* Zurich: Kurskommission der Schweiz. Gesellschaft für Urgeschichte.

STJERNQUIST, B.
1958. "Ornementation Métallique sur Vases d'Argile." In *Meddelanden Från Lunds Universitets Historiska Museum*, pp. 107–69. Lund.

VOGT, E.
1930. "Die Spätbronzezeitliche Keramik der Schweiz und Ihre Chronologie." *Denkschriften der Schweizerischen Naturforschenden Gesellschaft* (Zürich), Vol. LXVI, Abh. 1, pp. 1–80.

1950. "Der Beginn der Hallstattzeit in der Schweiz." *Jahrbuch der Schweizerischen Gesellschaft für Urgeschichte*, 40:209–31.

1956. "Die Mittlere Bronzezeit." In *Die Bronzezeit der Schweiz*, Vol. 2 of *Repertorium der Ur-und Frühgeschichte der Schweiz*, pp. 12–16, Pl. 5–7. Zürich. Kurskommission der Schweiz. Gesellschaft für Urgeschichte.

WAGNER, K. H
1943. *Nordtiroler Urnenfelder.* Vol. 15 of *Römisch-Germanische Forschungen.* Berlin: Walter de Gruyter.

PRECURSORS OF POLYCHROME PAINTED POTTERY: SOME EXAMPLES FROM THE PREHISTORY OF SWITZERLAND

WALTER TRACHSLER

WITHOUT a supplementary surface coating, clay pots often look rather unattractive. No wonder that potters from the very beginning of the ceramic era were thinking of means by which to decorate them. Lots of organic and inorganic pigments proved to have the negative quality of completely changing or even of disappearing in the heat of the potter's kiln. Since pigments added to the surface of vessels after firing tend to be fugitive, the potters thought of other means to get resistant colors on their wares. Ingenious ideas produced admirable polychrome effects. But a satisfactory solution of the problem of polychrome decoration was reached only when the potters succeeded in giving to easily available pigments the same imperishable resistance as fired clay proved to have by nature. In the region of present-day Switzerland the first attempts to produce polychrome effects on ceramic vessels date from the early time when Neolithic settlers of the Cortaillod Culture coil-built their clay gourds and beakers, but not until some 2000 years later did people of that same region succeed in adding to their pots polychrome effects which did not alter or fade out when they were fired.

Because of the special attention that is given in this publication to the technological side of pottery studies, the groups of vessels which we are going to consider will be taken out of their chronological context and will be looked at separately as technical phenomena, or—speaking properly—they will be presented by somebody who does not have a special technical background and therefore cannot, beyond the presentation of data available to him, give a reliable technological evaluation of his observations. They may, therefore, be taken as a preliminary communication *ad disputandum*.

Some of our "precursors of polychrome painted pottery" will probably prove to be more or less local inventions, while others will no doubt find their parallels in extra-European areas.

Starting points for the following study are the prehistoric materials available in the collections of the Swiss National Museum in Zürich.

BARK DECORATION

A number of Swiss prehistoric sherds show a white appliqué decoration which contrasts vividly with the black surface of the vessels (Pls. 12, 13). They have

PLATE 12
Goblet (completed) with rests of an appliqué decoration made of birch bark, from Egolzwil (canton of Lucerne). Earthenware, max. diam. 10 cm. Zürich, Swiss National Museum (Inv. no. 44441; photo from neg. no. 15830).

PLATE 13
Fragment of a goblet with appliqué decoration made of birch bark, from Egolzwil (canton of Lucerne). Earthenware, height (of the fragment) 6 cm. Lucerne, Naturhistorisches Museum. (Photo from Swiss National Museum, Zürich, neg. no. 10808.)

been found in lake-shore dwelling-places in the western and northwestern part of the Swiss Plateau, and they belong to the first half of the third millennium B.C. These vessels, the earliest ceramic wares found in prehistoric Switzerland, are primitive both in technique and shaping, and resemble calabashes and gourds (Wyss, 1959, Pls. 1–4). The appliqué material has been identified as birch bark; the adhesive connecting it with the surface of the vessel consists of tar extracted from the same trees. As far as we can determine, appliqué decoration consisting of white bark is restricted within the Swiss area to the Early Neolithic Age (i.e., to Cortaillod, particularly to the Egolzwil Culture).

COLORED VEGETABLE FIBERS

The affinity of Urnfield pottery with contemporary metalwork was the subject of the preceding report. Polychromy is an aspect of this relationship, showing the adaptation of a very popular metal technique to pottery. Threads are inlaid in small incised grooves that often run horizontally around the body of the vessels (Pl. 14). Each thread is tightened by a wooden pin which fixes its two ends into a small hole. Though nearly all of the organic material from the Urnfield period has disintegrated, it is possible to show that the material inserted into the grooves

PLATE 14

Two beakers with high cylindrical necks, from Zürich-Alpenquai, Urnfield period. Earthenware, graphite coated, with horizontal grooves for fiber inlay (reconstructed in the example on the left). Zürich, Swiss National Museum (left side, Inv. no. 26874 [height 19 cm.]; right side, Inv. no. 26887 [height 13 cm.]. (Photo from neg. no. 17079.)

consisted of a number of colored fibers. Their carbonized remains indicate that they were not really twisted; they could be wool, flax, or stinging nettle (*Urtica*). Fiber inlay was not only practiced on beakers and urns of the well-known Urnfield type (Pl. 14), it occurred also on small theriomorphic vessels, with grooves running in all directions.[1] The polychrome effect of those fiber inlays must have been very attractive, for we can imagine the bright colors of the threads contrasting with the black or graphite-coated surface.[2] Judging from the Swiss materials so far available, this inlay technique was restricted to the second part of the Hallstatt A phase.

METAL LAMINAE

In the transition period between the Bronze Age and the Iron Age an outstanding post-firing technique was used in a relatively small area of temperate Europe, i.e., in the Alpine region and its vicinity: in Switzerland, the adjacent regions of France and Italy, and in Austria (finds from Styria, cf. Szombathy, 1890, p. 183) and Yugoslavia (Stjernquist, 1958, pp. 111, 140).

It consists of the application of decoratively shaped laminae to the surface of

1. E.g., from Zürich-Alpenquai or from Corcelettes (Lake Neuchâtel) in the Swiss National Museum in Zürich (Cf. Kimmig, 1958, p. 64.).
2. Graphite coatings during the Urnfield period are discussed in the preceding paper.

ceramic objects by means of an adhesive (which seems to have been resin or tar pitch; Stjernquist, 1958, p. 152).

The laminae used were made of tin, sometimes alloyed with silver or lead; examples of bronze or lead are relatively rare (Stjernquist, 1958, pp. 140ff., 142ff.) and have not been found so far in Switzerland.

Very often the tin foil has a geometric decoration which—technically speaking —is derived from incised decoration applied to the surface of the pots before firing. Later, after the laminae were glued on and rubbed against the surface, the pattern again became visible (Pl. 15).

Swiss specimens of this appliqué technique are very rare and occur mainly on small vessels (Pl. 16); a few sherds belonging to large dishes are quite exceptional. The fragment reproduced in Plate 15 and reconstructed in Figure 1, showing geometric and maeander patterns, must have been of brilliant effect.

Tin appliqué decoration in the transitional period between the Bronze Age and the Iron Age seems to have been restricted, on the whole, to the so-called pile-dwellers' area. The Swiss examples from Lake Neuchâtel and its surroundings (Pl. 16) seem to be related to those found on the shores of Lake du Bourget (Savoy, France) (Stjernquist, 1958, p. 124, Fig. 17).

The finds from northern Italy come mostly from the Bologna region (Stjernquist, 1958, pp. 127–35). A considerable number of them, such as hut urns and cinerary urns, served a funeral or ritual purpose (Stjernquist, 1958, p. 168), and the same is true for some pieces found in France. As for the Swiss examples, we do not know whether they were used in the same sense.

FILLED INCISIONS

Filling prepared grooves of a fired clay surface with material of another color, a technique corresponding to certain kinds of enameling in metalwork, belongs to the standard repertoire of the prehistoric potter. It was practiced in eastern Europe from the Early Neolithic Age.[3] In the Alpine region, it was known in the later phases of that period (in the Michelsberg and Rössen Cultures), but it was practiced commonly only in Hallstatt C–D; i.e., at a time when potters even in this region were able to produce polychrome, at least bichrome, designs on their pots (Pl. 17). The incisions were made by simple engraving tools or by punches. Chemical analyses of the "incrusted" material (in the Swiss National Museum) showed that it consisted of fine flour obtained by grinding bone.

EARLY POTTERY PAINTING AND RESIST TECHNIQUE

Within the Swiss prehistoric material, painted pottery turns up as late as Hallstatt B, i.e., centuries or even millennia later than in eastern and southeastern Europe.

3. E.g., pottery from the Danube Basin (with spiral-maeander or stroke ornamentation) of Danubian I B. (Cf. Childe, 1929, pp. 39ff., 48ff.)

PLATE 15
Fragment of an earthenware plate with graphite coating and appliqué decoration made of tin laminae, from Cortaillod (Lake Neuchâtel). Diameter (of entire plate) 35 cm. Biel, Bienne (canton of Berne), Musée Schwab. (The reconstructed plate is shown in Fig. 1.) (Photo from Swiss National Museum, Zürich, neg. no. 9943.)

PLATE 16
Two small earthenware vessels with graphite coating and appliqué decoration made of tin laminae, from Hauterive (canton of Fribourg), end of the Bronze Age. Zürich, Swiss National Museum (left side, Inv. no. 6592 [height 3.5 cm., max. diam. 6.8 cm.]; right side, Inv. no. 6591 [height 8.5 cm., max. diam. 7.5 cm.].)
(Photo from Swiss National Museum, neg. no. 54597.)

FIGURE 1
Plate with graphite coating and appliqué decoration made of tin laminae,
from Cortaillod (Lake Neuchâtel). Diam. 35 cm. Reconstruction based on
the sherds in the Musée Schwab in Biel, Bienne (cf. Pls. 1 and 5).
(Reproduction from Vogt, 1956, Pl. 21, Fig. 2.)

From a technical viewpoint the Swiss pottery production of Hallstatt B (and
C) can be divided into two groups: one in the western part of the Swiss Plateau
with only painted decoration (Fig. 2), and the other in the eastern part of the
country very near southern Germany[4] with a mixed technique consisting of incision and additional painting, mainly in red and graphite black (Fig. 3).

A special painting technique which is found sporadically within the Swiss
Hallstatt C material is the "post-fire resist" (or negative painting).[5] Robert Sonin
of the Brooklyn Museum of Art has kindly studied a specimen from the Swiss
National Museum, (basing his observations on color transparencies which we put

4. German term: *Alb-Salem-Keramik*. (Cf. Drack, 1957, p. 8.)
5. E. Vogt was the first to mention the "Batik" sherds in the Swiss National Museum in an
article (1947, p. 1969).

PLATE 17

Two ceramic vessels with incrusted white decoration, from Lunkhofen (canton of Aargau), period Hallstatt C. Zürich, Swiss National Museum. Left side: plate with punched and incised decoration filled with white plastic material, from tumulus 14. Max. diam. 33 cm. (Inv. no. 3234). Right side: cinerary urn with incised decoration filled with white plastic material, from tumulus 61. Height 25 cm., max. diam. 28 cm. (Inv. no. 3229). (Photo from Swiss National Museum, neg. no. 11409.)

PLATE 18

Detail from a cinerary urn. Red painting with post-fire resist, from Wäldi (canton of Thurgau), tumulus 1, tomb 4. Zürich, Swiss National Museum (Inv. no. 26381). (Cf. cinerary urn of the type shown on the left in Fig. 3.) Total height 32 cm., max. diam. 35 cm. (Photo from Swiss National Museum, neg. no. 8084.)

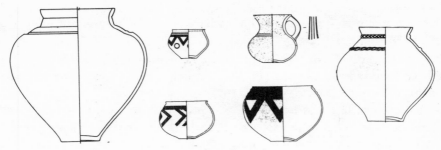

FIGURE 2

Pottery of period Hallstatt C (*ca.* 750–600 B.C.) from the western part of
the Swiss Plateau. Painted, graphite coated, or with relief decoration.
(Reproduction from Drack, 1957, Pl. 1.)

at his disposal). He describes this technique as follows (in a letter dated May
14, 1962):

In this technique the resist ("Batik"–"negative") pattern is applied to the fully fired
and otherwise completed vessel which may be of any sort of monochrome or polychrome fabric. The black resist pigment is organic in nature and if fired to a high
enough temperature it burns away. Because it is carbonaceous it is always black or a
dilution of black which diminishes through greys to invisibility. Only when it is applied
over a strong color such as ochre does it appear to be a darker shade of red or whatever
color happens to be seen through it.

About the character of the resist material Sonin writes:

. . . it would most likely be not wax but a water dispersible mineral substance such as
clay or wood ashes or a mixture of the two. Wax simply does not work in the post-fire
technique although it is employed in the pre-fire technique. The black post-fire pigments of the New World are evidently of two types. The first is a deposit from sooty
or resinous smoke to which the finished pottery is exposed with the resist (clay or ash)
in place. The second type is an organic substance which has been brushed or poured

FIGURE 3

Pottery of period Hallstatt C (*ca.* 750–600 B.C.) from northeastern Switzerland.
Incised and painted. (Reproduction from Drack, 1957, Pl. 1.)

over the surface, except where the clay resist has prevented it. It is then subjected to enough heat to scorch it to a black and insoluble state. The clay or ash resist is then washed away with water.[6]

"Negative painting" (or "Batik" painting), of which only a very few specimens have been found in Switzerland (Pl. 18), is much better documented in southern Germany (Kimmig, 1958, p. 92, Fig. 105).

Painted pottery in Swiss prehistory was produced during two relatively short periods; the first began with Hallstatt B (as mentioned above) and declined at the end of the Hallstatt period (about 450 B.C.); the second, bringing the first figured designs, began in La Tène D, about 50 B.C., and faded out with the Roman conquest of Switzerland at the beginning of our era.

6. I am very much obliged to Robert Sonin who gave me permission to publish his opinion.

BIBLIOGRAPHY

CHILDE, V. G.
   1929. *The Danube in Prehistory*. Oxford: Clarendon Press.
DRACK, W.
   1957. "Die Hallstattzeit im Mittelland und Jura." In *Die Eisenzeit der Schweiz.*, pp. 8–14, pl. 1–5. (Vol. 2 of *Repertorium der Ur-und Frühgeschichte der Schweiz.*) Zürich: Kurskommission der Schweiz. Gesellschaft für Urgeschichte.
KIMMIG, W.
   1958. *Vorzeit an Rhein und Donau. Südwestdeutschland, Nordschweiz, Ostfrankreich.* Lindau und Konstanz: Jan Thorbecke Verlag.
STJERNQUIST, B.
   1958. "Ornementation Métallique sur Vases d'Argile." In *Meddelanden Från Lunds Universitets Historiska Museum*, pp. 107–69. Lund: C. W. K. Gleerup.
SZOMBATHY, J.
   1890. "Urgeschichtliche Forschungen in der Umgebung von Wies." *Mitteilungen der Anthropologischen Gesellschaft*, Vol. XX: 170–93. Vienna.
VOGT, E.
   1947. " 'Batik' Patterns on Vessels of the Hallstatt Period." *Ciba-Review*, No. 54, p. 1969.
WYSS, R.
   1959. *Anfange des Bauertums in der Schweiz. Die Egolzwileskultur (um 2700 v. Chr. Geb.).* (Vol. 12 of *Aus dem Schweizerischen Landesmuseum.*) Bern: Paul Haupt.

ETHNOGRAPHICAL OBSERVATIONS IN NORTH AFRICA
AND ARCHAEOLOGICAL INTERPRETATION:
THE POTTERY OF THE MAGHREB

HÉLÈNE BALFET

B Y DEVOTING the second chapter of her book on ceramics and the archeologist to "Ceramic Processes and the Techniques of Prewheel Potters," it seems to me that Anna O. Shepard (1956, pp. 49–94) has definitely established the value of ethnographic data in the study of archeological pottery. This approach was initiated at least fifty years ago by L. Franchet, but there is still much to do. The following pages have no other aim but to add a small stone to the common project.

I have been fortunate in being able to carry out my investigations more or less equally in both directions, often making a most stimulating switch from one to the other. In addition, my ethnographic field—chosen with this double task in view—is in North Africa, or rather, to be precise, in the Maghreb, where at the present time there are to be found side by side pottery vessels that differ so much from each other that they could certainly pass for examples from different epochs if one were to study them out of context. I feel that I should take advantage of the privileged circumstances of these field studies to try to bring out certain points with respect to the conditions of archeological interpretation since the field stitches were particularly well-suited for this end.

MAGHREB POTTERY

The designation, "Maghreb Pottery," suggests vessels very different each from the other, but all having a right to the same designation. The most original are the painted wares from the Riff Mountains, the Kabylia, and the Kroumirie, though they are more widely spread since each region, still faithful to the traditional life of the Berbers, has its own ware recognizable by its peculiar style. (For Algeria, see Balfet, 1957). Hand-shaped porous pottery, often poorly finished for cooking purposes, usually has very carefully finished surfaces—on the inside of dishes and the outside of closed vessels. A slip covering all or part of the surface serves as a background for a rectilinear, geometric decoration, sometimes enhanced by an application of light yellow resin. The nature of the materials used and the procedures employed vary somewhat, but the decoration follows fairly strict rules of application, especially the cutting of surfaces and the filling in of these areas according to a fairly strict symmetry. Nevertheless, each region has its personal style which differs markedly from others within the great geographical ensemble. There may be minute variations from village to village, but they are clearly recognizable.

The North African wares also include faience and glazed pottery which are found in the homes and shops of all towns, although their present production is almost exclusively restricted to the peripheral regions, Tunisia and Morocco. The traditional pottery of Tunis and Fez are linked to those which were one of the glories of the Moslem civilization during the Middle Ages. On a white background of tin enamel, brilliant colors from a wide range of metallic oxides are used to design flowing plant and animal motifs. In Morocco, faience tends to follow more or less the traditional styles, but in Tunisia modern designs are being sought. Usually, utilitarian objects are produced in glazed pottery whose brown, yellow, and green tones are used to obtain decorative effects by simple contrast.

In order to get a picture of the varied ceramic production of the Maghreb, one must include some utilitarian objects with little or no decoration which can be found in the markets, particularly in those regions where the glazed type is lacking. The principal forms are pots, cooking vessels, and braziers which are hand-shaped and quite roughly molded and finished; their uniformity of shape and size approaches standardization. For decoration they have at the most a swiftly traced black or red band at the neck, some very simple painted motifs, or perhaps a few incisions. Standardized vessels transported in larger quantities also may appear. The most frequent forms are pitchers and water jars, just as poorly finished although they are not worked in the same way. These are wheel-made pieces which show by their color and "ring" that the firing has been uniform and prolonged even if not at a very high temperature. Several of their characteristics resemble those of the Punic era.

THE PRODUCTION OF POTTERY

These vessels, which sometimes occur together in the equipment of the same houses, come from potters' shops that are quite different from and independent of each other. We will draw a rapid sketch of them from the economic and professional points of view before examining their characteristic techniques.

1. Pottery-making is a *normal feminine domestic chore* wherever the traditional rural system exists; the family constitutes a closed economic unit which produces its own essential equipment (with the exception of metal objects). Annually, in each home, the women replace those vessels which have been chipped or broken in the course of the year. At that time, under the traditional local patriarchal family form of organization, a veritable workshop is organized under the direction of the mistress of the house. The work is shared according to the free time and the ability of individuals. This ensures the carrying-out of daily household tasks and the care of the children, and serves as an apprenticeship for the girls who learn the trade by watching and copying the procedures of the more skillful workers.

The pottery produced supplies the family with vessels for the preparation and the serving of meals, for the carrying and storing of water, and for preserving yearly provisions. They also provide adornment for the home and give proof of the foresight, care, and ability of its mistress, since the vessels are in full view, set out on shelves. The decorative and social role of pottery is far from negligible; it certainly helps explain the great care taken in the finishing process, and the richness of the painted decoration. Each woman does that which she can do best, giving to it all the time and attention that her self-respect demands.

2. We have brought together under the heading *elementary specialization* several cases, some of which differ but slightly from the one just described. This is the production of potters, "specialists" in the sociological rather than the technological sense. That is to say, they are recognized as specialists not because of any particular ability, but because they are widows, or, at any rate, obliged to contribute to the income of the home; they have to obtain financial support from a more intensive practice of an ordinary feminine activity. Their customers are women momentarily prevented from supplying their own needs, and who increase in numbers progressively as family groupings evolve. In a very small family, one woman alone cannot cope with the multiple traditional feminine tasks, and pottery-making, which is particularly absorbing and difficult, is one of the first to be given up. Sometimes women, if they need a little money, will fire pottery for a nearby market (more recently for offering to collectors who have tried to commercialize the traditional arts). Yet again, in the vicinity of the towns, some women have a modest livelihood making cooking pots and braziers, objects which the big specialized centers do not produce, but for which there is nevertheless a demand among the townspeople.

There is little or no difference in status between these women "specialists" and the village potters who are found particularly in Morocco and in southern Algeria and Tunisia. These are either peasant potters for whom pottery-making is a supplemental skill in the agricultural off-seasons, or nomadic potters, or potters living on the fringes of a community which feeds them in exchange for their products. With the simplest of implements, they produce utilitarian objects.

3. Finally, pottery is *a handicraft among others*. In the medieval-type urban structures which prevailed in North Africa until recently, the various handicrafts were organized into corporations of workers, whose strong cohesion ensured the observation and the transmission of the rules for production and sale. Every urban center of any importance had, therefore, its group of potters as it had its groups of weapon-makers, copper-beaters, and shoemakers. This is no longer true today, because some centers, benefiting locally from favorable circumstances, now supply a very large clientele. This regrouping has emphasized still further the specialization of craftsmen and the standardization of products which now consist of a large series of objects of fixed shapes and sizes. This does not exclude a plurality of quite distinct styles, some of which show a tendency to conserve the traditional style, whereas others follow passing fashions. There have even been cases of the sudden production of an entirely new type, as happened in Tunisia during the

last war when replacements were made for European objects which no longer reached North Africa. The tendency toward expansion of the most successful centers is followed by the increasing specialization of some of them in certain objects for which they have, in fact, a kind of monopoly (Djerba, for example, in the production of very large jars).

In summary, the Maghreb, from the point of view of the social position of men and women potters, offers a wide selection of possibilities. The independence of their evolution and the absence of mutual influence among these different traditions ·is certainly not the least remarkable fact about them.

THE PROCESSES OF POTTERY MANUFACTURE

The very loose character of the potters' relationships stands out particularly clearly in the examination of procedures. That is why we have decided not to separate the descriptions but to follow them all together through the successive stages of manufacture from the clay to the object ready for use.

1. *Raw materials and their preparation.*—In Kabylia, where the women make their pottery once a year, the season begins with the inevitable collecting of clay. Individually or in groups, they go out into the fields around the village or to the riverbank, wherever they have seen a good bed of clay. If the bed is exhausted, they dig haphazardly in its vicinity, never very far away, since such a rustic manufacture is not very demanding and the quantity needed is for a very limited production.

Very different are the demands of those potters whose commercial success is based on the utilization of a clay of special quality. To generalize, as soon as continuous production starts, there arises the problem of finding and systematically exploiting the clay-beds. The craftsmen of the specialized centers are generally installed in the neighborhood of an important deposit of which it sometimes happens they are, collectively, owners or tenants and controllers of its use. They all worry about a shortage of raw material, and stockpiling is frequent; this ensures a continuity of manufacture and also makes possible the use of the most suitable quality for each different product. The clay is seldom aged, and even the skilled potters seem to know little of the value of such a practice.

With regard to the preparation of clay, I have never known a potter, man or woman, who did not recognize its importance in the success of the procedures which follow it. The differences which can be observed in the choice and proportion of a tempering material (a large quantity of potsherds ground to fine powder, on the one hand; a small amount of sand on the other) appears to be due, at least partly, to the nature of the clays and to the correct requirements for the procedures employed. Hand-building demands a rather firm clay, but the majority of clays dug out in the fields, being mixed with humus and impregnated with organic materials, always have a high natural plasticity. Those potters who make very large vessels and who, as shall be seen, alternate turning and hand-building during construction, use more tempered clays than for normal wheel-made ware.

2. The distribution of *shaping* procedures corresponds roughly to the elementary sociological division between feminine hand-shaped pottery and masculine wheel-made pottery. However, a few variations must be noted in this outline, particularly with regard to the semispecialists.

At the present stage of our knowledge, no North African woman would appear to use a pivoting apparatus for making her pottery, which is usually formed by coiling. The work is carried out on a supporting stand, which can on occasions be made to turn, although it cannot be considered as even a very primitive wheel. In fact, the support is operated with an irregular movement during the molding, while the woman attempts to get the part on which she is working into the right position. It is only during the smoothing process and the final finishing of the rim that a continuous movement is used. It is imparted to the support by the left hand or sometimes by the foot, and is a slow movement to which the working of the hand offers little resistance, since the rough shape is already formed.

This general description leaves room for variations which appear very slight, but their various combinations with those of other steps suffice to give originality to each potter's work. There are variations, to begin with, in the posture of the woman who may be seated, squatting, or standing while leaning over her work, around which she moves. There are variations in the installation of the support which may be a simple disk placed on the ground, a slightly convex disk (which allows movement by hand or foot), or a raised disk, for example, on an upturned dish. Still other variations are in the thickness and the method of lengthening the coils.

At the other end of the scale, among the specialists, one can see common objects being turned on a kick-wheel which the seated potter moves by foot. For building very large jars, the Djerbian potters alternate for each ring segment of the wall, coil construction and wheel-shaping, an original method which in my opinion can be considered as true turning and not just as a simple smoothing by wheel (Balfet, 1963).

The greatest number of variations can be seen among the semispecialists, men and women. The only advantage these have over their nonspecialist neighbors, is the skill which an oft-repeated process gives and the achievement of a method of forming several vessels simultaneously which provides them with an already drying framework for every addition of a segment to the wall. It is not unusual to see men potters, contrary to the general rule, carrying out coil-building, either by hand-turning the pottery on a fairly high, wet support, or by moving around a fairly high support, or by using more or less perfected rotating supports with or without a pivot. Some of them alternate coiling and turning, rather in the style of the Djerba wheel, although with a slower rotation. To conclude, some of the peasant potters, both Moroccans and Tunisians, use a foot wheel, very primitive in appearance, but classical in its functioning.

3. The greatest variety is found in the *finishing and decorating* of the pottery.

Among the nonspecialist women potters, these variations are so great from one region to another that it would be irrelevant to give an account of them here. It may suffice to point out that each group has its own individual style, consciously different from the others. The finishing is always very carefully done, and the pottery objects, admittedly few in number, pass again and again through the hands of the part-time potters who devote hours to polishing the slip to get a uniformly smooth and brilliant surface. Moreover, they show great freedom in the choice of decorative compositions from among those in use. Thus in every village, each house normally has examples of five or six very different types: a smooth surface with a simple red border, decoration in relief, partial decoration painted in black on a red slip, varied compositions painted in black and red on a white slip. All this is done by one hand, that of the mistress of the house who knows exactly for what purpose she intends to use each of the objects.

But if that same woman makes a series of vessels for sale, she adopts for each a decoration which is sometimes simple, sometimes excessive, but always more artificial and less vivid, and she repeats it on each piece that she produces. However, when she works to order, she knows her customers and she generally keeps a personal style. Work for the marketplace evolves more quickly: one observes how the compositions get weaker, and how anecdotic motifs, which can amuse and hold a clientele, appear. On utilitarian objects, on the other hand, decoration tends to become less, and even to disappear.

Village potters produce a decoration which is simple and rapid and which can be, according to the regions, either painted, incised, stamped, or made of bands in relief. This is also so in the big specialized centers where glazes are added. Whether it be a question of matte or glazed pottery, every manufacturing center has, for each type of object, a decoration which is just as standardized as are the shapes of the pieces, and this decoration is applied as one of the necessary phases of manufacture and not as the personal mark of an individual or a group.

4. For the *firing*, as for the molding, an apparent distinction is made between two diverse procedures: that used by nonspecialist women, an open firing in which the pottery and the fuel are heaped together; and that of better-equipped potters who own solidly constructed kilns, with vaulted firing chambers that have a wide, regularly perforated floor. However, as before, detailed observations oblige one to make certain changes in this too simple picture. First it should be noted that the semispecialists are no more favored than the nonspecialists. To be more precise, it appears at the present stage of our knowledge that there is a perfect correlation between the use of the wheel and the kilns. By kiln is meant that, with differing details, the fundamental principle of the separation between the fire chamber and the pottery chamber is respected. But it can happen, for example, that instead of a permanent vault with vents, the firing chamber consists of a simple cylindrical wall leaving a wide, gaping opening at the top that is temporarily closed at each firing by the stacking of sherds above the pottery.

On the other hand, to reduce the difficulties of the most rudimentary form of firing, many devices have been used, principally at two points: the lowest layer and the covering of the pottery. A flat surface (sometimes limited by a ring of stones), a slight slope, or a true pit holds the pottery, which is very carefully placed on a bed of fuel. Above and around it is added the rest of the fuel—wood, straw or other dry plants, or dung cakes. These latter make possible a very effective arrangement: placed like a vault around the heap of pottery, kept in place by logs and buttressed by stones, they regulate combustion and prevent both loss of heat and drafts. An evenly distributed layer of straw can serve the same heat-regulating purpose, as can an insulating covering of earth, potsherds, etc., placed over the pottery. Finally, in certain rare cases, a kind of grating made out of iron bars holds the pottery, and it is then possible to keep a fire going under it. All these methods might suggest theoretical stages leading toward the construction of a kiln. However, in practice, they are found in dispersed order, but not generally in combinations which might serve as intermediate stages.

These descriptions of the different aspects of ceramic production in the Maghreb—the pottery, the potters, and the manufacturing processes—allow us now to try to define the relationships both between these aspects and between them and the environment; that is to say, to investigate the cultural significance of their diversity.

THE CULTURAL SIGNIFICANCE OF MAGHREB CERAMIC DIVERSITY

It is fitting to point out, first of all, that each one of these pottery-makers, co-existing in sometimes very restricted geographical areas, belongs to a specific environment, coresponding to different, although overlapping, techno-economic strata. One finds groups living in an elementary rural-type economy with largely autonomous family cells and with self-consumption of their own products. In a scarcely more differentiated rural organization one can observe a partial specialization in certain activities, usually undertaken only temporarily without giving up the usual tasks. The towns have a different professional structure which is based on a double complementary system: that of the town as a whole in relationship to the rural environment, and that of each group of workers in relationship to all the others.

North Africa, like other Mediterranean regions, has examples of these diverse strata which lived until recently in almost complete ignorance of one another, or, at any rate, with minimal commercial relationships among themselves.

We have seen that each one of the thus limited fractions could take care of its own essential ceramic needs. This explains, no doubt, why the limits of diffusion of the products are as clearly defined as those between their original groups. The conservatism, the apparent refusal to adopt pottery of better quality, or more perfected procedures, represents a problem only if one takes the technical facts into consideration separately. In a socioeconomic perspective, they become perfectly understandable. It is particularly hard to see how processes could be homogenized as long as the pottery-makers continue to be unaware of each other. Even if a piece from another potter reaches them, it is difficult for them to make creative use of it, so different are the conditions of production.

The distribution of the pottery is limited because the advantages offered are not sufficiently evident to justify even a very low price. In fact, the technical qualities count much less than one would suppose in *a priori* reasoning. The appeal of prestige or the picturesque must, on the one hand, struggle against the aesthetic and social role related to domestic production (in the town-country sense), and on the other, against the very poor technical quality of those same painted potteries (in the country-town sense).

Thus one sees the perpetuation of a plurality of traditions which go back many centuries, in the course of which some borrowings have been made, not always of the kind nor according to the criteria which it would seem should have been logically chosen. This absence of mutual influences connected with a definite historical and cultural situation certainly constitutes (*mutatis mutandis*) a valuable lesson for archeologists. In an attempt to specify its significance, we now propose to undertake an analysis of the variations described in the foregoing pages, showing a series of contrasts both between the types of production themselves, and within each type. Between the two extreme stages of domestic and artisan production particularly, a veritable inversion of certain characteristics takes place. The cases of elementary specialization hold a wavering position which seems to confirm the belief that they should be looked upon as holding a kind of intermediate place in the transition toward the craftsman .

*   *   *

One of the most obvious characteristics of domestic production is its great diversity of details against a background of a fairly restricted homogeneity of procedures and of style. Each region has its own very personal pottery, easily recognizable, freely adapted to the resources and needs of each home, even though from one end to the other of the Malghreb, all this handmade pottery belongs to one and the same stylistic and technical family. On the other hand, the production of the artisan-potters can be classified into certain clearly defined types which are distinct in appearance and in the processes used. Neither their overlapping, nor the widely spread geographic distribution of the production centers, prevent us from observing in each one of them a firm unity, leading to a standardization of production methods, and of shapes, sizes, and decoration. From this point of view, the semispecialist production diverges from both formulas; each center is noted for some adaptation made in a fairly rudimentary technique, and for a personal style, albeit a poor, monotonous one.

This same double contrast between extreme types is seen in the relationships between the techniques of forming the vessels and of finishing their surfaces. The poverty of the technical means contrasts with the extraordinary care put into the minute details of the women's domestic pottery. The artisans, on the other hand, who have better technical knowledge and equipment, finish their work much more quickly. They never take the time to work in detail on the surface finish or on the decoration. It is interesting to note here that elementary specialization shows two opposing formulas, both based on very crude technical means. The one takes advantage of these and simplifies to a maximum the details of the finish; the other puts the accent on decoration which will hide the defects caused by hasty and careless production.

The most remarkable inversion from the point of view of archeological interpretation is perhaps that which contrasts the relationships between degrees of spatial and temporal homogeneity to the two extreme stages, domestic and artisan production. The great stylistic and technical diversity of the pottery made by women in the Maghreb is accompanied by stagnation, or at least by an exceptional continuity in the same manner for many centuries. The procedures have not changed appreciably and the painted geometric decoration is more or less the the same as it was two millennia ago. On the other hand, the technical uniformity and the aesthetic standardization which, as we have seen, characterizes the work of the specialist-artisans, does not exclude either change or progress. Over the same period of time, they have gone a long way in the search for an ever more satisfying quality. Sometimes we learn of fairly exact dates when new procedures were discovered or adapted, or more often, when decorative styles were created, adapted, or abandoned.

Such a series of contrasts seems to me to justify, in the first place, the importance given to techno-economic disruptions; and, secondly, the hope placed in the ceramic evidence for the ethnological understanding of its original environment.

It will be seen even more clearly in a comparison of these observations with the way in which, at each level, a double relationship is established between the producer and the product on the one hand, and the producer and the user on the other. If it were possible to prove the existence of a fairly close tie between these two categories of phenomena, it should in fact be possible to infer from the techno-stylistic characteristics observed directly in the ceramics, certain conclusions on the economic and social structure of ancient societies.

*   *   *

If by the producer-product relationship is meant all the steps in pottery-making by which the potter selects and transforms little by little the raw material, it is obvious that between the annual production of a few vessels and the total artisan-specialization, this relationship is considerably compressed. From being episodic it becomes permanent, exclusive. The housewife who once a year replenishes her kitchenware certainly does not have to reinvent it all each time, but she has to reinstitute operational steps that had lapsed, bringing to mind again all that concerns the pottery-making cycle. This she had to do in the midst of her everyday chores. All her attention, all her available technical awareness,[1] is mobilized in this effort to reconstitute the chain of traditional steps,

1. This relationship between technical awareness and the repetition of operational steps has been observed here under the inspiration of the works of A. Leroi-Gourhan (as expressed in his lectures and in *Le Geste et la Parole,* in press).

the single, brief use of which, once a year, ensures their perpetuation and transmission from one generation to another. If occasionally an innovation is considered a success, it is integrated into the family or local stock-in-trade and gives rise to one of those minute variations which, in broad general outlines, distinguish one region or one village from another.

On the level of the elementary specialization of village potters, both men and women, we have seen that production occupies that part of their time which can be taken from their home tasks (women) and farm work (men). These seasonal operations, sometimes recurring at closer intervals, are repeated often enough to ensure a certain skill and even a certain routine, which leads to a work rhythm and often to a quality apparently at variance with the crudeness of the means employed.

When we come to the level of the artisan-specialist, a closer relationship can be observed between the producer and his product, since his whole time is devoted to his work. The frequency of the operations establishes such a routine that the chain of movements becomes mechanical. This freedom from technical awareness together with the repetition of experiences favors critical reflection. This, under the impulse of qualitative needs from the clientele and quantitative demands for productivity, spurs the search for improvements, attempts at rationalization, and adaptation of tools and of new procedures. To these conditions favorable to progress can be added the internal cohesion of the profession, proven by the uniformity and standardization previously pointed out, which permits the rapid diffusion of innovations and their conservation and accumulation by the whole group.

On the other hand, it is at the level of domestic manufacture that the producer-user relationship is limited to the point of coincidence, and functional and aesthetic adaptation show themselves to be very flexible. Each object is a direct response to the needs and taste of the user. A certain small pitcher is particularly well decorated because it is meant for a little girl who has reached the age at which she is allowed to go to the well with the women. The finely composed design in relief at the bottom of a certain dish will be found impressed every day on the family's bread. In general, the part played by personal interpretation is large enough to show the hand, the style, the skill, and the taste of each housewife, as well as the shapes and decorations characteristic of each village.

It has been seen earlier that a process of standardization starts from the most elementary form of specialization. Thus when diffusion depends on an appreciation of technical quality, the search for it can reach the point of eliminating all decoration on stereotyped-form vessels. The opposite is sometimes seen: for a tourist clientele which demands the most picturesque "souvenirs" possible, fancy objects are turned out whose abundant decoration compensates for their poor quality. As a continuation of these reflections, one might ask oneself whether, from the most ancient times, the production of nonfunctional objects (ritual objects, for example) has always been free from this type of deviation.

At the stage of craftsmanship, the relationships are more distant, without, however, reaching a total lack of recognition, since the clientele of the most specialized potters almost never oversteps the cultural limits. It is only very rarely that commissioned work is done for a private customer; as a general rule, it is a question of production in long impersonal series which scarcely ever go from the potters to the customers without the intervention of an intermediary, who transmits the preferences of the latter to the former by the rhythm of his restocking. Since they all live in the same environment and participate in the same kind of traditional life, function and style are, to a certain extent, the expression of this life, but production follows rules established as an end-product of the collective norms and the imperatives of productivity. These latter, it would seem, are at least partially responsible for the phenomena of evolution, slow progress or brusque stylistic changes, which have already been pointed out, in contrast to the stability of domestic production. To attract and hold a clientele which is being sought after by competitors, and thanks to the greater variety of procedures which technical progress allows, novelties are launched on the market; those which are considered successful are continued, and fashions are created and renewed.

After these reflections, it would appear that an affirmative answer might be given to the question as to whether techno-stylistic characteristics show certain kinds of techno-economic relationships. Nevertheless, we must define this conclusion and point out certain slight differences, and recall that the pottery in question has appeared to us as so many coherent, organic units, and not as the sum total of a variable number of traits that we could dissociate and consider separately. No doubt, given the variety of possible combinations, ceramics is a privileged document. It constitutes, in my opinion, one of the best material proofs of the unity of the inner milieu in which a human group lives, that dynamic, living balance which one always sees set up among the diverse sectors of activity. But that in itself prevents haphazard questioning. Putting oneself again in the original archeological perspective, one realizes that the very properties which increase the possibilities also impose conditions and limits on their interpretation.

SOME REFLECTIONS ON ARCHEOLOGICAL INTERPRETATION

It is not a question here, naturally, of drawing up an outline of these conditions and perspectives, but merely of emphasizing certain definite points which the ethnographic example of the Maghreb seems particularly to bring out.

First of all, as a direct result of the foregoing, the need for a global study of pottery becomes obvious. It has been seen that the different elements do not all play the same role, and what has the value of a criterion in some, perforce does not have it in others. To choose as an object of study such and such a part, such and such a law, such and such an isolated detail, is to run the risk of incurring serious errors of interpretation. At any rate, if this is done, then it is necessary that an attempt be made to limit its exact place and function in the original context.

The coexistence of several Maghrebian techniques of manufacture emphasizes a slightly different, although complementary, aspect of this preoccupation with totality. It is all these types of ceramics, at every one of the levels studied, which must be considered together, not only a few considered to be the most representative, if one really wishes to take advantage of these data and particularly to understand their cultural significance. In a given environment where various types are found, the very fact of their coexistence and the importance of divergencies between them will teach us at least as much, and possibly more, about their original culture as the specific study of each one of them.

The foregoing remarks can be applied particularly to that precise sector of the methods of study of ancient pottery which concerns the use of ethnographical data. Although it is an irreplaceable aid to archeological understanding, one should be aware of the danger of direct transpositions of such data, and particularly of all comparisons, feature by feature, between the modern and the ancient. However attractive the results may sometimes be, the comparison of isolated details errs especially through a lack of security, because it has no way of proving the equivalence of their level of significance in their respective contexts. If it does happen that an observation on modern pottery can be directly used to explain some detail of ancient pottery, the similarities should be very pronounced, since they will be used to explain more generalized situations.

The Maghrebian example emphasizes the great influence exercised by the complexity of the social and economic structures on several important characteristics of pottery. At the same time, there is considerable variation in the degree of fluidity, or on the other hand, of homogeneity and of stability in the pottery production. If contemporaneous and neighboring products show such differences in correlation with an alteration in the scale of social relationships between their respective environments, then all the more reason, it would seem, for not neglecting this element of appraisal in the choice of terms of comparison.

Rather than continue in this theoretical vein, it seems preferable to me to describe two archeological examples. I had the opportunity to study them under conditions particularly favorable for bringing out the possibilities of the technological and cultural interpretation of ancient ceramics.

*   *   *

In the field of technical understanding, however, a few preliminary remarks are necessary on the definition of technical environment (Leroi-Gourhan, 1945, pp. 362–67). This is a part of the inner milieu, the unity of which for any given human group we have already mentioned. It is a kind of guardian of the stock-in-trade accumulated by successive generations, stock-in-trade from which each one draws the elements needed for his innovations. Its homogeneity, the result of a tendency toward equilibrium of the various sectors, and its continuity are very important characteristics for us. Indeed, technological criticism depends on them for controlling the means which were really available at a given epoch—that is, what innovations were made possible by simple interplay of internal associations, and on the other hand, what progress most probably depended on the intervention of outside influence. In effect, progress is usually achieved by experimental attempts, starting with elements which are already known and mastered. It rarely represents a break with technical tradition, but rather uses this as its starting point, and favors in its turn, and within the measure of its true integration, the future stages of a continuous evolution.

Nevertheless, the rhythm is unequal, and it is known that certain conditions favor research or stagnation and withdrawal. This no doubt explains why neighboring groups having at their disposal appreciably equal means, show either immobility or dynamism. Or why, on the other hand, the simultaneity of comparable acquisitions sometimes gives the impression of contact between them, whereas a similar impulse has set in motion, by convergence, the same evolutive process. It is plain to see the reliability and the enrichment of means of study that such a criticism can provide in the presence of an important technical novelty, if one has the materials required for establishing it.

The archeological example chosen is that of pottery coming from Chalcolithic sites excavated by the French Archeological Mission in Israel, in the vicinity of Beersheba, in southern Palestine.[2] These are bowls shaped like truncated cones, giving the impression of wheel-made pottery, in contrast to all the other pieces from the stratum and of the period, which are handmade, generally of coils. The data we start with are: the proof of there having been pottery manufactured on the site itself; the similarity of the paste of the bowls with that of the other products, but the absence of any kind of a rotatory apparatus.

In the typological classification of Beersheba pottery, these bowls form a homogeneous group with respect to form (simple), size (small), and decoration (almost nonexistent). The proof of true forming on a wheel seems to me to be provided by the surest criteria, particularly the appearance of the fractured edges, whose organizational structure is clearly visible thanks to the fairly coarse texture of the paste. The bases are very roughly finished, and are emphasized by a thickening of the lowest part of the side walls and by a rough edge surrounding the base itself which is very slender and marked with irregular imprints. Their diameter averages 12 to 15 centimeters, and if occasionally they reach 20 or 22 centimeters, there is always some detail to show the difficulty that has had to be overcome in order for them to be this large. Certain rare pieces of other types show traces of probable turning in their lower body.

These marks of hesitancy, together with the ensemble of techno-economic conditions within which we believe Beersheba pottery can be placed, have led to a search, at the level of elementary specialization, for recent examples which might clarify this problem. In particular, we turned toward the Maghreb for practical personal reasons, as well as because of the reliability given by being within a common area of civilization, at least from Neolithic times onwards, and of which

2. J. Perrot, director of the excavations, has given me the technical study of his ceramic material. This work will appear as an appendix in the final publication on the site and is presented here very briefly and partly in resumé.

so many present-day features are living proofs. Without repeating details, let us recall only the great variety of adaptations observed for turning pottery, and especially several examples of shaping by rotation, although without a real wheel. It may not, therefore, be absolutely necessary to believe that a pivoting apparatus had existed and unfortunately been lost; maybe it is a question of turning without a wheel, an example of a technique in existence before the very tool which was later to become its attribute.

The proposed interpretation utilizes ethnographical examples freely, as suggested by their own flexibility at the stage under consideration, in order to try to reconstruct a process which could have been followed, since it was observed in an equivalent technical environment. The lump of earth placed on a narrow vegetal support was worked directly, by the left hand, onto the surface of a fixed disk lubricated with slip. (A stone plate, with a highly polished, slightly concave interior might have served this purpose.) The sizes and form seem to indicate that the potter, at the time of shaping, was working on the clay with one hand alone, since the height of the sides showing marks of turning corresponds exactly to that which the fingers of an average hand might reach.

This explanation has the advantage of not bringing forward a brusque creation out of nothing, nor a facile "outside influence," which in the present case would only serve to push the problem aside. In addition, it is interesting to note that it agrees with, and is the complement of, the picture which we can conjure up of Chalcolithic society. These groups in the process of socioeconomic diversification, bound by a network of very diverse exchanges, and with potters who knew their materials and their craft, trained and open to the search for improvements, constituted without any doubt a favorable environment for an innovation of such importance as this. Indeed, it seems that they combined the two essential conditions for any technical development: the need (the economic pressure of numerous customers), and the means of fulfilling it (by a decisive change in the rhythm of production).

*   *   *

We have enlarged at some length on the possibilities of a global cultural interpretation, although indirectly up to now, in order to offer here, very simply, certain points for reflection. When we asked previously if there were a tie-up between certain techno-stylistic characteristics of the wares and the economic and social conditions governing their manufacture, we were at the point of an archeological approach. If so, then it should be possible from the study of the pottery to draw conclusions as to the society in which it originated. I think it has been seen that this is so, and that such an association of many characteristics (rather than selected ones) signifies a certain relationship between the producer and the user of pottery, a certain techno-economic type. This, in spite of the many restrictions it has been seen fit to impose on it, constitutes, in itself, a very positive contribution.

Moreover, and in consequence, it is obvious that the characteristics thus held to be tied to the type of economic relationships, must be, for this very reason, discounted as being of any significance for the establishment of a stylistic and more especially, of a chronological typology. Thus, as a complement to technological criticism, the elimination of a new series of facts of convergence is effected, and the purely archeological interpretation (in an ultimate sense) gains in reliability what it loses in variety of criteria.

These two points will be illustrated by a single example, taken as previously from the archeology of the Near East, to be precise from the Syro-Palestinian hills and coast, during the period of at least three millennia which stretches from the first known ceramic documents to the end of the Early Bronze Age (about 2000 B.C.).[3]

The majority of the fundamental characteristics of the present contemporaneous strata of the Maghreb are found in successive periods, and rarely has the diachronic utilization of synchronic comparative data appeared more justified: in the Neolithic, against a common, rather poor, technical background, a very rich variety of procedures and decorative effects can be observed from one region to another and in the same stratum (especially at Byblos). Then, in the Chalcolithic, there appears everywhere, abruptly, a considerable impoverishment of decoration and of finish, while styles and manufacturing methods differ slightly according to the sites or the regional groups. In the Early Bronze Age, the overall picture is somewhat different: clearly defined types, chronologically more or less close to each other, are found, if not everywhere, at least in many sites, and constitute very good key-fossils for establishing comparative dating. The homogeneity, both technical and stylistic, of each one of these types is to be noted. One, which stands out increasingly clearly from the beginning to the latter part of the period, is remarkable for its beautiful technical quality which is accompanied by a rudimentary and stereotyped decoration.

It is striking to find among the stages of this chronological series some of the comparisons observed in North Africa. Taking in particular the two extreme periods of the Neolithic and the Early Bronze, one comes face to face with clearly different characteristics, and even with an inversion of the relationships both between the manufactures of the same period and their spatial and temporal distribution, and between the technical preoccupations and decorative research. Now these comparisons are the same as those which the example taken in modern times showed us between producer and product on the one hand, and between producer and users on the other. That is why their appearance among archeological documents makes one think that, doubtless, pottery was not put aside in the movement which marked the evolution of societies in the Near East between the fifth and the third millennia. While the human groups, for a long time limited to agricultural village cells, spread and organized themselves ever more strongly into villages and states, their activities became diversified and specialized, to give

3. The important collection of specimens from the Early Periods of Byblos will be used particularly. Their technical study, undertaken at the request of M. Dunand, will be published as an appendix in the final publication on the site.

rise to professional structures of the artisan type. The very characteristics of the pottery of the Early Bronze seem to me to prove that at about the middle of the third millennium, specialist-artisans produced them for a fairly large clientele (going outside the limits of the town and of the small region in all probability) and were perhaps in contact with each other over considerable distances.

In this respect, the intermediate period of the Chalcolithic is particularly interesting, because in it can be observed certain signs of a differentiation of activities in a structure which is still predominantly rural. The Chalcolithic pottery contrasts with the Neolithic at Byblos, for example, because of the sudden homogeneity of its shapes and decoration which make it possible for just a few pieces to represent the majority. The technical procedures show no change from the preceding period, but a greater regularity, together with the standardization and the rapidity of the finishing, seem to bear witness to products wrought by only a few hands, implying a certain degree of, as yet, very elementary artisanal specialization.

This same Chalcolithic example illustrates very well the limits that such a techno-economical interpretation imposes, in my opinion, on the chronological use of data. In the whole zone in which we are interested, one can observe the same contrast between the richness of the decorative formulas of the Neolithic and initial Chalcolithic and this pottery, whose mediocre sameness gives, at first sight, the impression of a general regression.

Now, if one holds these characteristics to be the criteria of a production already at least partially commercialized in contrast to a more independent stage, it seems obvious to me that one cannot be satisfied with them in maintaining either the hypothesis of contacts established between the production centers which presented them simultaneously, or the hypothesis of a sudden political or ethnic upheaval, at any rate not without examining very carefully the possibility of a parallel evolution under the influence of common conditions.

Speaking generally, a stylistic identity has very different significance according to whether it is seen in Neolithic products or in those of a later period, particularly those where the existence of political and commercial relationships is apparent. Thus, it seems to me very significant that there are great difficulties in the way when one wishes to establish chronological connections for the Neolithic where the ceramic styles are well differentiated, while in this respect later periods pose no problem. Perhaps we should see in this the proof that for a long time pottery was a local, even a family production, each decorative formula having its area of expansion within the frontiers of still limited social groups. Then these styles, although deficient as chronological documents, might be studied to find out the extent of intervillage relationships, blood relationships, or those of a complementary economy.

To end these remarks on the help which modern data can furnish in the interpretation of archeological ceramic documents, I will recall here the disappointment expressed by F. R. Matson (1951, pp. 113–14), among others, at the frequently incomplete character of the descriptions of which ethnographical literature is full; and in the same spirit, the refusal given by A. O. Shepard (1956, p. 93) to requests for a questionnaire for pottery observations. However long a list of questions may be, there is always the risk of leaving something out, hence of keeping from a conscientious observer the unexpected detail or the unusual association which might be the most significant thing in a given context. The author thus clearly indicates what the demands are for such an archeological set-up; an increase in the number and precision of the observations is of less importance in the long run than an understanding of their integration in the technical ensemble and the whole cultural environment, that is to say in a truly ethnological perspective.

BIBLIOGRAPHY

BALFET, H.

1952. "Problèmes Relatifs à la Position Sociale de la Potiére." *Comptes Rendus Sommaires des Séances de L'Institut Français d'Anthropologie*, 6:20–22.

1955. "La Poterie des Aït Smail du Djurdura. Éléments d'étude esthetique." *Revue Africaine*, 99:289–340.

1957. "Les Poteries Modelées d'Algérie dans les Collections du Musée du Bardo." Algiers: Département d'Ethnographie, Centre Algérien de Recherches Anthropologiques, Prehistoriques et Ethnographiques.

1963. "Fabrication de poterie à Djerba (Tunisie), Contribution aux recherches sur le tour de potier." *Actes du VI Congrés Internationel des Sciences. Anthropologiques et Ethnologiques* (Paris), T.II, Vol. 1:499–503.

LEROI-GOURHAN, A.

1945. *Milieu et Techniques*. Paris: A. Michel.

In press. *Le Geste et la Parole*. Paris: A. Michel.

MATSON, F. R.

1951. "Ceramic Technology as an Aid to Cultural Interpretation—Techniques and Problems." In *Essays on Archaeological Methods*, James B. Griffin, (ed.). Ann Arbor: Museum of Anthropology, University of Michigan, Anthropological Papers, No. 8:102–16.

SHEPARD, A. O.

1956. *Ceramics for the Archaeologist*. Washington, D.C.: Carnegie Institution of Washington, Publication 609.

THE POTTERY FOUND IN THE TOMB
OF NEFERWPTAH AND ITS SIGNIFICANCE

ZAKY ISKANDER

INTRODUCTION

THE TOMB of Princess Neferwptaḥ was discovered in April, 1956 at Hawaret El-Maqtaʻ which is about 13 kilometers to the southeast of the Fayûm city. This tomb lies in the center of some ruins of mud bricks which proved to be the remains of her pyramid.

The tomb was covered by seven huge limestone blocks each weighing about 15 tons, and was almost completely submerged in the infiltration water. It was divided by a partition wall into two subchambers, one small towards the north, which acted as an offering chamber, and the other large, which was the burial chamber (Fig. 1).

The offering chamber contained a tall "ḥs" vase of silver and a big granite offering table over which lay many fragments of pottery dishes containing small votive vases and surrounded by clay jars. The burial chamber contained two other silver vases and a huge sarcophagus of pink granite weighing about 35 tons. The offering table, the silver vases, and the sarcophagus were inscribed with the name of Neferwptaḥ, the daughter of King Amenemhet III of the XIIth Dynasty (1841–1792 B.C.).

The sarcophagus was found almost filled with infiltration water. After siphoning out this water, it was found that the original contents of the sarcophagus had been reduced to a muddy mass on its bottom, about 5 centimeters thick. These muddy remains contained a fair quantity of scattered gold leaf, fragments of a large alabaster jar full of a dark-brown material, some small alabaster vases, conical truncated beads of faience and carnelian, pieces of blue frit, and many beads of faience and blue frit (Fig. 2).

The author went down into the sarcophagus and carefully cleared its contents which were taken to the chemical laboratory of the Department of Antiquities at Cairo for restoration and study. From this study, it was concluded that the mummy of Neferwptaḥ had been adorned with a broad collar of gold, carnelian and feldspar; a necklace of gold, sard and carnelian beads; a pair of bracelets of gold, feldspar and carnelian beads; a pair of anklets of gold and carnelian beads; and a girdle of disk beads of faience and blue frit with a hawk pendant of carnelian. (The girdle, which was usually put around the abdomen over the embalming incision indicates that the owner of this tomb had been mummified.) Over the linen bandages, the mummy wore a funerary apron of faience and blue frit beads. (These were provided only for women.) The mummy was then put in a wooden

178

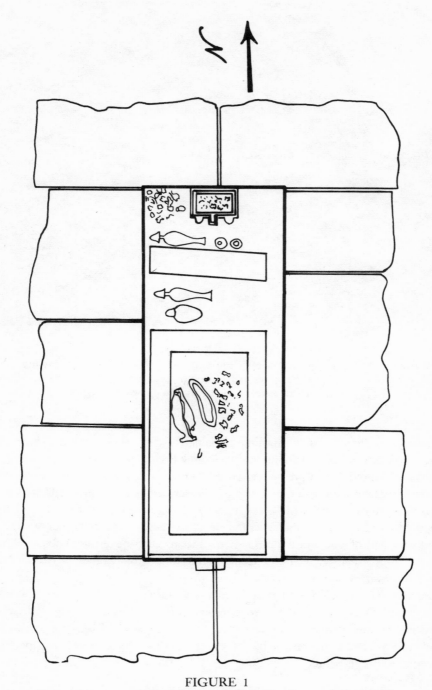

FIGURE 1
Plan of the tomb showing the offering chamber and the burial
chamber with their contents.

FIGURE 2

The inside of the sarcophagus after siphoning the water out of it, showing the broken parts of the large alabaster jar (a), and some parts of the flail (b) and eye-panel (c), beads of the apron (d), and the alabaster cosmetic vases (e).

anthropoid coffin of which nothing remained except a "sewrt" necklace and a broad carnelian collar, inlaid in the neck and breast areas respectively.

The anthropoid coffin was enclosed in a rectangular wooden coffin of which nothing remained except some of the gold-inscribed bands which adorned it and the parts of an eye-panel which was inlaid on its eastern side. Between the anthropoid coffin and the rectangular coffin was laid a set of ceremonial staves consisting of a flail of gilt wood and faience and carnelian beads, an alabaster headed mace, a "w',s" scepter, a "d'm" scepter and some other staves of wood coated with fine gesso plaster and overlaid with gold leaf.

The rectangular coffin with all its contents was then put in the large red granite sarcophagus. Over the lid of the rectangular coffin were put a large alabaster jar containing a medicament for removing the white spots from the eyes and a wooden box containing ten alabaster cosmetic vases for holding the perfumes, unguents, and eye-paints.

THE POTTERY

Since the pots had been lying in water for hundreds of years, they had become very friable, and some of them were found broken into many pieces, especially the wide dishes of coarse brown ware. They were, therefore, carefully washed with distilled water, dried, and then treated with 7 percent polyvinyl acetate (PVA) solution in organic solvents to consolidate them. The broken pieces were stuck together with a water emulsion of PVA, and the missing parts were completed with a mixture of plaster of Paris and the water emulsion of PVA.

The total number of pots originally placed in the offering chamber was most probably 69. These vessels are classified in Table 1.

TABLE 1

Type	Number of Pots	Fig.	Mouth diam. (cm.)	Height (cm.)
1	3	3	9.6–13.2	23.6–35.6
2	2	4	2.5	5.1
3	23	4	5.5	4.0
4	18	4	7.2	2.2
5	4	4	11.0	2.9
6	2	4	2.5	8.3
7	8	4	2.0	6.5
8	2	4	2.5	5.8
9	7	6	20.2–47.0	4.9–12.2

Type 1.—The three big jars belonging to Type 1 are ovoid, narrow-necked, and made of coarse brown ware coated on the exterior with a brick-red slip of red ochre (Fig. 3). They were found supported on ring-shaped stands of the same kind of ware, and they varied in external diameter from 15.3 to 16.5 centimeters, and in height from 6.5 to 7.0 centimeters. Similar jars and stands have been found in some tombs of the XIIth Dynasty (De Morgan, 1895, Vol. 1, Figs. 78, 82: 1903, Vol. II, Fig. 105; Petrie *et al.*, 1912, Pl. XXXIII; Petrie, 1890, Pl. XII).

Such jars were used in Ancient Egypt for keeping beer and wine. They are shown in some scenes of the Middle Kingdom illustrating brewing and the preparation of wine (Davies and Gardiner, 1920, Pls. XI, XII; Newberry, 1893, Vol. I, Pl. XII). As shown in these scenes and in the similar scenes from the Old Kingdom (Steindorff, 1913, Pls. 83, 84) and the New Kingdom (Davies, 1917, Pl. XXV), the wine jars were sealed with stoppers of clay, put on while wet, and usually plastered down over the shoulder of the jars. One or more holes were made in each stopper in order to provide a way for the escape of the carbon dioxide produced during fermentation, so that the jar would not burst. Such holes are shown in the wine jars from the tomb of Tut-ankh-Amun (Carter, 1933, Vol. III, pp. 148–49) and in some of those from the Monastery of Epiphanius at Thebes (Winlock and Crum, 1926, Vol. I, p. 79).

No remains of beer or wine, however, could be detected in the mud found in the three jars of Neferwptaḥ. They had, most probably, mud stoppers which vanished completely as a result of their long immersion in water.

Types 2–8.—The 59 dishes, vases, and cups belonging to Types 2–8 are made of smooth yellowish-brown ware (Fig. 4). Some pots of these types of Middle Kingdom date were found at Dahshûr (De Morgan, 1895, Vol. I, Figs. 17, 168),

FIGURE 3
The three ovoid pots on their stands (Type 1).

FIGURE 4
The different types of the small dishes, cups and vases (Types 2–8).

Hawara (Petrie *et al.*, 1912, Pls. XXXIII, XXXIV), Kahûn (Petrie, 1890, Pl. XIII), and Lisht (Mace and Winlock, 1916, Fig. 82, Pl. XXXIV).

The finding of these pots on or with the granite offering table in the tomb of Neferwptaḥ, helps to define the uses to which they were put. The upper surface of this offering table is surrounded with a frame containing the magical formula of offerings (Fig. 5). Enclosed by the frame are representations in relief of loaves, birds, meat, dining tables, and vases or cups similar to the small pots found with the offering table. In these reliefs the small vases are represented in rows beside each other or on the dining tables. The names of their contents were recorded on a similar alabaster offering table belonging to the same princess and previously discovered by Petrie in the Hawara Pyramid of her father (Petrie, 1890, pp. 8, 17, Pl. V; Kamal, 1909, T. I, pp. 10–15: T. II, Pl. VII). This offering table has the name of every kind of offering written on it. Although some of these names could not be translated with certainty, we can still conclude that the vases represented were used to contain beer, wine, water, natron, butter, bread, cakes, and different kinds of fruits.

These small cups, dishes, and vases might have been, therefore, the models of vessels used in everyday life for holding or serving such foods and drinks in

FIGURE 5
The grey granite offering table of Neferwptaḥ.

Ancient Egypt. This idea will be further confirmed by describing the vessels used in banquets as depicted on the walls of the Ancient Egyptian tombs.

Type 9.—The seven dishes belonging to this type are mostly made of coarse brown ware, and on their outer surfaces are traces of rope marks under the rim Fig. 6). These marks denote that the ancient Egyptian potter used the same system still used by the modern Egyptian potter who twists a short length of cord two or three times around the largest diameter of his pots before removing them from the wheel to keep them from collapsing while drying in the sun before baking. The fragments of the dishes which were still lying on the offering table contained nothing but some of the small votive vases. Dishes of the same kind containing such small votive pottery pots have also been found at Lisht (Mace and Winlock, 1916, pp. 111–12, Pl. XXXV) and Dahshûr (De Morgan, 1895, Vol. I, Figs. 250, 252: 1903 Vol. II, Fig. 105). The other contents of the dishes must have decomposed and vanished during their long immersion in the infiltration water.

Undoubtedly, however, some of these dishes were intended to hold food offerings, since dishes of the same kind containing remains of beef joints, ribs of beef, a goose, and trussed ducks have been found in the tomb of Senebtisi at Lisht (Mace and Winlock, 1916, Pl. XXXV), and some containing bones have been found in the tomb of Ita at Dahshûr (De Morgan, 1903, Vol. II, Fig. 105). Some others of these dishes might also have contained small clay pellets as imitation incense balls (Mace and Winlock, 1916, Pl. XXXV; De Morgan, 1903, Vol. II, Fig. 105).

SIGNIFICANCE OF THIS SET OF POTTERY

The ancient Egyptians enjoyed life to its utmost and they liked to put or picture in their tombs objects or scenes representing the pleasures which they enjoyed

FIGURE 6
One of the flat
dishes (Type 9).

during their life so that their souls might enjoy the same in the hereafter. The banquets depicted on the walls of many of their tombs give a true picture of their joyful days since they are identical in every detail with those at which the occupant of the tomb had presided during his life on earth (Montet, 1958, p. 91).

In these banquets, for example (Wilkinson, 1878, Vol. II, Fig. 305), we see a maid servant presenting a cup of wine to a gentleman seated beside a lady on chairs; another female attendant is offering wine to a guest, a napkin in her left hand for wiping his mouth after drinking. Other serving boys and girls go around offering ointment, wreaths, perfumes, etc., while the singers challenge the guests to "celebrate the joyful day with contented heart and a spirit full of gladness" (Erman, 1894, p. 255). In a corner of the banquet room is a table piled with cakes, bread, meat, geese and other birds, grapes in baskets, flowers, and big stoppered wine and beer jars. This is very similar to present-day cocktail parties where the guests go on talking while the servants go around serving drinks and foods from the tables containing them.

If we examine the offering table of Neferwptah (Fig. 5), we find that most of the foods, drinks, etc., offered in the Ancient Egyptian banquets are represented on it: namely, six dining tables piled with bread, cakes, and cups of beer and wine; twelve kinds of bread; eleven kinds of biscuits and pastry; fourteen kinds of liquid offerings, such as beer, wine, water, etc., contained in cups or vases; fifteen kinds of fruits, pastry, and natron contained in baskets; seven kinds of meat; five kinds of birds; and two bands of onions.

In the text of the magical formula on the offering table, it is mentioned that these offerings are given to the Ka of the princess. These offerings were, therefore, put in the pottery found with it in the offering chamber so that the Ka of the princess might enjoy them in the same way that her body had enjoyed them during her life. Beer and wine were put in the three big jars; meat, bread, fruits, incense, etc., were put in the flat dishes; and the small cups, dishes, and vases were perhaps the actual vessels, or more probably just models of the vessels, used for serving these foods and drinks as shown in the banquet scenes. This is confirmed by one of the scenes in the tomb of Antefoker and his wife Senet (Davies and Gardiner, 1920, Pl. XXXIII) of the Middle Kingdom at Thebes, in which we see three sealed wine jars (similar to the three jars of Type 1 shown in Fig. 3) on one of the tables and a maid pouring wine into a cup (similar to the cups of Type 3 in Fig. 4) from a fourth unstoppered jar for her mistress's refreshment.

The pottery found in the tomb of Neferwptah forms, therefore, a complete set of the different vessels used in common life during the Middle Kingdom in Ancient Egypt. It illustrates how the Egyptians kept their food and drink, how they served them, and lastly, how they enjoyed them in life and after death. (For a complete report on this excavation see Iskander and Farag, in press.)

BIBLIOGRAPHY

CARTER, H.
1933. *The Tomb of Tut-ankh-Amen*, III. London: Cassell.

DAVIES, N. DE G.
1917. *The Tomb of Nakht at Thebes*. New York: Metropolitan Museum of Art.

DAVIES, N. DE G., and A. H. GARDINER
1920. *The Tomb of Antefoker and His Wife Senet*. London: Egypt Exploration Society.

ERMAN, A.
1894. *Life in Ancient Egypt*. London: Macmillan.

ISKANDER, Z., and N. FARAG
In pres⸗ _he Tomb of Neferwptah*. Cairo: Department of Antiquities, U.A.R.

KAMAL, AHMED BEY
1909. *Tables d'Offrandes*. Catalogue Général des Antiquités Egyptiennes du Musée du Caire, T. I, No. 23013. Cairo: Service des Antiquités de l'Egypte.

MACE, A. C., and H. E. WINLOCK
1916. *The Tomb of Senebtisi at Lisht*. New York: Metropolitan Museum of Art.

MONTET, P.
1958. *Everyday Life in Egypt in the Days of Ramesses the Great*. London: Edward Arnold.

MORGAN, J. DE
1895. *Fouilles à Dahchour I, Mars-Juin, 1894*. Vienna: Adolphe Holzhausen.
1903. *Fouilles à Dahchour II, 1894–1895*. Vienna: Adolphe Holzhausen.

NEWBERRY, P. E.
1893. *Beni Hasan* I. London: Egypt Exploration Society.

PETRIE, W. M. F.
1890. *Kahûn, Gurob and Hawara*. London: Egypt Exploration Society.

PETRIE, W. M. F., G. A. WAINWRIGHT, and E. MACKAY
1912. *The Labyrinth, Gerzeh and Mazghuneh*. London: British School of Archaeology in Egypt.

STEINDORFF, G.
1913. *Das Grab des Ti*. Leipzig: Hinrichs'sche Buchhandlung.

WILKINSON, J. G.
1878. *The Manners and Customs of the Ancient Egyptians*, II. London: John Murray.

WINLOCK, H. E., and W. E. CRUM
1926. *The Monastery of Epiphanius at Thebes*. New York: Metropolitan Museum of Art.

CERAMICS AND THE SUPERNATURAL:
CULT AND BURIAL EVIDENCE IN THE AEGEAN WORLD

SAUL S. WEINBERG

GREEK pottery is, I believe, unique in the ancient world not so much for the quantity of it which was produced and which has survived, but rather for the amount of information concerning both the names and uses of the vessels which has come down to us. This information is embodied in two separate traditions, literary and pictorial. Many ancient authors supply the names of vessels, some describe them and explain their use. As a result there is complete certainty in many instances as to the type of vessel to which a name belongs, and even its use. For others there is less certainty, and there are still many types of vessels for which the proper name is not surely known; there are also names known which cannot certainly be identified with any known shapes. The pictorial tradition includes the numerous illustrations of vases in vase-painting, in mural-painting (especially Etruscan), and in sculpure. Here, too, there are sometimes written names with the pictures. The pictorial tradition is especially valuable for showing how pottery was used in daily life, in religion, or as burial offerings. Much of this information has been conveniently collected in a number of publications; the most useful single one is perhaps Gisela M. A. Richter's *Shapes and Names of Athenian Vases* (1935), in which texts, ancient illustrations, and the actual vases are all combined.

The pottery itself exists in very large quantities, and when found in controlled excavations it often has associated information on provenance which may either confirm or supplement what we know from other sources about the various uses to which pottery was put. Thus, pottery found in or about burials can usually be associated either with burial practices or with a cult of the dead; to distinguish between these uses is often more difficult. Commonly, much of the pottery which served as burial offerings was that of everyday use as well. On the other hand, the white-ground lekythoi are generally considered to have been incapable of standing daily use because of their evanescent colors (Cook, 1960, p. 233); their association with the tomb is well attested. The same is true of various Hellenistic polychrome wares, such as the Hadra polychrome hydrias and the Canosa vases of Apulia (Cook, 1960, pp. 209–10), both of which were used as containers of ashes. The latter often had large and unusual shapes, frequently with elaborate plastic additions. The large red-figured volute-kraters of Apulia seem also to have been made especially for burials (Cook, 1960, p. 231); their great size almost precludes usefulness. In the same category are the colossal Late Geometric

amphorae and kraters that were designed as grave markers, predecessors of the
stone stelae of the seventh century B.C. and later. Such vases commonly have a
hole in the bottom of the bowl, through which offerings to the dead were made.
Holes that render vessels useless for ordinary domestic purposes are common in
those meant for cult practices or for funerary offerings.[1] At the opposite extreme
are miniature vessels too small for practical use, except as toys, which are so often
found in the graves of the young, almost never in their houses. Thus, in the
period for which we have the most complete documentation, two characteristics
distinguish pottery associated primarily with burials: (1) a size too great or too
small to make the vases useful in daily life (for most of the large ones are hardly
portable, even without contents, and would be unusable except for storage when
filled, yet they are clearly not storage vessels); (2) decoration that is too delicate
or impermanent to withstand continuous use but which is sufficient for the single
handling of a burial offering.

Offerings common in Greek graves also include vases of types well known from
houses, clearly objects of daily use that were brought to the grave. These include
such small containers of oil or scents as the alabastron, the aryballos, and the
lekythos (other than the white-ground type), other toilet vases such as the
plemochoë, pouring vessels such as the oinochoë, many kinds of cups and bowls,
probably offered with their contents. But also found in the graves are a variety
of vessels which, while not exclusively for burial purposes, are not associated with
daily life but rather with some cult. In the tombs of the unmarried were often
placed those vessels which played a part in the marriage ceremony—the loutrophoros (Richter, 1935, p. 5), in which the nuptial bath was brought; the lebes
gamikos (Richter, 1935, p. 11), or marriage bowl; and the lekane (Richter, 1935,
p. 23), usually covered, in which gifts were brought to the newly wed. The chous
was offered to the child who did not live to receive it at the Anthesteria (Van
Hoorn, 1951), the blossom festival of early spring at which children in their
third year were initiated into the religious community. These are all offerings
which were part of the burial rite; other rites that followed burial were part of the
cult of the dead. Here, too, the white-ground lekythos played a prominent role,
but alabastra and aryballoi were also used, and the pyxis and oinochoë are frequently shown at the tomb.

With many cults, certain types of vessels are closely associated: the Panathenaic
amphora filled with oil was given as a prize to participants in the Panathenaic
games (Richter, 1935, p. 3); the kernos—a multiple recepticle for the first fruits
of the season (Harrison, 1927, p. 293)—was used in the Eleusinian festival; the
kantharos is intimately associated with Dionysos (Richter, 1935, pp. 25–26); at
the Isthmian sanctuary were found quantities of a special type of lamp apparently
used as a cult vessel in the mystery cult of Palaimon-Melikertes and not known

---

1. With regard to vessels with holes that render them incapable of holding contents, Matson
asked if these could not be measuring vessels. Such do exist, for instance, the "klepsydra" in
Greece, but in many instances such an explanation is precluded. Solheim mentioned the Philippine practice of "killing" a vase by means of a hole near the bottom.

elsewhere in Greece (Broneer, 1958, pp. 16–17). We have already mentioned those cult vessels which are at times found as grave offerings: loutrophoros, lebes gamikos, lekane, chous. Others, while not associated with a particular cult, are clearly special vessels for sacral use: the phial or libation bowl (Von Bothmer, 1962, p. 154), the perirrhanterion—a holy-water font (Weinberg, 1943, p. 50; Broneer, 1958, pp. 24–27). Cult-connected as well are the many thousands of miniature vessels found in the *favissae* of numerous sanctuaries in the Greek world (for instance, Verdelis, 1962);[2] these inexpensive votive offerings frequently reveal the nature of the worship and the special types of vessels associated with one or another cult. It is interesting to note how many of these vessels are handmade in a period when the wheel had long been in use. Handmade vessels also occur as offerings in graves, again alongside wheel-made vases. While this may represent a measure of economy, it is also highly probable that there was a certain sanctity associated with the older tradition of handmade ware.

Thus our picture of ceramics used as part of cult or burial rites in Classical Greece is fairly complete, though little special study has been devoted to the subject and much more could be learned. The record goes back, with diminishing detail, into the Geometric Period, but before about 800 B.C. the picture fades rapidly, and for the Dark Age following the Dorian Invasion, is most indistinct. It might be expected that the farther back one goes the less information would be available. Yet this is not so, for we have always had a fairly good idea of religious practices in the Minoan-Mycenaean world, and new light has been shed by the decipherment of the Linear B Script (Ventris and Chadwick, 1956, pp. 125–29). It is of interest that the famous Pylos Tablet which served as proof of Ventris' decipherment contains a list of vessels, for which both ideogram and name are given; although these are largely of metal, clay vessels are also listed among the tablets. Many of the tablets have to do with the gods as recipients of offerings; almost all the great gods and many of the lesser ones of later Greek religion are known (Jameson, 1960), thus establishing a continuity in cult which had not been expected.

Yet the major evidence for the cults of the now protohistoric Minoan-Mycenaean period still comes from the excavation of numerous shrines and other cult places and from the depiction of religious scenes in painting and glyptic art. While the evidence for Minoan religion is fairly plentiful for both the Middle and Late Minoan phases, from about 2000 B.C. to 1200 B.C., and there are significant indications of continuity of some elements from Early Minoan, perhaps as early as 3000 B.C., the evidence for Mycenaean religion is restricted to the Late Helladic phase, from 1600–1200 B.C. That Crete and the mainland had much in common in the Late Bronze Age is now clear. They had in common, too, certain types

---

2. Miniature vessels were discussed at length and Foster observed that in Mexico, all types of vessels were produced in miniature and sold in the markets, especially at fiestas, and that they were entirely unconnected with cult. This is true of many miniatures in the Aegean as well, but it is equally true that almost every sanctuary yields its hoards of miniature vessels and that inscriptions painted or scratched on them leave no doubt that they were votives.

of burial offerings; some of the finest products of Cretan workshops found their way into royal or princely burials on the mainland. These are largely of metal, often precious, but many fine Cretan pottery vases, or mainland imitations of them, also occur. How many, if any, of these were other than the vessels of daily life is difficult to determine. The rhyton has often been described as a ritual vessel (Nilsson, 1950, pp. 144–46), but it seems more than likely than many rhyta were luxury vessels of daily use which were often brought to the grave and which were at times dedicated to gods or used in the cult of one or another of them. It is not clear that any vessels used as burial offerings during these periods were made specifically for this purpose, except perhaps the miniature vessels often found in children's graves, and even these may have been their toys.

For various cults, including the cult of the dead, there is a variety of vessels, of clay as well as many more precious materials, that are believed to have been made for cult use only; this belief, in most instances, is based on circumstances of finding, in only a few cases on the illustration of their use in cult scenes. In his discussion of sacral vessels, Nilsson (1950, p. 147) states that the high-necked and high-handled libation jug is the only vessel shown in cult scenes. While most such ewers were of metal, they are known in pottery as well and from contexts that suggest sacral use. Although not a vessel, the triton or conch shell is shown being used by a priestess as a horn, and pottery imitations of such shells have also been found in cult deposits (Nilsson, 1950, pp. 153–54).

While tomb deposits are known from all Minoan periods, the earliest shrines excavated are of the Middle Minoan I phase, about 2000 B.C., and from then on there is a continuous sequence of shrines connected with palaces, houses, and tombs. Sir Arthur Evans (1921–35, *passim*) has described almost all of them, giving attention to the various types of cult vessels. Nilsson added the evidence which appeared subsequently (1950, pp. 117–54), and still more has accumulated in the last decade. The criteria by which Nilsson distinguished what vessels other than the oft-illustrated libation jugs are to be judged as cult-related are (1) shape, which usually makes such vessels unsuitable or unfit for practical use, and (2) provenance from sanctuaries or sacral deposits. Sometimes both conditions coincide.

As in the historic period, miniature vessels are frequently found, probably votives rather than cult vessels. Many votive bowls have plastic additions to the interior, guaranteeing their unfitness for practical use. Some have single animal or bird figures, some flowers; one remarkable example has a herdsman and his herd —some 160 animals, sheep or oxen. There are many examples of multiple vessels— small bowls or jugs attached to the rim or to the interior of a large vessel or to a ring or a slab of clay, bowls, or jugs clustered about a central support. These are clearly related to the kernoi of historic times, and their development can be traced through three millennia, beginning in Early Minoan I (Nilsson, 1950, pp. 134–43). Throughout, they seem to have served for offerings of first fruits, be it to the Great Minoan Goddess, to Rhea, or to Demeter. Besides those from sanctuaries, there are others both from tombs and from houses, but the sacral connection of the type is generally accepted. They come from all parts of the

Aegean world, though the Cycladic and Helladic examples are never so early as some of those from Crete.

Cult-connected, as well, are the many offering tables (Nilsson, 1950, pp.122–30), likewise known from Crete, the Cyclades, and the mainland of Greece. The tripod variety is common, but there are others with four legs or with a central support. A single central cupped depression, two or three depressions, or a whole row of them all occur. Such cupped depressions were at times replaced by shallow mini-ature bowls attached to the table. Some tables without cups have been classed as altars or movable hearths, both for domestic and cult use. Like the type with central support are the pedestaled vases, or "fruitstands," found in some shrines. Offertory bowls, often found with remains of food still inside them, occur frequently in sacral deposits. Whether the offerings were made to deities or to the dead, similar containers were used.

In the Aegean world a rich variety exists in the vessels associated with chthonic cults. The snake is the ever-present symbol of most such cults, and snakes abound in the plastic decoration of the vessels connected with them, vessels which in other respects present a bizarre appearance (Evans, 1921–35, Vol. IV, pp. 138–60). Many show the snakes drinking from small bowls placed about the rim of the vessel; similar "milk" bowls occur as offerings in the shrines, and Evans suggested that they were used for feeding household snakes as well. Evans also associated the bull's head rhyton with chthonic rites as a libation vase (Evans, 1921–35, Vol. II, p. 138). Clay votive bulls are well known as offerings, especially from some of the cave sanctuaries. Some bull rhyta have acrobats attached at the horns, asso-ciating them with the large variety of bull-vaulting scenes in the pictorial repre-sentations and also the various kinds of figurines showing bull and acrobat.

Incense burners (thymiateria) have been found both in shrines and in tombs; in the later case they have also been interpreted as fumigators for tombs that were opened for successive burials (Evans, 1921–35, Vol. IV, pp. 1011–12). Many have a deep-bowled form with a scalloped, wide-splaying lip and a large handle. Some are decorated with imperfectly fixed color, suggesting a parallel with vases of the historic period which have been judged as made for one-time use.

Lastly, there are the so-called hut urns, some of which have a figure of a god-dess inside, seen through an open doorway (Evans, 1921–35, Vol. II, pp. 128–32). These figures are like those well-known images of the Late Minoan III period which have their hands raised, representing either a goddess or her worshippers (Caskey, 1962).

Thus in the protohistoric period as well, the criteria which distinguish sacral pottery from domestic equipment are not unlike those for the historic period. Vessels too small for practical use are common both in graves and sanctuaries, but few vessels in the sacral group are too large for domestic use. Many of the cult-connected vessels have peculiar features which make them unfit for domestic use. In the case of at least one group, the painted decoration is too fugitive to withstand much handling,[3] suggesting that the vessels were perhaps used only

3. In discussing the use of fugitive paint on cult vessels, Solheim cited the practice in Borneo and Shepard noted its occurrence on Mayan mortuary pottery.

once, certainly not more than a few times. These criteria, together with provenance and group association, have helped to set apart a large number of Minoan
and Mycenaean pottery types which can be identified with good probability as
burial offerings or cult objects.

When we go back still farther to what must be considered the truly prehistoric
period, unilluminated either by written records or much, if any, pictorial tradition,
we become totally dependent on the objects themselves, and on the information
associated with them, for whatever we may learn about religious or burial
practices and the related ceramics. It is the Early Bronze Age, covering the entire
third millennium, with which we must first be concerned, though on the mainland
of Greece the Middle Helladic period, from 2000–1600 B.C., falls into this prehistoric phase as well. In following our plan of working backward, from the
better known to the less well known, we should consider first the mainland in
the Middle Helladic period. A large number of burials of this period have been
excavated, giving us a good idea of burial practices and of the offerings brought
to the grave. However, after a thorough study of the remains, Mylonas found no
evidence for a cult of the dead (Mylonas, 1951, pp. 68–82); others have seen
scattered evidence of such a cult. Offerings in these Middle Helladic graves are
very scant, perhaps because some of the objects brought to the burial were placed
around or above, rather than in the grave. What objects have been found suggest
the use of ordinary domestic vessels rather than the existence of any special types
as grave offerings. We are no better off with respect to the cults of Middle
Helladic Greece, and because of its comparative isolation from the rest of the
Aegean we are not in a position to extrapolate from what is known of Middle
Minoan Crete.

For the Early Bronze Age, before 2000 B.C., we have somewhat better information. We have already seen that in Crete certain cult vessels, such as the kernos
(Nilsson, 1950, pp. 135–37), have their origin in this early period and enjoy a
continuous use and development. The cultural continuity between Early and
Middle Minoan Crete is sufficient to allow us to conclude that many of the
practices of the later phase survive from the former. To a considerable extent
this is true in the Cyclades as well, but on the mainland there was a rather complete break between Early and Middle Helladic. Much that is Early Helladic
is closely connected with Early Cycladic; this is especially true in burial customs.
While literally thousands of Early Cycladic graves have been exposed, almost
nothing is known of the settlements of the period, though some sites have recently been tested. The reverse was for long true on the mainland, where many
Early Helladic settlements were excavated but few of their cemeteries were found
and Early Helladic graves were at a premium. More recently, sites like Aghios
Kosmas (Mylonas, 1959, pp. 64–120) and other Attic coastal settlements have
produced numerous graves of Cycladic type, full of pottery also very like that
found in Cycladic graves. These recent discoveries will, I believe, help to solve
an enigma, and the solution is pertinent to our present considerations.

The Early Cycladic pottery from graves, known in large quantities, consists largely of vessels made of rather coarse, gritty clay, not well fired, decorated with incised or impressed designs; some painted pottery of good quality also occurs. What excavation has been done in Early Cycladic settlements shows that thinner, better-fired pottery was in domestic use, pottery which is in fact very much like that found in Early Helladic settlements. Now that the Cycladic-type pottery has been found in Cycladic-type graves on the mainland, it seems pretty clear that much of this pottery was a special production for offering in the tombs, in a tradition quite independent of pottery for domestic use (Mylonas, 1959, p. 128). This might have been surmised earlier from the nature of the pottery itself, for its manufacture is much poorer than that of household pottery, and most probably it was unfit for domestic use. The repertory of shapes includes a variety of covered receptacles (pyxides and jars, footless or on a high base), pouring vessels, possibly drinking vessels as well (the sauceboat may be included in this class) and the so-called "frying pans," which seem to have served as mirrors. Nothing suggests any connection with a cult of the dead, and as in the Middle ,Helladic period, Mylonas sees no evidence for one in this period (1951, p. 68).

Further evidence that a special production of pottery to be used as grave offerings existed in the Early Bronze Age is forthcoming from Cyprus as well. In my trial excavations of both a settlement and a cemetery near ancient Kourion, there was found to be little correlation between the pottery from the two areas (Weinberg, 1956, p. 121). That from the settlement is well fired and in useful shapes. That from the tombs is seldom well fired and was often so poorly made that large cracks developed during firing. The fabric is thick and coarse. Many of the vessels are so large and so heavy that they can be moved only with difficulty even when empty; when filled they would have been too heavy for use and probably not sufficiently strong to hold the contents if moved. It seems clear that this pottery, and in fact most, if not all, of the Early Cypriote pottery found in tombs, was made specifically for offerings in graves. This does not imply that it is inferior pottery in all respects; much of it is elaborately decorated with incised patterns, a type of decoration common on the pottery found in Cycladic tombs as well; most of it has a good slip that is well polished; many of the shapes are very elaborate. Some of the shapes, in fact, are too bizarre to be practical for domestic use and they suggest a special use that may have cult significance. But together with the Cycladic vases from tombs, they indicate strongly that pottery made specifically for the purpose of depositing in burials, very likely with appropriate contents, was in common use in the East Mediterranean in the Early Bronze Age.[4]

---

4. Matson asked if inferior grave pottery might not be connected with the Egyptian principle of substitution. The occurrence of coarsely made, but elaborately decorated, pottery for ritual use was noted for Guatemala by Shepard. Weinberg added that the *Arkansas Archaeological Society Newsletter* II, No. 4 (April 1961), p. 14, in reporting on explorations in Panama, remarks: "almost all the pottery that they are finding is from habitation sites and is unlike that found in the graves of the same area."

When, on the other hand, we look for cult-connected ceramics in this period, we draw almost a complete blank. Even figurines, such as are so common in marble in the Cycladic tombs, are scarce on the mainland, and none can be associated with a cult rather than identified as burial offerings. It has been suggested that a large clay vessel, very well made and decorated, built into the floor of a building at Lerna may have been a ceremonial hearth used in some domestic religious rite (Caskey, 1958, p. 130). When one examines Early Helladic pottery, there are few, if any, nonutilitarian shapes and only a rare piece so elaborately decorated as to be unfit for use; the bull rhyton from Eutresis may be an exception, but rhyta are not necessarily cult vessels. There is nothing to indicate a lack of the usual religious observances, with rites in which pottery vessels were used, but thus far little evidence of them has been found.

Before 3000 B.C., the Aegean was in a Neolithic stage for some thousands of years. The record of this phase is uneven, very scant in parts, very full in others. Known burial places have until recently been scarce, but many have now been found on the mainland; thus far they reveal set burial practices, including contraction of the skeleton and the placing of offerings in the grave. There is little evidence as yet either for a cult of the dead or for a class of vessels made specially as grave offerings; an incised zoömorphic vase, a fragment of which was found in a Late Neolithic grave at Servia in Macedonia (Heurtley, 1937, p. 54), may be an exception. If we use the criterion of fugitive decoration, which we have

FIGURE 1
Drawings, including reconstructed profile, of black-on-red painted bowl on
pierced stand from Bothros in
Trench 3 at Elateia.

seen as an indication that pottery was made for offering in graves, then perhaps several Late Neolithic vases from graves at Lerna would fall into this class, for they were decorated with a powdery white incrusted paint, over which designs were painted in red or orange color (Caskey, 1958, p. 137).

Installations that might be termed sanctuaries or shrines are lacking for the Neolithic period, but deposits of such a nature as to suggest cult connections have long been known. Again, the criteria for judging them other than domestic are usually those which have been valid for later periods. In a deposit found at Phaistos in the first years of the Italian excavations, were many miniature vessels associated with a clay female figurine, shells, and a large lump of magnetic iron, an assemblage not unlike that found in later Minoan shrines (Evans, 1921–35, Vol. I, p. 37).

Perhaps the most recent such deposit is one which I excavated in 1959 at the Neolithic site of Elateia in Central Greece (Weinberg, 1962a). A very large oval pit, 2.15 meters by 1.80 meters and a little over a meter deep, was filled with a large variety of objects, including masses of pottery. The largest single object is a pillar of unbaked clay, about 0.14 meter in diameter and 0.26 meter high, having a core of coarser clay and an outer coating of finer clay with a well-rounded lip at the top and a splaying base. Unable to bear weight, it could have served as an altar, as an aniconic image, or even as a phallic symbol. There was much ash and carbon in the fill, great quantities of animal bones, including a boar's tusk and a large antler, several fragments of yellow and red coloring matter, the head of a figurine (the only head and one of the few fragments of figurines from the site). The large numbers of vases are of types not found elsewhere in the site, which suggests a special purpose. There are many examples of wide-open bowls on high pedestal bases, so-called "fruitstands," most of which have sections cut out in simple patterns such as triangles or lozenges (Fig. 1). While this suggests the use of fire within the base, there are no signs of burning on the underside; on the contrary, it is inside the bowls that there are clear traces both of burning and of scraping or rubbing (Fig. 2).[5]

Another group of pottery from the pit comprises large pieces of a number of carinated bowls of very finely burnished grey-black ware (Fig. 3), almost unknown outside this pit; peculiarly, each large piece forms a third to a half of a bowl, but none of them join and the other parts of the vessels must have been thrown elsewhere. It seems clear that we have to do here with a ritual breaking and casting asunder of parts of vessels used in a religious observance.[6] The oddest,

5. An extended discussion on so-called "fruitstands" or "tazzas" showed them to be very widespread, but particularly abundant in the East Mediterranean region. Hodges suggested that the "windows" in the bases may have a purely practical explanation as they would insure even firing. However, the pedestalled shape is often connected with sanctuaries, as at Ai and other sites in Israel, as observed by Amiran. Here, too, remains of ash were found in the bowls.

6. Ritual breaking and scattering of pottery was said by Hodges to be an established religious principle in Neolithic England; it was noted at Windmill Hill and at the entrance to many passage graves. Solheim mentioned the ritual breaking of clay figures in China, in cases where the heads were never found with the bodies.

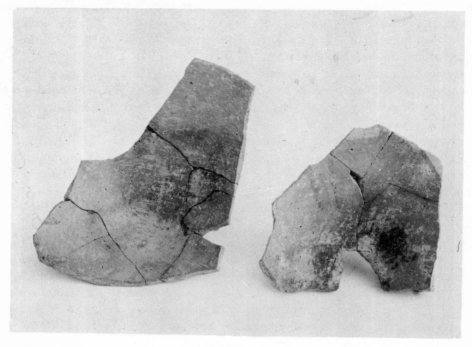

FIGURE 2
Burned and scraped interiors of "fruitstand" bowls from
Bothros in Trench 3 at Elateia.

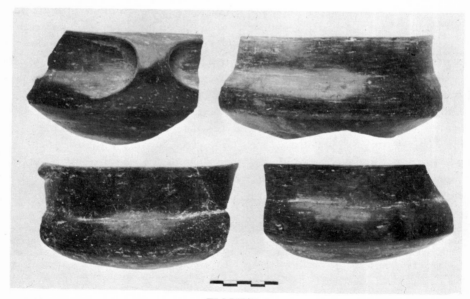

FIGURE 3
Large fragments of grey-black burnished bowls from Bothros in
Trench 3 at Elateia.

FIGURE 4

Reconstructed drawings, front and side, of four-
legged vase from Bothros in Trench 3 at Elateia.

and most important, remains are those of a four-legged vase which has a large,
oval mouth that rises almost vertically, and a domed top surmounted by a basket
handle (Fig. 4). The rear legs rise higher than the front ones, and all four are
decorated with incised, crosshatched bands, the incisions filled with white to
contrast with the polished black surface of the vase (Fig. 5a and 5d). The lip is
covered with a heavy, incrusted red paint, and the same paint fills incised bands
which outline the top of the legs and also cover the whole underside of the vase
among the legs (Fig. 5b). The interior is coated with a chalky white paint, and in
the cupped depression over each leg there is a broad stroke of red paint (Fig. 5c).
The underside of the handle is also coated with red. This richly, if impermanently,
decorated and oddly shaped vase seems to demand the explanation of a special use.

The fat, anthropomorphic legs of such vases have long been known from the
Kephissos Valley in central Greece, as well as from Neolithic Corinth (Weinberg,
1962, p. 192), but the form of vessel to which they belonged was not known and
some incorrect attempts at reconstruction were made. Now that the shape is evident, it is immediately clear that it is the same as that which has in recent years
been found in the repertory of the Danilo Culture of west-central Yugoslavia,
as seen in Figure 6 (Korošec, 1958, Pls. XVII–XXV). Not only the shape, but
the use of white-filled, incised patterns, of red and white incrusted paint, are all
the same. From their first appearance in Yugoslavia (Dujmovič, 1952), these have
been termed ritual vessels. It is my understanding that most recently, such vessels
have been found associated with large clay phalloi (Korošec, 1958, p. 157, Pl.

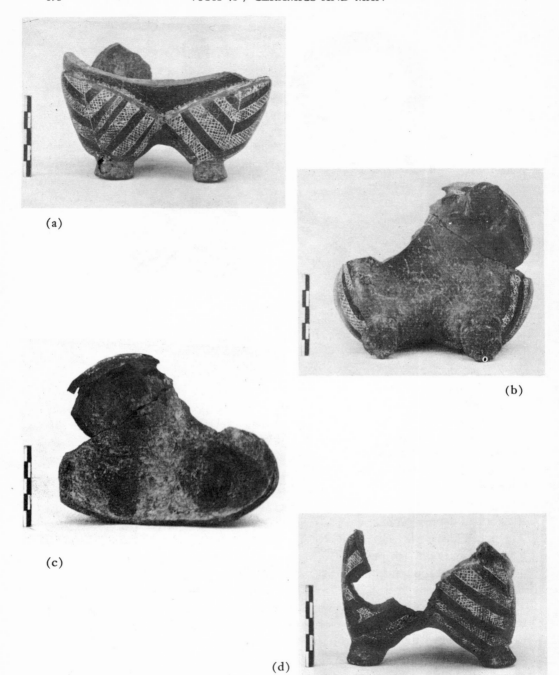

(a)

(b)

(c)

(d)

FIGURE 5
Large fragment of four-legged vase from Bothros in Trench 3 at Elateia: (a) front,
(b) bottom, (c) interior, (d) side.

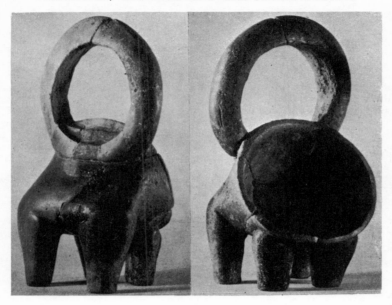

FIGURE 6
Four-legged vase found at Danilo, Yugoslavia. (Photographs
courtesy of Dr. H. J. Hundt.)

XXVII, 2–4), apparently the appurtenances of a fertility cult, of which the four-legged vessels may well have represented the female element.[7]

The whole character of the deposit in the large pit at Elateia, the nature of the pottery, the difference between it and the domestic pottery from other areas of the site, the association with the large clay pillar, all suggest that we have here the debris from a Neolithic shrine. It is the most considerable deposit of this nature yet known from the Aegean in the Neolithic period. Again, it illustrates the validity at even this early date of the two criteria that in all periods have separated the cult-connected from the domestic pottery—unusual size or shape, and bizarre or impermanent decoration.

This is but a brief summary of the evidence for the existence in the Aegean of special ceramic types used in cult or burial practices. No attempt has yet been made to apply the evidence from adjacent regions as a test of the criteria presented here, except in the case of our own experience in Cyprus. Yet the known relations of the Aegean in prehistoric times with the eastern Mediterranean and of widening contacts that embraced the entire Mediterranean world in the proto-historic and historic periods, suggest that parallel practices existed, which may

7. In discussion, the four-legged vase was thought to be either anthropomorphic or zoö-morphic. Mellaart suggested that an upper part similar to the figurines recently found at Hacilar in Turkey would fit well on the four-legged base and he sketched a hypothetical reconstruction.

well help to confirm or refute the ideas presented here. This preliminary survey, and the discussion which it hoped to engender, may form the basis for a more thorough and more widespread study of the subject.[8]

8. During the discussion, several questions and observations suggested further directions in which this subject might be pursued. Amiran noted that arm-shaped vessels occur in many parts of the East Mediterranean, always with jugs of a certain type, and wondered if this could mean that the rites in all these places were the same. Shepard wondered if it might be possible to distinguish any type of painting or any set of motives which would mark ritual pottery in a given area. Matson asked if ceramics might give some clue as to who is buried. Priest and shaman have been identified from the contents of burials; royal burials are identifiable. Might pottery make other identifications possible?

BIBLIOGRAPHY

BOTHMER, D. VON
  1962. "A Gold Libation Bowl." *Bulletin of the Metropolitan Museum of Art*, 21:154–66.

BRONEER, O.
  1958. "Excavations at Isthmia: Third Campaign, 1955–56." *Hesperia*, 27:1–37.

CASKEY, J. L.
  1958. "Excavations at Lerna, 1957." *Hesperia*, 27:125–44.
  1962. "The Goddess of Ceos." *Archaeology*, 15:223–26.

COOK, R. M.
  1960. *Greek Painted Pottery*. Chicago: Quadrangle Books.

DUJMOVIČ, F.
  1952. "Vase rituel néolithique provenant de Danilo (Dalmatie)." *Bulletin d'archéologie et d'histoire dalmate*, 54:73–75.

EVANS, SIR A. J.
  1921–35. *The Palace of Minos at Knossos*. London: Macmillan.

HARRISON, J. E.
  1927. *Themis: A Study of the Social Origins of Greek Religion*. (2d ed.) Cambridge: Cambridge University Press.

HEURTLEY, W. A.
  1937. *Prehistoric Macedonia*. Cambridge: Cambridge University Press.

HOORN, G. VAN
  1951. *Choes and Anthesteria*. Leiden: E. J. Brill.

JAMESON, M.
  1960. "Mycenaean Religion." *Archaeology*, 13:33–39.

KOROŠEC, J.
  1958. *The Neolithic Settlement at Danilo Bitinj: The Results of Excavations Performed in 1953*. Zagreb: Yugoslav Academy of Sciences and Arts.

MYLONAS, G. M.
  1951. "The Cult of the Dead in Helladic Times." In *Studies Presented to David M. Robinson*, G. E. Mylonas (ed.), 1:64–105. Saint Louis: Washington University.
  1959. *Aghios Kosmas*. Princeton: Princeton University Press.

NILSSON, M. P.
  1950. *The Minoan-Mycenaean Religion*. Lund: C. W. K. Gleerup.

RICHTER, G. M. A.

1935. *Shapes and Names of Athenian Vases*. New York: Metropolitan Museum of Art.

VENTRIS, M., and J. CHADWICK.

1956. *Documents in Mycenaean Greek*. Cambridge: Cambridge University Press.

VERDELIS, N. M.

1962. "A Sanctuary at Solygeia." *Archaeology*, 15:184–92.

WEINBERG, S. S.

1943. "The Geometric and Orientalizing Pottery." *Corinth*, Vol. VII, pt. 1. Cambridge: Harvard University Press.

1956. "Exploring the Early Bronze Age in Cyprus." *Archaeology*, 9:112–21.

1962a. "Excavations at Prehistoric Elateia, 1959." *Hesperia*, 31:158–209.

1962b. "Solving a Prehistoric Puzzle." *Archaeology*, 15:262–66.

CERAMIC ECOLOGY: AN APPROACH TO
THE STUDY OF THE EARLY CULTURES
OF THE NEAR EAST

FREDERICK R. MATSON

NLESS ceramic studies lead to a better understanding of the cultural context in which the objects were made and used, they form a sterile record of limited worth. At this symposium on "Ceramics and Man" several ways of using the ceramic data more effectively are being discussed in the hope that additional aids for archeological reconstructions of past cultures can be developed. A consideration of some of the ceramic products of man in their ecological context, or as some might say, in their ecosystem, may contribute to this discussion by examining the ceramic record of man's activities as they were influenced by the interaction of his culture and its environmental setting. For the purposes of this paper, regretfully, many ceramic items—brick, glass, glaze, enamel, faience, stoneware, porcelain, plaster, and cement—will be ignored. The environment will be that of the Near East, and the cultures will be some of those of roughly 6000–3000 B.C. in which people made and used pottery.

Ecological studies are appearing with increasing frequency in anthropological and related literature, and one reads of human, social, and cultural ecology, and even of the ecology of research. Over two decades ago, Kroeber's pioneer work, *Cultural and Natural Areas of Native North America*, redirected interest toward the importance of the environment in anthropological studies following the period of violent rejection of Huntington's geographical determinism. At the first of the Wenner-Gren Foundation's international symposia on anthropology, which was held in 1952, Marston Bates (1953, p. 701) presented a paper on "Human Ecology" in which he suggested that

It might be useful to regard ecology as a pervasive point of view rather than as a special subject matter. The ecological point of view—whereby the organism is regarded as a whole unit functioning in its environmental context—would carry over from the biological to the social sciences and might thus be especially helpful in relating the concepts of the one field to those of the other. The establishment of such relations is not easy, and most attempts to transfer concepts have possibly been misleading.

Julian Steward ably discussed "The Concept and Method of Cultural Ecology" in 1955. At the 1960 meetings of the American Association for the Advancement of Science one session of section H, with Paul T. Baker as organizer and chairman, was devoted to Ecology and Anthropology. The five papers presented at that symposium were published in 1962 in the *American Anthropologist* (64:15–69). And Coles concludes his recent brief but excellent survey with the statement ". . . environmental studies, using a number of scientific disciplines, are the only justifiable way with which to treat archaeological material" (1963, p. 97).

Ceramic ecology may be considered as one facet of cultural ecology, that which attempts to relate the raw materials and technologies that the local potter has available to the functions in his culture of the products he fashions. This temporary anthropomorphization of pottery may startle some, but an ecological elixir of life may help to increase our understanding of some cultures of the past. It should not be inferred that Steward's characterization of the objectives and methods of cultural ecology as he conceives them will be followed specifically. Instead, his stimulating discussions may be considered a point of departure, at present, for a ceramic study. The following quotations taken from his 1955 paper (pp. 36, 38) give an indication of Steward's approach:

Cultural ecology [seeks] to explain the origin of particular cultural features and patterns which characterize different areas. . . . The concept of cultural ecology, however, is less concerned with the origin and diffusion of technologies than with the fact that they may be used differently and entail different social arrangements in each environment.

ENVIRONMENT

The Near Eastern environment can be characterized in terms of factors that have affected or influenced the potters working there. The Near East, despite the great variations within it, may be said to be an area of mountains, plains, and deserts with wet cold winters and hot arid summers. Vegetation and water are available most of the year for man and his grazing animals at the higher elevations in the foothills and mountains and near the river banks on the plains. With the development of canals and irrigation systems, summer life became possible for more people in the lowlands. According to the agronomist Jack Harlan, wheat is the grain crop that was effectively developed in the Near East because it is adapted to a winter growing season and to winter moisture. In regions with a summer rainfall pattern, wheat disappears. The combination of a suitable crop, wheat, and a controlled water supply through irrigation made it possible for larger social groupings to develop in the Near East some eight thousand years ago, perhaps earlier. It is well to recall, however, that nomadic life based on the herding of sheep and goats continues in this area and that there is a close relationship between these two ways of life which are both focused on food production. The appearance of agriculture and a settled way of life with the resultant spectacular cultural development in the Near East have been extensively discussed by Braidwood and Reed (1957).

Pottery is found in the earliest settlements so far recognized, such as Jericho, Jarmo, Hacilar, and Çatal Hüyük. The fact that it does not appear in the lowest strata of these deposits does not necessarily mean that it was a later development. It could be that the small number of sites so far excavated represent settlements at which pottery was not used, but that similar villages did use pottery. As Childe pointed out, the very beginnings of a craft such as pottery will be difficult to recognize. At present, an extended discussion of pottery origins is pointless. The fact that it did appear early in the history of settled life in the ancient Near East is, however, important. Its study, in ecological terms, can be approached through a consideration of the needs of the people living in the region once food production had developed. In terms of the material aspects of these early cultures, containers—made of skin, wood, stone, basketry, gourds, or clay—were needed for some activities related to agricultural and animal-raising practices, but most importantly, for water and other liquids, and for food.

WATER

One is impressed today by the great importance that the availability of water in future hours or even days has for dwellers in many parts of the Near East. A stress situation of some intensity develops quickly when the water supply is threatened. This water is needed in this hot climate not only for human consumption, but also for the animals and for the cultivated fields. Therefore, material objects that will be useful in the procuring, conserving, and storing of water are required. Today one sees water jars of clay for bringing water from the wells, springs, streams, canals, *qanats, jooies,* or faucets. The size of the jars will depend in part on the method of transportation. Vessels to be carried on women's heads impose certain limitations in shape and size upon the potter. Jars for the storage of water in the home (or the present-day tea houses) will be much larger and of a different shape. Individual drinking vessels again will differ in size and shape.

The number of containers of each type will vary for many reasons, some of which are:

1. Size of the family; number of people transporting water.
2. Needs of the group—guest house or private dwelling; distance frrom water supply. Economic status of the family.
3. Replacement factor. Some vessels are "sweet" and can be used for a long time. Others quickly sour due to salts or to algae and bacterial growth in the porous vessel walls. In Beirut, the individual drinking jars (*brecks*) that are kept on the window sills to provide cool water are replaced about six times a year.
4. Social factors. Style changes; additions to the group such as a new wife from another village with somewhat different traditions. Visitors from another village.

This list could obviously be expanded. Perhaps it can be used by an archeologist in analyzing his collection of excavated vessels and sherds.

It will never be possible to assign specific functions to individual vessels, but the frequency with which open and closed-mouth vessels, for example, occur in several sizes can be suggestive. It should be possible, when reporting on the pottery excavated, to group it in terms of use. Spouted vessels, which first appeared in Ubaid times, can easily be classified. The size of the vessels must also be considered. When studying the pottery being excavated at Tepe Sarab near Kermanshah in western Iran, I was impressed by the fact that at this early site, approximately contemporary with Jarmo, there were but three principal diameters of the vessels. All slight variations could be assigned to these three groups which have definite implications as to use. The absence of large vessels that might have been water jars carried on the heads of the women, could suggest that water was transported in other ways, probably in animal skins as is still done today in Kurdistan and Afghanistan. Before drawing such a conclusion, however, one would have to consider the extent of the excavation that produced the pottery, and the nature of the settlement pattern as suggested by the simple architectural remnants that were found. The type of base—flat, rounded, or pointed—and the types of handles, or their absence, are also factors that help in classifying the pottery according to use. Each of these items could receive extended discussion for the Near East alone based on temporal and regional variations and on a knowledge of present-day practices.

This general discussion of water jars and related containers should include comments on the detailed observation of appearance of the sherds and vessels excavated, for they may offer clues as to use. The three general points that will be discussed are wear, surface treatment, and degree of firing.

Wear.—Evidence of wear is often overlooked in the field study of the entire mass of excavated sherds, but it can be of value, particularly if a low-power magnifying glass is used to examine carefully the more promising sherds. Evidence of abrasion or scratches should be sought on the interior and exterior of the base, around the handles, on the shoulder zone where cords might have been attached, and of course on the rims. The sludge deposits in the pointed bases of tall jars should be checked.

Surface treatment.—Various techniques have been and are being used to make the surfaces less porous, for the degree of porosity is of real concern to the users. Too porous a vessel will not contain its liquid very long, yet some porosity is needed for earthenware in hot climates so that the slow evaporation of water from the exterior surface will cool the water. In some cases, very fine textured clay is chosen by the potters so as to produce denser ware despite the danger of cracks developing during drying. Surface burnishing may help reduce the flow of water through the fired clay walls, but this may not be the chief reason for doing it from the viewpoint of the potter. A third method is to impregnate either or both surfaces with organic materials so as to fill many of the pores, and a great many different ways of doing this have been reported from most earthenware-producing parts of the world. It would be interesting at another time, and perhaps a good application of an ecological point of view, to analyze the various ways in which smoke, resins, oils, and other organic treatments have been applied to vessels in different environments and cultures. It is quite possible that the purposes behind these applications differ in many cases. Because such treatments are widespread, one should look for evidence on the sherds, although organic materials under some conditions of burial and in connection with some kinds of clays will disappear. The color of freshly broken cross-sections of sherds will often give one the best remaining evidence. Dark-surfacing occurred in the earliest ceramic horizons of the Near East at Sakje Geuze, Mersin, and the Amuq sites among others in Turkey, and occasionally at Nineveh and Hassuna. In the Uruk period, grey wares were intentionally produced. The beautiful Khirbet Kerak Ware that is found from Turkey south into Palestine in the first half of the third millennium, and the wide-spread Minyan Ware of Middle Helladic times about a thousand years later, were intentionally darkened.

The intentional darkening of the interior of jars has not been observed too often in archeological contexts except in wine jars. It might be advisable to look for such pieces, because the application of carbon to the interior of the vessel may have been a way of maintaining the flavor of the jar, probably because of the strong adsorptive properties of carbon. Lane's description, published in 1842, of the preparation of water bottles in Egypt at that time illustrates one such technique (p. 135):

The interior is often blackened with the smoke of some resinous wood, and then perfumed with the smoke of "kafal" wood and mastic; the latter used last. A small earthen vessel (called "mibkhar'ah") is employed in performing these operations, to contain the burning charcoal which is required to ignite the wood, and the mastic; and the water bottle is held inverted over it. A strip of rag is tied around the neck of the dorak, at a distance of about an inch from the mouth, to prevent the smoke-black from extending too far upon the exterior of the bottle. Many persons also put a little orange-flower-water into the bottles. The bottles have stoppers of silver, brass, tin, wood, or palm leaves; and are generally placed in a tray of tinned copper which receives the water that exudes from them. In cold weather china bottles are used in many houses instead of those above described, which then render the water too cold.

The presence or absence of a slip on vessels is a point that often troubles archeologists when they describe their wares. Perhaps such identifications are not important unless they can be related to use or to the degree of technological development evidenced. The earliest pottery so far known in the Near East often has a slip of red clay applied to its surface. This is frequently associated with straw-tempered ware and at times with burnished surfaces. The surfaces may be discolored with smoke stains or from varying degrees of oxidation. Sometimes the red slip has almost entirely disappeared and one has to look closely to detect its remnants. This was particularly true at Jarmo but is not unknown in the New World where the term "fugitive red" is at times used. The disappearance of the slip can be due to the friable nature of the pottery itself, the conditions of burial, the degree of adherence of the slip to the surface with or without burnishing, the physical and mineralogical properties of body and slip, and of course, to the energy and carelessness of the potter applying the slip and of the people washing the excavated sherds.

Red slip, often associated with chaff-tempered pottery, occurs on one of the characteristic wares of the early cultures of the Near East. The other wares are usually better made, better fired, and sometimes incised or decorated. This very general statement would not hold completely true for the pottery of any one site, but the contrast between the relatively simple and the better made wares is clear. Differences in use can sometimes be traced in terms of the shapes and sizes of the vessels. It is likely that more than one cultural tradition is here evidenced in ceramics. I would guess that the red-slipped ware, but not it alone, represents the work of the women, in all or most families, to provide without cost the essential vessel needs of the houshold. The better made wares, however, represent a specialized craft tradition. This can be illustrated by contemporary scenes.

The red clay for slips occurs in most parts of the Near East on the limestone mountain slopes as a weathering product. The dark-brown soils on these slopes contrast sharply with the tan valley soil. Many of these clays are more sticky than those in the valleys. This is not the place to discuss the processes by which such brown soils have been formed, but their availability to the potters should be mentioned. The mountain slopes are today used for small agricultural plots, for summer encampments at the higher elevations, and for grazing areas. The women of the villages thus have occasion to wander in such regions. The discovery that the brown earth will fire to a bright red color might have come from camp fires. It is quite possible that the red color was not the important factor; instead, the sticky adhering quality of this clay that incidentally burned red may have determined its use not only for pottery but also for resurfacing walls, roofs, and floors.

Life in many simple small villages today is intimately related to the agricultural cycle. After the harvest and the threshing of the grain is finished, activities that have used all the men and women of the villages as laborers in the field, the people begin to prepare for the next winter. A clay pit is dug in the village, water and chaff are added, and bricks to be sun-dried are made for the repair of houses and for the construction of new houses. Cracks in the roof and walls are plastered with a mixture of mud and straw. Storage bins, platforms, and wind shields for the hearth are rebuilt in the courtyards of the houses. And the women continue their preparation of dung cakes tempered with straw that will serve as the winter fuel. It is probable that similar dung-straw-clay mixtures were used to fashion pottery at home. This idea will be developed more extensively elsewhere, but it is possible that the red-slipped ware represents part of the activities of the agricultural cycle. One should not ignore the possibility that red clay was also used for body and clothing decoration, so it would be a familiar item procured from the mountain slopes and kept in the house. Today henna is widely used on the hands, feet, and hair in the Arab and Iranian areas. In India, pigments are thrown at people on festival occasions, and the body decoration of the American Indians and the Australian Aborigines is well known. Should one also mention the importance of red pigments in burial and ceremonial rites since prehistoric times, and wonder if there is a special significance attributed to the red-slipped wares? This has been a paragraph of suppositions—unprovable, but possible.

Degree of firing.—Once simple kilns had been developed, it was possible to control to some extent the temperature to which the vessels were fired and the

duration of the firing. (In ceramic studies, time and temperature are interdependent variables.) Porosity can be decreased through more intensive firing. I have
observed this at a potter's shop at Rachaiyah al Fakhar in southern Lebanon. There
the potter was making decorated jars about one and a half feet in height. Those
drawn from most parts of the kiln after firing were attractive in terms of
decoration and were sold as water jars. But some vessels were intentionally placed
on what were known to be the hottest parts of the kiln floor. These were discolored by the greater heat, but being well-fired, had low porosity and were
much desired for the storage of olive oil.

By Ubaid times in Mesopotamia, high-fired and over-fired pottery was common and is, in fact, characteristic of much of the Ubaid Ware that is preserved.
It would be interesting, when next an Ubaid site is excavated, to save all the
pottery until the degree of firing of the sherds can be correlated with the shapes.
When one visits the sherd-strewn excavated sites, he is impressed by the number
of low-fired sherds that can be seen on the surface and wonders if a disproportion-
ate amount of the higher-fired sherds had been saved. In the Uruk Culture period
which followed, high-fired pottery is rare, at least in terms of the so-called Uruk
Wares, and in the later Dynastic periods it constituted less than 5 per cent of the
sherds, often but 1 per cent. The range in firing temperature within a kiln may
be great, so a study of the degree of firing of pottery perhaps reflects the techniques of firing and fuel supply more strongly than the intential firing-tempera-
ture range for specific products. Lamps and figurines, for example, differ in their
degree of firing from that of pottery. In the pre-Ubaid cultures of the Near
East, however, in some of which kilns were not used, the degree to which the
black core of the vessel walls has been oxidized is the important item to observe.
It is remarkable how well oxidized the low-fired pottery is.

FOOD

Food production and the development of fired clay vessels are closely related,
but the uses to which these vessels were put is far from clear. Containers for water
have already been discussed. Similar containers for the storage of grain to protect
it from rodents and from moisture must have been used, and the large low-
shouldered vessels with small collared mouths found at Hassuna and Matarrah
have been considered grain storage jars. At Jarmo, the basal sherds of large storage
jars occurred chiefly in the lower portion of the ceramic horizons. It seems likely
that they represent the level at which the storage jars were embedded below house
floors. Aside from globular containers, open bowl shapes are the most common
ones found at the early sites. Although some of these could have been drinking
cups, it is probable that many were used for gruel or mush made from the seeds
of wild and cultivated plants. Parched grain was an early staple food. An interesting discussion of this food occurs in the notes prepared by Braidwood et al.
(1953) on the subject "Did Man Once Live By Beer Alone?"

Meat as a food in early communities was rare, if one may judge by present-day practices. Sick and dead domesticated animals were eaten, an animal might be killed for a feast for an honored guest or to inaugurate a new important project, and hunters provided wild game when possible. Much of the meat was roasted. The split long bones of sheep, goat, and other animals have been identified by zoölogists in the bone materials excavated, and the figures on the early painted pottery, particularly in Iran, attest to the interest in sheep and goats. Pots for stewing meat and other items have not been clearly identified so far in terms of fire stains on the exterior base or animal bones in the vessels. It would be nice to find a hippopotamus tusk in a cooking pot as did Miss Caton-Thompson at the Neolithic Fayum settlement. It is quite possible that there were few cooking pots in a small community, and their uninteresting fragments might be ignored in the sherd sortings. By Uruk times vessels that might be called cooking pots occur.

In later times, when dietary laws became ritually established, separate dishes were needed for meat and for milk foods. It would be interesting to know if such duplication of household vessels can be recognized in an archeological context. Some remnant of this tradition may exist today among the pastoral Galla in Ethiopia who, according to Huntingford (1955), do not put milk in pottery vessels but only in baskets made of closely-woven plant fibers. This custom may relate to the ritual status of the cattle and to the low status of potters, craft work being disdained.

Bread has long been the basic food item, together with dates and greens, of the Arabs and their neighbors. Presumably their predecessors in the same environment with no climatic difference used the same foods. Ceramic evidence for the baking of bread can be found in the coarse, crude fragments of ovens, *tannurs*, and perhaps of some vessels. There are some clay objects found in the early villages that may well have been used for bread-making.

In the small villages today there are relatively few food vessels. Copper caldrons for cooking rice and meat, containers for the soured milk (yoghurt or mast), tea cups, and a tea pot are the chief items in the inventory.

One gets the impression that much more pottery is found in the excavation of larger towns and certainly in city sites than in the villages. Population density, the need for vessels in the service of the temple, and perhaps the relative convenience of having clay vessels as contrasted to skins, etc., are factors relating to this ceramic abundance. The socioeconomic factors of cost, status, and consumption must also be recognized. The environmental factor may be the most important one, however. Large towns and later cities were located on the alluvial plain where fine water-deposited clay was abundantly available and fuel in the form of desert grass was easily obtained. But this present discussion concerns handmade pottery, some of which was lathe- or wheel-finished. With the advent of the wheel by Uruk times, the rapid production of pottery was possible, yet hand-formed vessels continued to be made in some villages and are still being made today.

FUEL

The potter's relationship to his biological environment is largely in terms of his need of fuel for firing the pottery. (The probability that much of the pottery was made by women is here subsumed in the male pronoun.) Dried grass and desert weeds such as camel thorn are easily gathered into large bundles and brought to the kiln area on the backs of the gatherers. Straw from the threshing floor can be used if it can be spared. Large quantities are needed, for such grass gives a hot quick fire with little ash. In villages where kilns were not used, and certainly in prekiln times, simple campfires were used to fire the pottery. Again grass and perhaps wood might be used. Wood, however, has never been abundant, although the rapid deforestation of later times was not then a problem. Aside from small branches, it is difficult to cut wood into short lengths. Until the analysis of charcoal fragments from ancient hearths show that wood was used commonly, it would be best not to consider it a probable fuel supply. On the irrigated plains where the greater part of the pottery was fired, wood was certainly scarce.

Dung has always been an available and useful raw material in areas where sheep, goats, and cattle or water buffalo are raised. Dung cakes are used today to fire pottery in Kurdistan on small hearths, but one cannot assume without evidence that such fuel was used by the potters in the past. However, at Bonahilk, a Halaf period site in northeastern Iraqi Kurdistan, I found ash cakes in a hearth that were like those remaining in a burned-out dung-cake fire today. It is probable that such fuel was used as soon as there was a sufficient number of animals to produce the needed material.

CLAY

The raw materials available to the potter—maybe one should say culturally available to the potter—are ample, judging from the large amount of pottery that has been produced in the Near East. The mountain villagers have clayey soil in their plowed fields and also right within their living areas. Clay pits for brickmaking in the village complex, often not far from a threshing floor, are still used. The villagers use the material for brick, for patching walls and roofs, for resurfacing floors, and for building various structures in their courtyards (as has already been mentioned), so they are familiar with what is available when in their role as potters they fashion vessels. At later times there may have been a more sophisticated selection of the clay. Sandy clays are found in coarser ware from some ancient villages, and this is available on the stream banks. On the alluvial plain it is easy to obtain fine-textured clay as there are few sandy or gravel-strewn areas. The major problem of the potter, if recognized as such, is the selection of material that does not contain too much salt since a salty incrustation is common on the surface of the ground. In the irrigated lands, the sludge that accumulates in the canals and is shoveled up onto the canal banks annually supplies nicely levigated material. In the marsh areas of southern Iraq, if pottery were made, there would be ample dried reed stalks available to crush and mix with the sticky clay.

Washing of the clay is done today in Lebanon, and in southern Turkey, but this may have been a Mediterranean-oriented technique for it is also employed by the Athenian potters. Clay from the mountain slopes is used, and at times two types of clay were mixed in the washing tanks. The potters in pre-wheel times were not concerned with this need for a fine, uniform clay. In Mesopotamia the river floodings produced it for them.

The re-use of clay from abandoned walls and houses that have been ruined by rains, floods, and neglect as a source of raw material must be recognized. Today, old mounds are trenched by nearby villagers to easily procure clay for brick-making. I have seen this taking place in Iraq, Iran, and Afghanistan.

The drying of the formed clay vessels in a hot climate is a problem that has to be solved by the potters. One potter in the Lebanon today makes his jars on the wheel before daybreak. The vessels are then placed outside at dawn so that they will begin to warm with the early morning sun. Throughout the morning an assistant turns them so that they will not dry too rapidly on one side. In most cases drying cracks do not seem to be a major problem in the Near East today. Some village women in Kurdistan place their dried water jars next to their cooking fires to dry them further. This step gives the vessels a smoked appearance before they are fired.

The archeologist examining sherds from the Near East in terms of their texture and types of clay used notes that the most common inclusions are small bits of limestone, the size varying with the texture of the clay. The degree to which the black core has been burned out of the pottery and the surface colors developed also help in making a preliminary sorting of the sherds in terms of the materials used.

Since many villagers, even today, spend their summers in tent camps in the mountains with their flocks, it is quite possible to find the same type of pottery, made by the same potters, but composed of different types of clay. It would be interesting to list vessels needed at the summer encampment as opposed to those in the permanent winter village, and then try to project these data into the past. The first part of such an analysis is underway, for Mrs. Patty Jo Watson included this material in her study of an Iranian village near Kermanshah in 1960.

THE POTTER

The pre-wheel potter of the ancient Near East must have been much like a woman of the mountain villages of Kurdistan and Anatolia today. Pottery-making is but one of their tasks, and such craft specialization as there may be relates to the production of vessels within a village area. There were special and fine quality painted wares in early times that had a wide distribution in terms of shapes and designs, such as the Samarra and the Halaf styles, followed in time by northern and southern variants of Ubaid. Any statement as to the role of the potters who produced such fine wares would be pure speculation, but there is no reason not to attempt controlled speculation.

In ancient Semitic tradition the Kenites were smiths and were extratribal in many respects. They were looked down upon but considered necessary. In Ethiopia today where there is a strong Semitic cultural tradition, the Amhara, for example, whose economic life is based on agriculture and animal husbandry, disdain craftwork of all kinds. In many parts of Ethiopia the potters are a lower status group, as are the smiths, both trades being considered menial by the Christians and the Moslems. There are wandering groups such as the Felasha, the "Black Jews of Ethiopia," who make the pottery for the others when they visit their villages. Simoons (1960) describes these practices. Recently I watched nomadic potters at work in northeastern Afghanistan; they summer in the Afghan villages, making large quantities of pottery, but winter in Pakistan. They are considered gypsies by Afghans. It is not impossible that the Samarra and Halaf styles may owe their wide distribution to wandering tribes with craft specialization such as those just mentioned.

THE PRODUCT

It is amazing to find the diversity of clay products made and used in the Near East in the past and today. The availability of clay in part accounts for this, as well as the relative lack of wood and the cost of imported materials; but also man's close identification with the soil must be recognized—he is clay-oriented of necessity. In southern Iraq, where stone as well as wood is scarce, sickles and hoes were made of hard high-fired clay in Ubaid times, but the reasons for using clay may perhaps be found in some other direction than in the scarcity of raw materials. Sherds were often reused as secondary tools. For example, scrapers with flaked edges have been made from sherds at the early village sites; disks were chipped or ground from sherds; and loom weights (so-called) were also made from them. Instead of trying to discuss the various products used in the cultures of the Near East that were and are made from clay, I should like to present an incomplete listing of items (below) in the hope that it may be added to by others. The purpose of such a listing is to emphasize the involvement and participation of the potter and other craftsmen in clay in many aspects of the life of their communities. When more sites are excavated in terms of the settlement pattern at one period of time, it will be possible to more intelligently prepare inventory lists of the material items of a culture as preserved in ceramic form.

Pottery in endless variety	Walls
Figurines	Granaries
Sculpture	Feeding troughs
Lamps	Chimney pots
Cones for wall decoration	Pot stands
Brick: sun-dried, fired, molded, glazed	Ovens, kilns, *tannurs*

Beads

Sickles

Hoes

Wall hooks

Molds for decorated bowls and figurines

Molds for metallurgy

Molds for bread

Waterwheel jars

Drains

Dovecotes

Beehives

Churns

Latrines

Qanats

Sling stones

Spit-holders for cooking

Livers for haruspicy

Potters' wheels

Pipes for smoking

Cuneiform tablets

Ostraca

Execration figures and bowls

Jar stamps

Ossuaries

Coffins

Libation vessels

Tax measures

Tokens as coin substitutes

Medicinal pastilles

Gaming pieces

INTERACTION

The state of transitory equilibrium existing between the three chief elements of a ceramic ecological study—the physical, biological, and cultural—is easily altered by a change in one of them. Since none of the three can be considered constant over extended time periods, it might be better to think of their continuing inter-action and to use ceramic data from historically documented cultures as a guide in the study of the far earlier ones.

Alterations in the physical environment are relatively rare. There have not been major climatic changes in the past ten thousand years in the Near East, so far as is known, and the minor ones have been well summarized by Butzer (1958). Floods and the alteration of river courses have always been destructive factors in Mesopotamia, and the progressive deforestation of the hills and mountains has been greatly accelerated in the past fifty years because of access roads, charcoal burners, and larger herds of tree-sprout-nibbling sheep and goats. None of these, however, should greatly affect the potter although they might result in a change in texture or even in the color of his wares, and could be the cause of the desertion of some villages and the establishment of new ones.

Changes in the biological environment, susceptible to drought, diseases, and acts of man would have a more direct impact on the ceramic products. Food and fuel are important for survival. There has been a drought for the past several years in Iran with resulting poor crops that were devastated by insects. Now the farmers are planting barley instead of wheat because there is a better chance of a harvest although the product is not as desirable. The only ceramic record of this or other reductions in the food supply might be that fewer vessels are made over a given period of time, in part as a result of a decrease in the population. When north Iranian villagers have used up their dung-cake fuel in an unexpectedly long and cold winter, they try to move to Teheran for aid. Similar problems in the past might have been solved by migration and the temporary abandonment of villages. Here, too, it would be difficult to trace these troubles in the ceramic record although new shapes or designs might be acquired by the potters from villages where life was more successful.

Adjustments in the cultural environment could be more susceptible to ceramic record. However, Shepard in her discussion of pottery as a clue to the interactions among peoples and cultures (1956, p. 348ff.) analyzes Tschopik's report on the lack of outside influence on the Aymara pottery in Peru from the period of Inca dominance through the Spanish colonization to the present day. "The Aymara ceramic tradition has been conspicuously insensitive and resistant to change throughout 500 years of drastic acculturation" (Tschopik, 1950, p. 217). Shepard is rightly concerned about the relationship between pottery traditions and warns against facile assumptions. In a study of culture change in a Lebanese village, Gulick (1955) found that material acculturation occurred only when (1) the change does not involve expense; (2) it is clearly conducive to greater comfort and convenience; and (3) it is not in conflict, functionally or symbolically, with other firmly established and unchanging norms. There was great conservatism in the material aspects of the culture that were concerned with diet, involving eating habits and cooking methods, and with farming techniques. In discussing cultural barriers to change, Foster gives examples of the emotionally based importance of the taste of food in retarding the introduction of improved wheat and maize seed (1962, p. 76). When he considers stimulants to change he pessimistically observes with respect to recent UNESCO programs in Mexican villages, "As a rule-of-thumb guide to community development work I would suggest that new community development programs avoid pottery-making villages as initial targets" (1962, p. 144). I have observed the resistance of some Egyptian villagers to the use of piped clean water provided by the government. They prefer the "sweet Nile water." And the people in southern Greece often rationalize the purchasing of widely distributed water jars made in certain villages, while rejecting those from other sources, in terms of the taste of the water stored in them.

If these widely separated examples were typical, one might assume that ceramic traditions are very conservative. However, that is not always the case as evidenced by the Tell-el-Amarna wares developed during the brief fluorescence of that city. At the Hellenistic capital city of Seleucia-on-the-Tigris there was a seven-year period of revolt from the Parthian rulers, A.D. 36 to 43. Prior to this struggle, the city was Hellenistic in its architecture, pottery, etc. Following the subjugation of Seleucia, the city became much more oriental in its architecture, and Parthian pottery became dominant. Ceramic studies may be able to help trace and explain several of the sharp cultural changes that occurred in the Near East. They can also show the opposite as is evidenced by Joan Oates's study (1960) of the Eridu and Ur prehistoric pottery in which she found that there was no evidence of foreign invaders causing the transition in southern Mesopotamia from the pre-Ubaid to the Ubaid-Sumerian Culture.

There is a residue of the ceramic past in the present, although not always as strongly preserved as among the Aymara. Therefore one can learn much by observing the village potters, brickmakers, and house builders at work. But Frankfort cautions in his pioneer work on Near Eastern ceramics (1924), when discussing ethnological parallels, that contemporary similarities to ancient traits are possessed by people who have not changed while most other groups have. This caution is useful, but the factors causing the stability of some culture traits, and a knowledge of what these present-day "primitives" had been like in the past is lacking. Studies of the stable and the variable traits in an ecosystem are important in considerations of culture change.

It is possible to become too socially oriented in ceramic studies, reading far more into the products than is justified. *The New Yorker* magazine for March 5, 1960 published the following excerpt from Von Hagen's "The Aztec: Man and Tribe":

Pottery was functional in this society of craftsmen. It brought psychological fulfillment —handcrafts are one of the therapeutic techniques of the psychiatrist; it had social utility—an economy based upon handcraft culture is not so liable to fluctuations as one based on mass-produced products. Naturally, the Aztec, who knew nothing of such reasoning, thought only of using the surplus pottery production as an exchange medium at the weekly market.

And the inimitable *New Yorker* commented, "He didn't even know why he felt good."

A more balanced approach can be found in Caldwell's comments in his paper on "The New American Archaeology" (1959) which summarizes some of the current interests in ecological studies.

The new archaeology in America is tending to be more concerned with culture process and less concerned with descriptive content of prehistoric cultures. . . . Another approach to cultural and historical process is seen in the wealth of inferences which can be derived from changes in cultural forms seen through time—that is, through stratigraphic and constructed sequences.

This approach could be applied more widely in the Near East, although at present, major contributions are being made to our understanding of the earliest food-producing cultures by the work of Kenyon, Braidwood, Mellaart and their associates. Dyson's current review (1961) summarizes well the present knowledge of the development of the early cultures, the Samarra, Halaf, Ubaid, etc., in the Near East.

CONCLUSION

An ecological point of view can be useful to archeologists studying their ceramic materials, for it emphasizes some of the unique properties of clay products that were recognized decades ago and were then well characterized by Frankfort, Childe, Harrison, and many others. For a long while potsherds have served as the raw data for stratigraphical and chronological studies, and the human aspects of this man-made and man-used product have been neglected. It should be possible for students of ancient ceramics to encompass in their interests an ecological approach to their studies even though, for the present, the results may not be spectacular. It is through a combination of many interests–historical, technological, artistic, and ecological, among others–that pottery can be made to serve our objective–the better understanding of man through a study of the material remains that have been left for us to excavate.

BIBLIOGRAPHY

BATES, M.
1953. "Human Ecology." In *Anthropology Today, An Encyclopedic Inventory*, A. L. Kroeber (chm.), pp. 700–13. Chicago: University of Chicago Press.

BRAIDWOOD, R. J., et al.
1953. "Did Man Once Live by Beer Alone?" *American Anthropologist*, 55:515–26.

BRAIDWOOD, R. J., and C. A. REED
1957. "The Achievement and Early Consequences of Food-Production: A Consideration of the Archaeological and Natural-Historical Evidence." *Cold Spring Harbor Symposia on Quantitative Biology*, 22:19–31.

BUTZER, K. W.
1958. *Quaternary Stratigraphy and Climate in the Near East*. In *Bonner Geographische Abhandlungen*, Vol. 24. Bonn: Ferd. Dümmlers Verlag.

CALDWELL, J. R.
1959. "The New American Archaeology." *Science*, 129:303–7.

COLES, J. M.
1963. "Environmental Studies and Archaeology." In *Science and Archaeology*, D. Brothwell and E. Higgs (eds.), pp. 93–8. New York: Basic Books.

DYSON, R. H., JR.
1961. Review of "Excavations in the Plain of Antioch" by R. J. and L. S. Braidwood. *American Anthropologist*, 63:630–41.

FOSTER, G. M.
1962. *Traditional Cultures: and the Impact of Technological Change*. New York: Harper and Row.

FRANKFORT, H.
1924. *Studies in Early Pottery of the Near East. I Mesopotamia, Syria, and Egypt and their Earliest Interrelations*. London: Royal Anthropological Institute, Occasional Papers No. 6.

GULICK, J.
1955. *Social Structure and Culture Change in a Lebanese Village*. Viking Fund Publications in Anthropology, No. 21. New York: Wenner-Gren Foundation For Anthropological Research.

HUNTINGFORD, G. W. B.
   1955. "The Galla of Ethiopia." In *Ethnographic Survey of Africa. North Eastern Africa*, pt. II, p. 25. London: International African Institute.

KROEBER, A. L.
   1947. *Cultural and Natural Areas of Native North America*. University of California Publications in American Archaeology and Ethnology, xxxviii. (First published 1939). Berkeley: University of California Press.

LANE, E. W.
   1842. *An Account of the Manners and Customs of the Modern Egyptians*. London: Ward, Lock.

OATES, J.
   1960. "Ur and Eridu, the Prehistory." *Iraq*, 22:32–50.

SHEPARD, A. O.
   1956. *Ceramics for the Archaeologist*. Washington, D. C.: Carnegie Institution of Washington, Publication 609.

SIMOONS, F. J.
   1960. *Northwest Ethiopia–Peoples and Economy*. Madison: University of Wisconsin Press.

STEWARD, J. H.
   1955. "The Concept and Method of Cultural Ecology." In *Theory of Cultural Change*, pp. 30–42. Urbana: University of Illinois Press.

TSCHOPIK, H., JR.
   1950. "An Andean Ceramic Tradition in Historical Perspective." *American Antiquity*, 15:196–218.

ANATOLIAN POTTERY AS
A BASIS FOR CULTURAL SYNTHESES

JAMES MELLAART

THE last decade of archeological research in Turkey has established beyond any doubt that previous theories about backwardness of the Anatolian Plateau or belated culture development there was not based on facts, but fantasy. The excavations conducted by the writer at Çatal Hüyük in the Konya Plain since 1961 have greatly helped to reinstate Anatolia in its proper place among the earliest cultures of the Near East.

Ten years of archeological survey have changed our knowledge of the archeology of Anatolia beyond recognition, and though excavation is only slowly catching up with the discovery of numerous cultures outlined by the survey material, it has pushed the beginnings of Anatolian civilization much farther back into the past than would previously have seemed possible. The one class of artifacts which has most contributed to this momentous change is, of course, pottery.

If any cultural relations are to be traced between Anatolia and its neighbors, pottery will take the first place in the absence of more specific and reliable cultural manifestations such as texts. It is therefore necessary to review briefly the ceramic development of southern Anatolia, which has recently been established through British excavations at the sites of Beycesultan, Hacilar, and Çatal Hüyük on the Anatolian Plateau (Lloyd and Mellaart, 1955–59, 1962; Mellaart, 1958–60, 1961a, pp. 160–64, 1961b, 1964a, 1964b).

1. An *aceramic culture* is so far only established at two sites: at Hacilar, where it occurs on virgin soil (Mellaart, 1961b, pp. 70–73) but is succeeded by a hiatus of unknown length before reoccupation takes place in the Late Neolithic period, and at Çatal Hüyük in the layers below Level X (Mellaart, 1964a, 1964b).

Although pottery is quite unknown, the aceramic people at Hacilar were quite familiar with the use of clay and plaster. Since mud brick of standardized sizes were used in the construction of rectangular houses, the brickmakers' mold must have been invented. Floors were made of mud, or, in the case of the main rooms, of a lime plaster laid on a bed of pebbles cemented together with lime. These lime plaster floors and the continuous wall plaster were stained red with red paint, and one small floor shows red-painted design on a cream background. Other fragments show patterns of red parallel stripes on cream. Mud brick, mud, and lime plaster were also widely used for the construction of hearths and ovens. The floor and wall plaster was burnished. In the damp, aceramic layers of the mound, it may be argued that had unbaked or sun-dried pottery been in use, it would not have survived. None of these seven superimposed building levels had been burnt. A few baked clay objects have survived, but they are too shapeless to suggest that they are parts of figurines. They certainly do not look like pottery.

For the sake of argument, it might be worth suggesting that unbaked sun-dried pottery may have been in use in the aceramic period. In view of the prevalent use of clay for building, this is not impossible, and unbaked clay bins are, after all, another form of pottery container, even if they cannot be moved. The fact that some fragments of stone bowls were found does not rule out the possibility of unbaked clay pots, for both occur frequently together, both in the Early and Late Neolithic periods as well as during the Early Chalcolithic period in Anatolia. Particularly interesting here is a sherd from Byblos that I was shown by Hélène Balfet, which was coated on the interior with white plaster. I suppose that a layer of white plaster, lining the interior of even an unbaked pot, could help to reduce its porosity and thus make it possible to boil water or other liquids in it by means of pot-boilers (such as occur commonly in Çatal Hüyük VI). However that may be, we have no such evidence from Hacilar's aceramic levels, where finds of any nature other than buildings were exceedingly scarce.

2. The *transition from aceramic to ceramic Neolithic* is now documented at Çatal Hüyük (Mellaart, 1964a, 1964b). Previously the appearance of exceedingly primitive pottery was noted during the B period at Beldibi (Bostanci, 1959, pp. 146–47, Pl. IV) in a context which, from the prevalence of microlithic stone tools, including sickle blades, may still be considered Mesolithic, although the author considers it very early Neolithic on the basis of the appearance of pottery. The writer had the opportunity, through the courtesy of Dr. Bostanci, to inspect this pottery and was struck by the "primitive" look of it, which is as pronounced as in the earliest pottery discovered at Catal Hüyük (Levels X and IX). The Beldibi pottery is, on the whole, very coarse and pockmarked with finger imprints. It has been pinched in the way a child would do if asked to produce a pot out of a lump of clay. Many large fragments look like daub and have the same unappetizing color. However, some of the smaller vessels were better made— though heavy and thick walled—and had flat bases and small perforated lugs. Some were given a summary burnish and all had been fired to some extent. Most of this pottery was red or brown, but a few rims were of the dark-burnished brown-to-black class familiar from Çatal Hüyük and the Kizilkaya group (Mellaart, 1961a, pp. 166–72). The Çatal Hüyük X–IX ware is better in quality than that of Beldibi with which it is probably contemporary. It may be dated to the beginning of the seventh millennium B.C.

After Period B the Beldibi rock-shelter was deserted, and at Çatal Hüyük there is virtually no pottery in Levels VIII, VII and VIB. A much improved version is introduced at the very end of Level VIA, but only from Level V onward can we talk of a fully "ceramic Neolithic" at Çatal Hüyük. It would appear that at Çatal Hüyük we can distinguish two phases of pottery production: an "experimental phase" in Levels X and IX (also attested at Beldibi, Belbaşi, and Reis Tumegi near Çatal Hüyük) and a "fully developed phase" from Level VIA onward. The one is evidently developed from the other, and further excavations will probably reveal the intermediate stages from Levels VIII–VIB.

The early Neolithic pottery of Çatal Hüyük shows a comparatively large number of shapes that would seem to be derived from prototypes in other materials, viz., wood and stone. Unfortunately stone is rare, for Çatal Hüyük lies in a great alluvial plain with the nearest mountains some thirty miles away. Judging by the fauna, wood must have been plentiful, but few wooden vessels have survived in the numerous burnt levels so far excavated. In the numerous burials of Levels VIA and B, wooden vessels have now been found in great numbers and the dependence of pottery shapes on prototypes in wood (and basketry) can now be satisfactorily demonstrated (Mellaart, 1964a, 1964b).

3. The *Early Neolithic period* is, unlike the two preceding phases, known from a widespread number of sites in southern Anatolia, both on and off the Plateau, the latter in Cilicia. A comparable but only roughly contemporary culture is attested for the Antioch Plain (Amuq A) and Ras Shamra, but there are enough fundamental differences to separate the Anatolian from the North Syrian group (Mellaart, 1964c). The term *dark-burnished*, frequently used for the pottery of this period, is misleading in that, besides the soot-coated cooking pots of this color, lighter colored wares are also in evidence. At Çatal Hüyük, at least, no dark-burnished pottery occurs exclusively, not even in the lowest layers reached (IX–X), where it is invariably accompanied by some buffs and browns. From Level V onward, creams and mottled grey occur, and from Level IV onward we have a wide variety of light colors—pinks, oranges, light greys, reds, mottled black, plum red, etc.—often variegated. These occur side by side with the brown-to-greyish-brown cooking pots, the dark-burnished ware.

All the pottery is invariably burnished, a technique applied to floors and walls long before it was used on pottery. Even the earliest pottery so far found is thin and sophisticated in technique, though not in shape. There is a gradual increase in size; most early pots are no deeper than the length of the potter's hand. There is a gradual development from a perforated knob handle (IX and Beldibi B) to a perforated ledge handle, first placed horizontally on the pot, and finally set at an oblique angle below the rim. Bases are invariably flat, like the floors; pyriform hole mouth shapes are more common than globular ones, and the pumpkin shapes of Mersin are not found. Nor do we find the decoration common in Cilicia: rouletted ornament, executed with the edge of a seashell, impressed ornament, excised blobs, etc. (Mellaart, 1961a, Fig. 4). Only in Levels IV–III do we find a number of horizontal incised lines round the rim of the vessel, and even this form of ornament is rare (Mellaart, 1961a, Fig. 4). Of painting we have two sherds in Level III which look as if someone has wiped his paint-stained fingers on a pot before it was baked.

These Early Neolithic pots were made by hand. The flat base shows that they were put on a flat object, and breaks show the use of the coil method. On the other hand, many are so thin that Matson has suggested the use of paddle and anvil. A characteristic of the fabric is that it never shows signs of straw or chaff.

Small grit particles are common, but they may have been in the clay and not intentionally added. The use of a slip would appear to be unknown. Conditions of firing must await the ceramic specialist's report, but it must be added that two kilns with separate firing chambers were found next to bread ovens in two separate instances at Çatal Hüyük, one in Level IV, the other in Level VI. The connection between baking bread and pottery suggested by Ruth Amiran (in this volume) is therefore confirmed by Anatolian Neolithic practices. The one other point worth making is the scarcity of pottery at Çatal Hüyük and its absence among burial gifts.

4. *Late Neolithic pottery* is best known from the excavated sites of Hacilar in southwest Turkey and Fikirtepe, near Istanbul, in northwest Turkey. Unfortunately the latter site is still unpublished (Bittel, 1960, pp. 29–36). The Late Neolithic of the Konya Plain is not yet known and its deposits are assumed to lie at the bottom of the later (Early Chalcolithic) mound of Çatal Hüyük West. Mersin also has two levels of this period (XXVI–XXV) (Garstang, 1935, pp. 27–40).

The Late Neolithic pottery of Hacilar IX–VI (Mellaart, 1961b, pp. 61–69) is the best known, and the following developments may be noted: A better firing control led to the production of light-colored cream wares, which lent themselves eminently to painted decoration. At the same time a red wash is frequently applied with a brush, coating the exterior of the pot and a band around the interior of the rim. Where the red paint is used for making patterns, one is most struck by the clumsiness of most of them—simple stripes, bands, V's, and chevrons—although it must be admitted that one or two pieces show the more advanced use of a "solid style" in which large curvilinear areas are filled with color. The simplicity of the first painted pottery, so notable at Hacilar, is equally striking at Mersin and offers a remarkable contrast to the artistic proficiency of the wall paintings of the previous period. Perhaps one might go so far as to suggest that there was a social as well as artistic distinction between the painter and the simple potter. At Hacilar, at least, one feels that it is not until the Early Chalcolithic period that professional painters decorate the now outstanding pottery. Equally noticeable is the increasing sophistication in shape: disk bases replace flat bases; jars are provided with at first a short and later a funnel neck; tubular lugs for fastening covers (the use of lids is unknown at this period) to keep out dust, flies, ants, etc., abound; bowls take on gracefully swung profiles often with slightly flaring rims. The prevailing colors are cream and light grey in Levels IX–VIII, and red, brown, and buff in VII and VI. Also noteworthy is the infrequent use of thick white paint on red or brown ware and fancy pots of anthropomorphic or theriomorphic shapes which may have been used in the rituals of the period (Mellaart, 1961b, p. 66, Fig. 27). Once again, the use of incision, grooving, ribbing, etc., is exceedingly rare.

It is particularly interesting to be able to compare this South Anatolian Late Neolithic pottery with approximately contemporary wares—or so we assume—made at Fikirtepe and a number of other sites in the northwestern part of the country. Once again, grit tempers predominate, but the firing is poor, the pottery crumbly, and the colors are, with a few exceptions, dark brown or a greyish brown. The surface treatment is burnishing and most of the pottery is undecorated. On such dark wares only white paint could have any effect, but painting appears to have been unknown. Instead we find incision, filled with a white material; scratching, so shallow that it could not hold a fill even if it was intended to; and pointillé. One might suggest that the differences between this northern pottery and that of its southern neighbors are merely the result of less developed techniques of pot-making. Numerous shapes, including ovals as well as such features as disk bases, tubular lugs, ledge handles, and S-profiles allow one to compare the Fikirtepe ware to the Late Neolithic of southern Anatolia, especially Hacilar, but certain other features such as the square boxes on feet seem to provide a link with some of the wooden shapes in use at Çatal Hüyük.

5. In the *Early Chalcolithic period* (roughly second half of sixth millennium B.C.), the characteristic product is a burnished red-on-cream painted ware which forms at least 50 per cent of the total sherd bulk and often more. This painted pottery is, needless to say, the development of the clumsy painted wares of the preceding period, and monochrome red, brown, and buff wares continue without much change. At least three groups can already be distinguished: one in Cilicia, south of the Taurus, best represented by Mersin Levels XXIV–XX; another in the Konya Plain at Catal Hüyük West and Can Hasan near Karaman; and a third in southwest Anatolia, in the Early Chalcolithic levels of Hacilar V–I. Each of these three groups has its own shapes and its own patterns, and artistically speaking, an increase in technical proficiency as well as artistic decoration progresses from east to west with the Cilician group noticeably lagging behind. Only the Hacilar pots of this period fall in the class of "art objects." The availability of excellent clays evidently has greatly contributed to the supreme quality of this ware. Compared to Hacilar pottery the Çatal Hüyük and Mersin wares of the same period are definitely inferior. Conditions of firing of the local clays often produced mottled effects with one part of the pot showing a brownish decoration on a greenish buff background which fades into a red or an orange on the other side. Evidently much less care was taken in the production of the pottery. Except in the latest Hacilar (I) pottery, coils are inconspicuous, but at Catal Hüyük, breaks at the junction of coils are frequent and easily noted. At Catal Hüyük and Mersin we notice another tendency: the gradual change of color from a red or light brown to a blackish-brown in the later half of the period, combined with a differentiation of the linear ornament in broad bands framing thin ones, such as was unknown before.

Both of the latter areas make almost exclusive use of linear ornament, whereas that of Hacilar V–II is predominantly solid and only that of Hacilar I is linear. Another feature of Hacilar I is the cheap reverse technique of painting in white-on-red, the single feature which survives the break between Early and Late Chalcolithic in western Anatolia.

6. Whereas a catastrophe marks the end of the early Chalcolithic period in southwestern Anatolia, traditions of painted pottery linger on in a part of the Konya

Plain and in Cilicia, where one might talk of a *Middle Chalcolithic*. During the earlier part of this phase, represented at Mersin by building-levels XIX–XVII, the tendencies of the end of the last period combine with imported and locally copied Halaf ware (including cream bowls) and with polychromy. There is also evidence for this phase in the Karaman area, but without Halaf imports, for they are not found on the Anatolian Plateau west of the Antitaurus.

The second half of the Mersin *Middle Chalcolithic* (XVI) would appear to be confined to Mersin and the Calycadnus Valley. Absent at Tarsus and farther east, this culture appears to be intrusive, coming most probably from somewhere in the Konya Plain. During its final phase (XVIA) there appear the first traces of Ubaid influence, which gives one a rough date of about 4000 B.C. for the end of the Middle Chalcolithic period in Cilicia. Characteristic of the Mersin XVI Culture is cream-slipped burnished pottery painted in black, brown, and red or in polychrome, red, buff, and brown-burnished monochrome wares, and a black-burnished ware with pointillé ornament. All these features now have an ancestry in the Konya plain, which also provides a possible prototype for the curious tab handles (Garstang, 1953, Fig. 93, Nos. 7, 8, 11) in the form of less stylized bulls' heads.

7. *Cilician Late Chalcolithic*. The final phase of the Chalcolithic in Cilicia is marked by decadence of painted pottery combined with uninspired Ubaid influence (Mersin XV–XIII). With it occur local burnished wares, plain wares etc., and in Mersin XII we once again see an intrusive Late Chalcolithic, with white-painted wares coming down from the Plateau to be submerged in turn by a later wave from the same Konya Plain introducing the Cilician Early Bronze Age (Mellaart, 1962, p. 5).

All the evidence at present available tends to suggest that the development from Early to Late Neolithic and from Late Neolithic to Early Chalcolithic on the Anatolian Plateau and in Cilicia took place without foreign stimulus or interference. On the other hand, we can see the work of foreign bands with different and inferior culture traditions in the destruction of the Hacilar and Çatal Hüyük West cultures and the establishment of Late Chalcolithic cultures in these parts. With them starts a new tradition which only after centuries of slow development will blossom into the Early Bronze Age civilization of Anatolia.

Until the Mersin XVI Culture (which is Late Chalcolithic in Plateau terms), all cultures just described in southern Anatolia show a number of traits which distinguish them from the wares in neighboring countries. Among these should be noted the use of a grit temper (Mersin XVI is the first painted pottery with a straw temper); the prevalent use of a good, and often brilliant burnish (always in the Neolithic at Hacilar, omitted at Çatal Hüyük West only on coarse ware, but less consistent at Mersin), and the rarity of incised ornament on the Anatolian Plateau. To this we may add the use of oval shapes (as well as ovoids, subrectangular, rectangular, square, etc., shapes) and the relative absence of jet-black burnished wares. Equally striking is the small proportion of coarse ware with increases in quantity eastward, and the early appearance of horned potstands

(Early Neolithic Catal Hüyük) which remained in use with little change until the end of the Bronze Age.

Distributed over an area extending from Cilicia to the Aegean, or about the same distance as separates the Zagros from the Mediterranean, all these cultures share features which, in the light of our new evidence, may be considered indicative of an Anatolian origin.

Foreign, i.e., northern Syrian-Mesopotamian influences, have not been detected before the Middle Chalcolithic Halaf period and then only in areas peripheral to its distribution such as Cilicia, the plain of Malatya, and Tilkitepe, south of the town of Van. This is as much as one could expect geographically. In the meantime, neither the ancestry nor the full distribution of the Halaf Culture are sufficiently known, and the investigation of these problems is much overdue (see Mellaart, 1961c, p. 64, for a distribution map of Halaf pottery). A detailed study of this ware with a new stratified sequence, full distribution patterns, regional variations, and local imitations, incorporating the publication of the unpublished Halaf material from Tilkitepe, Malatya, and the Adiyaman region, would be extremely useful.

ANATOLIA AND MESOPOTAMIA

In the previous paragraph we have already touched upon the relations between the Anatolian Highland zone and the vast Syro-Mesopotamian Plain. The relation between the earliest cultures of these two and other neighboring areas is of general importance for the cultural-historical interpretation of Near Eastern archeology as a whole. Old ideas and theories have changed in the last few years and will continue to change as more facts become available. This is inevitable and should not be regretted, for if archeology is to advance, it should be progressive and open to constant reinterpretation.

In the last few years, southern Anatolia has turned out to be as much a home of painted pottery cultures as northern Syria-Mesopotamia, Iran, and Thessaly. The one important difference is that we now have in Anatolia (as also in Thessaly) a long and distinguished ancestry for these painted wares in a monochrome series, which in normal archeological time estimates may occupy as much as a millennium, even though the beginnings of these sequences have not yet been found. Arguments about "time-lag" once familiar in archeology are unrealistic when applied to the regions between Mosul and Mersin, an open area with but one mountain range to cross.

With Mersin XIX–XVII anchored by imports and imitations to the Halaf, and Mersin XVIA (the last of three phases) marked by the first influence of Ubaid Ware, the previously Early Chalcolithic period (Mersin XXIV–XX) becomes the rough contemporary of Hassuna (Ib–V), as already pointed out by the excavators of Mersin and Hassuna. Imports from the Çatal Hüyük West Culture at Mersin are found in Levels XXIV–XXII so that both cultures may be assigned to the same period, and there are numerous resemblances between the latter culture and that of Hacilar V–I to suggest contemporaneity. Radiocarbon dates from Hacilar, Hassuna, Matarrah, and now Elateia in Greece all support such approximate contemporaneity of the earliest cultures with painted pottery in the Early Chalcolithic period.

At Hassuna, only the three superimposed camp sites of Level Ia, which produced coarse straw-tempered ware and jars of hole-mouth shape (as well as eight fragments of burnished bowls), are assigned to the "Neolithic" period. Hole-mouth shapes and light color may be compared to the Late Neolithic period of southern Anatolia with which this phase is probably roughly contemporary.

What, then, is the Mesopotamian equivalent for the Early Neolithic of Mersin and Çatal Hüyük, a period of long duration at both sites and of great cultural achievement at the latter site?

Pottery and architecture seem to indicate no gap between the Hassuna and Jarmo cultures, a suggestion further borne out by the stratigraphic sequence at Tell Shimshara. Jarmo is pottery-bearing only in its top five levels (out of sixteen) and this ware is considered to be ancestral to the plain simple ware of Matarrah, a southern and somewhat impoverished variant of Hassuna. Unless there is a serious gap in the record, and the excavators deny this (Braidwood, 1960, pp. 161–62), one cannot escape the possibility that Jarmo is, at least in part, contemporary with the Early Neolithic of Çatal Hüyük. Whatever the chronological correlation may be, it is already clear that earlier stages of pottery-making must precede the first pottery introduced at Jarmo, which includes painted wares. Moreover, if we compare the earliest pottery of Anatolia with that from either Jarmo or Tepe Sarab near Kermanshah, we are struck by the difference of tradition, technique, and finish, and it would seem at the present most unlikely that these different traditions go back to a common root. All one can say at the moment is that it certainly looks as if the discovery of pottery was made in the highland zone of the Near East. In spite of an intensive use of clay for floors, bins, bricks, and pisé as well as more delicate objects such as figurines, baked clay vessels would seem to have replaced stone vessels relatively late in time.

One can think of several reasons for this. Stone breaks less easily than pottery, especially the relatively thick-walled early vessels. Pre-pottery Neolithic cultures are nearly all found at sites where stone was easily available; and at Khirokitia in Cyprus, an early attempt at pottery-making was abandoned for the fashioning of stone bowls. Aesthetics and, more than this, religious beliefs may have contributed to this conservatism. Furthermore, firing may have provided great difficulties to the first potters, and so forth.

It is, however, interesting to notice the way in which stone vessels continue to be made, e.g., at Hacilar, during the Late Neolithic period, whereas they are comparatively much rarer at the earlier site of Çatal Hüyük. One is tempted to suggest that the position of Çatal Hüyük in the center of an alluvial plain with no good supply of workable stone for about fifty kilometers may have stimulated the first production of pottery. It would certainly have been no easy task to provide the entire population of this city-site with vessels of wood and stone! But Hacilar lies at the foot of limestone hills, and marble also can be found close at hand. This is but a theory, but one which in my opinion should be considered when one is dealing with the efficient beginnings of pottery production.

It is therefore perfectly possible that certain cultures should already be in the possession of pottery while others had not yet reached this stage of technological development. Such would seem to be the case with Anatolia's southern neighbors, Cyprus and Palestine and possibly parts of Syria. With the relative merit or height of a culture this has of course nothing to do, for pottery is often a cheap and unattractive product, and it may well have been so regarded by the people used to marble vessels. Archaic Egypt offers here a well-known parallel.

ANATOLIA AND HER SOUTHERN NEIGHBORS

If we may here ignore the primitive pottery in the bottom level of Khirokitia (sixth millennium), the production of which was abandoned in favor of stone vessels, the first general use of pottery in Cyprus begins at the end of the sixth millennium with a red-on-cream painted ware (Teoulli, Dhenia) that has close analogies with the Hacilar I Ware of southwest Anatolia. Prototypes for this painted pottery are lacking in Cyprus, and it was probably introduced by Anatolians from the mainland opposite. This tradition was maintained in the Erimi Culture which, although dated by carbon 14 to the late fourth millennium, one cannot help feeling may belong to an earlier period in spite of the relative chronology established for it. More excavations are needed to establish its position with greater precision.

Farther south, recent excavations at Ras Shamra, Tell Soukas, Byblos, T. Ramad (Damascus), and T. Munhatta and T. Eli in the Upper Jordan Valley have done much to establish a better sequence in Syria and Palestine, and this sequence is of great interest for it offers a parallel to Anatolian developments.

During the aceramic period (latest carbon-14 dates from Ras Shamra 6192 ± 100 B.C. [Stuckenrath, 1963, p. 83] and 5890 ± 160 B.C. from Jericho, limestone bowls and dishes prevailed. The very first "pottery" to be made from Ras Shamra to Damascus consisted of a heavy white chalky ware—evidently imitating the limestone vessels. This clumsy crumbly pottery soon gave way to a northern burnished ware, red or brown or light colored, which evidently derived from the north, and its Anatolian characteristics are unmistakable. Although the technique was derived from the north, local predilection for ornament was marked, especially at Ras Shamra, Byblos, T. Ramad, and in the coastal area of the plain of Esdraelon, with offshoots into the Jordan Valley just south of Tiberias. The incised or impressed ware probably imitated the texture of basketry. Other vessels of "dark-burnished type" were given a coat of white plaster on their interior or exterior—possibly to reduce their porosity or as a hangover from the "white chalky ware" prevalent in the previous phase. A carbon-14 date from Ras Shamra now dates this pottery to the early sixth millennium (5736 ± 112 B.C.), i.e., Late Neolithic in Anatolian terminology (Stuckenrath, 1963, p. 83).

The very appreciable time-lag between the first general use of pottery in Anatolia (Çatal Hüyük VI) *ca.* 6500 B.C. and that at Ras Shamra on the coast of Syria *ca.* 6000 B.C. perhaps suggests not so much the spread of a new technique as the gradual movement of farmers from the Anatolian Plateau southward in search of new land, first across the Taurus Mountains into Cilicia, then across the Amanus into inland North Syria or the coast, and gradually down south to Lebanon and northern Palestine.

The decorated pottery is coastal in distribution and a southern development on the plain Anatolian Plateau wares. In the following phase (Syrian Late Neolithic) we again see local fashions contrasting with the highland ones in which painted pottery predominated. Instead of the red-on-cream ware of South Anatolia (Hacilar, Çatal Hüyük West, Mersin XXIV–XX), painted pottery is rare in Amuq B or Ras Shamra, and absent farther south. Its place is taken by the pattern-burnished wares which produce the same patterns as those of the painted pottery but in a different medium. This pattern-burnished ware is characteristic of North Syria from Ras Shamra to the Khabur area—and it even occurs in the Middle Neolithic of Byblos, without gaining great popularity. According to a carbon-14 date from Ras Shamra (5234 ± 84 B.C. [Stuckenrath, 1963, p. 83]), in the second half of the sixth millennium, but it is likely to have survived into the fifth millennium at Byblos, for there are unmistakable imitations of Halaf shapes in Middle Neolithic Byblos. Halaf painted pottery itself spread over North Syria from the east during the 5th millennium, and was widely imitated there, but did not affect Lebanon or regions farther south such as Palestine. Here in the Middle Neolithic of Byblos (late sixth and early fifth millennia) the fine incised pottery develops into one with more advanced shapes and less decoration—which gradually coarsens. Herringbone-patterned red-washed wares predominate, and this same pottery characterises the Yarmukian Culture of Palestine and its variants known as Jericho VIII (or Pottery Neolithic B), Wado Rabah, etc. There are, however, a number of different wares found in Palestine in which painting is known (Jericho IX or Pottery Neolithic A and Ghrubba), and here we are either dealing with local developments or with influences from beyond Lebanon. All these various groups are probably contemporary and a number of features in shape and texture, such as the red wash or paint, the "bow-rims" and the great loop-handles link them to a new group which appeared first in North Syria (Amuq D) in the second half of the fifth millennium B.C. (carbon-14 Ras Shamra *before* 4200 B.C.). Associated with this late group of red-washed or painted pottery of ultimate North Syrian origin are peculiar subterranean round dwellings and a rather impoverished cultural inventory which many scholars have suggested possibly indicates a descent of seminomadic people from the north into South Syria, Lebanon, and Palestine perhaps *ca.* 4000 B.C. The entire ceramic history of Syria and Palestine in the sixth and fifth millennia B.C. thus appears to be one in which at first Anatolian and Late North Mesopotamian ceramic influences were being reshaped into a local Syrian or Palestinian mold.

ANATOLIA AND SOUTHEASTERN EUROPE

The recent emergence of Southern Anatolia as an important Neolithic and Early Chalcolithic culture center has significance for the origins of the earliest pottery of Greece and the Balkans and its chronology.

A glance at the shapes of the earliest pottery produced either in Thessaly, Greece, or the Balkans, shows that nearly every significant shape (i.e., excluding those so simple that anyone could have invented them independently) can be matched, not in Mesopotamia or Cilicia, but on the Anatolian Plateau, which is not only geographically but culturally nearer. It would then appear that it was Anatolian influence which was responsible for the first appearance of pottery in Europe at a date which according to new radiocarbon dates from Greece would still seem to fall just within the first half of the sixth millennium B.C., approximately at the time of transition between the Early and Late Neolithic of Anatolia, some time between about 6000 and 5600 B.C.—which is exactly the time when surface finds indicate a spread of Late Neolithic Culture to the Aegean and Marmara coast of Anatolia.

Even before this period, Anatolia may have exerted influences over its western neighbors, for aceramic Thessaly had already adopted the growing of grain and possibly animal husbandry. Pottery soon followed, and the whole character of the Thessalian sequence reflects the Anatolian one in that it also shows successive phases of dark to light or mottled monochrome wares, followed by painted pottery, most often red-on-cream, less frequently white-on-red. In Greece also, this phase is succeeded by matte-painted wares and polychromy and is finally submerged by a wave of black-burnished ware as in Late Chalcolithic Anatolia (Milojčić, 1959, Figs. 5–20). Allowing for local differences, the sequence is the same, whereas a comparison between Anatolia and its eastern or southern neighbors shows a somewhat different picture. The parallelism between Greece and Anatolia is too close to allow for independent origins. Similar parallels can be established with the Starčevo-Criş complex (Comşa, 1959, p. 11), but here we are on less sure ground as the sequences in the Balkans come on the whole not from great mound sites (Karanovo being the exception) but from sites with comparatively short occupation. The shapes of this complex, as well of the rest of its cultural inventory (tools, "stamp-seals," "altars," figurines, etc.) again find their best parallels in Neolithic Anatolia, but some of the primitive forms of decoration —barbotine, finger impressions, etc.,—would appear to be their own, as on the Levant coast.

Little is yet known of the way in which this cultural transfusion took place, but it is likely that we are dealing with two (or more) routes: one across the Aegean from the Izmir region via Skyros to Thessaly; the second from the area southeast of the Sea of Marmara to Thrace and Bulgaria.

SUMMARY

Summing up, we may now say that the South Anatolian Neolithic and Early Chalcolithic development is a purely Anatolian affair, unaffected by extraneous elements or influence. On the other hand, we may trace Anatolian influence in Cyprus, Syria, possibly Palestine, and certainly in southeastern Europe. Mesopotamian influence does not start until the Halaf period and is mainly confined to the Cilician area, not transgressing the Taurus Mountains.

CERAMIC CHANGES IN ANATOLIA

The examples quoted above show clearly that Anatolia possessed a vigorous native ceramic tradition during the Neolithic and Early Chalcolithic period. This tradition disappears in most of the area with the coming of Late Chalcolithic cultures. With a few notable exceptions, the pottery of this period shows a technique so far below that of the earlier wares that one can no longer doubt that the area was taken over by barbarians with a much inferior culture. Once again the Balkans provide interesting parallels, although it must be admitted that there the contrast in technique is less strong. Old traditions are swamped by bearers of new dark-burnished wares found in the Vinča, Boian, Karanovo II, Paradimi, and Hamangia cultures. In Anatolia it is out of this new tradition that after a long period of little or no development the Early Bronze Age is born.

The ceramic traditions of the Neolithic–Early Chalcolithic periods and that of the Late Chalcolithic to Early Bronze Age have nothing in common but the Anatolian preference for burnishing and the use of white paint for decoration. The decline and disappearance of painted pottery in the Late Chalcolithic period (except in Cilicia) in Anatolia is not necessarily the result of a change in taste, as was once thought, but of the inferior technique brought by the potters of the Late Chalcolithic, who were apparently unable to produce light-colored vessels that would lend themselves to painted decoration. In fact the Late Chalcolithic potter was back at the point where the Late Neolithic potter started producing light pottery. Unable to produce the fabric needed, he took to white paint, which frequently used to sink in. The motifs used were on the whole as unimaginative as the shapes, and the result remained unspectacular. It is not until the Early Bronze Age that West Anatolian potters learned to produce really attractive and graceful wares, and we find that side by side with white-painted ornament, incised ornament filled with a white substance was produced with greater effect. In the Yortan Culture of northwestern Anatolia during the Early Bronze Age I–II periods, these techniques reached their highest development. In the contemporary southwest, the potters at last awakened from their uninspired Late Chalcolithic slumber and fell under the spell of metalwork with ribbed, grooved, fluted, and embossed decoration, which made this pottery one of the most beautiful Anatolia has ever produced. Actual metal vessels of this period exist, coming almost entirely from royal tombs at Dorak, the Troad, Alaca, etc., and they show to what an extent the Early Bronze II potter was indebted to the contemporary metalwork of this rich and prosperous period.

As the result of the "Luvian" invasion which put an end to this period, we find a marked decline in West and South Anatolian Early Bronze III pottery, reflecting in its monotonous red, buff, and brown wares the simple tastes of the coppersmith of the time. Only at the end of the period, roughly the twentieth century B.C., do we again find a renaissance of metal working reflected in the grey wares of the Northwest and especially in the magnificent pottery of Kültepe

II. Throughout the second millennium B.C., West Anatolian pottery is frequently coated with grey, red, and gold micaceous washes imitating the silver, bronze, and gold vessels in use at the various courts. Elsewhere, a marked decline of pottery sets in as metal more and more comes to take its place, thus reducing it to cheap kitchen ware. Another sharp break occurs at the end of the Late Bronze Age.

POTTERY CYCLES

Where the evidence is both plentiful and unequivocal it is possible to talk in Anatolia of a number of ceramic cycles or traditions, for it will have become clear from the above account that we are not dealing with a single, let alone a straight, evolution of pottery (Fig. 1). Three main cycles can so far be distinguished in western and southern Anatolia:

1. Early Neolithic–Late Neolithic–Early Chalcolithic. If we tentatively put its beginning *ca.* 7000 and its end around 5000 B.C. it would have lasted about 2000 years.
2. Late Chalcolithic–Early Bronze Age I and II, *ca.* 5000–2300 B.C., a period of over two and a half millennia.
3. Early Bronze Age III–Middle Bronze Age–Late Bronze Age. In Southwest Anatolia *ca.* 2300–1000 B.C., but as the tradition started in Northwest Anatolia (in Late Troy II times) we may have to add another two hundred years or so. This would again give one a period of about fifteen hundred years or more.

These figures show the extraordinary tenacity and conservatism of the Anatolian potter, but comparisons with neighboring countries show that he was not unique in this respect: painted pottery was made in western Iran from the Tepe Sarab phase (contemporary with Jarmo?) until the Iron Age, and actually no country

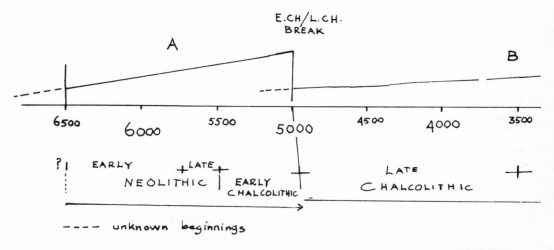

FIGURE 1

Diagram showing length and development of three successive pottery shows such a long tradition of painted pottery as Iran. The "Neolithic" of Knossos accumulated to a depth of ten meters, and at Beycesultan the Late Chalcolithic deposits reached to over eleven meters. The Neolithic of Mersin is at least ten meters thick, and that at Çatal Hüyük (without beginning or end) already fourteen meters. Earlier periods were no less long; over forty building levels (roughly half in phase A and the other half in B) form the Pre-pottery Neolithic mound of Jericho, again well over ten meters in height. None of the periods enumerated here seem to have lasted less than a millennium, and many lasted much longer. Man's rate of progress is often exaggerated in this modern age. As these early peoples were first of all agriculturalists or peasants, there was no need for rapid change, and to this day peasants are among the most conservative people in the world, especially in the Near East. This is a point that, I feel, is too often lost sight of by those who propose or adhere to the numerous "short chronologies," or those who dismiss radiocarbon dating.

THE USE OF POTTERY IN FIELD SURVEYS

Although many of the earlier explorers have left records of the presence of sites in numerous regions of Turkey, a systematic mound survey intended to cover more than a limited area was not undertaken until 1951.

During the last ten years members of the British Institute of Archaeology at Ankara have surveyed the greater part of Anatolia, and few large unknown areas remain except Turkish Thrace, the Black Sea coast, and the southwestern provinces of the country, where either military restrictions or the nature of the terrain made survey difficult if not impossible.

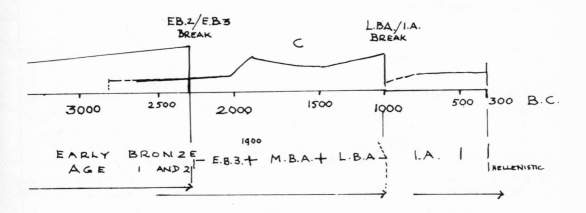

traditions (A–C) in southwestern Anatolia (including the Konya Plain).

Well over a thousand sites of pre-Iron Age date are now on record with details of the pottery collected on each mound (in contrast to the earlier explorers like E. O. Forrer or H. H. von der Osten who often simply registered the mere presence of a mound). As a result, it is now possible to produce maps of Anatolia for nearly every archeological period from the Neolithic to the Iron Age with a wealth of detail undreamed of before.

Needless to say, there are still very serious gaps, both geographically and chronologically, and such recently discovered periods of Anatolian prehistory as the Mesolithic or the Aceramic Neolithic are represented by only a single site. Nevertheless, this is a great advance over the state of things which existed before, when all one's knowledge about Anatolian prehistory was derived from a number of excavations and soundings with a sporadic distribution all over the country, each site separated from the other by vast areas of unexplored and totally unknown territory.

The use of a field survey as a preliminary to excavation is of comparatively recent origin. In the past, sites were frequently selected for excavation not on their own archeological merit, but because of a famous name, a chance find of importance, or because their sheer size impressed the archeologist during a journey through Anatolia. The idea of looking at every site in the area before choosing one for excavation is a new one, and we must therefore distinguish between pre- and post-excavation surveys. The latter can be very useful in widening the range of the cultures exposed during excavation, but on the whole they add little more to the distribution of the culture already known or to specific shapes. They are a useful appendix to an excavation report, and ideally such a survey should be made after each excavation. The pre-excavation survey, on the other hand, is not only more exciting as it takes place in unknown territory, but it is by far the cheapest form of archeology and can be practiced without large funds, motor transport (although it is far more comfortably done by car), or equipment. On the other hand, it demands time, perseverance, and a thorough practical knowledge of pottery, for sherds are the objects collected on the sites.

Pottery-collecting should be done by the archeologist himself, and mounds should be "combed," as one kind of pottery is often confined to one part of the site only. It is not enough to spend a few minutes on a good site and pick up a few pieces of each period thus proving that it was occupied from such to such a period. This method is out of date. We now want to know what sort of pottery can be picked up; how much of this and how little of that; what strange bits may be imports; and what occurs where and in what quantity or position. This takes time and there have been cases where I have visited a mound four times, on each occasion picking up bits of different periods which before were not visible because of recent plowing or dust. The prehistoric surveyor's work is never finished, and it is always possible to add another bit to the jigsaw puzzle that every mound presents. It frequently happens that surface sherds of a certain period collected on a mound do not occur in the trenches upon excavation. For example, pattern-burnished wares are not known in the Mersin XII assemblage as excavated at

Mersin, but they were found in this context on the site by visiting archeologists long after the excavation. At the neighboring site of Tarsus, several sherds of this ware were found, unfortunately "extrusive" and not stratigraphically datable. The chance find at Mersin now helps to date these sherds.

One of the chief requirements of the archeological surveyor is a good knowledge of the geography of the country, its natural divisions and their boundaries, its possibilities for early settlement or its limitations. Without this, no great progress can be made. One is no longer interested in being told that Early Bronze Age pottery occurs on such and such a site without further detail. "Red ware" or "black ware" is not enough. One wants rims and profiles and decorated pieces to determine (*a*) to what phase of the Early Bronze Age the pottery belongs and (*b*) to what regional culture. I remember once being shown bag after bag of utterly dull Central Anatolian Early Bronze Age pottery from the Aksaray region, all exactly the same until one bag was opened with different looking wares of the same period, but of quite distinct character. I remarked that this ware certainly belonged to the Konya Plain and asked from which site around Aksaray it came. The answer was that it was found across the watershed south of the Aksaray district in an area which was culturally part of the Konya Plain, as suspected. Around Aksaray, wares of this kind simply do not occur.

Provided the survey is conducted over a large enough area, the size of which may vary considerably in Turkey, the surveyor will normally find in moving from one plain to another that there are perceptible changes in fabric, shape, or decoration from plain to plain within a certain period. Apart from chronological distinctions, we have everywhere regional ones.

By noting the occurrence of such wares, features, etc., for each mound, one can build up a distribution pattern which may or may not eventually turn out to be significant, especially if it turns up again in a different area. To quote an example: When I was a member of Miss V. Seton-Williams' party surveying the Cilician Plain in 1951, I was much struck by a mauve overfired ware, then assigned to the Late Bronze Age, and kept some (fragmentary) notes on the sites where we collected it. During the survey of the Konya Plain, exactly the same ware turned up in much greater quantity but always associated with Early Bronze Age ware. This puzzle was eventually solved by a visit to the Adana Museum where I had the opportunity of going through the sherd material from Tarsus, and here I found the same "metallic or red gritty ware" firmly anchored by the Tarsus stratigraphy to Early Bronze Age periods I and II, just as in the Konya Plain. The Late Bronze Age ("Local Basering" Ware) attribution must therefore be revised (Seton-Williams, 1954, p. 135). The enormous quantities of this ware on sites in the eastern half of the Konya Plain show beyond any doubt that it was locally produced and not imported from Cilicia, where it is both much rarer and more badly made. A few sherds of it were found in the Aksaray region, and they are probably parts of imported vessels, but in the western part of the Konya Plain this ware, though present, is much less common (see distribution map, Fig. 2). Associated with this pottery in the Konya Plain is a coarse red ware,

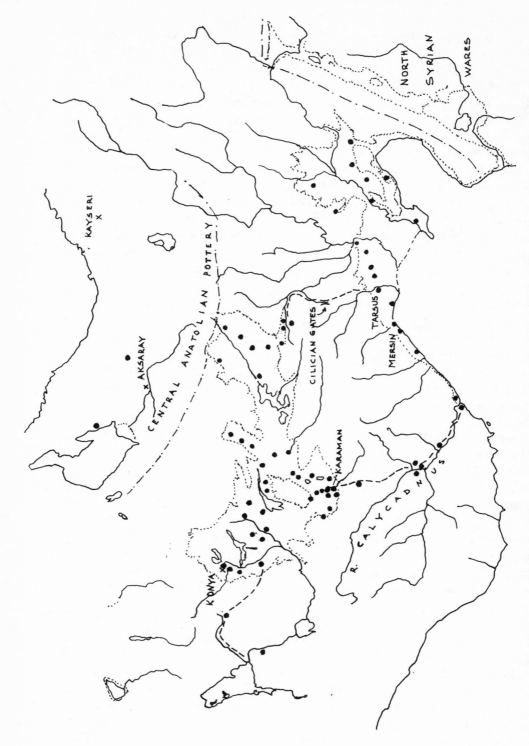

FIGURE 2. Distribution of the "metallic ware" in the plains of Konya and Cilicia and a few outlying sites.

frequently scored, which has an ancestry there that can be traced back to the
end of the Early Chalcolithic period (Çatal Hüyük West), and fine thin burnished
bowls, often with black interiors, which there can be traced back to a Late
Chalcolithic origin.

These three main classes of pottery appear in Cilicia for the first time at the
beginning of the Early Bronze Age I period side by side with local Late Chalcolithic survivors, and it would seem therefore that the Cilician Early Bronze Age
pottery was introduced from the eastern end of the Konya Plain. This theory,
based entirely on surface finds, is in our opinion to be preferred to that of Miss
Goldman (1956), who considers likely a North Syrian origin for the "red gritty
ware." All I need point out here is that a leading shape among this pottery is the
jug with "beak spout," completely unknown in Syrian pottery or before this
period in Cilicia, but typical of the Konya Plain and other more western Anatolian cultures.

Cuts or holes in mounds not infrequently give one a rough idea of the stratigraphy of certain wares, and more often than not, an even rougher stratigraphy
can be established by comparing the pottery from the top of the mound with that
found at the bottom. Fortunately one-period sites are common, and it is therefore possible to build up a corpus of shapes for each period which can serve as
a basis for comparison with others. Dangerous as a procedure of this sort may be
on a few sites, conditions change when identical pottery is found consistently on
forty or fifty or even a hundred sites, as in the Konya Plain. The bulk of pottery
collected is often greater than that found in a small sounding, and as only sherds
of value (rims and profiles) are usually picked up, its importance is often greater
than that from a small trench on a mound, although ideally all one's conclusions
should be tested by excavation. The surface material from about 250 mounds of
the Early Bronze Age II period in southwestern Anatolia gives one a better idea
of the forms and ceramic variety current at this period than the finds from an excavated village site of the same period, even though the latter material may be
stratified. Often it is the sheer bulk of the material which gives one the confidence
needed for drawing conclusions from surface finds.

Conditions often are not as favorable as they are in the greater part of Turkey.
Mounds are absent on the north and south coast except in certain stretches, and
where mounds are absent, the discovery of sites is pure chance. Where mounds
are covered by modern villages—a practice fortunately rare in Turkey, but
frequent in Syria and Mesopotamia—sherd-collecting is exceedingly difficult. In
many parts of eastern Anatolia, turf covers mounds and sherds can only be collected from the earth thrown out by burrowing animals. In other areas, such as
the southwest coast or the Karasu Valley, clays are poor, and when sherds are
water-worn they may belong to almost any period. Classical sites are notoriously
bad for the collection of possible earlier underlying material because of a blanket
of later debris. And finally, there are cases where so little is known of the
archeology of the region that any new and unfamiliar material cannot be dated
without prior excavation.

By plotting the sites of each pottery complex (most cultures use more than one ware) on a physical map (and not a blank one!) one can, more often than not, roughly define the boundaries of their geographical distribution. Within the culture group thus defined it is frequently possible to determine by the quantity in which it occurs the probable center of production of a certain ware, e.g., that of "metallic ware" in the eastern part of the Konya Plain. In the Cilician Plain, both the Mersin XVI and the Mersin XII wares are confined to the Mersin site and are absent at Tarsus, twenty miles farther east, or for that matter anywhere east of Mersin. On the other hand, one can trace these wares westward and up the Calycadnus Valley to the Karaman area, which suggests that they came from the Anatolian Plateau. One can thus demonstrate that a number of cultures appear to have come from the Plateau, viz. the vast and rich Konya Plain whose population appears periodically to have spilled over the rim of the Plateau down to the Mediterranean. One would like to know what caused this, if not overpopulation. Overpopulation is suggested by the huge number of settlements in this plain as revealed by archeological survey. All these deductions are based ultimately on the collection of pottery during field surveys. They remain to be substantiated by excavation, but they are nevertheless highly suggestive.

As a result of ten years of field survey in Anatolia, a host of new and mainly unexcavated cultures have been placed on the map. Many of these may be combined into larger complexes, such as the Northwest, Southwest or Central Anatolian groups. Important differences have been established not only in pottery, but in architecture, burial habits, etc., between western and southern Anatolia on the one hand and central and Eastern Anatolia on the other. Such differences would seem to be more fundamental and may be based on different ethnical groupings. Periods of pronounced regional differentiation are followed by those with more homogeneous culture, or vice versa. Different economic backgrounds are suggested by such vast culture areas as that of east Anatolia, which at one period extends from the Euphrates watershed to Tiflis and Tabriz, including much of Transcaucasia and part of the Iranian Azerbaijan. The greater part of these regions are unfit for agriculture, so we may therefore expect a greater interest in pastoralism. Seasonal migrations of part of the population may have been instrumental in keeping the not very numerous areas of settled agriculturalists in close contact with each other, thus preventing for a time the development of strong regional differentiations which are such a feature of the more western parts of the country.

Noticeable also are the fluctuating borders of the spheres of cultural influence, which often extend far beyond the present frontiers of Turkey. Anatolian influence in Thrace, Macedonia, and eastern Bulgaria is often attested and matched in the east by influence in western Transcaucasia or Azerbaijan. At times this process is reversed; Caucasian and Iranian influences are found in the Van-Kars area, and western barbarians overflow into the basin of the Sea of Marmara.

Anatolian prehistory cannot be studied in a vacuum, and its maximum zone of influence reaches from Thessaly and Macedonia to the Caspian watershed.

The distribution of the Troy I Culture illustrates this point (Fig. 3). It includes the Troad and the west coast of Anatolia down to the Erythraean Peninsula

FIGURE 3

Distribution map of the maritime Troy I Culture, as known in 1961. (For clarity, other cultures have been omitted.)

(Karaburun) as well as the offshore islands: Chios, Lesbos, Lemnos (and probably also Tenedos and Imbros, both unexplored). Nowhere does this purely maritime culture penetrate inland across a mountain range. It also covers the Thracian Chersonese, Turkish Thrace, Greek Thrace, and part of Macedonia (both Greek and Yugoslav) where it pushed up the Vardar and Haliakmon valleys. As a result of this crescent-like maritime distribution, the northern Aegean might well be called a Trojan Sea, but it should be noted that no remains of the Troy I Culture have been found south of the island bridge which runs from Samos to Thessaly. In a previous period, remains of the Kumtepe Culture, the ancestor of both the Troy I and Yortan cultures, extended over the greater part of northwestern Anatolia and some of its remains have been found even on Paros, Naxos, and Amorgos in the Cyclades.

One of the most interesting features of field surveys is the tracing of catastrophes and migrations. On the basis of the results of the excavations at Beycesultan and field surveys in northwestern Anatolia, one can now say that the Early Bronze II Culture of southwestern Anatolia was brought by a wave of northwesterners, probably from the Akhisar-Manisa area. Bringing with them a northwestern culture akin to that of Troy I, one can see the full flowering of northwest Anatolian Early Bronze I Culture in the Early Bronze II Culture of the southwest (Mellaart, in Lloyd and Mellaart, 1962, pp. 135–39). My reconstruction of a Luvian invasion into Anatolia at the end of the Early Bronze II period, *ca.* 2300 b.c., is based almost entirely on survey material combined with excavated evidence from the excavations at Troy, Beycesultan, and Tarsus (Mellaart, 1962, pp. 46–50).

Among such points of general interest for the prehistory of Anatolia as were revealed by field surveys we may just quote the following:

1. Bronze Age and earlier sites in Anatolia are generally found on or near alluvial soil, i.e., in the plains. Settlements on rocks, indicative of need for defense are generally few, but increase enormously in number in the Iron Age and Classical periods.

2. Classical conditions are immaterial and irrelevant for conditions in the prehistoric period. The south coast of Turkey, e.g., west of Silifke, did not acquire any importance until the Iron Age when it became a refuge for people driven off the Plateau.

3. All the main cultures of Anatolia (with the exception of those in the northwest) are essentially plateau cultures, and a decrease in the size of sites is notable as soon as one leaves the Plateau.

4. The great routes to the west coast were in use since the Neolithic period, and the passes were generally controlled by the plateau cultures. The distribution of the sites of these cultures belies the popular concept of difficult communications with the west coast.

BIBLIOGRAPHY

BITTEL, K.
    1960. "Fikirtepe Kazisi," *V Türk Tarih Kongresi*, pp. 29–35. Ankara: Türk Tarih Kurumu.

BOSTANCI, E. Y.
1959. "Prehistoric Researches on the Mediterranean Coast of Anatolia. A new Palaeo-lithic Site at Beldibi near Antalya." *Anatolia, Ankara Dil Tarih-Coğrafya Fakültesi,* pp. 129–78.

BRAIDWOOD, R. J., B. HOWE, *et al.*
1960. *Prehistoric Investigations in Iraqi Kurdistan.* Studies in Ancient Oriental Civili-zation, No. 31. Chicago: The University of Chicago Press.

COMŞA, E.
1959. "La Civilisation Criş sur le Territoire de la R. P. Roumaine." *Acta Arch. Carpatica,* I:2, pp. 173–90.

GARSTANG, J.
1953. *Prehistoric Mersin.* Oxford: Clarendon Press.

GOLDMAN, H.
1956. *Excavations at Gözlü Kule, Tarsus.* Vol. II, *From the Neolithic Through the Bronze Age.* Princeton: Princeton University Press.

LLOYD, S., and J. MELLAART
1955–59. "Preliminary Reports on Excavations at Beycesultan." *Anatolian Studies,* V:39–92; VI:101–135; VII:27–36; VIII:93–125; IX:35–50.
1962. *Excavations at Beycesultan. I. The Late Chalcolithic and Early Bronze Ages.* London: British Institute of Archaeology at Ankara.

MELLAART, J.
1958–60. "Preliminary Reports. Excavations at Hacilar." *Anatolian Studies,* VIII–X.
1961a. "Early Cultures of the South Anatolian Plateau." *Anatolian Studies,* XI:159–84.
1961b. "Excavations at Hacilar, 1960." *Anatolian Studies,* XI:39–75.
1961c. "The Beginnings of Village and Urban Communities." In *Dawn of Civilisation,* S. Piggott (ed.), chap. ii. London: Thames and Hudson.
1962. "Anatolia c. 4000–2300 B.C." In *Cambridge Ancient History* (rev. ed.), Vol. 1, chap. xviii (Fascicle 8).
1963. "Early Cultures of the South Anatolian Plateau. The Early Bronze Age in the Konya Plain." *Anatolian Studies,* XIII:199–236.
1964a. "Earliest of Neolithic Cities: The Origins of Pottery in Chatal Huyuk. Part III —Wooden Vessels in Many Shapes." *The Illustrated London News,* Vol. 244, No. 6498: 232–34.
1964b. "Excavations at Çatal Hüyük, 1963." *Anatolian Studies,* XIV:39–119.
1964c. "Anatolia before 4000 B.C." In *Cambridge Ancient History* (rev. ed.), Vol. I, chap. vii (Fascicle 20).

MILOJČIĆ, V.
1959. "Ergebnisse der Deutschen Ausgrabungen in Thessalien, 1953–1958." *Jahrbuch des Römisch–Germanischen Zentralmuseum Mainz,* VI:1–56.

SETON-WILLIAMS, V.
1954. "Cilician Survey." *Anatolian Studies,* IV:121–74.

STUCKENRATH, R., JR.
1963. "University of Pennsylvania Radiocarbon Dates VI." *Radiocarbon,* 5:82–103.

THE BEGINNINGS OF POTTERY-MAKING
IN THE NEAR EAST

RUTH AMIRAN

T HE QUEST for the beginnings of human civilization devotes much study and research to the "why and how" of the invention or discovery of pottery-making. As Scott (1954) points out, we must emphasize the fact that pottery-making is only one item in the complex picture of community life in its earliest stages. Furthermore, these items are interdependent and have developed out of mutual influence.

The problem now is not only to sort out this picture into separate items, and to organize these items in their sequential development, but also to clarify the character of the relationship between them. Our objective here is to isolate a certain part of the complex picture of crafts and achievements, and to demonstrate that it is a group of crafts of interrelated inventions. These may constitute another gauge with which to measure the intellectual progress of the human mind. The group is: the craft of preparing bread/porridge and the craft of making pottery. The resemblance which exists between the two, both in the processes together—preparing, grinding, mixing with water, kneading, shaping, and firing— and in the auxiliary instruments, has been taken as a basis for grouping the two crafts together.

We shall present the evidence for this thesis by analyzing the progressive stages of development of the two crafts from the Natufian through the Pre-Pottery and Pottery Neolithic phases.

NATUFIAN

The sources for our knowledge of the way of life of the Natufian community are constantly increasing. The basic works of Garrod and Neuville revealed an amazingly complete picture of the Natufian cave life, and the recent discoveries of open-site Natufian life at Jericho (Kenyon, 1960, pp. 36–43), at Eynan in the Hula Basin (Perrot, 1960, pp. 14–22), and in Nahal Oren in the Carmel (Stekelis, 1960, pp. 118–19) have complemented that interesting picture.

The Natufian context does not as yet show signs of the use of clay in any of its manifestations. As for the other craft, however—the making/cooking of bread/porridge—an excursus into one of the cardinal problems of protohistoric times is unavoidable: the question of the character of the Natufian Culture. Garrod, the discoverer of the Natufian Culture, recently expressed her attitude. She "agrees with Neuville in thinking that the Lower Natufian people were the first

240

agriculturists" (Garrod, 1957, p. 216). The Braidwood school (Braidwood and Howe, 1960, p. 182) has abstained from shaping a categoric attitude toward the question, but is inclined, apparently, to the idea of "incipient cultivation." It seems to me that the data accumulating pertinent to this question is steadily corroborating the Garrod-Neuville conception. The artifactual evidence on the one hand (reaping and grinding tools are very prolific in all the sites mentioned above), and theoretical conclusions such as those of Helbaek on the other hand, do much to throw light on the Natufian Culture in the direction of the Garrod-Neuville conception. The problem of the luster on the sickle-blades is an old one. Braidwood's suggestion, that it may have been imparted to the blades from the reaping of reeds, has already been rejected by Garrod.

The Terrace of Level B in Mugharet el-Wad on Mount Carmel is a good example, it seems, of a Natufian baking/cooking unit. Garrod's lucid description of the Terrace (Garrod and Bates, 1937, p. 9ff.) speaks for itself. This terrace seems to be provided with all the equipment required for the processes: the pavement, partly preserved (described in *ibid.*, pp. 11–12), would be suitable for hand-threshing and husking; the cup basins (*ibid.*, Basins 2–5, p. 11) and the numerous stone mortars (*ibid.*, p. 10) would be suitable for the grinding or milling of the grain; the one larger basin (*ibid.*, p. 10, Basin 1) would serve for mixing the ground grits or rough "flour" with water; and all this was found not far from ovens (*ibid.*, pp. 10, 12). The excavator looked for an explanation for this scheme, so complete in itself, and suggested the ritual of the dead, discarding Guy's notion (*ibid.*, p. 13) that similar installations (though of much later date) at Megiddo were cooking places. It may not be superfluous to point out in this connection that the grinding technique, developed by the Natufians, apparently became a dominant one, employed in many aspects of daily life. All instruments and various personal accessories were manufactured by the meticulous grinding of stone on stone, or stone on bone. In imitation of natural holes and cavities, the Natufians shaped mortars in movable stones by patiently grinding stone on stone, and then used them for grinding wheat or barley. They must have first tasted these grains by grinding them between their teeth. It has been mentioned above that theoretical conclusions like those of Helbaek corroborate the Garrod-Neuville conception. In his studies of the grains and grain-impressions from Jarmo, Helbaek came to the conclusion (in Braidwood and Howe, 1960, pp. 102–3) that, "there seems to be no reason to doubt that at Jarmo we are faced with the earliest stage of plant husbandry yet discovered. . . . However, that even Jarmo does not represent the very first steps in the agricultural economy is suggested by the fact that its wheat spikelets seem to belong to a crop of a conspicuously mixed character. . . ." It seems, therefore, inescapable to look for the beginning of cultivation in a stage prior to Jarmo.

PRE-POTTERY NEOLITHIC

The Jericho Pre-Pottery Neolithic Levels A and B, the Jarmo Levels XVI–VI, and the aceramic Levels I–VII of Hacilar (Mellaart, 1961, pp. 70–73) were farming communities in many, if not all, respects. One point, new with these communities, is of special significance for our thesis—another product of the grain-bearing grasses entered the economic circle of life, the straw-and-chaff-and-husks, a by-product of any type of threshing activity. We find the straw-and-chaff-and-husks in various phases of Pre-Pottery Neolithic life, and always in some relationship to or dependence upon another new commodity, clay. Clay mixed with straw was the main material used in building all three dimensions of the spaces in which they lived: walls made of mud bricks laid in clay, mud floors, and roofs made of the same material. The immediate proximity or close relationship between the craft of which straw-chaff-husks is a by-product—the threshing of wheat or barley—and the use of straw-tempered clay is evidenced, it seems to me, by the occurrence of grain in the clay of floors and ovens discovered at Jarmo (Helbaek, in Braidwood and Howe, 1960, pp. 42–102). An enlarged example of an impression of a grain of two-row barley from a clay floor is seen in Figure 1. Out of the same clay the man of the Pre-Pottery Neolithic stages made figurines and statues to fulfill his growing elementary religious and aesthetic needs. We would like now to suggest that the clue for the most crucial question in the use of clay—its transformation to pottery by physical actions—is to be sought in another clay phenomenon of the Pre-Pottery Neolithic levels, both at Jarmo and Jericho. This is the clay-lined depressions of the floors, made in one piece with the clay floors themselves, which were uncovered both in Jarmo (Braidwood and Howe, 1960, p. 43) and in Jericho (Kenyon, 1957, p. 56). A floor with a basin in it from Jericho is shown in Figure 2. Whether used as basins for household activities, or as bins, or as ovens with "boiling stones," the main interest lies in the fact that these immovable receptacles are located together with the ovens and hearths in the courtyards, the working spaces of the houses. We may now conclude, confident in the logic of our inference, that some accidental firing, due to the proximity of the various acts of preparing–cooking–baking the ground wheat or barley in the immovable basins and the oven, was the cause of the transformation of the mud clay to pottery.

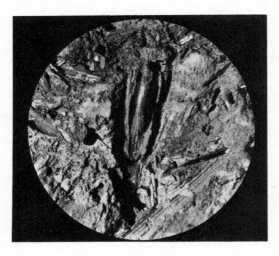

FIGURE 1
Impression of two-row barley in a clay floor at Jarmo. (Courtesy of Dr. H. Helbaek.)

FIGURE 2
Floor with basin, Pre-Pottery Neolithic B at Jericho.
(Courtesy of Dr. K. M. Kenyon.)

POTTERY NEOLITHIC[1]

Having surveyed the preparatory stages (from the standpoint of the subject
of our symposium, pottery is somehow nimbused as a kind of goal!) of long and
slow evolution, in which any revolutionary moments are very difficult to pinpoint,
we are faced now with pottery, which is made of the cheapest, most ubiquitous,
and most accessible material on earth—clay. The excavators of the sites where a
first pottery-bearing stratum was reached were confronted with the question of
whether they had discovered the "absolute" first, or only a "relative" first appearance of pottery. There always exists the logical possibility that the first pottery-
bearing stratum, like any other stratum, may represent an intrusion, as maintained
by Kenyon in her explanation of the Pottery Neolithic A stage at Jericho. Even
in the case of Jarmo, where the excavators maintain an "overall consistency of
the Jarmo assemblage from bottom to top" (Braidwood and Howe, 1960, p. 49),

1. A general remark must be interposed here which pertains also to the preceding para-
graphs, and concerns absolute chronological correlations between the cultures mentioned.
Mellaart, in this volume, proposes an interesting set of correlations between the early cultures
of the Near East. His Anatolian-Mesopotamian correlations are convincing; those with Syria-
Palestine, on the other hand, would call for some comment which should be kept for another
occasion since they are not directly relevant to our present subject.

they express the opinion that the "sherds are obviously early, but good examples of the potter's craft. We do not see on Jarmo the fumbling beginning of this craft. They may not, of course, be very far back," thus allowing for the possibility of a gap between the Pre-Pottery Neolithic settlement and that of the Pottery Neolithic.

The expression "fumbling beginnings" raises another point which is an integral part of our thesis. It is the fact that the potter's craft is *not* the earliest of man's crafts, and is therefore not to be expected to represent any characteristics of primitiveness in the absolute sense of the word. Techniques and aesthetics were inherent in man's feelings and perhaps in his concepts. Man's hands were already skilled in fine grinding and drilling techniques, shaping complicated forms, and executing decorations, variegated and refined, in stone, bone, and shell (we should only recall the Natufian, Karim Shahir, Pre-Pottery Jarmo assemblages, etc.). Man was already, as we have seen, in possession of the knowledge of mixing and preparing his clay, and modeling from it his figurines and statues. In discovering the potentialities of fired clay, man had only to translate his acquired knowledge and skill to the newly gained material. He was spared the necessity of inventing shapes, as he had at his disposal stone mortars, stone bowls, and natural shapes such as gourds which were used as containers, and the like. He was also already familiar with the use of color, especially red. We remember the burnished red slip of the Pre-Pottery Neolithic floors at Jericho, or the red and black paints used on the statues of the same stages. It seems, therefore, that such definitions as "fumbling beginnings" are not clear enough. Neither theoretically nor empirically are we in a position to give any clear definition of what the "missing link" of Jarmo pottery should look like. In shapes and decorations, as already explained, we may expect very unfumbling products. Neither the consistency of the clay nor its need for tempering was new with them. Only one step was new: firing the clay objects, whether figurines or vessels. With this new step they had to experiment, understand the results, and achieve progress. And we are not amazed to find that man is is conservatively or inertially continuing to work and experiment at the same location where he first acquired the notion of firing: near the cooking/baking oven. At Early Neolithic Çatal Hüyük on the Konya Plain, Mellaart (in information helpfully supplied) is reporting

The occurrences in various levels of the Pottery Early Neolithic of two types of ovens, one built next to the other. One is the normal vaulted type of baking oven. The second is different in that it has a fire chamber divided into two compartments by a half brick some 15 cm. high below the main chamber. The front part of these ovens and kilns, which evidently protruded into the room, was destroyed, and was evidently removed to take out whatever was baked in them, whether pots or bread. With the next firing/baking, the front part would be covered over again, which is of course easily done in mud.

This evidence from Çatal Hüyük is of the greatest significance, since its chronological position at the beginning of the Pottery Neolithic stage is clear.

All the Neolithic pottery, of Jarmo V–I, of Jericho Pottery Neolithic A

FIGURE 3
Sherd made by the coil method.
Jericho Stratum IX—Pre-Pottery
Neolithic A. (Photograph from the
Palestine Archaeological Museum.)

and B, and of Çatal Hüyük is handmade. Figure 3 shows the inner face of a sherd made of coils that was excavated by Garstang in his Level IX—Kenyon's Pottery Neolithic A. The method of building by coils or rings is attested also in other cases. Very often the smoothing of the surface of the vessel has eliminated almost all traces of the coiling construction, but is recognizable on the broken edges of sherds.

Thus we have tried to follow bread and pottery through their early steps from the Natufian to the Neolithic. It does not seem to us that this "pairing" ceases here, but a chapter in their development, and in human development in general, is about to end here. In the coming period, the Chalcolithic, human society in all its facets is gradually emerging into what we know of it in historic periods. In the Chalcolithic period we have, side by side, continuation of the old Neolithic traditions and manifestations of the new in its process of development. In the village of Teleilat Ghassul we see, on the one hand, its growth, its "modern" measurements and layout, and on the other hand, as in Figure 4, the agricultural tools that village was using. Here we still feel very much in the Neolithic tradition. We see here the hoes, the mortars known from the Natufian times, and the querns with their rubbers known from Neolithic times. In the craft of the potter many of the old ways also continue. However, we see the very first signs of a forerunner of the potter's wheel in the impressions it has left on the potter's products. Vessels from Ghassul with the impressions of a mat on the base are seen in Figure 5. One of the rudimentary problems in the process of building a vessel by hand with coils or rings is the separation of the ball of clay from the floor on which the potter is working. This necessity brought the mat between the ball of clay and the floor. The potter was now free to work on his vessel with his two hands while the mat stuck to the base during the whole operation, including perhaps the firing. On this observation

FIGURE 4
Heavy Stone Tools from Teleilat Ghassul (reproduced from Malon, Koeppel, and Neuville, 1934, Vol. I, Pl. 34).

FIGURE 5
Mat impressions on vessel bases from Teleilat Ghassul. (Photographs from the Palestine Archaeological Museum.)

we could theorize a whole series of forerunners to the wheel, or more exactly to the pivoted tournette, the first manifestations of which appear in Palestine at the beginning of Early Bronze I (around 3200 B.C.). It has to be said that the mat as such is also of a long known Pre-Pottery Neolithic traditional craft, if we remember the rush mats covering the floors of the rooms of that period at Jericho (Kenyon, 1957, p. 56 and Pls. 12–13). But the complicated story of the wheel and tournette is part of the next chapter in the development of human society.

BIBLIOGRAPHY

BRAIDWOOD, R. J., B. HOWE, *et al.*
1960. *Prehistoric Investigations in Iraqi Kurdistan.* Studies in Ancient Oriental Civilization, No. 31. Chicago: University of Chicago Press.

GARROD, D. A. E.
1957. "The Natufian Culture: The Life and Economy of a Mesolithic People in the Near East." *Proceedings of the British Academy*, XLIII:216.

GARROD, D. A. E., and D. M. A. BATES
1937. *The Stone Age of Mount Carmel. Excavations at the Wady El-Mughara.* Oxford: Clarendon Press.

KENYON, K. M.
1957. *Digging Up Jericho.* London: Ernst Benn Ltd.

1960. *Archaeology in the Holy Land.* London: Ernst Benn Ltd.

MALLON, A., R. KOEPPEL, and R. NEUVILLE
1934. *Teleilat Ghassul I.* Rome: Pontifical Biblical Institute.

MELLAART, J.
1961. "Excavations at Hacilar, 1960." *Anatolian Studies*, XI:39–75.

PERROT, J.
1960. "Excavations at Eynan (Ein Mallaha), Preliminary Report on the 1959 Season." *Israel Exploration Journal*, 10:14–22, pls. 1–2.

SCOTT, SIR L.
1954. "Pottery." In *History of Technology*, C. Singer, E. J. Holmyard, A. R. Hall (eds.), I:376–412. Oxford: Clarendon Press.

STEKELIS, M.
1960. "Oren Valley (Wadi Fallah)." *Israel Exploration Journal*, 10:118–19.

SOME CERAMIC CONTRIBUTIONS TO
A KNOWLEDGE OF CULTURE
IN PREHISTORIC IRAN

LOUIS VANDEN BERGHE

INTRODUCTION

CIVILIZATIONS of the greatest antiquity have been made known by excavations carried out in the Near East. For a knowledge of the expansion and development of these civilizations we are limited to material remains, among which those of ceramics, and particularly of painted ceramics, constitute the principal element. It is, consequently, of great importance that pottery should be studied systematically. For that reason, a classification into schools or styles, as well as a meticulous study of their chronological positions, is essential. The study of Iranian ceramics is especially important since there the prehistoric period was very long, stretching over nearly forty centuries. Ceramics, being the most characteristic phenomenon of agricultural communities and their cemeteries, therefore constitutes the main element for establishing the dates of material remains and the characterization of the various cultures.

The first thing that strikes us is the great number of styles and schools all over Iran. Contrary to developments in Mesopotamia, Iran produced a great variety of them. This can be explained by a geographical factor, for Iran is a country of boxed-in mountains and deep valleys, whereas Mesopotamia is just an immense plain. In Iran, each valley or each region has, in spite of mutual contacts, its own characteristics. In Mesopotamia, we know only seven styles for pre- and proto-history, especially the pre-Ubaid style represented in the north by Hassuna, Samarra, and Halaf; and in the south by Eridu; and the Ubaid, Uruk, and Jem-det Nasr styles. In Iran, on the other hand, for a corresponding period extending from 4500 to 2900 B.C., we can count no less than fifteen styles. Ten other styles can be added if one defines the prehistoric period as extending up to the arrival of the Iranians, and we are far from knowing them all. While excavations in Mesopotamia have produced no styles other than those already known, we can still hope for new discoveries in Iran. In addition to a greater variety, we can observe that the Iranian styles, as opposed to those of Mesopotamia, show a richer and more diverse decoration. In the question of geometric designs, for example, let us recall the Tall-i-Bakūn motifs; in floral and animal decoration, the Hisār I and Siyalk III designs.

The method for a scientific study of these styles can be summarized as follows: the heterogeneous material from excavations must be grouped and classified, taking as a basis the characteristics of technique, shapes of vessels, and decoration. For each style, we find it useful to take as a starting point the locality which has provided the most typical and abundant material in the course of scientific excavations.

It is obviously important to study the evolution of each style, that is to say, to establish a relative chronology, relative because of the lack of definite dates. Two methods may be used:

1. The direct method is applied to the styles represented by localities which, scientifically excavated, have yielded sufficient materials in clear strata. This has been done, for example, for the Siyalk I, II, III, Hisār I, Giyān, T. Bakūn and T. Taimurān styles.

2. The indirect method is employed for the styles which are not represented by localities with clear or precise stratified deposits. On comparing the materials of these places to that of the neighboring styles, where strata have been found, a chronological development can be recognized, as in the case of the Bampūr-Khurāb, Susa II, etc., styles. It goes without saying that this second method is less effective and that it should be used with the greatest precaution, because two localities having the same ceramics are not necessarily on the same chronological level.

The geographical expansion of each style presents yet another problem since, up to the present, it has not been possible to delimit with any certainty the stylistic regions, since vast regions have not yet been systematically surveyed. The establishment of the limits of expansion of each style is a basic need.

FĀRS

We have chosen the province Fārs as an example for discussion, because we have had occasion, over several years, to prospect and to excavate in this region of southwestern Iran. Our investigations have demonstrated the almost uninterrupted evolution of cultures from the end of the Neolithic period until the arrival of the Iranians.[1] (A comparative table of this culture sequence is given in Table 1.)

The study of the evolution and expansion of styles is not only of interest in acquiring a knowledge of pottery itself and for establishing the dates of material cultures, but it also gives us a better understanding of other cultural factors. We

1. In his original paper prepared for the "Ceramics and Man" symposium, Dr. Vanden Berghe described in some detail the prehistoric pottery from Fārs for each of the cultures he has listed in the Fārs–Tall-i-Bakūn column in Table 1, citing extensive bibliographic references within the field of Iranian ceramic studies and presenting evidence for the culture sequence he has established. Unfortunately Dr. Vanden Berghe was unable to present his paper, but his slides were shown and discussed. Since the materials that he planned to discuss and illustrate concerning the cultural sequence in Fārs, based largely on his extensive field studies, is reported in his excellent volume *Archéologie de l'Iran Ancien* (Leiden, 1959), pp. 41–45, this material will not be presented in this volume. As in so many regions where the archeological data are fast accumulating, the dates which Dr. Vanden Berghe has suggested (revised in March, 1964) in Table 1 may not be entirely acceptable to some of his colleagues because of the ever-developing and changing chronological picture being obtained from radiocarbon dating.   F.R.M.

TABLE 1. COMPARATIVE CHRONOLOGICAL TABLE OF EARLY IRANIAN CULTURE SEQUENCES

	Mesopotamia	Geoy Tepe	Hasanlū	Chashmah-i 'Ali Tepe	Tepe Siyalk	Tepe Hisār	Anau	Tūrang Tepe	Shāh Tepe	Tepe Giyān	Khūzistān Susa	Fārs T. Bakūn	Bampūr Khurāb
Early Neolithic	M'lefaat												
Late Neolithic	Jarmo												
Early Chalcolithic 5500-5000	Samarra	M		IA	I: 1, 2, 3, 4, 5 — II: 1, 2, 3		IA					T. Djari B — T. Mushkī	
Middle Chalcolithic 5000-4000	T. Halaf			IB	IIIB: A 1, 2, 3; 4, 5, 6	I: A, B, C	IB			V: A, B	T. Djaffarābād 6-3 50 m. Musyān A — T. Djaffarābād 3 50-2 m. Musyān B	T. Bakūn B2	
Late Chalcolithic 4000-3500	El Ubaid				IIIB: C 7; 7b	II: A	II			V: C, D	T. Djaffarābād 2-0 m. — Musyān C Susa I	T. Bakūn A1-4 — T. Bakūn A5	
Early Bronze I 3500-2800	Uruk / Djamdat Nasr				Hiatus — IV	II: B	Hiatus	97 m.	III	Hiatus	"couche intermédiaire"	T. Kaftari	

Chronological correlation chart:

Period	Date	Mesopotamia			
Early Bronze II	2800-2300/2200	Early Dynastic (Old Sumerian)	K		
		Akkadian			
Early Bronze III	2300/2200-1900	Guti / III Dynasty of Ur	G	VI	
Middle Bronze	1900-1600	Dynasty of Isin-Larsa	D		
		Old Babylonian			
Late Bronze	1600-1200	Kassite	C	V	
			B		
Iron Age	1200-800	Assyrian	A	IV	

| III A | III B | III C | | | 106 m. | II B | II A | IV | III | II | I A | I B | I C | | V | VI | Kalār Dasht |

Sites:
Susa II — Hiatus — Khurāb — Bampūr — T. Qal'ah — T. Shughā — Taimurān A — Taimurān B — Djalābād

251

want to cite the most important of these factors, together with some examples. It is not our intention to give an exhaustive list, since these examples could be multiplied.

In the field of *domestic and social life,* pottery allows us to get a glimpse of certain facts, among them:

1. The relative density of populations and their prosperity at a given period: It can be observed that the distribution of population is not the same in different regions. For example, Tall-i-Bakūn pottery is found all over Fārs, while that of Tall-i-Shughā is limited to the plains in the neighborhood of Persopolis. The Marv Dasht Plain has known every phase of pottery evolution. On the other hand, prehistoric settlements are not found, one might almost say, in the Buluk Kurbal, situated to the north of the salt lake of Niriz, while mounds of the Islamic period are very numerous. One is thus justified in supposing that this region, properly speaking, was still a part of the lake in the prehistoric period.

2. The reciprocal relations of different civilizations: There are striking examples of the contacts established between distant populations, with regard to the spread of the same techniques, the same shapes, and the same characteristic designs. In the section dealing with Fārs, we have stressed several times the fact that there were contacts with other regions of Iran and even with Mesopotamia and Syria.

3. Population movements and the communication routes taken: This observation comes from the previous one.

4. The daily life of the people: The designs represented on this pottery furnish us with indications of the activities of the population. They may show fishermen in a boat, hunters pursuing wild beasts, or agricultural workers. The nomads have left their traces in the Shāh Tepe and Tūrang Tepe styles.

Daily life was carried on in beautiful countrysides or in homes on river banks (Tall-i-Bakūn, Tall-i-Shughā). A baker occupied with his chores comes to our mind (Susa II). It is probable that bull-fighting was already being practiced (Susa II). It should be mentioned here that the flower and animal designs of painted pottery give us some knowledge of the flora and fauna of the period and provide us with limiting dates for deciding on the presence of this or that plant or animal.

In the field of *religion,* iconography provides us with some information, although vague, about the beliefs of these peoples.

1. Certain styles have a preference for astral designs; these are found most often on the Tall-i-Bakūn, Shahi-Tump, and Susa I pottery.

2. Others prefer designs relating to the fertility and fecundity cult (Siyalk III).

3. Designs recalling magic are to be found relatively frequently. Representations of mountain goats, wild sheep, goats, ibexes, sheep, and gazelles are explained by the belief held by the hunters that by representing the animals pictorially, they were thus captured in advance by the power of magic. On several vessels from Tepe Siyalk II and Tepe Hisār, one sees panthers without heads. Should one read

into this the intention of making magic to prevent these animals from ever being dangerous again?

The survival of ancient pottery in techniques, shapes, and decorations: In certain regions of Iran, pottery is still made which by its shape recalls that of ancient times. In Baluchistan, modern pottery evokes in its designs the ancient pottery of Bampūr-Khurāb and of Mohenjo-daro, although the time span between the production of the old and the new is one of some 4000 years. The carpets which are still made in Fārs continue to use the designs, thousands of years old, that were popular on the Tall-i-Bakūn pottery.

THE FUNCTIONS OF POTTERY IN SOUTHEAST ASIA: FROM THE PRESENT TO THE PAST

WILHELM G. SOLHEIM, II

Two general purposes in the excavation of most archeological sites are to place the site in a time and cultural context with other sites and to discover as much as possible about the internal organization, or the culture, of the society whose remains are being excavated. In those sites where pottery is present it often makes up the majority of the portable artifacts recovered and so should be one of the most important sources of information. The use of ceramic evidence for placing sites in context is widespread and of long standing, but pottery, of itself, has only recently and rather narrowly been used to gain insight into the internal organization of a community. It is the purpose of this paper to examine one general approach for the greater use of pottery to gain information on internal organization.

The approach suggested here is to examine the uses of pottery in living communities, observing how this is related to the organization of these communities; and from this to work backwards in time to see what can be said about and from the pottery of the past. This report can best be called suggestive, with the possibility that the subject will warrant more extensive and detailed examination in the future. Data are presented from Southeast Asia using the area as a whole without attempting to examine even one community in depth. Only portable pottery is considered, omitting any form of architectural ceramics, such as bricks, tiles, molded or modeled elements of architectural decoration, etc.

THE FUNCTIONS OF POTTERY IN THE HISTORICAL PRESENT

Pottery performs a number of different functions in a society, which, for the purposes of this paper, are classified in three different levels from the point of view of the pottery: (1) its functions to the user, i.e., the physical functions of the pottery; (2) its functions to the manufacturer, i.e., economic and psychological; and (3) its functions to the community, both within the community and outside it, in its relations with other communities.

The functions of pottery in terms of its use must be further subdivided, and here one must be arbitrary. Two major subdivisions are used, partially because there is a certain amount of tradition behind them. These are "utilitarian" and "ceremonial." These terms carry certain ethnocentric viewpoints with them which are undesirable. For example, certainly ceremonial items are of utility, though these two terms give the feeling that one group is useful and the other is not. Possibly "profane" and "sacred" would be better, but similar value judgments that are not all necessarily correct go with these terms as well. However, any terms will do as long as one keeps in mind one's own bias. Similar difficulties are present for each level of subdivision.

There are also difficulties as to the subdivision into which a specific function should be placed. For example, the use of pottery as a wealth item is included as a subdivision of "ceremonial" because this pottery in Southeast Asia often plays an important role on ceremonial occasions. Good arguments could be put forward for forming a third "wealth item" category at the same level as "utilitarian" and "ceremonial." At the more abstract levels of classification it is at times necessary to be arbitrary.

Utilitarian Functions

Food.—The major uses to which pottery is put in Southeast Asia are in connection with food. It may be used for the packaging and transportation of food, for its storage, preservation, fermentation, cooking, serving, and for eating and drinking. In some communities, all these functions are present; in others, only one or two.

The majority of communities in Southeast Asia that include any specialized commercial functions have one or more Chinese stores. In virtually all these stores a number of food items are displayed in large glazed stoneware jars. Many of the jars originally served as package containers for transportation of one or more of the foods displayed. When the jars are emptied they are used as storage and display containers for locally produced products such as vegetables and dried fish, or for products shipped from a distance in basketry containers. Many varieties of Asian and European alcoholic beverages, packaged in glass or stoneware bottles, are found in small stores in the most remote areas as well as in quantity in the more central locations. After their first use, the bottles are often collected and re-used for numerous purposes. Individual rooms in the long houses of Sarawak usually include a number of such bottles being used for a variety of storage purposes, after having been purchased for the second or later contents of the bottle. The great majority of the Chinese stores also have large, transparent glass jars, square in cross section, for the display of various sweets and other small items. Most, if not all, of these ceramic containers are either manufactured in large numbers in centralized locations in Southeast Asia with western technology or come from China.

One use of locally made earthenware pottery for transportation is to bring water from its source to the house (Cole, 1922, P1. XLII–XLIII; Colani, 1940, P1. XXXVIII–XXXIX). This is no longer common, as bamboo containers or kerosene tins are widely available, inexpensive, and not as liable to break as the pottery. In Ilocos Norte in the Philippines, the inner walls of many wells are formed by heavy earthware-pottery cylinders.

The impression gathered about the storage of food items is that pottery vessels are more often used for liquid storage than for dry. Preservation is here the major consideration, and for preservation of dry organic substances in a moist climate, ventilation is important to avoid the development of mold. In the Chinese store the turnover is relatively rapid for such items as vegetables and dry fish, so they are unlikely to mold during the short time of their storage. Another common item stored (and displayed) in the jars are the various kinds of eggs preserved in their shells, which do not need ventilation. Uncooked rice is stored in a jar by the Bajau of North Borneo (Alman, 1961, p. 597).

Liquid storage includes water, alcoholic beverages, and the preservation-storage in liquids of meats and vegetables. The containers for each of these purposes differ. The usual water storage jar is as much for dispensing water as for storage. In the Philippines large earthenware jars are often made with a common water tap at the base. These jars are porous, without glaze, so that the water soaks through the jar and evaporation keeps the water cool. A common water storage jar for general purpose water is a stoneware jar made in Thailand. These jars are found in the Philippines, Sarawak, Malaya, and probably elsewhere. They have an olive-green glaze, a flat bottom, a wide mouth, and a patterned surface (usually vertically ribbed) from a carved paddle.

A common form of beverage container found in several areas of Southeast Asia is a large glazed porcelain or stoneware jar used to store rice or fruit wines. Many of these jars, for many different tribes in the Philippines and Borneo, are heirloom pieces of great value, having been made in China or Indochina centuries ago. Just outside of Kuching in Sarawak, there is a Chinese potter who makes good imitations of these jars for sale. The local groups who value the old jars can tell the difference and use these new jars for storage, but apparently not as wealth items. These same jars are used for fermenting the wine before storage. In markets in Kuala Lumpur, Malaya, similar imitations of old Chinese jars can be seen. The usual small glass or stoneware bottles are also used for storage of both fermented and distilled beverages commercially or privately manufactured. The beverages may be stored for only a few days or for many years. In Ifugao in the Mountain Province of the Philippines, rice-wine jars full of wine are buried in the ground to be saved for special ceremonies. Folklore has it that the older the wine the better, and cases have been noted of jars with wine well over fifty years old still buried awaiting some major occasion for their consumption.

In the Philippines, a widely used method of temporary preservation-storage of fresh meat is to cook it in vinegar and then keep it in a container of vinegar for up to two weeks or more. In a relatively short time the meat turns a very dark brown but does not spoil. When it is recooked for eating it is fried with a great deal of garlic, producing the common Philippine *adobo*. Any kind of flesh may be kept in this way, as, for example, beef, carabao, pork, chicken, dog, lizard, and fruit bat. The container may be any of several kinds of pottery, including earthenware. In Ifugao, an old earthenware jar was seen in which were kept preserved old pieces of meat which had come from animals used in former important ceremonies. On the occasion of some of the major religious ceremonies held at the present time, these pieces of meat are displayed as a part of the ceremony. From these ceremonies, in turn, a new piece of meat is added to the others. Vegetables of many kinds are pickled and kept by the Chinese in ceramic containers of many varieties.

Cooking is probably the major use for locally made earthenware pottery in Southeast Asia today. Many groups in the Philippines do not feel that rice can be properly cooked except in an earthenware pot. Only when so cooked does it have the "good" taste. This applies to other foods in other areas. In Sarawak ". . . it is recognized that certain kinds of foods (such as some of the relishes, or *enkayu,* which the Iban eat with their rice) taste much the best if they are cooked in an Iban earthenware pot" (Freeman, 1957, p. 172). In other areas in Southeast Asia, rice is now cooked in aluminum pots, in the large cast-iron Chinese round bottom pan, or, as of old, in bamboo tubes. It is not uncommon that particular pots are used only to cook a specific food. Cooking pots of different sizes may be used for different purposes. In Amotag, Masbate: "All the pots made are of the same shape and without decoration. There are three different sizes. The smallest is called *anglet* and is used to cook porridge for children or to cook fish. A slightly larger pot, called *korron,* is used for cooking rice or a larger amount of fish. The largest, called *banga* (jar), is used as a water jar" (Solheim, 1952, p. 51). All this cooking is apparently done by boiling. The Chinese, and possibly others in some areas, cook their rice by steaming, using a double connected pot with perforations in the base of the upper portion. Pottery vessels used for frying or baking have not been noted in this area.

The other widespread use of a distinct pottery form in connection with cooking in Southeast Asia is the stove. Stoves vary considerably in size, but they have one basic form with many variations. The basic form has two functioning levels. The lower level is a flat bottom on which the burning charcoal rests. Toward one end or in the middle, the sides and the end (or ends) are built up in a thick wall; toward the top of this wall and projecting from it, is some form of support where the pot is set (Alman, 1961, p. 596). This forms the second level of the stove. The paste of these stoves is usually coarse and the walls are thick. The flat base may be raised off the ground by an oblong or ring foot, depending on the shape of the base, or there may be three or four separate feet. The pot may be held above the charcoal by the construction of the three walls, or supports may extend inward from the top of the walls, from three or four sides.

On special occasions involving eating, food is displayed before it is eaten. This varies from the tremendous display before cooking of yams and other foods in Melanesia and eastern Indonesia (Du Bois, 1944, plates between pp. 32–33), or of pigs before butchering in the Mountain Province of the Philippines, to the relatively simply display of prepared food before a party. The display of unprepared foods at the beginning of major social ceremonies is for obvious purposes of seeking or confirming prestige and status, and does not ordinarily involve pottery. This food is ordinarily divided in the raw state and cooked, and then consumed by family groups in the general area of the display and/or taken home for later consumption. It is not difficult to see the remnants of this practice at most private parties given in the Philippines, particularly those in celebration of a wedding, christening, or other family ceremony of the nature of a public announcement. Arriving at the party some hours before the time to eat, one first sees the display of the food to be eaten. Here the food is displayed in the best porcelain bowls and serving dishes. Many of these bowls are on high ring stands and are not used in the usual family serving and eating situations. Eating comes only at the end of the party, after which everyone departs, taking with them food presented by the host, there always being much more prepared than can be eaten by the invited guests and the friends they often bring with them. This same procedure was—and probably still is—found in a political setting in the provinces. Here a common vote-attracting procedure was to give large public parties before an election with a tremendous display of food before eating, with guests taking home much that they were not able to eat (Bulosan, 1944).

Porcelain or metal enamelware bowls are the common containers used for serving and for eating. The porcelain is now primarily of Chinese origin, though in historic times a fair amount of this type of porcelain came from Indochina and possibly Thailand. Eating also includes the use of the Chinese type of porcelain spoon which is now also commonly found copied in metal. The use of earthenware for either of these two functions has not been noted.

Drinking utensils are commonly of glass or porcelain. These are primarily in the usual western forms of cup or glass. Among the Chinese in Southeast Asia, the Chinese-style teacup of porcelain or stoneware is used, and the usual Chinese teapot of hard reddish earthenware or of porcelain is used for making and pouring the tea. Where straws are not used, rice wine is usually now served in glasses or metal enamelware cups. The *kendi*, or kendi-like vessel, with a narrow neck and a spout which is drunk from directly, is used in Indonesia and Malaya (Alman, 1961, p. 600).

Miscellaneous.—There are a variety of uses of pottery not connected with food, the majority of which involve porcelain or stoneware rather than the locally made earthenware. Possibly the most widespread function of locally made earthenware in Southeast Asia at the present time is as flowerpots. The local manufacturers of these pots often make no other kind of pottery than the two major types of flowerpots. The orchid pots have numerous openings to allow for free entrance of air, while regular flowerpots have ordinarily only one perforation, if that, for drainage of water. Flowerpots and the growing of potted flowers in Southeast Asia would make an interesting study.

The Tinguian (in the Philippines) use earthenware pottery for rat guards on their granaries. "Just below the floor, each post supports a close fitting jar—without top or bottom. . . ." (Cole, 1922, p. 394 and Pl. LV). There is no indication whether these jars are specially made for this purpose.

Some portions of the Iban of Sarawak still make special earthenware pots for the preparation of mordants during an important ceremony concerning *ikat* weaving. Here the pots appear to be serving both a ceremonial and utilitarian function (Freeman, 1957, p. 172–73).

The many other uses of porcelain and stoneware vessels would appear to be primarily of Chinese origin. A partial listing of these would include umbrella stands, drum-shaped seats, stands for flowerpots, large bathtubs often found in surprisingly remote areas, containers for betel-chewing requirements, Chinese writing sets with ink and brush, and containers for many kinds of cosmetics and unguents.

Pottery manufacture.—Pottery is used to a slight degree in many areas in Southeast Asia in the manufacture of pottery. No example is known where potsherds are used for temper, but a very similar purpose has been noted for pottery manufacture near Vientiane, Laos. In July, 1960, information was gathered on pottery manufacture just outside the capital of Laos. Here, one variety of clay is mixed with rice chaff, formed into balls about six inches in diameter, and then fired in a large pile. This firing lasts about twenty hours. After the firing and cooling, these clay balls are crushed, and the resulting fragments are used as a temper for a different clay in the making of pottery vessels.

In many areas, portions of broken pottery vessels are used at different stages in manufacture. Large sherds are used for water containers to supply water to the hand or to a wooden paddle to prevent the clay from sticking to the hand or paddle. Complete rims of vessels with the body broken off evenly below the neck are used as stands for unfired pots while they dry, or to hold them off the ground during the different stages of manufacture. These whole rims are occasionally used for stands to hold the rounded-bottom pots on the floor in the house.

The Buhid of Mindoro, Philippines, use fairly large pieces of broken pots "as small frying pans in which maize and other foods such as termites may be toasted" (Conklin, 1953, p. 9).

In the Philippines, and probably elsewhere, potsherds are used as markers in various types of games or in a game vaguely like quoits or bowling, where sherds are tossed to come as close as possible to a mark or previously thrown sherd, or to knock a sherd out of a ring. The sherds so used are often worked and are sometimes very nicely polished into disks.

Uncracked portions of large storage jars or large pots are often used to store rice hulls for chicken food or as containers to feed pigs or chickens. Porcelain collectors in the Philippine lowlands occasionally found large celadon or blue-on-white porcelain bowls or platters being used to give pigs food, the pigs eating directly out of the bowls.

CEREMONIAL FUNCTIONS

Recurring use.—Pottery may be in constant use as part of altar furniture or it may be found on special occasions. Most Chinese altars, whether private or public, have a ceramic or metal container containing sand in which joss sticks are placed.

Offerings of fruit are often made at these altars, in some cases held or displayed in porcelain bowls. Liquid offerings are also made from porcelain cups or bowls. In connection with animistic beliefs on the mainland of Southeast Asia, a number of small offering locations for local spirits have been noted which include a pottery bowl or two, again to hold fruit offerings and joss sticks.

Some of the Tinguian of northern Luzon in the Philippines have specially made earthenware vessels which would, to a certain extent, fit into the category of constant use.

In Buneg . . . small incised pottery houses are found among the rice jars, and are said to be the residences of the spirits, who multiply the rice. They are sometimes replaced with incised jars decorated with vines. The idea seems to be an intrusion into the Tinguian belt. (Cole, 1922, 313, Pl. XXIX.)

No mention is made of their use in particular ceremonies, but they appear to have a constant religious function. The shapes of the pottery houses differ from any other recently made pottery of northern Luzon, and the substitute jars, while of a common shape, are apparently the only Tinguian pottery that is decorated. (Such jars are on display in the Chicago Museum of Natural History.)

A number of tribes in Southeast Asia use special plates and bowls as part of their numerous religious ceremonies. These vessels are, in most cases, porcelain or stoneware. On them are placed offerings of rice, in varying forms, and eggs. In the ceremonies of the Tinguian, Cole (1922, pp. 295–314) mentions and provides pictures of numerous occasions (Pls. XXX and XXXII) on which plates (Pl. XIX) or pots (Pl. XXV) are used. He also pictures a bowl with a high ring foot in use during a ceremony (Pl. XIV) but does not state of what it is made. A similarly shaped bowl used in the wedding ceremony (Pl. XIV) is stated to be made of wood (*ibid*, p. 280).

While in Sarawak in 1959, Solheim made collections of material culture for the American Museum of Natural History and purchased a number of small plates and bowls of porcelain which were said to be for use during ceremonies. He stayed at one Land Dayak long house for several weeks while excavating in a cave nearby. The first night after his arrival, a ceremony was held to contact the spirits of the cave in order to inform them that there would be digging there and to make sure that this would be all right. At the beginning of the ceremony, a number of large enamelware metal bowls and brass bowls were brought out and set up in a row. On each bowl was piled *palay* (unhusked rice), and on the *palay* were several porcelain bowls, each of them containing some husked rice; and finally, topping it all, was a small green plate of stoneware in which was placed a cooked egg still in its shell. These were the offerings displayed for the spirits. The hardboiled eggs were eaten after the ceremony. The bowls and plates used in the ceremonies are apparently not used for any other purpose. Several of the larger bowls and plates were cracked or were missing a fair-sized piece or two. They had been broken by the children, but as long as they remained primarily in one piece they were still kept for use, while the sherd broken from the bowl was thrown away.

In the baptistery of an old Catholic church in northern Luzon was seen an old Ming blue-on-white jar used in baptisms as a container for holy water. In several of these old churches the holy water containers just inside the front door are old porcelain bowls, often cemented into the structure of the church.

Funeral use.—The pottery associated with funerals can be divided into two distinct categories: funeral furniture and the actual containers for the bones or body itself. The use of pottery as funeral furniture in Southeast Asia at the present time has not been noted, though similar funeral practices have been observed in Sarawak. "The placing of porcelain bowls and dishes onto secondary burial 'posts' is common in the upper Rejang—the projections on these posts being intended partly for this purpose" (B. Harrisson, 1956, p. 154). This article by Harrisson concerns the excavation of a pair of burials with a number of porcelain vessels as funeral furniture, the graves being less than 100 years old.

In some areas, jars of stoneware or earthenware are still used for coffins, and it is a practice that has only recently died out in many other areas. In Vietnam, secondary burial in jars was quite frequent until recent times (Janse, 1961, pp. 109–10). In Formosa in July 1960, while proceeding to an archeological site in the outskirts of Taipei, it was necessary to cross over the area surrounding a small tower. All around the tower and inside of it were many well-fired earthenware jars containing the cleansed bones of recent secondary burials. This is a custom among some groups of South Chinese and is also widespread in Ryukyus (Takiguchi, 1960, p. 3). In Sagada, Mountain Province, Philippines, only some years before the war, there occurred the primary burial of a child in a jar. After a Christian ceremony for the child, whose body was then in an ordinary coffin, the parents wished to transfer the body to a jar. "At the *campo santo* the body of the child was cut up . . . and transferred to the jar, which was said to be a very old one" (Solheim, 1960a, p. 129).

Present-day remnants of the Cham in Vietnam make use of an unusually shaped pottery vessel (Solheim, 1961a, Fig. *2k–p*) in connection with the purification of a corpse. "The vases are used for mixing *sea water* with the *white* sediments produced in the nearby health sources of Vinh-hoa, of ancient reputation. The concoction is used for washing (purifying) the corpses of individuals, who in lifetime had important positions" (Janse, 1961, p. 110).

Wealth items.—The importance of old Chinese and Southeast Asian stoneware and porcelain jars as items of wealth among many different groups of people in Southeast Asia is well known. In many areas these jars are also used for storing and fermenting rice wine or other varieties of wine. Where these jars are valued they are often important in the exchange ceremonies at betrothals and weddings. They are displayed on important occasions, usually ceremonial in nature, not only for the benefit of the living but for the spirits as well. In many areas, the drinking of rice wine and offering it to the attending spirits is a part of the ceremony, and the rice wine is always contained in a valuable old jar which is present at the ceremony. In several articles, Tom Harrisson has mentioned a number of different kinds of jars and other kinds of vessels which are of great value to various tribes in Borneo, as well as mentioning some vessels of ceremonial use which are not considered of great value (1950, pp. 272–73; 1951, pp. 546–47; 1954, pp. 108–10). In Mindanao, in the Philippines, some of the jars that are in themselves wealth items have had iron lids attached which can be locked with a padlock and are used for storage of other wealth items.

The Functions of Pottery to the Manufacturer

There is a considerable amount of scattered published information concerning the functions of pottery in terms of its use, but there is much less information available on the function of the pottery to the individuals who manufacture it. While there is some information as to the economic function of the pottery to the potter, no examples have been noted to the psychological function of pottery manufacture to the potter.

Economic Functions

The majority of the reports which include information on pottery manufacture mention whether the pottery is sold or bartered, and often for how much, but they go little further than that. It would be well worth the trouble to study the economics of both a full-time potter and a part-time potter.

Full-time potter.—To make a full study of the economic aspects of the life of a full-time potter would require an ethnographic study of a community of such specialists. Two such communities in northern Luzon in the Philippines are known. Both use the old method of paddle-and-anvil manufacture without apparent specialization within the manufacture of one pot. There is one barrio just south of Laoag, Ilocos Norte, that produces pottery the year around. A few kilometers north of San Fernando in La Union is a small community of about a dozen houses, all engaged in producing pottery the year round. Either one would be an ideal location for such a study. Here one could get accurate information in quantity which would lend itself to detailed statistical analysis of all factors in pottery manufacture, all of which would be in some way involved with the economics of pottery manufacture to the full-time specialist.

Part-time potter—There are two different kinds of part-time potters: one who works at it seasonally, i.e., who works full-time for a specific period each year and little or not at all for the rest of the year; and one who works at it occasionally as time allows or as demand requires. The economic situation is different between the two and quite different from that of the full-time potter. The occasional potter is probably the most common in Southeast Asia, though far from the largest producer. In Amotag, Masbate, Philippines, a potter-informant ". . . had been making pottery for many years as a secondary source of income, and is the only potter in town" (Solheim, 1952, p. 49). In Makebog, Masbate, the potters ". . . no longer manufacture pottery as they did for themselves and their neighbors before the war" (Solheim, 1952, p. 51). In the Batanes Islands north of Luzon in the Philippines: "There is little trade for pottery on the island [Batan] as most of the women make the pottery needed for their own use" (Solheim, 1952, p. 52). Among the Buhid of Mindoro: "In areas where pottery making is possible, all women are usually potters, and as one might infer, there are no full time potter-specialists. After years of imitating and helping her elders, an average girl of fourteen may be considered an experienced potter. Most women continue making pots throughout their adult lives" (Conklin, 1953, p. 10).

PSYCHOLOGICAL FUNCTIONS

The psychological function of pottery manufacture to the potter, as far as Southeast Asia is concerned, is a matter for possible future study and present conjecture. At this stage two questions would be of interest: What is the personal importance of quality (craftsmanship), and what is the possibility of artistic expression? These factors would probably vary in importance among the full-time potters, the seasonally full-time, and the occasional potters.

Craftsmanship—We have heard a great deal about the psychological implications of industrialization, where a worker has become so specialized in making a small portion of the finished product that he no longer receives personal satisfaction from his work. The craftsman, who is proud when he turns out a fine product, receives much personal satisfaction from his work as well as an economic return. Does the potter have similar feelings? Does she feel an identification with her product? Are different degrees of pottery-making ability recognized by the community and the market? And what effect, if any, does this have on the comparative status of potters in one community? Are there economic advantages to the worker of higher potting status? Obviously there are many questions of this nature that one could ask, and expect much variation in the answers. This would necessarily require a study in depth of a number of potters in a community as well as a number of different communities.

Artistic expression.—On this subject there should be much of interest, both as it affects the artist and as it reflects the mores, feelings, and possibly even the philosophy of the culture. Unfortunately, there remains little possibility for the potter to give free reign to artistic feelings. The great majority of the pottery made in Southeast Asia today is plain with considerable standardization in form. It would be of much interest to study this subject in any society where pottery is found. Since this is a matter of individual psychology and artistic ability as acted upon by the culture, studies from other major culture areas would produce information valuable to Southeast Asia. Such studies need not be restricted to pottery but could include wood carving or weaving or other craft products which have a traditional form and pattern in a culture. There is enough artistic expression in wood carving and weaving in Southeast Asia to throw light on the potters' situation.

If there is a possibility of artistic expression, it could be examined in terms of its quality of expression and the mastery of different techniques both in decoration and form. If the potter has a freedom of personal expression within the overall tradition, what does that expression mean to the person? What sort of societies allow personal expression, and what sort do not? What does the rest of the society think of the individual's expression and how does this affect the individual and his or her pottery? Again, a large number of questions can be asked. Possibly such studies have been made in other areas, or on different crafts in Southeast Asia. It so, they would present a much better idea as to where to start on this problem.

THE FUNCTIONS OF POTTERY TO THE COMMUNITY

Probably the primary function of pottery manufacture to a community as a whole is economic. However, other less obvious functions connected with the presence of potters in the community could be of importance to the community or could provide information about the community. If the pottery is traded outside of the community, the persons involved in the trade will also furnish a channel of communication with other communities. Returning to the question of artistic expression in pottery, the possibility or artistic expression or lack of it must present information on the community, and the symbolic or realistic content of the artistry must present further information.

ECONOMIC FUNCTIONS

The study of pottery manufacture in a community would present two important insights as to the total economy of this community. First, it would throw light on the internal organization of that small society. What is the relationship of the potters to the community as a whole? Does each nuclear family produce its own pottery, or does the extended kinship group take care of its own needs? Is the pottery bartered or sold? Is it sold to anyone or only to particular people? Is there a particular exchange relationship between potter and customer, or does the customer shop for what he wants? Is payment made in kind with traditional values as in India, or is the pottery a subject for bargaining? This, and much other detailed economic information on the pottery, can only lead to the study of the economy of the community as a whole and how the movement or non-movement of pottery within a community is interrelated with the rest of the economy.

An interesting beginning on those problems has been made by Conklin in his study of Buhid pottery (1953, pp. 11–12). The surplus pots made by the part-time potters are most important items for barter and trade with others of the same tribe and with people of other tribes.

The Buhid and Bangon desirous of these pots usually go directly to the potters and return home carrying the earthenware themselves. In trading with the pagans to the south, however, the Buhid potter's male relatives take the pots with them on peddling

trips into Hanunoo territory. . . . Such transactions are of great economic importance
to the Buhid who depend heavily on Hanunoo for knives, other metal implements, and
salt. . . . Among all but some of the more coastal dwelling Hanunoo, Buhid pots are
common items of material culture, and in many homes they are important household
necessities. This holds true particularly for the interior Hanunoo communities within
ten or twelve kilometers of Buhid territory. Consequently, a Buhid visitor with pottery
for trade is always welcome in a Hanunoo settlement. Long standing friendships often
result from repeated visits by the same trader. I know of three instances where Buhid
traders finally decided to settle with their Hanunoo friends permanently. . . . Among
the Buhid, pottery provides . . . an economic surplus which is the most important
single commodity in a relatively far-reaching series of trade relations among southern
Mindoro pagans.

From the study of the economic position of pottery within the community,
it is an obvious step to study the use and importance of pottery in the economic
relations between the community and the non-community. Pottery may well be
the only item through which there is a constant or cyclical source of money or
goods from outside the community. The study of the external trade in pottery
will present information on the larger society and culture of which the community is a part, and help to explain the relationship of that community to the
larger units or higher levels of organization. Again, it would be of importance to
study not only the trade in pottery but the position of the pottery trade in the
total trade of the community and the higher levels of greater overall organization.
The type of study made by Malinowski on the *Kula* is the best example of this
level of study.

DIFFUSIONAL FUNCTIONS

The diffusional function is not so much a function of the pottery as it is of
the trader in pottery. The same function would probably be filled by the trader,
whatever craft ware was moving out of a community. As pottery in Southeast
Asia appears to have been, at least until recently, one of the most common of
traded items, the diffusional function of the pottery trader is used as if it were
a function of the pottery.

While the study of economic functions of pottery on a community scale would
be relatively straightforward, the study of diffusional functions of pottery would
be most difficult at the present time because of the relatively simple and widely
used channels of communication now open throughout most of Southeast Asia.
In the not far distant past, when pottery was one of the few items involved in
relatively wide trade patterns, and when communication was on a much smaller
scale, the traders, whether coming in for the pottery or going out with it, must
have been a most important channel of communication with the outside and a
major source of contact for diffusion. Conklin's remarks above on the traders of
pottery among the Buhid, convey some idea of the extent of contacts between the
trader and his market. This channel of diffusion was probably of importance to
the potter as well as to the society as a whole, as the trader could well present
requests for changes or suggestions for change in the pottery itself to better

satisfy the distant consumer. These outside preferences would affect at least the relative quantities of the different vessels the potter produced. The trader could have a further effect on pottery change, since in many cases he could be in contact with the potters from more than one community, and through him might spread bits of technological information among different pottery-trading centers. The sort of study needed to examine the possible influence of the trader in pottery could probably still be made in interior areas of New Guinea and would be of interest to a much wider audience than just those interested in pottery.

ARTISTIC FUNCTIONS

While the economic and diffusional functions of pottery are of more importance to the community where pottery is internally manufactured, the artistic functions to the community expand to include the imported pottery. In connection with the rice-wine jars used as wealth items in the Mountain Province in the Philippines, different tribes certainly have different tastes in the jars which to them have the highest values. From what information has been noted, taste seems to be primarily concerned with the color and texture of the glaze on these jars. These jars have little in the way of decoration other than the glaze. Data have not been furnished on differences in value placed on the different types of dragon jars, but no doubt there is again variation in taste between different ethnic groups as to the type and style of dragon jar deemed the best. The difference in preference for different styles and forms of pottery, changing through space and time, is of course the basis for seriation techniques used in the United States to help place archeological sites in time and cultural context. These changing preferences probably express more than drift and diffusion.

Fischer (1961, p. 79) has recently published a most interesting article on the possible "connections between art forms and sociocultural conditions." In this article he presents a series of hypothesized correlations between specific pictorial elements of design and specific elements of social organization and then tests these correlations statistically.

Here is something that needs testing in the field and which should not be too difficult to test on pottery as used in present-day Southeast Asian societies. It should be extended to form as well as design. If it tests out, the importance of its use for the past is obvious.

THE EXTENSION OF PRESENT DAY FUNCTIONS OF POTTERY INTO THE PAST

The more accurate way to extrapolate backward in time is to move back gradually rather than to take large leaps. By moving back slowly and using bits of information in ethnographic reports and reports of the earlier voyagers, we may possibly be able to make out trends in the direction of change in specific functions of pottery. This would certainly be a major study in itself. It should at least restore to pottery, or possibly to wooden containers, some of the use functions now held by the widespread enamelware utensils and aluminum pots and pans. For Southeast Asia, documentation will not go back far enough to reveal conditions before porcelain and stoneware started coming from China in large quantities or before the use of brass trays and containers which may have displaced some of the earlier uses of pottery.

Archeological excavation will not stop while all these studies are being made. If functional studies of excavated pottery are not made at the same time that the rest of the laboratory work is done on the pottery, it is likely that they never will be done. Therefore, it is desirable that what functional analysis is possible at the present time should be utilized along with the more traditional methods of analysis. The same three levels of classification as used previously are examined for possible analytical methods that may distinguish some of the specific functions of pottery in the past from the archeological record.

The type and condition of a site will naturally have considerable influence on the pottery functions discovered from that site. A burial site will obviously contain different information than a living site or a refuse dump. The pottery from any site in which there are distinct units should be studied by unit as if each unit were completely independent of the others.

There are good possibilities for functional analysis of the pottery in any site that was quickly destroyed as by volcanic eruption, landslide, or fire. In these cases, excavation should often locate pottery in its functioning or storage location, and the position of such pottery relative to the position of other implements and to the boundaries of the unit in which it is contained will furnish valuable information. Burial sites not mixed with living or refuse sites will always contain valuable information. However, this is all common-sense archeology and the source of the major portion of our knowledge on the functions of pottery in the past. It is for the mixed sites, disturbed sites, refuse dumps, and abandoned sites, that little analysis has been done in the past.

UTILITARIAN FUNCTIONS

Food.—It is likely that the major use for pottery in prehistoric times was in connection with food, as it is today. It is also likely that all of the major subdivisions used in examining present-day pottery uses in Southeast Asia were present in the recent prehistoric past. However, the importance of some of these subdivisions is different, and moving a bit farther back in time, it is likely that two or three of them no longer exist.

The Chinese have been in contact with Southeast Asia for about 2000 years, but for most of this time their presence was in extremely restricted areas—for trading, political, or military purposes. Their spread into the hinterland as relatively permanent residents did not come until the advent of the European. In the major port towns of Southeast Asia, small, relatively permanent Chinese settlements may have started by A.D. 500 or even earlier in such a place as Oc-Eo in Funan. Fragments of large and heavy stoneware jars have been found at a number of such sites. These fragments indicate jars with a plain glazed surface not much different from those used today in Chinese stores. Very little has been published about this ware because so little is known about it and because it is so "undistinguished" in general appearance. It may be possible, through Chinese records, to find out when they started shipping in ceramic containers, and what it was that was shipped in these containers. The present-day use of ceramics for packaging, for transportation of items other than water, and for display, all takes place in stoneware, porcelain, or glass, and primarily involves products of Chinese or European origin. It is probable that these functions of pottery were not present before Chinese contact brought them in. It is desirable that future reports on archeological excavations in Southeast Asia include analysis of the heavy stoneware. If some effort were made, it is probable that restoration of the stoneware jars from which the sherds came would be possible, or at least enough to enable probable reconstruction of their form and size.

Earthenware pottery was probably more commonly used in the past than it is today for bringing water from its source to the house. The use of kerosene tins does not go back in time. Stoneware jars are in most cases too heavy, and bamboo is not everywhere available or used where it is available. The present-day pots used for carrying water are not unusual in any way, so that it would be doubtful that they would be distinguishable in an archeological site. The use of cylindrical pottery walls for wells is not known to be widespread in Southeast Asia and probably came into the northern Philippines from China or Japan. Archeologists in Southeast Asia have not paid particular attention to wells—with one exception. Madeliene Colani (1940), in a book on the use of stone in ancient days, included wells lined with stone in her study, but the wells were not her primary interest.

Liquid storage is found today in both vitrified and unvitrified ceramic containers and probably goes far back in time. Storage of dry food materials seems to be considerably less common and is in vitrified containers where the food does not have to remain for long. A specific study should be made on this before attempting to work back in time.

The jars used today for wine fermentation and storage are all stoneware or porcelain. Does this mean that previous to the entrance of these jars from China and Indochina there was no use made of rice wine? The making and use of rice wine, and its importance in ceremonies, is so widespread in Southeast Asia that this seems doubtful. It would be worth experimentation to see whether one set of earthenware jars could be used for fermentation and another set for storage. The advantage of vitrified jars in this case may be primarily in that they allow indefinite storage, which might well be difficult in nonvitrified jars. Because of the importance and position of fermented drinks in Southeast Asian societies it would be most interesting to know the background of this wine. It may well be related to the use of *kava*, which is brewed in wooden containers but not kept for any length of time.

The semipickling process for preservation of meat found in the Philippines could well go far back in time. It is not known whether this method is widespread in Southeast Asia. However, this is probably correlated with the spread of the coconut tree, as the common vinegar in the Philippines is made from coconuts. In a number of areas in Southeast Asia coconuts have only recently been planted for use.

Cooking was no doubt the primary use for pottery. The use of pottery for cooking was certainly considerably more important only a relatively few years ago, before cheap aluminum and cast-iron pots became available. The large cast-iron "skillets" of the Chinese probably do not antedate the entrance of the Chinese themselves. Frying is an important method of Chinese cooking but is much less important for non-Chinese in Southeast Asia. It would seem likely that both the iron skillet and the method were brought in by the Chinese. However, the two do not necessarily go along together. Many long houses in Sarawak have the cast-iron skillets, yet they are apparently not used for frying but for boiling rice. Many of these same people do not make pottery and have not done so for a long time, if ever, as they do not have any indication of pottery manufacture in their folklore. Cooking rice in bamboo tubes is common for special occasions and was probably the usual method before the skillets came to be used.

Cooking pots in Southeast Asia are the simple rounded-bottom semispherical pots, the only variation being in the form of the rim and the proportion of the diameter to the total height. In cooking, they are ordinarily placed directly on or over the fire, either on the pottery stoves or held up by three stones. They are often soot incrusted on the outside, though under intense heat from time to time this soot may be burned off or it may flake off. Sherds which have considerable soot on the outside and are relatively clean on the inner surface probably came from pots used for cooking. On the other hand, the lack of a soot coating does not necessarily mean that the sherds were not from cooking vessels. Over a period of time, mechanical and chemical agents in the soil should be able to remove most of the soot, and only in more recent sites or in well-protected cases will the soot remain in any quantity.

The widely found pottery stove of Southeast Asia is probably archeologically recent and may well have come in with the Chinese. Sherds from these stoves, when in any quantity, are easily recognizable because of the distinct form of the stove.

Ceramics used in serving, eating, and drinking in Southeast Asia do not include earthenware utensils. From this it would seem likely that these functions for ceramics developed after porcelain and stoneware became a trade item. This goes back as far as Han times in Indonesia. Very rare Han stoneware is on exhibit in the museum in Djakarta. However, the Han objects are not of a utensil nature. Sung bowls were common funeral furniture in Tanjong Kubor in Sarawak (Harrisson and Harrisson, 1957), though this does not necessarily mean that they were used for serving or eating. This usage probably spread first to the local aristocracy, if any existed, and from them to the general population.

There are two major pottery traditions in Southeast Asia (Solheim, 1959);

one with little variety in form and the other with great variety. The forms of the vessels belonging to the tradition with little variety suggest primarily cooking and possibly storage functions. The variety of form in the other traditions suggests a great number of functions. The shallow bowls with ring feet of the Kalanay pottery complex in the Philippines (Solheim, 1957, p. 285, Fig. 3) and other forms, of themselves suggest the serving and display functions which porcelain serves today. However, the great majority of the pottery from this tradition has been excavated from burial sites, and this pottery may have only funeral and religious significance. When living sites with pottery of this tradition have been excavated, we will be able to say much more about the possible functions of this pottery.

Pottery manufacture.—The infrequent use of pottery temper in pottery manufacture is probably old. While sherd temper, as such, is not known to me to be in use at the present time, it was used in the past. Pottery excavated at a number of sites in the Santubong region of Sarawak show the use of pottery temper. A neck sherd from Tanjong Kubor contained such a large piece of a rim sherd that it was possible to see the form of the rim (Solheim, in press). Ground-up sherd or fired-clay temper was not uncommon in sherds excavated at Johore Lama, a sixteenth-century Malay fort in Johore, Malaya.

Miscellaneous.—The majority of the functions not having to do with food seem likely to have come in with the Chinese. As mentioned before, the earthenware flowerpots do not appear to be old. Nothing of this nature has been recognized from excavation. Worked sherds in the form of flat disks do go back some time. They are extremely common in sites of the last few hundred years in the Philippines, and are made from earthenware, stoneware, or porcelain sherds. One possible function that could have been served by earthenware prior to Chinese contact is that of a container for betel-chewing requirements. Box-like vessels of the Kalanay pottery complex have been excavated from a site in Marinduque, Philippines (Solheim, 1961b, p. 164).

While most of the present-day miscellaneous functions of pottery entered the area relatively recently, there were probably non-food functions of pottery in the past that have disappeared. The tremendous variety of form of the Kalanay complex pottery and its related pottery complexes in Southeast Asia suggest that there were numerous functions of this pottery which are no longer found today (see *Asian Perspectives*, Vol. III, No. 2).

CEREMONIAL FUNCTIONS

All three of the present-day major ceremonial functions of pottery were probably present in the past. However, since the great majority of the sites excavated in Southeast Asia have been burial sites, it is only safe to talk about funeral uses of pottery. It is very likely that, prior to its use as funeral furniture, some of the pottery associated with burials had other functions, particularly as wealth items. However, until similar pottery vessels are found in living sites, it is always possible that all burial furniture was specifically made or obtained for that purpose alone.

Funeral use.—The use of pottery as burial furniture has been very common in Southeast Asia and goes back at least 2000 years or more. It has been found associated with specific burials in the Philippines in Early Iron Age sites (third century B.C. to fourth century A.D.) (Beyer, 1947, p. 234) and Porcelain Age sites of the fifteenth century (Fox, 1959, Pls. 3–21); in Malaya, with Late Neolithic (possibly *ca.* 500 B.C.) burials (Sieveking, 1954–55, Pls. 2–10); and in Sarawak, from Late Neolithic burials (500 B.C.) (Solheim, Harrisson, and Wall, 1961, Pl. I) and burials of only a hundred years ago (B. Harrisson, 1956, p. 154). The great majority of the archeological sites excavated in Southeast Asia have been burial caves which have been much disturbed but where the pottery had probably been associated, at least to some extent, with individual burials.

Burial in jars is also common in Southeast Asia from around the beginning of the Christian era or earlier up to recent times. This jar burial has involved adult primary and secondary burial and child burial (Solheim, 1961c).

The great size, the quality of workmanship in both decoration and form of many of the vessels belonging to the Kalanay pottery complex in the Philippines, and the related complexes elsewhere in Southeast Asia suggest that some of the vessels had also been wealth items. For the Philippines, this high quality pottery disappeared from the scene very quickly after Chinese stoneware and porcelain started entering. It looks very much like the quality Chinese pottery replaced the quality locally made pottery of this one tradition. Nowhere is this pottery made today, though a few elements of this pottery tradition remain in some Sumatran and Malayan pottery. The simple pottery of the other tradition apparently continued relatively undisturbed.

THE FUNCTIONS OF POTTERY TO THE MANUFACTURER

There is little reason for attempting to carry this level of pottery function back in time before we know what the present functions are. Once they are known for the present it may be possible to work them back into the past, but certainly not before, with any accuracy.

Once much more local and detailed archeology is accomplished in Southeast Asia, it may become possible, as in classical archeology, to recognize the pottery of specific potters. At that time, and with an understanding of the present-day functions, it may be possible to examine psychological functions of pottery in the past as well as to arrive at some ideas on the economic functions as far as individual potters are concerned.

THE FUNCTIONS OF POTTERY TO THE COMMUNITY

Much more archeological work is needed in Southeast Asia before it will be possible to examine economic functions of pottery to the community. The present-

day economic organization connected with earthenware pottery probably goes
well back in time, and by comparative analysis of pottery from a number of sites
in a restricted area it may be possible to work out an approximation of the
economic organization of pottery on a community level at an approximate point
in time for the past. Diffusional functions will probably have to remain primarily
theoretical.

The artistic functions of pottery to a community should be determinable as
soon as its present-day artistic functions are understood, and by Fischer's (1961)
suggested correlations between art forms and sociocultural conditions it should
be possible to tell something right now about individual communities and about
cultures as a whole, if his correlations are correct.

BIBLIOGRAPHY

ALMAN, J. H.
1961. "Bajau Pottery." *Sarawak Museum Journal*, IX (15–16) (n.s.):583–602.

BEYER, H. O.
1947. "Outline Review of Philippine Archaeology by Islands and Provinces." *Philippine Journal of Science*, 77:205–374.

BULOSAN, C.
1944. *The Laughter of My Father*. New York: Harcourt, Brace.

COLANI, M.
1940. *Emploie de la Pierre en des Temps Recules; Annam-Indonesie-Assam*. Hanoi: Publications des Amis du Vieux Hue.

COLE, FAY-COOPER
1922. "The Tinguian; Social, Religious, and Economic Life of a Philippine Tribe." *Fieldiana: Anthrōpology*, Vol. XIV, No. 2. Chicago: Chicago Natural History Museum, Pub. 209.

CONKLIN, H. C.
1953. "Buhid Pottery." *Journal of East Asiatic Studies*, III (1):1–12.

DU BOIS, C.
1944. *The People of Alor*. Minneapolis: The University of Minnesota Press.

FISCHER, J. L.
1961. "Art Styles as Cultural Cognitive Maps." *American Anthropologist*, 63:79–93.

FOX, R. B.
1959. "The Calatagan Excavations: Two 15th Century Burial Sites in Batangas, Philippines." *Philippine Studies*, 7:325–90.

FREEMAN, D.
1957. "Iban Pottery." *Sarawak Museum Journal*, VIII (10) (n.s.):151–76.

HARRISSON, B.
1956. "Song Excavations (and Secondary Burial)." *Sarawak Museum Journal*, VII (7) (n.s.):153–65.

HARRISSON, T.
1950. "Some Borneo Ceramic Objects." *Sarawak Museum Journal*, V (2) (n.s.):270–73.

1951. "Some Ceramic Objects recently acquired for the Sarawak Museum." *Ibid.*, V (3) (n.s.):541–52.

1954. "Outside Influences on the Upland Culture of Kelabits of North Central Borneo." *Ibid.*, VI (4) (n.s.):104–25.

HARRISSON, T., and B. HARRISSON
1957. "The Pre-historic Cemetery of Tanjong Kubor." *Sarawak Museum Journal*, VIII (10) (n.s.):18–50.

JANSE, O. R. T.
1961. "Some Notes on the Sa-huynh Complex." *Asian Perspectives*, III:109–12.

SIEVEKING, G. DE G.
1954–55. "Excavations at Gua Cha, Kelantan." *Federation Museums Journal*, I and II:75–138.

SOLHEIM, W. G., II
1952. "Pottery Manufacturing in the Islands of Masbate and Batan, Philippines." *Journal of East Asiatic Studies*, I (3):49–53.

1957. "The Kulanay Pottery Complex in the Philippines." *Artibus Asiae*, XX:279–88.

1959. "Two Major Problems in Bornean (and Asian) Ethnology and Archaeology." *Sarawak Museum Journal*, IX (13–14) (n.s.):1–5.

1960a. "Notes on Burial Customs in and near Sagada Mountain Province." *Philippine Journal of Science*, 88 (1959):123–31.

1960b. "The Use of Sherd Weights and Counts in the Handling of Archaeological Data." *Current Anthropology*, I:325–29.

1961a. "Introduction to Sa-huynh." *Asian Perspectives*, III:97–108.

1961b. "Further Notes on the Kalanay Pottery Complex in the Philippines." *Asian Perspectives*, III:157–66.

1961c. "Jar Burial in the Babuyan and Batanes Islands and in Central Philippines, and its Relationship to Jar Burial Elsewhere in the Far East." *Philippine Journal of Science*, 89:115–48.

In press. "The Earthenware Pottery of Tanjong Kubor." *Sarawak Museum Journal.*

SOLHEIM, W. G., II, B. HARRISSON, and L. WALL
1961. "Niah 'Three Colour Ware' and Related Prehistoric Pottery from Borneo." *Asian Perspectives*, III:167–76.

TAKIGUCHI, H.
1960. (ed.) *Yaeyama.* Tokyo: Waseda University.

THE NEW YORK PLANNING CONFERENCE

IRVING ROUSE

As indicated in the Preface, a transcription of the discussions of the Planning Conference was distributed to the symposiasts together with the preprinted papers that would be discussed at Burg Wartenstein. During one of the sessions at the castle Dr. Rouse kindly undertook to summarize the results of the New York meeting. I have attempted here to present a very brief resumé of Dr. Rouse's presentation. The names of the twenty-five people present at the New York meeting are appended to this chapter. F.R.M.[1]

THE PEOPLE attending the New York Planning Conference were mostly from the eastern United States. Since the nature of the discussion was bound to be determined to some extent by their interests, these should be indicated. Fourteen of the participants were specialists in New World archeology; Griffin and Rouse were among them. Ehrich was one of the three in attendance specializing in either the prehistoric or protohistoric archeology of the Old World. Five were interested in the later periods of Old World archeology —Classical, Egyptian and Chinese. There was one art historian present and two people, including Matson, who were interested in technology. There were no ethnologists present, nor anyone, so far as I know (except for the art historian), with European training. All had worked with pottery but could not be called specialists in pottery in the sense that most of us here are. The meeting was chaired by Fred Matson. In his opening statement concerning the nature of the conference he implied that there is a need to convince many anthropologists that ceramic studies extend beyond simple description and classification, and I certainly think that we have succeeded in doing that.

In going over that transcription, I found that thirty topics were discussed at the meeting, and I have attempted to classify them into major areas as follows:

—Methods of studying pottery
—The functions of pottery
—The use of pottery as a record of other aspects of culture
—Problems of ceramic change (This group includes the largest number of topics.)

1. A quotation was suggested by Dr. Erik Reed as appropriate for the conference:
   Your honours have seen such dishes; they are not China dishes, but very good dishes.
   Measure for Measure, Act II, Scene 1, lines 96–97.
   Although the two stewed prunes therein contained and the woman under discussion in the play may not be pertinent to our discussion, it is encouraging to know that Shakespeare thought well of ceramics! F.R.M.

One point, first introduced in New York by Jimmy Griffin, was the desirability of having a group of specialists to correlate on a world-wide basis the level of ceramic complexity and development with the level of development and complexity in the rest of each culture. In the extended discussion of this point Evans pointed out that he and his wife, Dr. Meggers, had attempted to do this in a little-known article written in 1956 which they had published in Portuguese. An abstract of this paper, "Identificação Das Areas Culturais E Dos Tipos De Cultura Na Base Da Cerâmica Das Jazidas Arqueológicas" [Identification of Culture Areas and Types of Cultures Using Pottery from Archeological Sites] by Betty J. Meggers and Clifford Evans, *Arquivos do Museu Nacional*, 46:9–33 (Rio de Janeiro, 1958), appears in *Abstracts of New World Archaeology*, 1:10, item 32 (1960). The same summary in English was appended to the preprint of Matson's paper so that it would be available for use here during the discussion of Griffin's paper.

I am surprised and pleased to find that at Burg Wartenstein we have covered or can be expected to cover practically everything that was suggested at the New York meeting. Technology was not discussed there because our chairman specifically ruled it out. I detect a difference in the general attitude of the two conferences. In New York the main concern was with what we can learn from pottery. Here, at least for myself, one of the major things I have gained is appreciation of what we can't learn from pottery. A very strong interest in the need for publications of many kinds related to these various topics was expressed.

LIST OF PARTICIPANTS

Jacques Bordaz, New York University
Mary Butler, University of Pennsylvania
Douglas Byers, Robert S. Peabody Foundation, Andover, Massachusetts
Robert H. Dyson, Jr., University of Pennsylvania
Robert W. Ehrich, Brooklyn College
Gordon F. Ekholm, American Museum of Natural History
Clifford Evans, United States National Museum
Paul Fejos, Wenner-Gren Foundation
Henry Fischer, Metropolitan Museum of Art
James B. Griffin, University of Michigan
Emil W. Haury, University of Arizona
Jotham Johnson, New York University
Jean G. Lee, Philadelphia Museum of Art
Frederick R. Matson, The Pennsylvania State University
Betty J. Meggers, United States National Museum
Edith Porada, Columbia University
Erik K. Reed, United States National Park Service
Irving Rouse, Yale University
Rose Lilien Solecki, Columbia University

Robert Sonin, Brooklyn Museum of Art
Albert Spaulding, University of Oregon
Homer A. Thompson, Institute for Advanced Study, Princeton
Gus Van Beek, United States National Museum
Stephen Williams, Harvard University
John Witthoft, Pennsylvania State Museum

CERAMIC QUERIES

FREDERICK R. MATSON

ANY of the symposiasts said that a valuable result of the discussions held at Burg Wartenstein was a broadening of their world view of ceramic products in their artistic and technological aspects and in their cultural significance. An increasing awareness of the uncertainties often lurking behind firmly published interpretations of ceramic data in archeological and ethnological reports was a bit unsettling. Our combined efforts to apply these data to the study of cultural processes was stimulating. We agreed that the materials appearing in the transcriptions of our discussions, a record of over forty-six hours of analysis, argument, illustrative examples, and the showing of slides and movies, should be synthesized insofar as was possible. We also felt that reference to the individuals making the contributions was unnecessary, for many of the evolving ideas and questions reappeared in several sessions in varied form.

Since the book is designed to be of service to professional anthropologists, I thought it best to condense some of the voluminous materials that were not incorporated in the revised papers prepared for publication into a series of questions and statements grouped by general topic rather than by reference to a specific paper. Phrases appearing in the transcriptions have been used directly whenever possible. Some of the statements selected from the transcriptions would not be acceptable to all of the conferees, but they illustrate points that were discussed, often at length. Many of the questions here presented would need further qualification before they could be answered specifically. They are intentionally phrased in general terms, but some would be pertinent only within limited time periods and restricted world areas. These materials are gleanings; some of the harvest has been incorporated in the papers themselves. No attempt has been made to augment and organize them in a comprehensive form such as one might find in *Notes and Queries on Anthropology* that is published by the Royal Anthropological Institute of Great Britain and Ireland (6th ed., 1951). Perhaps the Index, which emphasizes topics rather than fleeting references to people and sites, may help integrate this chapter of supplementary material with the individual papers.

In the time since the conference and the final revision of their manuscripts, several of the symposiasts have published books or articles relevant to our ceramic interests. I have included those items with which I am familiar in the Bibliography for this chapter.

GENERAL

There is need for a closer collaboration between the subdisciplines within anthropology in order to better understand and interpret the materials being studied. Anthropology as a field of study for a European from the Germanic regions is quite different in concept than that for an American. The former is accustomed to consider it as a philosophical discipline which poses the question "What is man as a spiritual and psychological being?"

How useful is pottery in the study of past cultures when it is the major sensitive item found in archeological contexts? Can we more clearly understand the range in relationship by an examination of the present and immediately past ethnographic record? (In the United States there are fairly well marked regional boundaries for the contemporary culture pattern that are almost identical with the American Indian culture area boundaries. Might these be reflected in the Indian pottery types, or in the lack of pottery, as in much of California?)

That there is real danger in always applying rational explanations to ceramic traits can be well documented in the ethnographic literature.

Regional differences today in some countries parallel similar diversity in the archeologically known cultures from the same areas. Can the knowledge of the present-day patterns help in the better understanding of the distribution of ancient pottery wares?

How valuable are the collections of surface sherds that have been made in extensive site surveys in view of the purpose for which they had been gathered?

Is there sufficient ethnographic information to make it possible to recognize subregions in southeast Asia and their communication patterns, which would then aid in archeological ceramic studies?

Do the radioactive-carbon dates of archeological sites conflict with the relative chronologies established with aid of stratigraphic ceramic evidence?

Are there serious misuses of ceramic evidence?

Is there need to resolve trilingual terminological differences in ceramic descriptions which at times cause misunderstanding of the information being presented? ("You can't legislate a vocabulary.")

In assessing the significance of ceramic data for cultural studies one must rely on archeological evidence, literary sources preserved from past cultures, native tradition, early observers of unacculturated groups, and the activities and attitudes of contemporary village potters.

ORIGINS

Might there have been several independent developments of fired pottery? How and why did man begin using clay as a medium for the manufacture of containers? Wattle-and-daub construction could well relate to the development of clay containers in many parts of the world. What is the relationship in terms of shape and function of the clay and stone vessels found at early sites in the Near East?

What are the possible relationships between the domestication of animals, agriculture, and the development of pottery in the early village-farming and village-pastoral communities?

Myths pertaining to the origins of pottery making.

CLAY

How important are the nature of the clay available and the skill of the individual potter on the long-range development of ceramic products?

How important is technological development in the production of uniform kinds of pottery in regions where there are distinct differences in the properties of the clays available?

Does the so-called "grit tempering" often consist of only the natural materials that were part of the potter's clay?

What is the significance of the darkening of vessel surfaces? How was it produced? Can one be sure that this was intentionally done to obtain dark surfaces?

How can one differentiate between a slipped ware and one with a salt-bleached surface?

What is the significance of the range in firing color of the pottery found at a site?

Fuels: sources, quantities, seasonal variations, archeological evidences. Why is dung used as a fuel when other materials may be available? (It provides a slow burning fire.)

North African potters making hand-formed vessels are not familiar with other processes of manufacture and attribute the differences in products to the quality of the clay. "If we had better clay, we could do the same."

POTTERY PRODUCTION

Rotary motion techniques in the shaping of non-wheel-made pottery.

What are the possible variations in meaning of the term "wheel-made pottery" and their technological significance? You can have a technique before having the tool. Evidences of the first uses of the potter's wheel. Was its use related to the stimulus of market demand?

Can one determine the relative roles of men and women in the manufacture and distribution of pottery?

The nature and extent of the use of molds in forming vessels.

Potters' tools.

Potters are not particularly susceptible to influence from the work being done by neighboring potters.

What is the effect of itinerant potters with their manufacturing and decorating techniques on the local ceramic production?

In preparing an exhibit of polychrome Swiss ceramics of the sixteenth and seventeenth centuries at the Landesmuseum in Zürich, the intent was to show the men who produced these wares. Therefore documents and potters' tools were incorporated in the exhibits.

SHAPE

What are useful criteria for determining the cultural significance of shape and decoration? (There is an overall similarity in appearance of Thessalian pottery with that of the American Southwest.)

Why do some cultures have a rich variety of pottery forms while others have very few? Is it a function of the market—pleasing customers? Conservatism? Exposure through trade to other cultural stimuli?

Might the pottery shapes which have been extensively published for many archeological sites be grouped for each site into simpler units that have cultural significance—"pottery phonemes"? (At Tsintzuntzan there are but four basic ceramic forms—the griddle, casserole, cooking pot and water jar. But for each of these there are twelve to fourteen recognized principal sizes, so there are about fifty forms that could be recognized archeologically. The differences are a function of the market.)

DECORATION

Is there a relationship between the occurrence of painted decoration on vessels and the dark or light color (when fired) of the clays available to the ancient potters?

What factors relate to the disappearance of painted decoration from Near Eastern pottery in Late Chalcolithic times?

When one recognizes revivals in painted pottery decoration, might they really be the reflourishing of techniques or patterns that had survived so obscurely that they had not been apparent in the archeological record? Are there fashions in painted pottery?

What are the local relationships between mural decoration in rooms and pottery from the same site? Is this relationship the same in Egypt, Greece, and Central

America (to name but three sample areas)? Might polychrome ware have some association with wall decoration?

What is the distribution of the technique of post-firing application of decoration to pottery? (Is this a priestly function in Central America?)

Are there cultural clues in the appearance of polychromy, negative painting, or "resist" decoration?

How early do signed pots appear?

TECHNOLOGY

Technological ceramic evidence must be interpreted culturally by the same standards as the artistic evidence, and not be relegated to a report isolated in the appendix of a publication.

Can a study of the orientation of clay particles in pottery help determine how the vessels were made?

What has been learned of cultural significance from the microscopic study of thin sections of pottery?

ECOLOGY

Can an ecological approach be more than a general one? Can you actually put it to use when faced with a specific problem?

Do the natural conditions of cultural communication *within* a geographically delimited area influence ceramic differences or uniformity?

Is ecology more of a limiting factor in the advanced stages of pottery-making than in the earlier stages?

Man has caused changes in his environment in many areas—the ancient damming of Lake Van, silting and the increasing salinity of waters, changes in the level of the water table, deforestations, soil erosion. De we have ceramic evidence of such changes?

May the decline in habitation sites with the accompanying reduction in pottery found be related to increasing pastoral economies and nomadic migrations? Is the ceramic uniformity in the Early Bronze Age from eastern Anatolia into northern Iran as far as Tabriz the result of pastoral nomadism and perhaps itinerant potters?

TIME SPAN

What is the life expectancy of cooking pots, water jars, fiesta ware, and figurines within a culture? How does the habit in some regions of having domestic animals intimately associated in the household affect this? What is the disposition of broken ware? (In Greece it was used to fill dry wells.) Can such data be used when studying stratigraphic deposits of sherds?

What variables affect the life span of a ceramic style?

RITUAL

Does the occurrence of large numbers of like vessels in a deposit indicate the single use of each vessel in some ritual?

How early can one recognize the appearance of libation vessels?

Can one recognize the ritual breaking of vessels and figurines and the scattering of fragments of the sherds?

Are wares intended for burial with the dead inferior in quality of material but not inferior in their decoration?

Might lime stucco and impermanent painted decoration have been applied to mortuary pottery? Was there a fugitive red surfacing on more ceramic objects than have been so described, since long burial in some soils and vigorous cleaning after excavation may have removed much of this coating?

What criteria are useful in differentiating between ritual and household pottery? May some pottery have served as containers for foundation deposits?

What was the motivation for the manufacture of miniature vessels which duplicate the full-size pieces in shape and decoration—votive objects, toys, souvenirs?

COOKING

Is there a technical interdependence between the preparing and cooking of food and the making of pottery in the same courtyard when both skills are in their earlier stages of development, and the two tasks probably performed by the same woman? Could hearths for cooking be associated with the firing of pottery?

Is there a relationship between the baking of bread and the development of kilns?

Might gruel or beer, which would require containers, have preceded bread? (Braidwood, 1953)

Cooking ware: methods of manufacture, relative abundance, relationship to metal containers, uses, traditional aspects, archeological recognition of such ware.

What is the significance of the thickness of vessel walls in cooking ware and other utilitarian pottery?

Cooking pots are rare in Saxon England from the end of the Roman period until about A.D. 800. Then quite suddenly they appear in large quantities.

Bamboo was used for the cooking of food in southeast Asia in both ancient and modern times. Cooking pots were used in many of the islands. These facts may be of interpretative use.

METALS

Were there reciprocal influences on vessel shapes in the production and use of clay and metal containers?

May the appearance of rivet heads, etc., on pottery be surer indications of the imitation of metallic ware than are the highly angular shapes? (Yet there are bosses on some stone vessels and on the handles of baskets.)

Have crucible fragments been found in sufficient quantities in archeological contexts to be of use in tracing developments in metallurgical practices?

Social differences may be implied from the relative richness and abundance of metal grave goods in the Hallstatt Period, but the closeness of the site being excavated to the center of production may be a conditioning factor.

STATUS

In a peasant society in which land or work on the land is readily available, is the potter of low status?

The potters of Tzintzuntzan complained of dirty work, while the old Swedish craft ironworkers, who were still making files and rasps up until 1940, complained of unhealthy work. In Sweden handicraft work is undergoing a renaissance, but underestimation of their trade by the craftsmen is still quite usual.

The rate of intermarriage of the potters and people of other trades might constitute a criterion for status determination. (In many villages, however, potting is the only craft.)

While other craftsmen are mentioned, there is only one record of a potter in ancient Greek texts. The potter himself, insofar as is known, had no particular status despite the fact that he produced much valued work that he often signed. The painters who decorated the finest pottery were apparently itinerant, not only traveling from one potter's shop to another, but also voyaging to other countries.

TRADE AND DIFFUSION

In what ways can one distinguish between trade wares and the diffusion of a style or technique?

Do stylistic traits diffuse more readily than basic ceramic techniques which may be dependent upon the properties of local clays?

Are ceramic traits valid criteria on which to base suggestions about population movements?

Should not one assume a migration of peoples when there is a demonstrated diffusion of pottery-making techniques?

Are there ceramic evidences for some of the great "invasions"—such as the Indo-European, Amorite, Hyksos, Dorian, Luvian, Anglo-Saxon, Pueblo, and Mongol?

A "nativistic" phase has been recognized in some Peruvian pottery by Professor John H. Rowe—the re-establishment of identity after outside conquests.

Roger of Sicily's raiding of Corinth in the twelfth century A.D.—in part to acquire artisans—hastened the spread of Majolica production throughout the Mediterranean area.

The origin and distribution of Bell Beakers received extended discussion.

Are unique pieces necessarily imports?

CULTURE CHANGE

Within what limits can ceramics serve as an index of cultural changes?

Can one have marked cultural changes, historically documented, with no significant changes in the archeologically documented pottery? (Example: In the Lesser Antilles the Carib conquered the Arawak, killed the men and married the women; no sharp ceramic change can be observed in the deposits of that period. But the women were the potters, and the present-day Caribs really speak a form of Arawak, so the persistence of the women's language and probably of their pottery styles seems likely.)

It might be interesting to compare ceramic change with linguistic change within a single group. When the language changes rapidly is there any change in the ceramic products?

Is there a correlation between the complexity of the pottery and the degree of cultural development?

Perhaps we should be comparing the complexity of a single element of the non-ceramic culture with a single element of the ceramic complex. Trends might be traced through correlation studies.

What is a ceramic complex—materials, techniques, forms, decorative art, uses, distribution patterns? The isolation of such aspects in ceramic comparisons would help in evaluating the relationship of ceramics to cultural development.

The change in Maya ceramics from monochrome to polychrome ware must certainly reflect a change in technique as well as style, and must eventually be correlated with other changes in the culture at the time.

Cultural development is often not linear, but cyclical; this is particularly true of style.

In the gradual recognition of the cultural periods in the southwestern United States, house forms and ceremonial structures were used to define the culture periods, and only later was the pottery of each used to symbolize the stages. Pottery did not play a major role in defining the cultural developments, but was of great stratigraphic use in establishing the chronology of the events.

RESISTANCE TO CHANGE

Can factors be recognized that affect resistance to ceramic change?

Was the Germanic resistance to the manufacture of Roman wares due to the fact that there was such a great technical difference between the two that it precluded adoption?

Motor patterns—the ways in which we use our bodies—are among the most resistant to change of all the elements of culture. The use of the wheel is widespread in many parts of Mexico, but the non-wheel-using potters are not interested in adopting it and are incurious concerning it. The motor patterns that the potter first learns may in some cases make it difficult for him to adopt a drastically different set of patterns. The commercial factor is also very important. The Mexican mold technique is very efficient and rapid, so the potters are able to meet the market demand, and no premium is placed on adopting the wheel.

If a peasant group is in acculturational contact with an industrial society, and commercially produced vessels (pottery, glass, enamel, plastic) are introduced into the village shops or markets, how is the local ceramic industry affected?

ECONOMICS

When does pottery manufacture cease to be a home industry and become organized as a shop? Criteria are needed for recognizing this stage with its economic implications if we are to compare pottery from different cultures.

It is a mistake to think of the artist as someone who is quite apart from the culture in which he lives. The artist is very much a part of the economy.

What was the immediate stimulus that led Nampeyo to successfully develop her pottery style which was based on ancient examples?

What criteria are important to potters in evaluating their own ware and that of their competitors?

What criteria are important to the purchaser of pottery when he makes his selection?

If a vessel cracks in firing, the crack is repaired with a paste, or holes may be drilled on either side of it to tie it together. Such salvaged vessels are sold and used. How early does such salvaging occur?

Pottery made for a specific market in another community is often called by the name of the market village.

How has urban development influenced or affected pottery production in peripheral villages?

How do changes in the local economy affect pottery production? Miss Olga Tufnell has observed that the manufacture of pottery in some parts of the Near East has been resumed in areas where it had essentially disappeared. Discarded *tinnakas* (the five-gallon gasoline containers) have long been used to store water, oil, etc., and were at times modified to form specialized containers. The oil companies have recently been improving their methods of distribution, filling stations are being established in the larger towns, and *tinnakas* are becoming much scarcer. There again is a commercial need for storage jars.

*   *   *

This conference on "Ceramics and Man" is but a start. It represented to some degree all major world areas in which ceramic products have been an important item in the archeological and ethnographic records except central and south Africa, India, and central to eastern Asia. Perhaps there would be value in arranging similar future meetings that are more limited in scope. A laboratory conference, possibly for advanced graduate students, to which those invited came only after having experimented with the local clays which concerned them, might be useful. The more we know of the ceramic aspects of cultures other than those with which we are specifically concerned in our own studies, the better we can use our materials in broader cultural terms. We can then appraise more effectively the point that Dr. Paul Fejos emphasized in several conversations—"What has ceramics done *for* man?"

BIBLIOGRAPHY

BALFET, H.
1962. *Ceramique Ancienne en Proche-Orient Israel et Liban, VI⁰–III⁰ "Millenaires",
Etude Technique.* Paris.

BRAIDWOOD, R. J., *et al.*
1953. "Symposium. Did Man Once Live by Beer Alone?" *American Anthropologist,*
55:515–26.

CORNWALL, I. W., and H. W. M. HODGES
1964. "Thin Sections of British Neolithic Pottery: Windmill Hill—A Test Site."
University of London, *Bulletin of the Institute of Archaeology,* 4:29–34.

EHRICH, R. W. (ed.)
1965. *Relative Chronologies in Old World Archaeology.* (2nd ed.) Chicago: University of Chicago Press.

Foster, G. M.
1962. *Traditional Cultures: and the Impact of Technological Change.* New York: Harper and Row.
1965. "Peasant Society and the Image of Limited Good." *American Anthropologist,* 67:293–315.

Hodges, H.
1964. *Artifacts: An Introduction to Early Materials and Technology.* London: John Baker.

Linné, S.
1961. " 'Ceramics and Man' Conference at Burg Wartenstein, 1961." *Ethnos,* 4:227–38.

Matson, F. R.
1963. "Some Aspects of Ceramic Technology." *Science in Archaeology,* D. Brothwell and E. Higgs (eds.), pp. 489–98. New York: Basic Books.

Shepard, A. O.
1963. "Beginnings of Ceramic Industrialization: An Example from the Oaxaca Valley." *Notes from a Ceramic Laboratory,* No. 2. Washington, D.C.: Carnegie Institution of Washington.
1964a. "Ceramic Development of the Lowland and Highland Maya." *XXXV Congreso Internacional de Americanistas, Mexico, 1962. Actas y Memorias,* pp. 249–62.
1964b. "Temper Identification: 'Technological Sherd-Splitting' or an Unanswered Challenge." *American Antiquity,* 29:518–20.

Solheim, W. G., II
1964a. *The Archaeology of Central Philippines. A Study Chiefly of the Iron Age and Its Relationships.* Manila: National Institute of Science and Technology, Monograph 10.
1964b. "Formosan Relationships with Southeast Asia." *Asian Perspectives,* VII:251–60.

Vanden Berghe, L.
1963. "A la découverte des civilisations anciennes dans l'Iran méridional." *l'Annuaire des amitiés belgo-iraniennes,* I:5–43.

Van der Waals, J. D.
1964. *Prehistoric Disc Wheels in the Netherlands.* Groningen: J. B. Wolters.

INDEX

A

Acatlán, 46, 53
Acapulco, 53
Aceramic culture, 218, 228
Adana Museum, 233
Afghanistan, 205, 212
Aghios Kosmas, 192
Aitken, M. J., 81
Aiyappan, A., 55
Aksaray, 233
Alabama, 106
Alaca, 229
Alb-Salem-Keramic, 157
Albuquerque, 73
Algeria, 161
Alman, J. H., 257
Alpine region, 141–146, 154, 155
   Hallstatt A-B, 144
   Hallstatt B, 150, 155, 157, 160
   Hallstatt B-C, 146, 150
   Hallstatt C-D, 148, 150
Alumina, microchemical test for, 79
Amazon River system, communications, 31
American Indians, 20 ff., 62 ff., 207
   Andean influence, 36
   Cholula, 25
   lack of humor, 38
   types of pottery, Black on Red, 79
      Fine Orange Ware, 25
      Plumbate, 24–25
      Sikyatki, 33
      Thin Orange Ware, 24
   (*See also* Mexico, United States)
American Museum of Natural History, 157, 260
Amiran, R., 195, 221, 240–247
Amotag (Masbate), 257
Anatolia, 7, 218 ff., 238
   Amuq B, 227
   Amuq D, 227
   Belbaşi, 219
   Beldibi, 219–220
   Çatal Hüyük, 203, 218–235, 244
   ceramic Neolithic, 219
   Cilicia, 4, 13, 222 ff.

cycles, 230
Early Bronze Age, 229 ff.
   I, 230, 238
   II, 229, 230, 235, 238
   III, 230
Early Chalcolithic, 219, 221, 222, 224, 227, 229, 235
Early Neolithic, 219–220, 223–224, 228, 230
Hacilar, 203, 218–227
Halaf, 224, 228, 248
influence on other cultures, 227
Iron Age, 230
Kizilkaya, 219
Late Bronze Age, 230, 233
Late Chalcolithic, 229, 230, 231
Late Neolithic, 219, 221, 223, 225, 227, 228, 230
Mesopotamian influence, 228
Middle Bronze Age, 230
Middle Chalcolithic, 224
Minyan Grey, 4
Neolithic, 175, 223, 228, 229, 231
prehistory, 220, 232, 238
Sakje Geuze, 206
Tarsus, 233, 238
Anatolian plateau, 223, 227, 236
   use of pottery in field surveys, 232–238
   Vinča figurines, 10
Ancón, 21
Anthesteria, 188
Apulia, 187
Arabs, 6
Archaeological Institute of the Czechoslovakian Academy of Sciences, 6
Archeological interpretation in North Africa, 161 ff.
Archeologist, relation to analyst, 62, 83
Arequipa, 51
Argentine, 14, 36
Asboe, W., 47
Atzompa, 46, 52, 53, 55
Australian Aborigines, 207
Aymara, 22, 50, 215
Aztecs, 25

289